GOOD COOKERY

GOOD COOKERY

BY

W. G. R. FRANCILLON

&

G. T. C. D. S.

LONDON

J. M. DENT & SONS LTD.

© Revisions, J. M, Dent & Sons Ltd, 1960

Printed by
Robert Cunningham & Sons Ltd
Alva · Clackmannanshire
for
J. M. DENT & SONS LTD
Aldine House · Bedford Street · London
First published 1920
First published in this edition 1933
Revised edition 1936
Further revised 1938
Further revised 1955
Last reprinted 1960

PREFACE

I was taught to cook against my own wish; and that this training was insisted on, is one of the things for which I am most thankful. I was told that within a week I was to take up the study of cookery at the Gloucester School of Domestic Science. I went, reluctantly, but from the first morning was keenly interested, and I can never be sufficiently grateful to Miss Baddeley and to Mrs. Booth for all they taught me. On leaving Gloucester I spent some years in cooking high-class dinners, and in teaching both mistresses and their cooks, thus collecting much knowledge and a vast variety of recipes. A few years ago some of my friends insisted that I should take their daughters and train them in my own home, and from this small beginning a School of Cookery here at Harcombe has evolved.

In an endeavour to carry out exactly the Gloucester methods, our standard hitherto has been Mrs. Booth's Cookery Book. Unfortunately that valuable work has been out of print for some time, and owing to so many demands for a book of its type, but modified to suit the present difficult and expensive times, I have been asked to publish the following. It is written for the practical use of students or of those who undertake, or are compelled to do their own cooking without having been sufficiently fortunate to have had a training. For these the necessary terms and methods are clearly explained, but the professional cook will also find the book of great value for its many carefully tested recipes. Many pre-war recipes have been slightly altered and re-arranged with a view to economy and saving of labour; many others of the same type have been added. The busy housewife who wants to feed her family economically and well, and who, at the same time, with her many duties cannot give much time to cookery, will find here what she wants; and for her benefit some of the less expensive and quicker recipes have been marked with an asterisk.

Recipes for sweet-making have not been included in this book. It is a separate art and there are many excellent books on the subject.

I hope the book may be of use to many, and I must again thank all those who have been good enough to give me their help and advice and above all I must thank Mrs. Booth, on whose training my knowledge was originally founded.

1920. W. G. R. FRANCILLON.

PREFACE TO THE EIGHTH EDITION

Originally issued in 1920, this book has been revised and enlarged at each successive edition.

In 1924 it was adopted by the Gloucestershire Training College of Domestic Science as the official text-book of the college—and the cookery staff then became my co-editors.

The publication of the book is now in the hands of Messrs. J. M. Dent & Sons Ltd. The present edition, which makes the eighth and for which the work has again been revised and improved, is the second for the general public.

W. G. R. FRANCILLON.

HARCOMBE HOUSE,
  UPLYME, DEVON.
  1936.

PREFACE TO THE NINTH EDITION

Again this book has been revised and brought up to date. Economies in recipes have been made where these can be done without in any way sacrificing results.

The Cookery Staff of the Gloucestershire Training College of Domestic Science have rewritten much of the section on Breads and Buns giving a basic recipe for the dough and showing how a wide variety can be obtained by suitable adaptations. The rather simpler and shorter methods also indicated are most valuable: such delicious and inexpensive results can be obtained. I feel many housewives will enjoy experimenting with these simpler and more speedy processes.

W. G. R. FRANCILLON.

32 QUEEN'S PARK,
  WEST DRIVE,
  BOURNEMOUTH.
  1955.

CONTENTS

		PAGE
PREFACE	. . . .	v
TEMPERATURES	. . . . . .	viii
I. STOCKS AND SOUPS	. . . . .	1
II. FISH	. . . .	28
III. MEATS (HOT OR COLD)	. . . .	51
IV. POULTRY, GAME, AND RABBITS	. . .	89
V. ENTRÉES (HOT AND COLD)	. . . .	97
VI. SAUCES	. . . . . .	109
VII. VEGETABLES	. . . . . .	129
VIII. VEGETARIAN COOKERY	. . . .	152
IX. PASTRY AND PUDDINGS	. . . .	164
X. BATTERS, OMELETS, AND SOUFFLÉS	. .	229
XI. JELLIES, CREAMS, MERINGUES, AND ICES	.	241
XII. EGG COOKERY	. . . . .	270
XIII. HORS D'ŒUVRES AND SAVOURIES	. .	279
XIV. BREAKFAST DISHES	. . . .	290
XV. BREAD, SCONES, CAKES PLAIN AND RICH	.	296
XVI. FILLINGS AND ICINGS FOR CAKES	. .	340
XVII. BEVERAGES	. . . . .	347
XVIII. INVALID COOKERY	. . . .	351
XIX. JAMS, FRUIT JELLIES, AND FRUIT CHEESES	.	362
XX. BOTTLING OF FRUITS AND VEGETABLES	.	372
XXI. PICKLES AND CHUTNEY	. . . .	380
XXII. BUTTERS, FORCEMEATS AND FARCES	. .	386
XXIII. MISCELLANEOUS RECIPES AND HAY BOX COOKERY	391
XXIV. FOOD VALUES	. . . . .	396
XXV. MEALS AND MENUS	. . . .	398
XXVI. FOODS IN SEASON	. . . .	403
XXVII. COOKERY TERMS	. . . .	409
APPENDIX	. . . . . .	414
INDEX	. . . . . .	422

TEMPERATURES

The following temperatures will be constantly referred to:

Blood heat	98·4° F.
Sterilizing point	150° F.
Scalding point for Devonshire Cream .	170° to 180° F.
Simmering point	180° to 190° F.
Boiling point of water	212° F.
Sugar syrup	220° F.

RECIPES

Read throughout:

1 glass	sherry *or* madeira	$=\frac{1}{2}$ gill
1 ,,	brandy, rum, *or* liqueur	$=1$ tablesp.
1 ,,	white wine	$=1$ gill
1 ,,	port	$=\frac{3}{4}$ gill

*The recipes marked with an asterisk are particularly inexpensive,
satisfactory and quickly made (see page* v).

I. STOCKS AND SOUPS

BEFORE making a soup it is necessary to know what stock is, as this is the essential ingredient for good soup. There are various kinds of stocks, and these will be given in due order.

First Stock is the best kind, and this is obtained from the first boiling of meat, bones and vegetables. Good first stock is necessary for the making of clear soups, and the following ingredients will be required: 1 lb. meat (shin of beef, meat and bone together, or a mixture of shin of beef and knuckle of veal); 1 qt. cold water. (Sufficient for 4 people.)

METHOD. Scrape the meat finely or mince it, removing any fat. Break the bones and place these with the minced meat in a saucepan, adding the cold water. Leave these to stand for at least half an hour. (This process allows the albumen and other juices of the meat to dissolve.) Place the pan on the fire and bring to boiling point. Boil for a few moments and skim well; then reduce to simmering point, and simmer gently for three hours, keeping the lid on the pan. Then add:

1 slice carrot.	1 clove.	
1 ,, onion.	Bunch of herbs.	Tied all
1 ,, turnip.	Blade of mace.	together
1 stick celery.	About 10 peppercorns.	in a
Salt to taste.	Small bay leaf.	muslin bag

and simmer the whole gently for two hours. This time allows the vegetables and spices to give their full flavour to the stock, without giving them time to become a pulp, which would cloud a clear soup. When the process is complete, remove the pan from the fire, strain the stock, and leave it in a bowl till next day. Leave the meat and bones on a plate for further use, and throw away the vegetables, herbs and spices.

NEXT DAY remove any fat that may have risen on the cold stock, and the good, first stock is now ready for the soup.

Second Stock. Take the same meat and bones that have been left from the first stock, and exactly repeat the process, adding fresh vegetables, herbs and spices. Again save the meat and bones for further use.

Household Stock. Take the same meat and bones that have been left over from the second stock, and to these add any household bones, i.e. cooked or uncooked bones from joints, poultry, game, etc. Again repeat the process given for first stock, allowing 1 qt. of water to each lb. of meat and bones. This stock is excellent for vegetable soups, but is usually too poor in flavour for clear soups.

*Plain Household Stock can be continually made entirely from the supply of bones that every household gets with its daily meat. The bones should be used again and again for stock until each bone becomes porous and easily breakable and crumbly. They are then no use except for bone manure, which is excellent for a garden. As one porous bone is removed it will usually be found that there are others available, so a stock pot should really be inexhaustible, and should cost nothing except when clear soups are needed. Certain things should never be put in a stock pot:

(1) Any form of starch. Therefore, if a chicken has been served with white sauce, any sauce clinging to the bones should be carefully washed off before the bones are put in the stock pot, owing to the flour, which contains starch, in the sauce. Bread and toast, also potato (raw or cooked), rice, macaroni, etc. are also starch and must not be added.

(2) Cabbage, cooked or uncooked.

(3) Any excess of fat.

(4) Milk or cream in any form.

Care of the Stock Pot. This must be emptied and well washed every night, and it is advisable once a week to stand it out in the open air or sunshine. Otherwise it is liable to become sour.

Fish Stock may be made much in the same way as meat stock, but as it does not need so much cooking, the fish bones, vegetables and spices (in the same proportion as for First Stock) should all be put on together in cold water and simmered gently for 2 hours or even less. As Fish Stock does not keep well, it should be made and used the same day.

Vegetable Stock (Brown). Take 1 lb. of flavouring vegetables, onion, carrot, turnip, celery, etc., and fry these. When a good brown, cover them with 1 qt. of water, add any herbs and spices, and salt to taste, and simmer 1 or 2 hours. Strain this; cool the stock and remove any fat and it will be ready for use. Like Fish

Stock, this does not keep, and should be made and used the same day.

Vegetable Stock (White). Make exactly as above, but do not fry the vegetables. Simply cover them with water, add any herbs, spices and salt and simmer gently for 1 or 2 hours.

SOUPS

Soups may be divided into 4 classes:

I. Purées, i.e. soups composed largely of sieved substance.
II. Thickened soups, i.e. those thickened by the addition either of starchy material (flour, etc.) or egg.
III. Clear Soups (Consommé).
IV. Broths, which are obtained by cooking meat, bones, vegetables, etc. in water until the nourishment from these ingredients is dissolved into the water.
v. Fish Soups.

For household use allow ½ pt. per head; for dinner-party just over ¼ pt.

CLASS I

PURÉES

These may be thickened entirely by the sieved substance, e.g. potato soup, by sieved potato; but as this purée is inclined to settle and separate from the stock, it is advisable to add a binding or 'liaison' of (1) starchy material, (2) egg, (3) blood (hare soup), which prevents this.

A purée consists of various parts:

(1) Fat.
(2) The Foundation. Vegetable, fish, or meat.
(3) The Flavouring. Onion, herbs, etc.
(4) Liquid. Stock, milk, or water, or a mixture of these.
(5) The Liaison.

THE METHOD for making all vegetable purées is as follows, and the quantities given are enough for 4 to 6 people:

(1) Fat. ½ oz. butter, margarine, or dripping.
(2) Foundation. { 2 lb. green vegetable.
1 lb. starchy vegetable.
1–1½ gills dried vegetable.

(3) Flavouring. Usually 1 onion and various herbs and spices, but flavourings vary.
(4) Liquid. 1 qt. Preferably ¾ stock and ¼ milk.
(5) Liaison. 1 oz. sago, or 1 oz. flour mixed to a smooth cream with a little cold milk.

METHOD:

(1) Melt the fat.

(2) Add the raw (sliced, if necessary) vegetables, also the flavouring, and cook gently in the fat about 10 minutes, keeping the saucepan covered, and shaking it frequently to prevent burning. This process is known as SAUTÉING. This term will be used in future to save repetition in explaining the method. When sufficiently SAUTÉD, the vegetables will be seen to have absorbed the fat, but without being at all browned or discoloured.

(3) Cover with the stock or water, NOT MILK, and cook till the vegetables are tender. Milk must not be added yet, as long cooking with vegetables, owing to the acid in them, will always curdle milk.

(4) Sieve the vegetables and stock. If convenient, a better texture is given if the soup is sieved through a hair sieve, but a fine wire one answers for household purposes.

(5) Return the sieved mixture or 'purée' to the saucepan and re-heat, adding the milk.

(6) Add the liaison. If sago, boil gently, stirring for 10 minutes. If flour, mix it to a smooth cream with cold milk, and add it, stirring, till the soup boils.

(7) Taste and season to taste, and serve at once.

If the liaison added should be egg, e.g., 1 yolk, ¼ pt. cream, beaten together, the method is slightly different after process (4).

Instead of, as in (5), returning the purée to the pan at once, cool it a little, and add the mixed cream and yolk. Return all to the pan, and carefully re-heat until the egg is sufficiently cooked, but on no account allow the soup to boil or the egg will curdle.

N.B. (1). If VEGETARIAN SOUPS are required, any of the following recipes, or vegetable ones, can be adapted by using water instead of stock. The addition of extra milk or egg or cream would add to their nourishment.

N.B. (2). If cream is added to soups it should go in last. Soup may then be re-heated, but not re-boiled, as the latter might cause the cream to oil and resemble grease on the surface of the soup.

CLASS II

The Second Class of Soups, i.e. those thickened by the addition either of starchy material (flour, etc.) or egg.

CLASS III

CONSOMMÉS or CLEAR SOUPS

For these specially made first stock is essential. See rules for first stock (page 1).

The stock must be quite cold so that it can be freed from all fat.

CLASS IV

BROTHS

This class of soup is neither sieved nor thickened with flour, etc., but consists of the liquid in which meat has been cooked slowly, with or without the diced meat, with nicely cut vegetables and a thickening of whole grain, generally rice or pearl barley.

CLASS V

FISH SOUPS

These are made from fish: if shell fish are used they are called 'bisques'.

SOUPS—CLASS I

PURÉES

*ARTICHOKE SOUP (about 7 people)

2 lb. Jerusalem artichokes.	Seasoning.
1 oz. butter.	½ oz. to 1 oz. flour.
1 onion.	1 qt. white stock or water.
1 stick celery (white part).	3 gills milk.
Pinch of sugar.	½ gill cream.

Sauté the peeled and sliced artichokes. Cover them with stock and water, and boil till tender. Sieve them. Return to the pan adding most of the milk. Make a liaison of the flour and the rest of the milk. Add this, re-boil, and season. If the cream is added, it should go in last. Avoid re-boiling after the addition of the cream.

N.B. Peel artichokes under water, as they discolour so quickly, and keep them in cold water (to which one teasp. lemon juice or vinegar has been added) until required. This recipe can be used for Potato Soup.

ASPARAGUS SOUP (4 or 5 people)

1 bundle of asparagus.	1 oz. flour.
1 qt. white stock or water.	1 gill of cream or 'Ideal' milk.
¼ teasp. of salt.	¼ teasp. of sugar.
1 oz. margarine or butter.	

Boil the asparagus in the water with a little salt. When tender remove the heads and boil the remainder till soft. Sieve this. Mix the flour and fat in a pan and add the sieved asparagus, including the water it has boiled in. Boil up, add sugar and seasoning and cream or unsweetened 'Ideal' milk. Use the heads of asparagus as a garnish. If the soup is a little thick add more milk or water.

*BROWN VEGETABLE SOUP (4 or 5 people)

2 potatoes.	¼ head of celery.
1 turnip, 1 carrot.	2 tomatoes.
1 to 2 oz. fat.	1 slice toasted bread
Seasoning.	1 inch thick.
1 qt. stock or water.	

Cut up the vegetables and fry them in the fat. Pour the stock or water over, and add the toast and tomatoes. Simmer for about 2 hours, until the vegetables are quite tender. Sieve, re-heat, adding seasoning to taste. Serve with fried croûtons.

*CAULIFLOWER SOUP (5 or 6 people)

1 cauliflower.	1 pt. milk.
1 small onion.	½ oz. fat.
Bunch of herbs.	1 oz. flour.
Seasoning.	1 pt. stock or water.

Wash and blanch the cauliflower. Cut it up and sauté it with the chopped onion and herbs in the fat. Add the stock and cook till tender. Sieve, re-heat, adding part of the milk and the seasoning. When boiling, add the flour, mixed to a smooth cream into some of the cold milk. Boil for 5 minutes, stirring, garnish with sprigs of cauliflower, and serve with fried croûtons.

*CELERY SOUP (4 people)

2 heads of celery.	1½ pt. stock.
1 shallot.	½ pt. milk.
½ oz. fat.	2 tablesp. cream.
1 oz. flour.	Seasoning.

Wash and slice the celery. Chop the shallot. Sauté these in the fat. Add the stock and cook till tender. Add the flour mixed to a smooth cream with the cold milk. Stir and boil; then sieve. Re-heat, adding the cream (if used). Serve with fried croûtons.

CHEAP PEA SOUP (Cheap dinners for 50 people)

3 lb. peas.	2d. or 3d. worth of bones.
2 lb. onions.	3 gallons water.
1 lb. carrots and turnips.	¾ lb. flour.
A head celery.	About 1 oz. salt (to taste).

Soak the peas (if possible) overnight. If the water is hard, add ½ teasp. bicarbonate soda to it. Wash and slice the vegetables and break up bones, tying them in muslin to keep out the splinters from the soup.

Cook gently vegetables, bones, and water for at least 3 hours. Mix the flour to a smooth cream with 1 pt. cold water, and add this. Stir well for at least 10 minutes.

N.B. Any other pulse (e.g. lentils) could be substituted for peas.

Sieve the soup and serve. If impossible to sieve it, serve it as it is. Small suet dumplings add to the nourishment and should be cooked in the soup.

*Cheap Dumplings

2 lb. flour.	1 lb. suet.
½ pt. water.	2 teasp. baking
2 teasp. salt.	powder.

Chop the suet. Add it to the flour, baking powder and salt. Mix well, and add the water to form a dough. Form into little balls and cook them for at least 40 minutes in the soup.

CHESTNUT SOUP (Purée de Marrons)
(4 or 5 people)

1 pt. chestnuts.	¼ pt. milk.
½ to 1 oz. butter.	¼ pt. cream.
1 qt. white stock.	Seasoning.
Pinch of sugar.	½ oz. flour or cornflour.

Split the nuts at both ends. Boil for 10 minutes, then skin them. Sauté them in butter, add the stock, and cook till tender (30 to 50 minutes). Rub through a hair sieve. Mix the flour or cornflour to a smooth cream with the milk. Re-boil the sieved purée, adding the liaison of flour or cornflour; boil, cool a little, add the cream and seasoning. Serve with fried croûtons of bread.

*CRESSY SOUP (Purée à la Cressy)
(4 or 5 people)

4 large red carrots.	¼ pt. milk or cream.
1 large onion.	½ oz. fat.
1 stick celery.	1 qt. stock.
1 slice raw ham.	1 oz. cornflour, if necessary.

Pinch of sugar.

Cut finely the red part of the carrot, the onion and celery, also the ham. Sauté these in the butter. Add the stock and cook gently for about ½ hour till quite tender. Pound and sieve the vegetables, and sieve the stock. Return to the pan, re-boil and skim. Add the cornflour, mixed to a smooth cream with a little cold milk, and boil well (if a liaison is needed). Then add the cream and seasoning Re-heat (do not boil) and serve.

GAME PURÉES

Make as for ordinary Game or Hare Soup, but after the meat has been simmered take it from the bones, and pound and sieve it. Add it to the soup, and re-heat without boiling.

GREEN PEA SOUP (4 people)

1 lb. peas.	½ teasp. sugar.
1½ pt. white stock.	1 gill milk.
1 small onion.	½ oz. flour.
1 sprig mint.	1 tablesp. cream (or more).
2 or 3 spinach leaves or green colouring.	¼ oz. butter.
	Salt and pepper.

Wash the shells well. Shell a few pods and cook the peas as a garnish. Put peas and shells, onion and stock into a saucepan and simmer till tender. Sieve, return to pan. Add the butter, creamed flour and milk. Boil up well. Add cream and a few whole peas and serve.

*HARICOT SOUP (about 6 people)

See Lentil Soup.

*HARICOT AND TOMATO SOUP (6 people)

½ pt. haricot beans.	1 lb. tomatoes.
1 turnip. ⎫	1 oz. fat.
1 carrot. ⎬ optional.	1 qt. stock or water.
1 onion. ⎭	½ oz. cornflour or flour.

Seasoning.

Wash the beans and soak them for 12 hours. Sauté them with the tomatoes, cut up, and the other vegetables (if added) chopped. Add the stock; boil till tender. Sieve. Add the cornflour, mixed to a smooth cream with a little cold milk or water. Re-boil, stirring, season and serve.

*IMITATION HARE SOUP (A Purée)

(about 4 people)

¼ lb. lean gravy beef.	2 oz. fat.
1 carrot, turnip, onion.	1 qt. good stock.
Bouquet garni.	2 oz. oatmeal flour.
Seasoning.	1 teasp. red currant jelly.

Cut the meat and onion into small pieces. Fry these in the fat, remove them, and brown the oatmeal flour. Add the stock and boil up. Add the meat and vegetables again and simmer for 2 or more hours until all is tender. Rub through a sieve. Add seasoning and jelly, re-heat and serve with small force-meat balls.

KIDNEY SOUP (5 or 6 people)

1 lb. ox kidney.	½ turnip.
2 oz. dripping.	1 carrot.
2 oz. flour.	1 onion.
1 qt. stock (or water).	Bunch herbs (thyme, marjoram,
1 blade mace.	parsley, and 1 bay leaf).
½ teasp. black peppercorns.	Salt.

Remove skin, wash and dry the kidney and cut it into small dice, keeping back the core. Skin, scald and dry the onion and cut it into rings. Make the dripping smoking hot in a large, deep pan. Toss the kidney lightly in the flour and fry a good brown colour. Lift the pieces out and fry the onion and remaining flour until well browned. Return the kidney, add stock and salt and bring slowly to the boil. Skim carefully. Cut the carrot and turnip into blocks and add to the soup with the herbs and peppercorns. Simmer 4 or 5 hours. Strain

through a sieve and when cold remove all fat.   Return soup to
the pan, rinse the pieces of kidney and add them to the soup, or
the kidney may be sieved and added.   Re-heat and serve.

*LENTIL SOUP (5 or 6 people)

½ pt. lentils.	1 oz. flour.
Sprig thyme and parsley.	1 onion.
1 pt. milk.	1 qt. stock or water.
1 carrot.	1 bacon bone.

½ oz. fat.

Sauté the washed lentils and vegetables, cut small.   Add
cold stock or water and bring gently to the boil.   Skim and
cook about 2 hours till very tender.   Sieve, re-heat, adding the
milk.   When boiling add the flour, mixed to a smooth cream
with a little cold water.   Stir and boil for 5 minutes.   Season
and serve with fried croûtons.

*MULLIGATAWNY SOUP (Thick)
(4 or 5 people)

1 oz. fat.	A squeeze of lemon juice.
1 onion, 1 sour apple.	1 tablesp. coconut infused in a
1 dessertsp. curry powder (more or less to taste).	cup of boiling water.
	1 qt. stock.
¼ pt. milk.	2 oz. pea flour or flour.

Seasoning.

Fry meat, chopped onion, etc., add the curry powder, fry
this, add the chopped apple, and fry carefully.   Add the stock
by degrees and the coconut infusion.   Boil.   Add the pea flour
mixed to a smooth cream with cold water.   Boil all gently for an
hour or so, skimming and stirring frequently.   Sieve, re-heat,
add the cream, lemon, seasoning, and serve.   Hand boiled
rice with it.

N.B.   This soup is improved by the addition of any fresh
summer vegetables, tomatoes, chutney, etc.

*ONION SOUP (6 or 8 people)

4 large onions.	1 lb. potatoes.
Bacon rind (2 oz.).	½ pt. milk or cream.
4 pt. stock or water.	Bay leaf.

Seasoning.

Slice the onions and potatoes.   Sauté them with the bacon
rind, or with 2 oz. fat.   Cover with stock or water, and when

tender sieve them. Re-boil, add the milk or cream, and serve. 2 oz. grated cheese may be added if liked.

PALERMO, SOUP À LA (about 6 people)

2 oz. vermicelli.	4 tomatoes.
1 qt. white stock.	Seasoning.

Yolks of 2 or 3 eggs and } For a liaison, but a cheaper
½ pt. milk.   } one of flour can be used.

Break the vermicelli into short lengths and cook it in the boiling water for 5 minutes. Drain it, throw away the water, and put it in a pan with some of the stock, and cook till tender (20 minutes). Simmer the tomatoes separately in a little of the stock, and when tender, sieve them, and add them to the stock and vermicelli. Re-heat and add the liaison. If egg, do not re-boil; if flour, boil for 5 minutes.

POTATO SOUP

½ oz. butter or margarine.	1 qt. white stock.
1 lb. potatoes.	½ pt. milk.
1 onion.	½ oz. flour.
1 stick celery.	½ gill cream, if liked.

Method.—Follow recipe for Artichoke Soup.

PURÉE D'ARTOISE (about 6 people)

For this an equal quantity of the following three things is needed:

(1) 1 pt. béchamel sauce.
(2) 1 pt. haricot bean or lentil purée (¼ pt. beans or lentils cooked in ¾ to 1 pt. stock, and sieved).
(3) ¼ pt. finely cut julienne strips of vegetables, cooked till tender in 1 pt. stock. These must be tender but unbroken.

Make these three things quite separately, then mix them together, season, re-boil. Add cream, if wished, and serve.

This is an excellent soup.

*SPINACH SOUP (6 or 8 people)

1 lb. spinach.	1 qt. stock or water.
6 Spring onions.	2 tablesp. of lightly
1 oz. fat.	browned roux.

Salt to taste.

Sauté the onions and spinach. Mix the stock to the roux, and add this to the sautéd vegetables. Cook gently 30 to 40 minutes. Sieve, re-heat, season to taste. If possible, lastly add 1 tablesp. cream. Serve with fried croûtons.

TOMATO SOUP (I)

(4 to 5 people)

1 lb. fresh or tinned tomatoes.	½ teasp. sugar.
½ oz. fat.	1 carrot.
1 oz. lean bacon or bacon bone.	1 onion.
	1 stick celery.
1 pt. stock.	½ oz. fine sago.
2 tablesp. cream.	1 clove, 1 blade mace, bunch herbs.

Salt, pepper.

Sauté carrot, onion, celery (previously cut into slices). Add tomatoes, stock and seasonings. Simmer till tender (1 hour). Then sieve. Add sago, simmer till clear. Add cream and serve.

TOMATO SOUP (II)

(4 or 5 people)

1 lb. fresh or tinned tomatoes.	½ teasp. sugar.
½ oz. fat.	1 carrot.
½ oz. lean bacon or bacon bone.	1 onion. } Cut into slices.
	1 stick celery.
1 pt. stock.	Salt, pepper.
½ pt. stock or water.	1 clove, 1 blade mace, bunch herbs.
1 oz. flour.	

Sauté carrot, onion and celery in the fat. Add tomatoes, stock and seasoning. Simmer till tender. Sieve. Blend flour and water or stock, put into rinsed pan, stir till boiling. Add tomato purée. Re-boil and serve.

*VEGETABLE MARROW SOUP (4 or 5 people)

2 small marrows (about 2 lb.), peeled and sliced.	1 pt. stock or water.
	1 pt. milk.
Bunch of herbs.	1 oz. flour.
1 onion.	½ oz. fat.

Seasoning.

Sauté the marrows in the butter. Add the stock and herbs. Cook till tender. Sieve, re-heat, adding the milk. When boiling add the liaison of the flour, mixed to a smooth cream with cold milk. Boil for 5 minutes. Season and serve.

SOUPS—CLASS II

BARLEY CREAM SOUP (4 or 5 people)

3 oz. pearl barley.	½ oz. fat.
1 qt. white stock.	Dust of nutmeg.
1 small onion.	1 egg and 4 tablesp. of
1 small carrot.	milk, or 1 egg and
Stick of celery.	¼ pt. cream (or less).

Salt and pepper to taste.

Wash the barley, then blanch it. Sauté the vegetables in the fat. Add the barley and stock. Cook gently for two hours. Strain. Add eggs and cream (beaten together). Re-heat, but do not boil again. Serve with fried croûtons.

BEEF SOUP (4 or 5 people)

1 lb. beef.	1 onion.
1 qt. well-flavoured second	Bunch of herbs.
stock.	Salt.
1 carrot, 1 small turnip.	1 oz. cornflour or flour.

Cut the meat into very small pieces and the vegetables into dice. Put these in a saucepan with the stock and herbs. Simmer gently for about 3 hours till the meat is quite tender. Strain. Thicken the soup with the cornflour or flour mixed to a smooth cream with cold water. Re-boil, stirring, for 5 minutes. Add the meat and vegetables and serve.

CABBAGE SOUP (5 or 6 people)

1 cabbage (small).	3 pt. boiling water
½ oz. fat.	or white stock.
1 onion.	1 oz. fine sago.
1 pt. milk.	Chopped parsley.

Seasoning, salt and pepper.

Wash and shred the cabbage; if old, blanching it first. Melt the fat in a saucepan, add the shredded cabbage and finely sliced onion, sauté this for about 10 minutes over gentle heat, shaking frequently. Add the boiling water or stock. Cook gently till the cabbage is tender (about 30 minutes). Add the milk and fine sago and boil and stir well for about 10 minutes till the sago is clear. Add the chopped parsley, seasoning and serve.

*CALF'S HEAD (Thick) or MOCK TURTLE (12 or more people)

Half a calf's head.	Bunch of herbs.
3 qt. second stock.	Blade of mace.
1 large carrot, turnip, onion, shallot.	4 cloves, 10 peppercorns.
1 clove of garlic.	4 oz. butter.
2 sticks celery.	3 oz. flour.
6 mushrooms.	½ pt. sherry (or less).
	Forcemeat balls.
Bay leaf.	

Wash the head well. Cut off the meat and chop the bones. Put these with the stock and a teasp. of salt into a pan. Bring to the boil and skim. Cook for at least 3 to 4 hours gently. Strain off the stock, cut meat into dice; when stock is cold remove all fat from surface. Fry the vegetables and ham, cut into small pieces, in the butter, also the herbs, spices and flour until the flour is a good, rich brown. Add the stock, stir and boil. Simmer for 1 hour or more, skimming frequently. Strain it into another pan, add the meat from the head. Season with the wine, lemon juice and salt and cayenne. Re-boil the soup. Serve it with tiny forcemeat balls, made of veal forcemeat, to which the calf's brain has been added. Egg and crumb and fry the balls before serving them in the soup.

CHESTNUT SOUP (Not Purée)
(4 or 5 people)

1 cup of rice.	1 qt. water.
1 onion, 1 turnip.	1 stick celery.
3 tablesp. chestnut flour.	½ pt. milk or cream.
	Seasoning.

Wash the rice. Put it in a pan with the water and vegetables. Simmer gently for an hour. Strain it and return it to the saucepan. Mix the chestnut flour to a smooth cream with the milk or cream, and add it to the soup. Boil for 10 minutes, stirring constantly. Season and serve with fried croûtons.

COCK-A-LEEKIE (11 to 12 people)

2 qt. chicken liquor.	1 large bunch leeks.
1 or more chicken carcasses.	1 cup rice. Seasoning.

Trim off roots and green part of leeks, wash well. Cut into thin slices and place with chicken bones and seasoning into stock. Cook gently for 1 hour. Remove bones and add rice. Continue till tender. Stir and skim soup while cooking.

GAME SOUPS

Follow the recipe for Hare Soup. If a white soup is required follow the recipe for Rabbit Soup, using game stock.

GIBLET SOUP (8 or 10 people)

4 sets giblets.	2 oz. fat.
1 carrot.	1 blade mace.
1 onion, stuck with	1 bunch herbs.
3 cloves.	Juice of half lemon.
1 turnip.	2 qt. stock.
¼ head celery.	2 oz. flour.

Seasoning.

Wash the giblets and cut them up. Slice the vegetables and put them with the giblets into a pan with the stock. Simmer 2 or 3 hours till cooked. Make a roux with the fat and flour. Add some of the soup to this. Boil and return this to the rest of the soup. Stir and skim for 20 minutes. Strain, re-heat; add a glass of sherry if wished; season to taste, and add the giblets cut into neat dice.

GRAVY SOUP

This should be made from good stock, to which is added any remains of meat gravy, or of the gravy to be found under dripping. To this must be added a brown roux, and vegetables in the proportion of ¼ pt. vegetables to each pt. of soup.

A very satisfactory recipe would be as follows for 4 or 5 people.

1 lb. lean beef (shin of beef without the bone, or gravy beef).	
1½ pt. good gravy stock.	Bunch of herbs, 10 pepper-
Small carrot, turnip, onion,	corns.
celery.	Salt and pepper.
1 oz. fat. 1 oz. flour.	2 cloves, blade of mace.

Cut or mince the meat finely. Cover it with the cold stock (if the stock is jellied put the meat with ½ pt. cold water to draw out the juices and then add the stock). Leave for ½ hour or more. Bring gently to the boil and skim. Then simmer gently for 3 hours. Make a brown roux of the fat and flour, add the vegetables, cut up and fry these lightly. Then add part of the soup, stir and boil. Add this to the remainder of the soup, and simmer the whole for another hour. Strain or sieve, skim well, season, and serve. If a thicker soup is desired, ½ oz. fine sago may be sprinkled and boiled in the soup for 10 minutes until clear.

HARE SOUP (20 people)

1 hare.	12–20 peppercorns.
2 slices ham.	Blade mace.
3 oz. fat.	6 cloves.
1 carrot, turnip, onion.	4 qt. stock, or water.
Stick celery.	4 oz. flour.
Bunch of herbs.	¼ pt. port wine.
Seasoning.	Red currant jelly.

Cut the hare in joints, and the ham and vegetables into slices. Fry these in the fat till slightly browned, then remove them. Add the flour and brown this. Add the stock, herbs, spices, and return the hare and vegetables to the pan. Simmer gently for at least 4 hours. (If possible, it is better to do this prolonged cooking in a casserole in the oven, which prevents any danger of burning. If so, do the preliminary frying in a large frying pan, and lift the hare, etc., into the casserole when browned.) Strain. Leave till cold. Remove all fat. Either sieve the meat or cut it into dice, re-boil it with the soup, adding a teaspoon of red currant jelly and the wine. Serve with small forcemeat balls.

HOLLANDAISE SOUP (I)
(5 or 6 people)

1 qt. very well-flavoured white stock.	1 gill cream
	Seasoning to taste.
1½ oz. butter.	½ pt. carefully cooked
1 oz. flour.	vegetables, cut into
4 egg yolks.	small fancy shapes.

Melt the butter, add the flour to make a white roux. Add the stock. Stir and boil for 5 minutes. Cool, and strain the eggs and cream beaten together to the soup. Re-heat without boiling to cook the egg. Add a pinch of sugar, the seasoning, and, if liked, a squeeze of lemon, and garnish with the vegetables.

HOLLANDAISE SOUP (II)
(5 or 6 people)

1 qt. thin béchamel sauce. This must be hardly thicker than milk. 1½ oz. flour to the qt. should be quite sufficient.

4 egg yolks.	1 gill stock.
Seasoning.	Lemon juice.

Boil the sauce, cool it slightly, and add the stock and yolks beaten together. Season, and re-heat, without boiling. Lastly add a squeeze of lemon, and, if wished, ½ gill cream. Serve as before with the prettily cut cooked vegetables.

*MOCK HARE SOUP (4 or 5 people)

½ lb. lean beef.	1½ oz. dripping.
1 qt. stock.	1 oz. flour.
1 carrot, onion, ½ turnip.	1 tablesp. mushroom ketchup.
Strip of lemon rind.	
Bunch herbs.	1 tablesp. red currant jelly.
3 cloves.	
1 wine-glass port wine.	Seasoning.

Fry the meat till brown on both sides. Add the onion stuck with the cloves, and fry also. Remove the meat and onion. Make a roux with the fat and flour. Add the stock, stir and boil well. Cool this, and add the vegetables and meat cut into small pieces. Add the flavourings, and simmer for 2 to 3 hours. Strain and add the wine and jelly. Re-heat and serve with forcemeat balls.

*NORMANDY SOUP (4 or 5 people)

½ oz. fat.	1 pt. white stock.
2 large carrots.	1 pt. milk.
2 teasp. chopped onion.	1 oz. flour.
1 bay leaf.	Seasoning.

Scoop out the red parts of the carrots with a pea cutter. Grate 2 tablesp. of the remaining parts.

Sauté the grated carrot and chopped onion in the fat. Add the stock, carrot balls, bay leaf, and seasoning. Simmer this until the carrot is quite tender. Mix the flour to a smooth cream with the milk. Add this, and stir till the soup boils.

Serve with fried croûtons of bread.

*OX-TAIL SOUP (8 or 10 people)

1 ox-tail.	2 oz. flour.
2 qt. stock.	1 oz. lean ham or bacon.
1 carrot, turnip, onion.	6 peppercorns, 2 cloves,
Stick of celery.	blade mace.
Bunch of herbs and	2 oz. fat.
bay leaf.	½ lemon.

Salt and pepper.

Divide tail into joints. Wash, blanch, and dry them. Fry these with the vegetables, cut into small pieces.

Put all these in a large pan with the stock, herbs and spices, and cook gently for 4 or 5 hours. Strain, and when quite cold, skim all fat from the stock. Return it to the saucepan, and, when boiling, add the flour, mixed to a smooth cream with cold stock or water. Boil for five minutes.

Season with lemon juice, salt and cayenne. Serve with small pieces of the tail in the soup and some cooked rounds of carrot and turnip the size of a shilling.

A glass of wine may be added to the soup.

POTAGE À LA BONNE FEMME (5 or 6 people)

2 lettuces.	The crust of a French
½ cucumber.	roll cut into small
2 or 3 sprigs tarragon	rounds.
and chervil.	1 qt. white stock.
2 leaves of sorrel.	½ oz. butter.
Small teasp. sugar (white).	2 yolks of eggs.
Seasoning.	¼ pt. cream.

Shred finely the washed lettuces, tarragon, chervil and cucumber. Sauté these in the butter. Add the salt and sugar, and pour the boiling stock over them. Cook gently for 20 to 30 minutes, till all the vegetables are tender. Cool the soup. Beat the eggs and cream together, and add them. Re-heat to thicken, but not to boil. Brown the rounds of French roll in the oven, and serve them in the soup.

POTAGE D'AMANDES (A good winter soup)
(4 people)

2 oz. almonds.	½ oz. flour.
1 gill milk.	1 pt. white stock.
1 tablesp. bread-	½ gill cream.
crumbs.	Lemon juice.
½ oz. butter.	Pepper and salt.

Blanch almonds and put through mincer. Pound with a few drops of water to prevent oiling, then stew with the milk for 1 hour, adding more liquid if required. It should be a thick pulp when cooked. Add the breadcrumbs and simmer for a few minutes. Melt the butter, add the flour and almond pulp, then the stock gradually. Boil, season, add the cream and re-heat without boiling.

POTAGE REINE MARGOT (6 people)

1 chicken carcass.	½ pt. milk.
1 qt. stock.	2 egg yolks.
2 oz. butter.	2 oz. cream of rice.

Vegetables for flavouring.

Sauté the carcass of a roast chicken and any vegetables for

flavouring in 1 oz. butter. Add this to the stock. Boil gently
for 15 minutes. Cool. Beat 2 egg yolks with 2 tablesp. cream.
Add to the soup. Re-heat. Do not boil.

*RABBIT SOUP (10 people)

1 rabbit.	1 pt. milk.
3 pt. stock or water.	Bunch of herbs.
1 slice pork or ham.	A piece of celery
2 onions.	(white part).
2 oz. flour.	Salt to taste.

Wash the rabbit and divide it into neat joints. Put these in
a pan with the onions, herbs, ham and celery. Add the stock
and simmer gently for quite three hours. Strain, and when
cold, remove all fat. Re-boil, then add the flour, mixed to a
smooth cream with the milk. Cook well. Season and serve
with fried croûtons.

*SAGO SOUP (6 or 7 people)

3 pt. very good stock and 1½ oz. fine sago.

Sprinkle the well-washed sago into the boiling stock. Simmer
for 20 to 30 minutes, stirring occasionally, and serve.

TAPIOCA CREAM SOUP (5 or 6 people)

1 qt. well flavoured	1 oz. crushed tapioca.
white stock.	2 egg yolks.
¼ pt. cream.	Seasoning.

Boil the stock and sprinkle in the tapioca. Stir and cook for
20 minutes. Beat the yolks and cream together. Cool the
soup and add these. Re-heat carefully but do not boil.

TURTLE SOUP, Thick (8 to 10 people)

Six oz. dried turtle will make about 2 qt. of soup. Soak the
turtle for 3 or 4 days, changing the water daily. Then cut it
into neat pieces and cook gently in well-flavoured stock made
from fish and beef, adding the usual (see Consommé à la Tortue)
vegetables and herbs. The latter should include basil. Cook
for 4 or 5 hours.

To each qt. allow 1 oz. fat, 1 oz. flour for thickening. Make
a brown roux with these, and to the roux add the soup. Boil
up and skim well. Add a glass of Madeira and some lemon
juice and cayenne. Serve with some pieces of turtle in the soup,
and, if liked, with forcemeat balls.

WHITE FOAM SOUP (4 or 5 people)

1 qt. milk.	1 tablesp. chopped
1 oz. flour.	parsley.
1½ oz. butter.	1 onion.
1 clove of garlic.	Stick celery.
2 eggs.	Blade of mace.
2 oz. cheese.	Seasoning.

Melt the butter, add the flour, then the milk by degrees and stir thoroughly. Boil well. Add the garlic, celery and mace. Barely simmer for 20 to 30 minutes till the soup is well flavoured. Cool slightly and add the yolks. Re-heat without boiling. Add the seasoning and grated cheese. Beat the whites to a stiff froth. Fold half into soup, put the rest into hot tureen and pour soup over and sprinkle a little very finely chopped parsley on the top. Serve with fried croûtons of bread.

*WHITE VEGETABLE SOUP (Vegetarian) or SOUP MAIGRE
(4 people)

1 carrot, turnip, and onion.	½ oz. fat.
2 leeks (white part).	1 oz. cornflour or 1¼ oz.
2 white sticks of celery.	flour.
Small bay leaf, small blade	1½ pt. vegetable stock.
of mace.	½ pt. milk.
Seasoning.	Pinch sugar, 2 cloves.

Cut the vegetables into equal sized match-like strips. Sauté these in the butter, then add the stock, bay leaf, mace, and cloves (known as the bouquet garni). Cook gently until the vegetables are tender but unbroken (½ hour or so), removing the bouquet garni after 15 minutes. Mix the cornflour or flour to a smooth cream with the milk and add it. Boil for 5 minutes. Season and serve.

SOUPS—Class III

CONSOMMÉS or CLEAR SOUPS

CLEAR SOUP (4 or 5 people)

To each qt. of first stock allow:

½ lb. lean gravy beef (entirely freed from all fat), the whites and shells of 2 eggs.

A thick slice of each of the following vegetables: Onion, carrot, turnip, celery, a bunch of herbs (parsley, thyme, and bay leaf),

12 peppercorns and 2 cloves. Seasoning (salt and cayenne) to taste.

The herbs, peppercorns and cloves should be tied in muslin, and if no celery is available, tie ½ teasp. celery seed with them.

METHOD. Mince the meat very finely, putting it several times through a mincing machine.

Wash the egg shells and carefully divide the yolks from the whites (any yolk would cloud the soup).

Place all the ingredients in a large pan, season carefully with salt, cayenne and a squeeze of lemon, and whisk all together over the fire until a light froth rises and remains when all whisking ceases (temperature should be about 170° F.). Stop whisking, and leave undisturbed until the soup commences to boil, then watch carefully and allow the scum to rise up nearly to the top of the pan. When this occurs, move the pan carefully to the side of the fire and simmer gently for about 40 minutes, then strain through a fine cloth. Strain twice if necessary.

The strained soup should be sparklingly clear. Any specks of grease can be removed by passing blotting paper or any clean white paper over the surface.

Taste it and add more seasoning if necessary. A glass of sherry is usually added, or this may simply be poured into the hot tureen, as boiling evaporates the spirit in wine.

Colour the soup if necessary; one drop of caramel is usually sufficient, as the colour required is a golden one. Re-heat and serve very hot.

Consommé made exactly in this manner can be used for any clear soup, the flavour can be varied by using chicken or veal stock, etc., but the NAME given to each consommé is derived from its garnish, the actual soup in most cases being exactly the same.

The garnish must NEVER be cooked in the soup or it will cloud and spoil it. It must be cooked quite separately, and if suitable then rinsed several times in warm water.

CONSOMMÉ À LA BRUNOISE (4 or 5 people)

| 1 qt. clear soup. | The white part of half a |
| 2 carrots.   1 turnip. | head of celery. |

Cut the vegetables into small dice. Cook these separately, rinse them well and serve them in the soup.

CONSOMMÉ CARMEN

Make a double strength consommé, adding 2 or 3 ripe, shredded tomatoes before clarifying.

GARNISH. Shred sweet Spanish pepper and hard-boiled white of egg into very thin shreds; cook a little rice and rinse it well and add these with finely shredded tarragon and chervil to the soup.

Shredded tomato may be used if Spanish pepper is unobtainable.

CONSOMMÉ À LA CONDÉ

Consommé, clarified as usual, but the stock made from game.

GARNISH, very small quenelles of haricot bean purée and fine julienne strips of partridge.

CONSOMMÉ FLEURI

Prepare a 'Consommé à la Jardinière,' put 3 tablesp. of cooked well-rinsed rice into a hot tureen, and pour the consommé over and serve.

CONSOMMÉ À LA JARDINIÈRE

Cook the following vegetables: sprigs of cauliflower, rounds cut from the white leaves of cabbage, carrots or turnips cut into pea shapes, green peas and asparagus tips, and, if possible, a few tarragon and chervil leaves.

Rinse them well and allow ½ pt. of vegetables to 3 pt. consommé.

CONSOMMÉ JULIENNE

Cut the following vegetables into very thin matchlike shreds, equal in length, cook them, rinse and add them to the soup: 2 carrots, ½ turnip, 1 leek, ½ onion, and, if liked, a small part of a cabbage.

CONSOMMÉ AU MACARONI

Cook some macaroni in salted water. Rinse it in several waters, cut into very thin rings and put these in the consommé.

CONSOMMÉ À LA PRINCESSE

1 qt. consommé.	1 tablesp. pearl barley.
1 fillet off the breast of chicken, cooked.	1 tablesp. cooked asparagus points.

Boil the barley in stock till quite tender. Rinse it well and add it with the fillet cut into dice, and the separately cooked asparagus points, to the soup.

CONSOMMÉ AUX QUENELLES FRITES

Make a Choux Paste (see recipe p. 175). Put it in a forcing bag and cut off tiny pieces, dropping them into hot fat. Fry them. They should be the size of small marbles or peas. Drain very thoroughly to free from all grease. Pour the consommé into a hot tureen, and add the fried quenelles just before serving.

CONSOMMÉ À LA ROYALE

GARNISH.

1 yolk of egg.	Seasoning.
2 tablesp. of cream or strained stock.	

Make the liquid blood heat. Pour it on to the beaten egg. Season and strain into a buttered cup. Cover with a greased paper and steam very gently for about 20 to 30 minutes (or bake in a cool oven, standing the cup in water). When quite firm, turn out the custard and when cold cut it into fancy shapes. Leave the custards in cold water until required for the soup. Drain them, pour hot water on to warm them, drain again, put them into a hot tureen and pour the consommé (1 qt.) over.

CONSOMMÉ AU RIZ

Clear soup garnished with plain boiled rice.

CONSOMMÉ ROTHSCHILD

Consommé garnished with finely cut shreds of breast of pheasant, chestnuts and strips of truffle.

CONSOMMÉ À LA TORTUE (12 to 16 people)
(Turtle Soup. Made with dried turtle)

½ lb. best sun-dried turtle.	1 glass brandy.
2 carrots.	5 qt. 1st stock.
1 stick celery.	2 turnips.
3 onions.	1 leek.
10–20 peppercorns.	4 cloves.
Bunch of herbs, including basil.	2 blades mace.
	½ lb. lean gravy beef.
½ lb. veal.	4 whites of egg.
½ lemon.	2 glasses sherry.
	Seasoning.

Wash the turtle (cold water) and soak it in cold water for 3 or 4 days, changing the water daily. Put it in a large stew pan, bring to the boil, skim, and then add the vegetables, herbs, and spices (tie the last two in muslin). Cook gently for 8 to 10 hours.

Remove some fat, strain the stock and put the turtle on a dish, and when cold cut it into convenient pieces.

Next day skim the stock free of all fat. Mince the veal and beef 2 or 3 times and exactly follow the directions given on page 21 under Clear Soup.

When finished and strained, re-heat it, adding the wine, brandy and meat from the turtle. Season and serve.

CALF'S HEAD SOUP (Clear)
(8 to 10 people)
(Sometimes known as Clear Mock Turtle)

½ calf's head.	3 qt. of second stock.
A knuckle of veal.	½ pt. sherry (or less).
A large slice of ham.	½ lemon.
A large carrot, turnip, onion.	1 lb. lean gravy beef.
2 sticks of celery.	Whites and shells of 3 eggs,
Bunch of herbs, blade of	for clearing.
mace, etc.	Cayenne and salt.

Thoroughly wash and then blanch the head. Place it with the ham, veal and vegetables in a large pot with 1 qt. stock. Boil this rapidly and reduce the stock to a glaze.

Add the rest of the stock and cook gently for 3 or 4 hours until the meat is very tender. Strain and when cold remove all fat from the soup. Finish it by clearing, following the rules given on page 21. Garnish with small pieces of the calf's head, and, if liked, with egg balls.

FOR THE EGG BALLS. Hard boil 3 eggs. Pound these with salt, cayenne and a few drops of lemon juice. Add the raw yolks (left from clearing the soup) and pound again. Sieve the mixture and form it into balls. Poach these carefully and serve them in the soup.

SOUPS—CLASS IV

BROTHS

*CROÛTE-AU-POT (5 or 6 people)

1 qt. good stock.	1 French roll cut into thin
1 small carrot, turnip.	rounds and browned in
½ cabbage.	the oven.
1 teasp. chopped parsley.	1 oz. butter.
Salt, pepper.	Nutmeg.

Wash and shred the cabbage. Cut the carrot and turnip into rounds the size of a shilling. Sauté these in the butter. Add the stock, seasoning and nutmeg, and simmer gently for about 40 minutes (or until tender). Place the slices of roll in the soup tureen and pour the soup over and sprinkle with chopped parsley.

*HOTCH POTCH

This is made like Mutton Broth, but many more vegetables are added to it. If seasonable, shredded lettuce, green peas, French beans cut small, etc., should all be added, as well as carrots and turnips.

*MUTTON BROTH (6 people)

2 lb. scrag end of mutton.	3 pt. water.
Medium-sized onion ⎫ cut into	2 oz. pearl barley, or rice.[1]
,, carrot ⎬ small	1 teasp. chopped parsley.
,, turnip ⎭ dice.	Seasoning.

Wipe the mutton, trim off any extra fat. Place it in a saucepan with the water and barley. Bring to the boil and skim. Add the vegetables and a teasp. salt. Cook gently for 1½ to 2 hours. Remove the meat and serve it separately coated with parsley or caper sauce.

Leave the broth till cold. Remove all fat. Season to taste and add the parsley. Serve with very thin three-cornered slices of bread in the soup.

*POT AU FEU (about 8 people)

This is a ' standing dish ' in many European countries and simmers all day in many households. Much that would be wasted otherwise is put into it, and an excellent and nourishing soup results.

2 lb. shin of beef or brisket.	About 2 qt. water.
	1 clove.
1 onion, carrot, turnip and leek.	10 or 12 peppercorns.
	Salt to taste.
Stick of celery.	1 French roll.
½ or ¼ cabbage.	Bunch of herbs.

Place the meat in a saucepan and cover it with cold water. Bring gently to the boil and skim well. Wash the vegetables. Stick the clove in the onion and tie up the leek, celery and cabbage. Simmer gently for at least 4 hours. Remove the meat to serve separately, or to use later. Strain the broth, season it to taste, remove any fat and serve it with rounds of

[1] If rice is added instead of barley, it should be added *after* the vegetables, as rice does not take long to cook.

the leek, turnip and carrot in it. Cut some roll into very thin slices and put these into the tureen. Pour the broth over, add some finely chopped parsley and serve.

*SCOTCH BROTH (6 people)

2 lb. scrag end of mutton.	Medium-sized onion ⎫ cut into
3 pt. water.	,, carrot ⎬ small
2 oz. rice or pearl barley.	,, turnip ⎭ dice.
1 teasp. chopped parsley.	Salt.

Cut the meat into small pieces, removing the fat. Cook these with the water 2 to 3 hours. Add the rice and vegetables (cut into dice) and cook till tender, about 1 hour. Remove the bones. Cool and remove the fat. Re-heat and serve with the chopped parsley. If pearl barley is substituted for rice, it requires washing and cooking as long as the meat.

*SHEEP'S HEAD BROTH (12 people)

1 sheep's head.	¼ lb. rice, pearl barley
3 qt. water.	or oatmeal.
2 carrots.	6 peppercorns.
2 turnips.	1 teasp. chopped
2 onions.	parsley.
Celery. 2 cloves.	Salt.

Prepare the head (see recipe Sheep's Head, p. 78) and cook gently 1 hour, skimming occasionally. Cut the vegetables into neat pieces and add these with the rice, spices and salt. Cook slowly 2 hours. Remove the head. Add a teaspoonful of parsley before serving.

The head can be served separately with brain sauce, or the meat from it can be cut into small pieces and served with the soup.

SOUPS—CLASS V

FISH SOUPS

LOBSTER BISQUE [1] (Bisque de Homard)
(6 people)

1 hen lobster.	2 oz. butter.
1 qt. fish stock.	2 oz. flour.
½ oz. spawn.	1 teasp. anchovy
1 onion or shallot.	essence.
Bunch of herbs.	½ gill cream.

Remove the meat from the lobster. Pound the shell and

[1] Soups made of shell-fish are called *bisques*. Crabs, prawns or crayfish may replace lobster in the recipe.

add it when making the stock. Fry the onion and herbs lightly in the butter. Add the flour and fry to a pale brown. Add the stock (straining it to the soup) and cook for 40 minutes. Rub the spawn and $\frac{1}{2}$ oz. butter through a hair sieve and add it to the soup. Re-heat, adding the anchovy essence, lemon juice and cream. Serve small pieces of meat in the soup.

OYSTER SOUP (6 people)

2 doz. oysters.	$\frac{1}{2}$ pt. cream, or $\frac{1}{4}$ pt.
$1\frac{1}{2}$ pt. fish stock.	and 2 egg yolks.
2 oz. butter.	1 teasp. lemon juice.
2 oz. flour.	Salt to taste.

Beard the oysters and add the beards in making the stock, which must be flavoured with fish, vegetables, herbs, and spices.

Make a white roux of the fat and flour and add the stock by degrees. Stir and boil for 5 minutes. Add the cream, or yolks and cream. Re-heat (do not boil). Blanch the oysters in their own liquor (which must first be strained). Add these to the soup. Season with salt, pepper, and lemon juice and serve.

WHITE FISH SOUP (4 or 5 people)

1 lb. fish or bones and skin of fish.	Bunch herbs.
	6 peppercorns, 2 cloves.
1 qt. stock or water.	Blade of mace.
1 onion, carrot, turnip.	1 oz. flour.
Stick celery, 1 teasp. chopped parsley.	$\frac{1}{2}$ pt. milk.
	Seasoning.

Cook the fish with the vegetables, herbs, and spices. When done remove the flesh and continue cooking the rest for an hour. Strain. Return to the pan, boil and thicken with the flour mixed to a smooth cream with the milk. Boil for 5 minutes, add the chopped parsley, season and serve with the fish broken into neat pieces in it.

A cod's head will make twice this amount of soup.

II. FISH

FISH contains a varying amount of water and mineral and nitrogenous matter. The latter is mostly gelatine; isinglass, for instance, is made from the bones of sturgeon.

Fish, though not so satisfying a food as meat, is more digestible and therefore better for those whose work is sedentary.

Fishes are in season before their spawning time, after that their flesh becomes flabby.

There are 3 classes of fish:

    I. White fish, e.g. sole, whiting.

    II. Oily fish, e.g. mackerel, salmon.

    III. Shell-fish, e.g. lobster.

Fish vary in shape:

    (1) Flat.
    (2) Round.

The Choice of Fish:

    (1) There must be no unpleasant smell.
    (2) The eyes should be full and bright.
    (3) The flesh should be firm and plump.
    (4) The scales should be abundant.
    (5) The skin must not be wrinkled.
    (6) The colours should be bright and fresh, and with plaice the spots should be bright red and not dull orange.
    (7) The gills should be red.

Medium-sized fish are better in flavour than very large fish, which are apt to be coarse, and small ones tasteless. Shell-fish should weigh heavily in proportion to their size. Whitebait should not cling together.

Preparation of Fish. Fish should be cleaned as soon as possible. There are three exceptions: whitebait, smelts, and red mullet, which are not cleaned but cooked with the insides left in.

To SCALE fish, scrape with a knife from the tail to the head; scale in cold water.

To CLEAN, remove the head, or if the head is to be left on, remove the eyes. To do this latter, snip the skin over the eye and press out with the thumb, taking care not to burst the eye. Open the fish, with scissors or a knife, cutting to the tail. Remove all the inside till the backbone is clear; then clean under cold water. Take away any black skin, rubbing with salt until perfectly clean, giving special attention to the clot of blood sometimes found near the tail. Remove and wash the roes—replace unless otherwise required.

TRIM the fish. To do this, cut off the fins, cutting towards the head. Trim tail neatly.

Preparation of Freshwater Fish. After cleaning the fish it must be well washed in salt and water and freed from blood. Salt removes any slime; and also with freshwater fish the plentiful use of salt removes any muddy flavour.

Flat Fish require skinning and filleting. To do this trim off the outside fin with scissors, then make an incision across the tail, slip a knife under the skin and loosen from the tail and all round the edges of the fish.

Dip the fingers in salt to prevent slipping and raise a large enough flap of skin at the tail to take a firm hold of, and draw the skin off by pulling it upwards from the tail to the head. A sole skins easily; a plaice is difficult, therefore fillet plaice before skinning it.

To Fillet Fish. A sharp knife will be required. A flat fish has 4 'fillets', that is to say, the flesh is more easily removed in 4 parts, whereas a round fish has 2; or the flesh is removed in 2 divisions.

To Fillet Round Fish (herrings, whiting). Cut down the centre of the back to the bone, and with a sharp knife work all the flesh off the bones.

To Fillet Flat Fish (sole or plaice). Cut down the mid-rib from the head to the tail. Then carefully remove the flesh on either side of the backbone, cutting with firm strokes and leaving the bone quite clean. Turn the fish over and repeat this process on the other side. Thus two fillets are obtained from each side of the fish. Plaice must be skinned after being filleted. To do this lay the fillet, skin side downwards, and with a sharp knife cut the flesh off the skin from the tail upwards to the head.

THE COOKING

The methods of cookery that are detailed for meat (pages 52–59) are also applicable to fish. Various small differences should be noted.

(1) BAKING. This is suitable for all fish. It may be done by wrapping the fish in greased paper, OR by laying it on a greased fireproof dish or tin and closely covering it with greased paper.

There are many modifications of the above two methods, e.g. small fillets may be rolled and stuffed, placed in a greased fireproof dish, surrounded by a little water, milk or white wine (to prevent them from getting too dry), covered well with a buttered paper; but these variations will be enumerated in the different recipes.

TIME: Allow about 6 minutes to the lb. and 6 minutes over. Very thick cuts of fish, such as salmon and cod, will require 10 minutes to the lb. and 10 minutes over.

(2) GRILLING OR BROILING. The fish should first be brushed with melted butter, then thinly coated with flour and grilled over a hot clear fire or broiled before one. When cooked the marks of the gridiron should plainly be seen on the fish.

(3) FRYING. This is probably the most popular method. Before being fried the fish must be well dried, first in a clean cloth and then by covering it with flour. Any surplus flour should be shaken off. The fish may then be SAUTÉD or fried in shallow fat with the exception of Whitebait (see page 40), allowing one side to brown in a small quantity of smoking fat, then turning and browning the other side. But to be fried properly in deep fat a light casing of flour should still be put to dry the fish, which is then egged and crumbed and fried in hot deep fat until of a golden colour. Fillets of fish may be seasoned with salt, pepper and a squeeze of lemon juice before being floured. This much improves their flavour.

Fish may also be enclosed in batter before being fried.

(4) BOILING. There are several points of difference in boiling fish and meat. RULES FOR FISH:

AVERAGE TIME, 6 minutes to the lb. and 6 minutes over, except for thick cuts of cod and salmon, when 10 minutes to the lb. and 10 minutes over must be allowed.

(a) Fish are never skinned before boiling. The heads must
    be left on and only the eyes removed.

(b) Fish before being boiled must be seasoned, sprinkled with
    lemon juice, if liked, and wrapped in greased paper.
    This prevents the loss of much flavour.

(c) Some drainer is required on which to place the fish for the
    purpose of lifting it out of the pan. If no proper one is
    available a coarse cloth may be used. Let the fish lie
    on this and lower it into the pan (placing an enamel dish
    or any 'false bottom' so that the cloth does not rest on
    the bottom of the pan, where it would stick and burn),
    allowing the corners of the cloth to rest on the edges of
    the pan, fixed in their places by the lid.

(d) Only sufficient water to just cover the fish is required.

(e) Allow salt in the proportion of 1 oz. to each qt. of water,
    also 1 tablesp. of vinegar to 1 gal. of water (not for
    salmon). N.B. The acid makes the flesh white and firm.

(f) The water must be hot BUT NOT BOILING when fish is put
    into it. Boiling water would break the delicate skins.

   Exceptions: (i) Salmon. Owing to its tough skin the water
       should actually boil gently when it is first put in. (ii)
       Mackerel has a very tender skin, and must go into
       TEPID water.

(g) The water must only SIMMER throughout the cooking of
    fish or the outside will be broken before the inside is done.

(5) STEAMING. Allow nearly twice the times given for boiling.
Sprinkle the fish with lemon juice, salt, and pepper, and wrap it
in greased paper. This is a particularly good and nourishing
method of cooking, as there is very little loss of flavour and
nourishment. It is particularly suited to small fish and cuts
of fish.

(6) STEWING may be defined as 'long slow cooking in a
covered pan'. The best method of stewing is by means of a
covered casserole in the oven. Coarse or tasteless fish may be
so cooked with vegetables, with a very savoury result. TIME:
allow the same as for steaming.

(7) BRAISING. Follow the recipe for braised meat; allowing
12 minutes to the lb. and 12 minutes over, or even rather longer.

DIFFERENT KINDS OF FISH AND THE BEST WAYS OF SERVING THEM

BARTLE

This fish should be fried.

BREAM

Do not scale this. Boil or bake it; if the latter it should be stuffed with veal forcemeat.

BRILL

Follow the directions given for Turbot.

CARP

This fish will have a bitter taste unless the small gall-stone is removed from the head. Bake or boil it and serve with good sauce.

COD

This can be cooked in a large variety of ways.

*If BOILED serve on a napkin garnished with cut lemon and parsley; or it may be coated with a thick sauce and decorated. With boiled cod the following sauces may be served: anchovy, egg, lobster.

*If BAKED it may be stuffed with any good forcemeat. If small enough to bake whole, truss into shape of an S, place on a well-greased tin or fireproof dish, coated with browned bread-crumbs, covered with a greased paper. For further details see Baking, page 30. Serve with a good brown sauce.

Small cuts of cod should be baked as described on page 41, and coated with white sauce.

*COD'S ROE

Wash this well, tie in butter muslin and cook gently in salted water for ½ hour to 1 hour according to thickness. Drain and serve in any of the following ways: *(a) on toast with any good sauce; (b) sliced (when cold) and dipped in fine oatmeal, OR in batter, and fried; *(c) fried in bacon fat with bacon for breakfast.

COD, *SALT

Soak in cold water overnight. Place in cold water and blanch. Then in fresh cold water and cook as for cod. Egg sauce should be served with salt cod.

COD SOUNDS

Soak for several hours. Cook in milk or water till tender (about 40 minutes). Divide into neat squares, marinade these, dip in coating batter and fry. Garnish with lemon and hard-boiled egg.

CRAB, DRESSED

1 crab (large).	1 teasp. made mustard.
Parsley.	1 oz. breadcrumbs.
1 or 2 tablesp. vinegar.	1 tablesp. butter or
Seasoning.	salad oil.

Throw away apron, gills and bag near head. Remove the meat from the shell and the flesh from the claws. Mix the ingredients, wipe the shell and fill it with the mixture. Dish on folded napkin and garnish with parsley and the small claws.

DABS

Fry, preferably in batter.

DACE

These should be fried.

EELS

These can be fried, baked, or stewed, or made into pies. A good sauce such as hollandaise, tartare, piquante, etc., should accompany them.

Eel Pie

Follow the directions for Beefsteak Pie, page 170, putting in eels instead of meat and adding lemon juice.

Eels, Stewed (4 people)

1 lb. eels.	¾ pt. stock.
1½ oz. fat.	1½ oz. flour.
Lemon juice.	Salt and pepper.
1 teasp. anchovy essence.	

Wash and dry the eels. Cut into pieces 2½ ins. long. Flour and fry these till brown. Make a brown sauce of the fat, flour and stock. Boil well and skim. Add the flavourings, then the fish, and stew gently for about 1½ hours or more until tender. Half a glass of port improves this stew.

*B

FINNAN HADDOCK

Wash this well and cover it with hot water. Leave for 10 to 15 minutes. Brush with butter, and grill, or bake if preferred in milk, or divide into neat pieces and stew in milk.

FLOUNDERS

Fry, preferably in batter.

GURNET

Usually stuffed and baked, but may be cooked in any way.

HADDOCKS

Any methods applied to cod are suitable for haddock (fresh). Baked and stuffed haddock (see recipe for Cod, Baked) may be served with parsley or anchovy sauce instead of gravy if preferred.

HAKE

This fish is excellent and resembles a small cod. Follow any rules for cod.

HERRINGS

May be boiled (securing them with their tails in their mouths) and served with mustard, shrimp or parsley sauce. They may also be fried and served with any of the above sauces; or grilled and served with any butters. Scale them before cooking. They may also be split down the middle, opened flat, floured, fried, and served with maître d'hôtel butter.

*HERRINGS (Soused)

(4 people)

Four fresh herrings. Bone and divide each into 2 parts. Season and roll up neatly with the roes inside. Place in a casserole. Add the following: 1 bay leaf, 10 peppercorns, blade of mace, 2 cloves, and sufficient vinegar or vinegar and water to cover the fish. Cover with a greased paper and place a lid on the casserole. Bake gently for 1 hour. The same recipe is excellent for mackerel.

JOHN DORY

Choose a fish 5 or 6 lb. in weight. Cook and serve as for turbot.

LOBSTER (Homard)

If alive, drop quickly into fast-boiling water and boil 20 to 30 minutes.

Usually preferred cold with salad. Remove the head, cut down the centre of the back, break the claws, remove the meat from the body and claws. Mix these with mayonnaise and salad and garnish with small claws and a head.

*MACKEREL

If boiled serve with mustard or parsley sauce. See directions for boiling (page 31), and note that it must be put into tepid and not hot water and gradually brought up to simmering point.

Fried Mackerel. (1) Divide in half, remove bones, flour, egg, crumb, and fry. Garnish with lemon and parsley, and hand separately gooseberry, brown caper, tartare or mustard sauce. Wash and blanch the roes and cook them in the oven. Serve them in the centre of the dish. (2) Split the mackerel in half, but do not divide or bone them. Flour them and fry in shallow fat. Serve with any of the above sauces or with maître d'hôtel butter.

Grilled Mackerel. Follow rules for grilled fish. Serve with maître d'hôtel butter and hand mustard, tomato, fennel, or gooseberry sauce separately.

Mackerel à l'Anvers (or baked and stuffed). (Sufficient for 2 or more people, according to size of mackerel.) Two mackerel. Remove the heads, cut off the fins, split down under side, remove bones, and lightly flour and season them. Place one mackerel on a baking tin, add plenty of dripping for basting. Make the following stuffing:

1 tablesp. breadcrumbs.	2 roes (washed and cooked in salted water for 5 minutes).
½ teasp. grated lemon rind.	
½ teasp. chopped parsley.	1 egg yolk.

Seasoning.

Place this, all the ingredients having been mixed together, on one fish and cover with the other, placing the top one skin side uppermost. Cover the surface with browned breadcrumbs, and bake 20 to 30 minutes. Serve with any good sauce poured round.

MULLET, GREY

This differs entirely from the red variety, and may be cooked in any way suitable for fish, and served with any sauce.

MULLET, RED

These fish are not cleaned. Remove the eyes and fins and wipe the fish gently. A usual way to cook them is in cases.

Red Mullet en Caisses. Notch the fish here and there, sprinkle with salt, pepper, and cover it with oiled butter. Leave for one hour. Wrap each fish securely in a piece of greased paper, lay them on a greased tin, cover with another greased paper, and bake in a moderate oven for 15 to 20 minutes. Serve in the paper cases, garnished with parsley.

The mullets may be prepared and then grilled instead.

*Red Mullets Baked (2 people).

2 mullets.	1 small onion, chopped.
2 teasp. chopped mush-rooms.	2 teasp. chopped parsley.
	Lemon juice.

Prepare as for mullets in cases. After notching the fish, sprinkle half the ingredients on a greased fireproof dish, lay the fish on these, place small pieces of butter over it, and add the rest of the ingredients over the fish. Bake for 15 minutes. Serve in the same dish, garnished with cut lemon and parsley, and serve tomato or any good brown sauce.

Red Mullets Fried. Egg, crumb, and fry these.

*Red Mullets au Gratin. Follow recipe for Sole au Gratin.

OYSTERS

These are usually served raw in one half of the shell. The beards should be removed. Thin brown bread and butter and quarters of lemon are handed with them. They form one of the most popular hors d'oeuvre. If fresh, the shells are very difficult to open; if stale, they will be found slightly open. If possible, eat them at once, but if they have to be kept, place them in salt and water, changing the water daily. Discard any if the shells are open.

PERCH

Follow any recipe given for Trout.

PIKE

Follow any method of cooking suitable for fish, but preferably stuff and bake them.

*PLAICE

See directions at the beginning of this section for filleting and skinning. Any recipe given for sole is suitable for plaice, and if the fillets are well seasoned, plaice may often replace sole.

POUT

This fish is also called 'Whiting Pout' or 'Blind Whiting'. It is a fish that is only obtained locally where caught, as it will not keep or travel. It is distinguished by having eyes that protrude right out of its head. When killed, at once they begin to recede and look dull. Otherwise, the pout much resembles whiting. It has rather a strong smell, even when quite fresh, but is really a most excellent fish when freshly caught, and as it is so little known and appreciated, it can be bought very cheaply. Cook in any of the ways applicable to whiting.

PRAWNS

These are usually eaten cold and freshly boiled as bought in the shops. They may also be curried (see recipes for Crab, Curried), made into patties, cutlets (see Lobster Cutlets), or put in aspic (see recipe for Aspic, page 244).

ROACH

This fish is usually fried.

SALMON

May be cooked in any of the ways given for fish. It is more often boiled or steamed and served with hollandaise, tartare, or other piquante sauces. Cold salmon is excellent for mayonnaise, salads, cold soufflés. Salmon steaks are excellent grilled (see Cod Steaks). These may be served with any good butters instead of sauces.

See rules on Boiling and Baking fish (page 30).

SCALLOPS

These somewhat resemble a large oyster, but are yellow and white. They are not at all wholesome unless quite fresh. Open the shells, remove any beards and the black parts, only the yellow and white portions being edible. Wash and dry them and allow one or two for each shell. Replace them in the shells which have been washed, buttered and sprinkled with breadcrumbs.

Cover the fish with a good tablespoonful of any suitable sauce. Cover this with more crumbs, and small pieces of butter, and brown the surface in a very hot oven. Hand cut lemon with them. This method is called 'scalloping' and may be applied to any other fish, the scallop shells being used for the purpose.

Scallops may also be stewed, or boiled in milk, and used as a garnish.

SHAD

Make one or two cuts across the back, and leave it in a marinade of oil, lemon juice, and seasoning for an hour. Then brush with oil, flour lightly and grill or broil, or fry. Hand brown caper sauce with it.

It may also be cooked in any way suitable for salmon.

SKATE

Skin it, and boil, steam, or fry it. If fried, marinade it first. Serve with shrimp, lobster, caper or piquante sauce, or with any good butter.

SMELTS

These are usually egged, crumbed, and fried, and served with fried parsley and hollandaise or tomato or any good brown sauce, to which fish stock is added.

OR, serve au gratin (see Sole au Gratin).

SOLE

See directions at the beginning of this section for filleting and skinning, page 29.

Fried Sole. A small or medium-sized sole is usually fried whole. To do this, skin the fish, trim the fins and, if large, cut off the head. Wash, dry and flour the sole; dip it into beaten egg; then into fine white crumbs, and fry in hot fat for about six minutes, when it should be golden brown. Drain on paper and serve on a dish, paper, or folded napkin, and garnish with parsley and cut lemon.

Fillets of Sole, Fried. These may be done in several ways: (1) Dip into flour, egg and crumb, and fry flat. (2) Lay the fillets flat on a board, putting the side where the skin has been uppermost. Lay any good stuffing on this, and roll up the fillet. Season, flour, egg and crumb it, and fry in hot fat. (3) **Sole à la Whitebait.** Cut the fillets into narrow strips to resemble Whitebait. Flour these and cook as for Whitebait (see recipe). Garnish with cut lemon, parsley (fried), and hand brown bread and butter with this dish. (4) Dip the seasoned fillets into batter and fry them. The fillets are improved if marinaded first.

SPRATS

Wash and draw them at the gills. Dry them well. Dust with flour and fry, a few at a time, in hot fat. Sprinkle with lemon and cayenne. Serve very hot. Sprats may also be thus prepared and grilled, or broiled before the fire fastened in rows by the heads on a skewer.

STURGEON

Wash and scale the fish. Remove the spikes. Soak it for some hours in salt and water. Wipe it and rub it with lemon juice. Divide it into pieces, and form into cutlets. Place these on a buttered tin or fireproof dish. Sprinkle with salt, pepper, and lemon juice. Cover with a greased paper, and bake in a moderate oven. Pour a white sauce or anchovy sauce over.

Sturgeon is excellent when braised.

TENCH

Cook in any manner suitable for Trout.

TROUT

See notes on freshwater fish (page 29). Trout is usually fried or grilled.

Grilled Trout. Clean and wash it well in salt and water. Cut it down the back. Season with salt, pepper, and lemon. Brush with melted butter or salad oil, flour lightly and grill or broil. Serve with beurre noir sauce, or with maître d'hôtel butter.

Fried Trout. (1) Fillet the fish. Flour, egg and crumb it. Fry in hot deep fat, garnished with fried parsley. Serve with sauce hollandaise, anchovy sauce, or any suitable butter. (2) Clean the fish. Flour it and fry in shallow fat, turning it when one side is brown, to brown the other. Serve with cut lemon or maître d'hôtel butter.

Fillets of trout may also be stuffed, rolled and cooked in the oven (see recipes for Sole). When cold these can be coated with mayonnaise, or they can be egged and crumbed, and fried, or served plainly with any good sauce.

TURBOT

This is an expensive and very delicious fish. If possible a small turbot should be cooked whole, either steamed or cooked in the oven, and served with hollandaise sauce. A good example of the latter method is the following: Procure a young turbot. Remove the black skin, trim off the fins. Cut down the centre of the fish, loosen the flesh and remove any bones that come easily away. Fill this cavity with any good farce. Place the fish on a greased fireproof dish, season it well, cover with ½ glass wine or milk or fish stock, cover with a buttered paper and cook for about 20 minutes in a moderate oven. Add some of the liquor surrounding the fish to a good béchamel or other sauce, pour this round the fish and garnish the top of it with cut lemon and parsley or any more elaborate decoration.

WHITEBAIT

Keep these on ice or in a very cold place till wanted. Wash them in salt and water, handling as little as possible, and lay each one apart on a cloth to dry. Then shake them gently on to another dry cloth and dust them carefully all over with very fine flour. Heat deep fat till it smokes well (about 380° F.). Place some of the fish (they should not touch) in a frying basket and plunge them in the fat to cook them, i.e. 1 or 2 minutes. Turn them on to a sieve and repeat until all are cooked. Then re-heat the fat up to 400° F. A great deal of smoke will rise at that temperature. All the fish may now be put together into the frying basket and re-heated for a moment. This will serve to crisp and slightly brown them. Drain well, first by shaking the basket over the fat, and then by tossing them gently on paper. Sprinkle them with salt and cayenne and serve. Thin brown bread and butter and cut lemon are handed with whitebait.

WHITING (Merlan)

These are very delicate fish and may be cooked in any way. Probably the nicest is to clean them, then curl them, putting the tail through the eye socket. Flour them lightly and egg and crumb them and fry them whole in deep fat. Serve with maître d'hôtel butter. They may be filleted and served au gratin, and are also excellent for soufflés, being a very light fish. See recipes for Chicken Soufflé; substitute sieved and pounded whiting for the chicken and make the panada with fish stock instead of milk.

FISH DISHES

*COD CUTLETS

Divide the fish into slices about 1½ inches thick. These may be grilled, fried and served with any suitable sauce. E.g.

Cod Cutlets à la Crevette (with shrimps). 4 or 5 people.

1½ lb. cod cut into cutlets.	1 teasp. chopped parsley.
½ pt. shelled shrimps.	1 teacup breadcrumbs.
Beaten egg.	Seasoning.

Dry the cutlets, pound the shrimps with egg, breadcrumbs, seasoning, and parsley. Coat one surface of the cutlets with this mixture. Dip them into flour, then into beaten egg and breadcrumbs. Fry in deep fat. Serve with anchovy butter.

COD, *DRESSED (Baked)
(4 or 5 people)

1½ lb. thick cod.	2 tablesp. bread-
½ tablesp. dripping.	crumbs.
1 egg.	1 tablesp. chopped
Brown crumbs.	parsley.
Lemon. Salt.	Seasoning.

Wash the cod. Mix the breadcrumbs, dripping, parsley, salt, with a beaten egg. Stuff the cod with this. Sprinkle with lemon and seasoning. Coat with egg and crumbs. Bake on a tin with some dripping for about ½ hour, basting. Serve with brown gravy.

COD STEAKS GRILLED À LA MAÎTRE D'HÔTEL

Dip the cod steaks into melted butter, then into flour. Grill and serve them with maître d'hôtel butter.

*Another Recipe for Cod Steaks. Grill or fry and serve with tomato sauce.

CRAB, CURRIED
(4 or 5 people)

2 medium crabs.	¼ pt. curry sauce.
1 tablesp. cream.	Lemon juice.

Prepare as for Crab, Dressed. Remove the meat and make it hot in the curry sauce. Add the cream and lemon juice. Serve with boiled rice.

CRAB, SCRAMBLED (5 or 6 people)

1 crab.	6 eggs.
1 oz. butter.	½ teasp. chopped.
½ cup milk.	parsley.
Cayenne.	Seasoning.

Mix the milk, butter and seasoning. Heat the meat of the crab (broken up) in this. Add the eggs, lightly beaten, and stir till sufficiently thick. Add the parsley and a dash of cayenne and serve hot.

LOBSTER CROQUETTES

Form the cutlet mixture (see below) into balls. Flour, egg and crumb, and fry these. Serve with fried parsley and cut lemon.

LOBSTER CUTLETS (4 or 5 people)

1 lobster.	Lemon juice.
1 oz. flour.	1 oz. fat.
1 tablesp. cream	¼ pt. fish stock.
Seasoning.	

Make a thick sauce (panada) with the fat, flour and stock. Boil well. Add the cream. Season, and lastly add the meat of the lobster, cut up. Turn on to a plate, cover with greased paper, and when cold form into cutlets. Flour, egg, crumb and fry these. Insert a small piece of the lobster feeler to represent the cutlet bone.

*MACKEREL PICKLED

This method is excellent for using up cold, cooked mackerel. Take:

½ pt. water.	½ pt. vinegar.
1 blade of mace.	2 cloves.
Bunch of herbs.	12 peppercorns.

Boil these ingredients for ½ hour, and when cold pour them over four mackerel. Herring and salmon may be treated in the same way.

OYSTER BASKETS

Halve some good tomatoes. Scoop out the centres. Cut some oysters into dice and mix them with a good white panada (see Patties). Season well. Fill the half-tomatoes with this mixture. Make handles of long stalks of parsley and decorate prettily. Serve hot.

OYSTER FRITTERS

Sprinkle the oysters with salt, cayenne and lemon. Dip them into any good coating batter and fry in hot fat. Drain well, and serve with fried parsley.

OYSTER PATTIES (8 people)

Make patties. See recipe for Puff Paste, page 170. Bake these, and prepare the following filling:

2 doz. oysters.	⅓ pt. milk or cream.
1 oz. flour.	1 oz. fat.

Make a thick sauce (panada) of these ingredients. Blanch the oysters, removing the beards, in their own liquor (i.e. the water that remains in the shells), and add this liquor to the sauce. Add the oysters and fill the hot-baked cases with this. Re-heat quickly and serve.

OYSTERS STEWED

Prepare the same mixture as given in the previous recipe for the filling of the patties. Serve this, surrounded by fried croûtons of bread.

*SOLE À L'OLGA (4 people)

4 large mealy potatoes.	2 oz. grated cheese.
1½ gills béchamel sauce.	4 fillets of sole (small), cooked
½ gill shelled shrimps.	as in Sole au Vin Blanc.

Bake the potatoes in their skins. Cut off the tops lengthways. Remove some of the potato. Fill the skins with the sauce, cheese, fish, and shrimps in layers. The last layer must be sauce. Sprinkle grated cheese on this and put a few small pieces of butter on each potato. Bake in a hot oven till brown, and serve on a folded napkin.

SOLE À L'ORLY

Fillet one or two soles (allow 1 medium sole for 3 people). Lay the fillets for an hour in the following marinade: 1 tablesp. of salad oil; 1 teasp. of each of the following: lemon juice, tarragon vinegar, chopped parsley, chopped shallot. Mix all these together.

When marinaded, coat the fillets in any good frying batter and fry. Garnish with fried parsley and hand tomato sauce with this dish.

SOLE À LA SUPRÊME (6 people)

| 2 soles. | Lemon juice. |
| Seasoning. | Sauce suprême. |

Season the fillets and sprinkle them with lemon and cayenne. Roll them neatly (see Sole au Vin Blanc), and bake as described in that recipe, pouring a tablesp. of milk or water round instead of the wine. Cover closely with a greased paper and cook for 10 to 15 minutes. Dish and coat with sauce suprême.

*SOLE AU GRATIN

This may be done in two ways: (1) Skin the fish, remove the head and fins. Make a cut down the centre of one side only and slip a knife in, loosening the flesh from the bone. Do this on each side of the backbone, so making two pockets. (2) Fillet the fish. Lay the two bottom fillets together, and keep the top two, to replace afterwards. This method has the advantage of removing all bone, and the shape of the fish can be kept by laying the fillets carefully together; but the former way looks plumper and neater. Finish both ways as follows: Lay the fish on a fireproof dish. Make a stuffing of the following:

> 4 tablesp. of chopped mushrooms.
> 1 tablesp. finely chopped parsley.
> 1 dessertsp. finely chopped shallot or onion.

Lay this either in the pockets made in (1), or spread it over the fillets (2), and in (2) replace the top two fillets. Sprinkle the fish with salt, pepper and lemon. Cover it with ½ gill wine and some good brown sauce. Sprinkle some fine browned breadcrumbs over the top, place some small pieces of butter here and there, and bake for about 20 minutes, covered with a greased paper. Serve in the fireproof dish.

Many fish and some vegetables may be served in this manner.

SOLE AU VIN BLANC (3 or 4 people)

4 fillets of sole.	¼ to ½ pt. white wine.
Lemon juice.	½ pt. béchamel or
Seasoning.	veloutée sauce.

Season the fillets and sprinkle them with the lemon. Roll up neatly, from the thick to the thin end of the fillet, keeping the side where the skin was, inwards.

Place these on a lightly greased tin or fireproof dish. Pour the wine (or fish stock, milk or water) over and cover closely with a greased paper. Bake in a moderate oven for about 15 minutes. Add the wine in which the fish was cooked to the sauce; reduce this by boiling and skimming. Dish the fillets neatly, pour the sauce over, and decorate to taste.

SOLE FILLETS WITH CHEESE

Cook the fillets as for Sole au Vin Blanc, placing them on a fireproof dish. Make a mixture for Welsh Rarebit (see Savouries, page 289) and pour this on to each fillet. Put them for a moment under a hot gas grill or salamander, and send slightly browned to table (or brown for a moment in a very hot oven).

SOLE FILLETS À LA MICHEL

Stuff the fillets and roll them. The stuffing may be of a mixture of foie-gras, ham, tongue, or anything available. Cook the fillets either by baking (see Sole au Vin Blanc) or by poaching in boiling water.

Dish them on a border of green pea purée, coat them with sauce suprême. Force roses of purée between each fillet, and in the centre put a ragout of prawns.

SOLE FILLETS WITH TOMATO

Fillets, stuffed with shrimps, etc.; roll and cook these as for Sole au Vin Blanc. Bake some large tomatoes. When hot, but unbroken, cut neatly in half; remove some of the tomato, and place a small cooked fillet in each half tomato. Mask it entirely with forced roses of good purée of potato mixed with a little egg and cream. Brown for a few moments in a very hot oven and serve with a thin purée of spinach (or other sauce) poured round.

SOLE EN MAYONNAISE (3 or 4 people)

1 sole.	Lobster Cutlet mixture
Lemon juice.	(see recipe).
Aspic jelly.	Chili, gherkin, etc., for
1 gill mayonnaise sauce.	decoration.

Stuff the fillets with the lobster mixture, season and bake them (see Sole au Vin Blanc). When cold, coat with mayonnaise sauce, decorate with thin slices or fancy shapes of chili, gherkin and aspic. Dish on a bed of lettuce, etc., garnished with cucumber and tomato.

SPRATS AND RICE PIE (4 to 6 people)

½ lb. rice. When tender line a greased pie-dish with this.
he dish with sprats, sprinkling them with salt, pepper,
lemon and cayenne. Pour ½ pt. béchamel or other sauce over
them, and cover with the rest of the rice. Bake in a hot oven.

TURBOT À LA FLORENTINE

(8 to 10 people, according to size of turbot)

Cut the turbot into small fillets, season well and place these
on a greased fireproof dish. Add a glass of wine or water, cover
with greased paper and bake about 20 minutes till tender. Put
a layer of spinach purée over the fillets, then a thin layer of
béchamel sauce, adding grated cheese to taste. Cover with
breadcrumbs, grated cheese and small pieces of butter, and bake
in a very hot oven (about 10 minutes) until browned.

RÉCHAUFFÉ OF FISH

(Warmed-up dishes)

There are many nice ways of reheating cooked fish. The
following recipes are not only good in themselves, but can be
freely modified and should give many ideas for other dishes.

*FISH CAKES (Plain Recipe)

(4 or 5 people)

Equal quantities of cooked fish and mashed potato. To each
pound of the mixed fish and potato allow:

1 oz. butter. 1 yolk of egg.	Salt, cayenne, and if liked
½ teasp. dry mustard.	a squeeze of lemon.

Melt the butter, add the sieved potato and flaked fish (this
last must be quite free from skin and bones). Mix thoroughly
with the egg, add the seasoning. Turn on to a greased plate,
cover with greased paper and when cold form into 6 even-sized
flat round cakes. These may be floured only, and fried in
shallow fat; but they are nicer if egged and crumbed and fried in
deep fat. Serve with fried parsley. Boiled rice may replace
potato: if so it must be chopped and moistened with 1 tablesp.
or more of white sauce flavoured, if liked, with anchovy.

*FISH CAKES (Richer Recipe)
(4 people)

¼ lb. cooked fish.	½ oz. melted butter.
¼ lb. mashed potato.	A little thick white sauce to bind
1 teasp. chopped parsley.	the mixture (this may be omitted
1 egg yolk (can be omitted).	if the fish mixture is moist).

Salt, pepper, and lemon juice.

Flake the fish finely and free it from bone and skin. Add the potato, parsley and seasoning. Bind with the melted butter, sauce (if used) and egg yolk (beaten). Turn on to a round plate. When cold divide into 6 equal portions. Shape neatly into round flat cakes. Coat twice with egg and crumb. Fry and serve garnished with fried parsley and cut lemon.

*FISH CROQUETTES and CUTLETS (4 or 5 people)

½ lb. cooked fish, finely flaked, and freed from skin and bone.

PANADA
- ½ oz. butter OR margarine.
- ½ oz. flour.
- ½ gill milk.

Seasonings.
½ teasp. of finely chopped parsley.
Squeeze of lemon juice.

Make the panada. Add the fish, seasoning, and turn out on to a plate. Cover with a greased paper. When cool shape into:

(a) Croquettes, i.e. form into small cylinders or balls (about 5).
(b) Cutlets, i.e. shape to resemble cutlets.

In either case flour these and coat twice with egg and crumbs. Fry in deep fat and serve, garnished with fried parsley and cut lemon. Cutlets may have a small piece of macaroni inserted to resemble a bone, place a cutlet frill on each and dish, if wished, on a potato border and serve with a suitable sauce poured round.

*FISH KEDGEREE (4 or 5 people)

½ lb. cooked fish (any fish will do, but dried haddock is one of the best for this).	1 gill thick sauce.
	1 or 2 hard-boiled eggs.
6 oz. cooked rice (3 oz. raw rice)	1–2 oz. butter.
	Salt, pepper, and cayenne.

Flake the fish, removing all skin and bone. Put it into a saucepan with the boiled rice (this must be well cooked and quite dry), sauce and butter. Stir over the fire until very hot. Turn on to a hot dish, pile up, mark with a fork. Decorate with the yolk and white of 1 egg, both sieved separately; a second egg can be cut into a fancy flower shape and used to garnish the dish.

Kedgeree may be made with meat (such as ham) instead of fish.

FISH KROMESKIES

Prepare a mixture as for Fish Cakes (Richer Recipe). Form this, when cold, into cork-like shapes. Roll these in very thin bacon, dip in coating batter and fry.

*FISH PIE (5 or 6 people)

½ lb. cooked fish.	1 lb. cooked potatoes.
¼ pt. white sauce (cold fish sauce).	½ oz. butter or margarine. A little milk.

Salt and pepper.

Carefully remove the skin and bone from the fish. Mix it with the sauce, season well and put in a pie-dish. Sieve the potatoes, melt the butter in a saucepan and add the potato, seasonings and sufficient milk to make a soft creamy consistency. Beat well and pile on the fish as for cottage pie. Smooth with a knife, mark neatly, brush with egg or milk, and brown in a moderate oven.

FISH PIE (Russian)

(6 to 8 people)

FLAKY PASTRY. 8 oz. flour, etc.

FILLING

¾ lb. white fish (cooked and roughly flaked).	1 hard-boiled egg. A little grated lemon rind.
1 teasp. chopped parsley.	2 tablesp. white sauce.

Pepper and salt.

Mix all the ingredients together. Roll the pastry into a square, trim and turn it. Lay mixture in centre. Brush edges with egg and fold corners to the centre. Close joins firmly, brush with egg and cover joins with leaves of pastry. Bake in a hot oven about 40 minutes.

NOTE. Oysters, prawns, etc., may be added. Raw fish may be used if liked.

*FISH PUDDING (I)

(4 or 5 people)

½ lb. cooked fish.	2 oz. breadcrumbs.
1 oz. melted butter.	1 egg.
¾ gill milk.	Anchovy essence to taste.
1 teasp. chopped parsley.	Seasoning.

Grease a mould. If liked, cover it with browned breadcrumbs.

Flake the fish and mix it with all the other dry ingredients. Mix with the anchovy, beaten egg, melted butter and milk. Put this into the greased mould, cover with a greased paper and steam for ½ hour or 40 minutes. Serve with sauce poured over it.

FISH PUDDING (II)
(5 or 6 people)

½ lb. cold cooked fish, flaked finely.	½ lb. cold cooked rice (boiled very dry).
2 raw beaten eggs.	A little milk, or sauce.
1 hard-boiled egg.	Seasoning and lemon juice.

Mix all the dry ingredients. Grease a mould and decorate it with the hard-boiled egg. Add the beaten eggs to the dry ingredients, adding milk or sauce until the mixture drops from the spoon; ¼ to ½ pt. liquid is usual. Steam for 1 hour. Turn out and pour a good sauce round.

FISH SOUFFLÉ (Cold)
(6 or 7 people)

1½ lb. fish cooked, as for Sole au Vin Blanc. Flake and sieve the fish when cooked, and with it sieve 1 or 2 hard-boiled eggs and 3 anchovies. Dissolve ½ oz. of gelatine in ¼ pt. fish stock and add this to the sieved mixture. Season with salt, pepper, cayenne and lemon. Add ½ pt. whipped cream or ¼ pt. thick white (cold) sauce and ¼ pt. whipped cream. Pour this into a china soufflé case round which a stiff band of paper has been tied—the paper must project 2 inches over the top of the case. Leave the soufflé till set. Carefully remove the paper and decorate with whipped cream, prawns and aspic. Garnish with good salad.

If made with salmon, colour the soufflé to a salmon pink colour.

FISH SOUFFLÉ (Cold) WITH ASPARAGUS (6 or 7 people)
(Fish Charlotte Russe)

Make the soufflé as above, adding 5 or 6 sheets of gelatine instead of 4. Rinse a plain charlotte mould with cold water and line it carefully with cooked unbroken asparagus, cut into even lengths, and slightly flavoured with mayonnaise. Arrange asparagus tips prettily round the top. Fill the mould with the fish soufflé. Set on ice or in cold salted water.

Turn out on to a bed of salad. Decorate with a very little forced cream.

The same dish is excellent made of cold chicken mousse or any other light meat mixture. If liked, a little mayonnaise may be incorporated with the soufflé.

SALMON MOULD (4 or 5 people)

1 tin salmon.	2 tablesp. tarragon vinegar.
Pinch ground mace.	2 tablesp. chili vinegar.
½ oz. gelatine dissolved in 3 tablesp. stock or water.	Salt Pepper } to taste.

Mix all the ingredients well together. When nearly setting pour into a wet mould. Turn out when firm and serve with a good salad round.

III. MEATS (HOT OR COLD)

The two elementary methods of cooking are roasting and boiling.

From roasting the following have been derived: (1) baking, (2) frying, (3) broiling; and from boiling we get (1) stewing, (2) braising, (3) steaming.

CHOICE OF MEATS

Beef. The fat should be bright yellow and the lean bright red and close grained. In foreign beef the lean is slightly purple.

Lamb. The fat should be white and firm, and the lean a nice pink. With all the good joints of lamb some of the ' leaf ' or ' caul ' (see page 53) should be supplied.

Mutton. The fat in home-grown mutton should be very white and firm. The lean should be of a darkish red, tinged with brown. The meat should be finely grained. Joints that have been well hung change in colour, and the lean, if cut, looks very dark. Well hung meat is excellent for cooking, and very tender, but in hot weather meat will not keep long enough to hang it. When choosing meat, test largely by smell. It should smell quite good.

New Zealand mutton, etc., while still frozen, has very hard firm white fat and pale pink lean; when melted the fat looks dirty and the lean purple.

Pork. Choose meat, if possible, from a small animal. The fat should be white, and the lean pink and close grained, and devoid of any spots, as these will show that the animal was infested with some parasite.

Veal. The fat is not of such a pure white and the lean is softer than in other meats. The meat must be finely grained.

Internal Organs. These have a very high food value and most of them are economical. They must be eaten while quite fresh and need to be thoroughly washed before cooking.

51

THE COOKING OF MEAT

ROASTING AND BAKING

ROASTING. This term means cooking by direct or radiant heat in front of an open fire. E.g.: The old-fashioned roasting jack.

BAKING is cooking by reflected heat, i.e. cooking in a closed oven, where the heat is reflected from the sides of the oven.

The rules for roasting and baking are practically the same, and are as follows:

(1) First wipe the meat with a damp cloth to remove dirt or dust. (Meat should only be washed if necessary.)

(2) Beat thin pieces (steak, etc.) with an old rolling pin to break the sinews and make the meat tender.

(3) Weigh the meat and allow TIME for cooking according to the following table:

If the meat is to be ROASTED it is hung on a roasting jack, and so turned before a quick fire. If BAKED it is placed on a grid, which in its turn is placed on the top of 2 tins, the lower of which is filled with water. This prevents burning.

Beef and Mutton. 15 to 20 minutes for each pound, and 15 to 20 minutes over. Foreign meat requires 20 to 25 minutes to each pound and 20 to 25 minutes over.

(N.B. The variation in time depends upon: (a) the thickness of the meat and the size of the joint—a large sirloin would need 20 minutes where a small joint would require only 15; (b) the taste of the individual to be served, some preferring well-done and others underdone meat.)

Veal and Pork. 25 minutes to the lb. and 25 minutes over.

(N.B. The meat of young animals is indigestible unless well cooked, and pork, particularly the internal organs, if under-cooked is unwholesome owing to pigs being unclean feeders and so liable to parasites, which may not be killed unless the meat is well cooked, and which would then possibly infect human beings.)

Imported Meat. This should not be cooked until thoroughly thawed or it will be hard. The thawing should be done slowly by keeping it in the warmth of the kitchen for several hours. Never attempt to thaw by placing the meat in water, as this causes loss of juice. After thawing, it should be cooked as soon as possible, as it decomposes quickly.

Method of Roasting and Baking

Expose the meat at first to a high temperature. This seals the outside albumen in the meat and so prevents the escape of juices.

The heat must be reduced after the first 15 to 20 minutes to prevent the inside albumen from hardening, which would make the meat tough. Hot air rises; therefore, when baking meat in an oven, it is usually convenient to place the meat on the top or hottest shelf at first, and afterwards to put it on a lower, and so cooler shelf. The meat should be basted about once in every 20 minutes. The term BASTE means to pour the hot fat (dripping) that escapes from the meat on to the top of it. This is done with a long iron spoon, and it prevents the meat from drying up and burning.

Water may be used instead of dripping for basting. Proceed in exactly the same way till the meat is cooked. To make gravy: Skim off the fat very carefully. To $\frac{1}{2}$ pt. liquor add 1 teasp. flour blended with a little cold water or stock. Boil up, stirring all the time, add seasoning and a touch of browning.

Some joints are deficient in natural fat and in this case extra fat must be cooked with them, e.g. the LEAF or caul (a lining of fat taken from the inside of the animal) should be sold with all best joints of lamb and veal; this should be placed over the joint before baking. Otherwise extra dripping must be added. Fat bacon may also be used to supply a deficiency of natural fat. It should always be put with chickens, game, etc., and may be applied in two ways:

(1) BARDING. This means that slices of bacon should be slit crosswise (to prevent the bacon curling up in cooking) and then tied over the breast of the chicken, etc.

(2) LARDING. For this a special larding needle is required. Into this, pieces of fat bacon are affixed and these are then threaded into the flesh—the pieces of bacon so threaded being called lardoons.

GRILLING

This method is suitable for small joints such as cutlets (of fish or meat), steaks, etc.

A clear smokeless fire or a good electric or gas grill is needed. The joints must be:

(1) wiped;
(2) trimmed of surplus fat;

(3) beaten;
(4) seasoned (salt, pepper, and sometimes lemon juice);
(5) brushed with oil or melted fat.

They should be placed on an oiled grid (salad oil if possible should be used) which is held OVER a bright fire. The grid must be turned frequently (or the joints on the grid) to harden the outside albumen and to prevent burning.

Avoid pricking with a fork or the juices will escape.

A steak should be 1½ inches in thickness, but must not exceed this. It should be surrounded by fat. A well-cooked piece of steak of the above thickness will take 18 minutes; if under-done, 15 minutes.

A chop 1 inch thick will take: 'well done', 10 minutes; 'under-done', 8 minutes.

A ½-inch cutlet ' well done', 8 minutes; ' underdone', 6 minutes.

The meat should look plump after cooking. This shows the outside albumen has been sealed, and the heat expanding the steam inside the meat, gives this appearance.

BROILING

Is exactly the same as grilling, except that the meat is cooked BEFORE, not OVER, a bright fire. The flavour of broiled meat is not quite so good as that of grilled meat.

FRYING

There are two methods of frying:

(1) **Wet or French Frying.**

In this method the cooking takes place by totally immersing whatever is to be cooked in hot fat. A pan is required of sufficient depth to allow this. Into the pan a frying basket should fit loosely. The pan is filled rather more than ½ full with fat.

The best fat is olive oil, but this being expensive, the following are good substitutes:

    (a) Home-made clarified fat. (See page 56.)
    (b) Block Atora suet.
    (c) Lard.
    (d) Clarified dripping.
    (e) Trex, Spry, etc.

Two or three lb. of fat will be needed for a pan 8 inches in diameter. With proper care the fat can be used again and again.

Much is talked of ' Boiling Fat ' in Cookery Books. Fat will burn before it boils, and any bubbling seen, shows it contains water, which boils as the fat heats. It will be remembered that 212° F. is the temperature of boiling water, whereas 380° is the usual temperature for frying rissoles and 400° is needed for whitebait and potato chips.

Heat may be tested by watching the smoke that rises from the fat. At first it is very faint, but when it is clearly seen, the temperature is about 380° and ready for ordinary purposes. Without practice, the heat cannot be determined by the colour and amount of smoke. Then it is wiser to throw in a small piece of bread. If the fat bubbles quickly round it, and the bread turns brown in about 1 minute, the heat is right for rissoles.

Things to be fried in deep fat should usually be encased in batter or in egg and crumb.

If batter is used avoid a frying basket, and place the coated substance direct into the fat. As it fries, it will rise to the top, and can be removed with a wire spoon.

If egged and crumbed, things should be placed in the frying basket and then gently lowered into the smoking fat. When sufficiently browned, they are usually sufficiently cooked. They must be thoroughly drained—this is done by shaking the frying basket—and then turned on to kitchen paper. This is then placed on a tin and the things kept warm till ready to be served.

To keep the fat in good condition, cool it slightly after use, and strain through a strainer into a jar. The pan should be rubbed hard with clean paper and put aside. This usually suffices, but occasionally the pan must be boiled with soda. If fat loses its frying power and becomes coarse and dark in appearance, and the things when fried look dark and greasy, the fat is useless. This is probably caused by burning or by lack of straining.

(2) English or Dry Frying.

This is suitable for such things as kippers, pancakes, eggs, etc. In fact it must be used for everything the surface of which is not protected by a casing such as egg, batter, etc.

For this method, a SMALL quantity of fat is placed in the pan. This must be allowed to get hot as in the French or deep frying, until a faint blue smoke arises. Whatever is to be fried is then put into the pan, and as soon as one side is sufficiently browned, it must be turned to allow the other side to cook.

Flour is not an effective casing; if floured fish is fried in deep fat, the fat is soon spoilt, so that the English method is more economical for floured fish. As previously stated, the French method is far preferable for anything enclosed in a case, and for these it is more economical as, should they be fried in shallow fat, only a portion of their surface is covered with fat at one time and, therefore, more fat is absorbed into whatever is being fried, giving a more greasy and less good result, using at the same time more fat.

Coating with Egg and Crumbs.

To do this well requires care. First carefully dry the substance to be egged and crumbed—or if this is not possible, flour it all over, shaking off any surplus flour. Prepare the following things:

(1) A plate on which an egg is beaten with a palette knife.
(2) Some finely sieved white breadcrumbs.
(3) A baking tin covered with clean unprinted paper.

Then proceed in either of the following ways:

(I)

Dip the floured substance into the egg, seeing that the whole surface is covered with egg. To do this use a brush.

(II)

Lift the substance with a knife, or two knives, drain it over the egg to let any surplus egg slip off, and place it on to the breadcrumbs.

(III)

Entirely cover it with crumbs—not touching with the hands till all egg is hidden by crumbs. Then pat in as many crumbs as are necessary to coat the whole surface and shake the rest off, being careful to see that no loose crumbs remain on. This latter is important, as any loose crumbs would fall into the fat and, being so small, when the drying basket was lifted with the first batch of, say, cutlets, the crumbs would continue getting darker, and, when the next batch was fried, the cutlets would be covered with dark specks—composed of the burnt crumbs.

Home-made Clarified Fat.

Cut any raw fat into small dice. Mutton fat is better than beef, but any fat can be used.

Put this in a thick saucepan with cold water and bring it to the boil. Continue boiling steadily, filling up the pan as the water evaporates. No lid must be put on the pan. Boil for several hours—often a second day's boiling is required—until the particles of fat have lost their shape and the oil rises to the surface and the particles of skin sink. When this happens, the particles will stick to the bottom of the pan, and as the fat is above the temperature of boiling water, the heat will make the particles spurt out.

At the first sign of this, commence stirring and continue to stir fast and carefully until the fierce bubbling dies down and the particles of skin begin to turn a chestnut brown. This shows that all water has evaporated and that the fat is frying the particles.

Strain the fat, pressing the particles to get all fat from them. It will be noticed that they rustle like dried paper. When cold the fat will appear white and firm.

An inferior method is to cut the fat up, to cover it with water and to cook it (' render it down ') in the oven. But by this means much fat is left in the particles when they are strained and much waste thereby takes place.

Small quantities of fat may also be ' rendered down ' without water, on a tin in the oven.

BOILING

Boiling may be defined as cooking by immersion in boiling water. The temperature of boiling water is 212° F.

The principles of boiling are similar to those of roasting, i.e. the surface albumen must be sealed by plunging the meat into boiling water.

The RULES are similar:

(1) Wipe the meat.

(2) Beat the meat. (Not for large joints.)

(3) Weigh it and place it in the boiling water and boil it rapidly 10 to 15 minutes, then reduce the heat to simmering point (180° to 190° F.) and keep at this for the remainder of the time.

TIMES for boiling meat:

20 minutes to the lb. and 20 minutes over is the shortest time that should be allowed, as boiled meat should be fully cooked, and very tender. This applies to beef, mutton, poultry, etc.

Very large joints, hams, etc., require longer, and these should have 25 to 30 minutes to the lb. and 20 minutes over.

c

To TEST BOILING POINT WITHOUT A THERMOMETER. If bubbles rise rapidly all over the water, it is boiling.

To TEST SIMMERING POINT WITHOUT A THERMOMETER. At the side of the pan nearest to the fire an occasional bubble will rise, whereas at the side away from the fire the liquid is still.

Boiling of Salt Meat.

Salt meat must be washed when it is removed from the pickle and soaked in fresh cold water for several hours or overnight, according to the saltness. If it is very salt and hard, put it on in cold water, bring to the boil and throw this water away. This removes some of the salt. Then put it on again in warm water, bring to the boil, and allow 25 to 30 minutes to the lb. and 20 minutes over.

STEAMING

This means cooking in the steam that rises from boiling water. This method has advantages over boiling for the following reasons:

(a) The cooking is more gradual.

(b) Water cannot get into contact with the foods cooked.

(c) Less nourishment is lost, as, by boiling, certain nutriments escape into the water.

(d) Puddings, etc., if steamed are lighter than when boiled.

It has some disadvantages:

(a) It is a much longer process, therefore requires more fuel.

(b) It is more uncertain than boiling, as, should water go off the boil, all cooking ceases.

RULES for steaming:

(1) Wipe the meat.

(2) Beat the meat.

(3) Weigh it and allow nearly double the time allowed for boiling.

(4) Season the meat.

(5) Wrap the meat in greased paper, to prevent the escape of any flavour and goodness.

STEWING

Stewing means cooking in a small quantity of liquid in a covered pan. This is a very excellent and economical method,

Beat two yolks with ½ gill of cream and add these to the cooled sauce. Mix well. Re-heat carefully, then add a very little lemon juice or vinegar, drop by drop, to taste, and serve.

LEMON, SUPERIOR—SWEET (4 people)

2 eggs.	1 or 2 oz. sugar.
1 large lemon.	1 oz. butter.
¼ pt. water.	

Cut the lemon rind very thinly, and boil it in the water for five minutes. Add the sugar, butter, lemon juice and beaten eggs. Stir carefully over gentle heat till the mixture thickens. Strain and serve.

NORMANDY SAUCE (Sauce Normande)
(5 or 6 people)

1 oz. butter.	1 oz. flour.
About 1 pt. fish stock	2 yolks of eggs.
or white stock.	Lemon juice.

Make a white sauce of the butter, flour and stock. Boil well, skimming. Then cool and add the 2 egg yolks. Re-heat carefully, add a squeeze of lemon, and, if liked, another oz. of butter in small pieces.

Tammy and serve.

SAUCES—Class III

(Whipped Custard or 'Mousseline' Sauces)

GERMAN EGG SAUCE (4 people)

1 wineglass wine.	2 yolks of eggs or
Sugar to taste.	1 whole egg.

Put these in a bowl over boiling water and whisk till a light froth is obtained. Serve at once.

SABAYON SAUCE (Sauce Mousseline)
(4 or 5 people)

2 oz. fine castor sugar.	2 yolks.
½ gill of cream.	Flavouring to taste.

Whisk these in a double saucepan till they are frothy. Add 1 wineglass Madeira or other wine; whisk till the sauce begins to thicken, and serve it with hot sweets.

N.B. Fruit syrups can be substituted for wine, if wished.

E

as vegetables may be put in with the meat, and as the whole is eaten, no flavour is lost.

There are two kinds of stews, white and brown.

White Stew, e.g. **Irish Stew.** For this the meat is cut into neat pieces and the vegetables (potatoes and onions) are sliced. These are placed uncooked in layers in a pan, sufficient seasoning is added, with about ½ to 1 pt. of warm water.

Place pan on the fire and bring slowly to simmering point and simmer gently for 1½ to 2 hours at least. Cheaper and coarser cuts of meat need 4 hours' cooking or even longer. The stew may be turned out or served in a casserole.

Brown Stew. For brown stews, the meat is first floured and then fried a golden brown on each side. Any vegetables may then be fried. These with the meat are then placed in a pan or casserole half covered with a good made gravy and gently simmered for 2 hours or longer. A typical example is haricot of mutton.

BRAISING

Braising is a combination of baking and steaming. Special braising pans may be obtained with sunk lids to hold charcoal so that top and bottom heat may be applied at the same time. But braising can be successfully carried out in various ways.

(I)

Place a layer of vegetables on a baking tin, lay the meat on these, and place the tin in a quick oven. Baste well, and when the meat is a rich brown, remove it. Place the vegetables in a pan or casserole. Lay the meat on the vegetables and make a good gravy. Pour this over the vegetables. It should barely cover them. Cook gently (preferably in the oven) for 3 to 4 hours, or according to the size of the joint. Cutlets require about 1 hour.

TIME to allow for braising: 30 to 40 minutes to the lb. and 30 to 40 minutes over.

(II)

Place a small piece of fat in a pan and place in this a layer of vegetables and on the bed of vegetables lay the meat.

Sauté the vegetables and cover them with stock or water (this should barely touch the meat), place a greased paper, which fits the pan, closely pressed on to the meat, and simmer gently

for the full time, occasionally raising the paper and basting the meat with the gravy.

Whichever of these methods is employed, the method of dishing is the same. Lift the meat on to a hot dish, keep it hot. Strain the vegetables from the gravy, thickening the latter if necessary. Brush the meat with meat glaze and pour the gravy round. Braised vegetables are not very suitable as a garnish, so small heaps of separately cooked, neatly cut vegetables should be used for garnishing.

(III) Braised Meat

2 lb. (more or less) of lean meat, e.g. small fillet of mutton.

1 large carrot.	
1 large turnip.	
1 large onion.	These form the mirepoix.
1 stick celery.	
1 oz. dripping.	
½ oz. lean bacon or ham.	
⅓ teasp. peppercorns.	
1 blade mace.	Tied in muslin.
Bunch herbs.	
Salt. Stock.	

Melt the dripping in a pan or casserole. In this fry the bacon cut into dice, and the vegetables cut into *thick* slices (this bed of vegetables is known as a 'mirepoix'). When slightly browned, pour off any surplus fat, add just sufficient stock barely to cover the vegetables. Add the herbs and seasoning and bring to the boil.

The meat may be prepared as desired—by boning, stuffing, larding, etc. Weigh and allow for cooking 30 to 40 minutes to the lb. and 30 to 40 minutes over.

Place the meat on the mirepoix, cover with a round of greased paper, place a closely fitting lid on the pan and simmer gently over gentle heat for two-thirds of the time required for cooking. Baste occasionally. Then place the casserole in the oven for the remainder of the time, removing the lid 10 minutes before dishing to brown the meat. At the same time as the lid is removed take out about 1 gill of the stock surrounding the vegetables and boil this rapidly and reduce to glaze.

To Dish. Place the joint on a hot dish, glaze the surface, skim the stock and strain it round the meat. Garnish with neatly cut vegetables that have been cooked separately. The vegetables from the braise may also be served if wished.

Cutlets and small pieces of meat may be *fried first* before

placing them on the mirepoix—the browning by removing the lid for the last 10 minutes is then omitted. This prevents the meat from drying up.

TIME allowed for cutlets and small pieces of meat—about 1 hour.

GRAVIES FOR ROAST MEAT

Clear gravies, strictly speaking, resemble soups more than sauces, but as they are served with meats, they are placed in this section.

The simplest form of making a gravy for roast meat is as follows: Remove the meat from the baking tin. Pour off the fat from the tin and add boiling stock or water to the thickened meat juice that remains. Boil this for a few moments and season to taste. The stock should be flavoured with beef, if for beef gravy, with chicken (by boiling the gizzard, neck, etc.), for chicken, etc., and so on.

The actual GRAVY so made is excellent, but owing to some fat remaining with the meat juices, on cooling, the surface of the gravy becomes greasy. Therefore it should be left to get cold, all fat can then be removed, and the gravy re-heated, seasoned to taste and served. To do this it is necessary to use a gravy made the day before.

Of course, in small households this might not always be possible, but in large ones, where there is daily roasting, it would be a simpler matter than making the fresh gravy while dishing up.

Thickened Gravy

This can be made in several ways:

(1) Brown ½ oz. flour on a paper in the oven. This requires care, as the flour is apt to brown unequally. Add the flour so browned to 1 oz. hot dripping, left, as above described, in the meat tin. Mix these and add stock or water, and boil. (This is quicker, which is important, as it does away with time taken in browning a roux.)

(2) Leave 1 tablesp. fat and sediment from meat in the tin. Add 2 tablesp. flour and stir well all over the tin till dark golden brown. Add 1 pt. brown stock and stir till mixture boils up. Season and strain round dish and into gravy boat.

(3) Use 'Bisto'. This is a prepared thickening for gravies, sold in packets. The method is: Leave the tablesp. of dripping, as already described, in the tin, add a tablesp. of 'Bisto' (do

not cook these together), and at once add some boiling stock or water. Mix till smooth, then re-boil, thin down to the desired consistency and serve. This is a most quick and useful method.

Unthickened Gravy

Pour off all the fat from the meat tin, leaving the browned sediment. Add boiling water, or hot stock, scrape and stir well. Boil, season, and remove grease by passing unprinted paper over the surface to absorb fat. Pour a little round the joint if wished and serve the rest in a hot sauce boat.

Slightly Thickened Gravy

Leave 1 tablesp. fat in the pan with the meat sediment.
Add ½ oz. flour. Brown this in the tin, stirring over gentle heat. Add 1 pt. brown stock and boil, stirring well. Season and strain round the meat.

*BEEF, BOILED

See page 57. Two hours before the meat is done, vegetables should be added, i.e. carrots, turnips, onions and celery. These should not be cut up, but require careful cleaning. Simmer these with the meat for the remaining 2 hours. Half an hour before the meat is done, small suet dumplings may also be added.

Recipe for Dumplings

½ an onion, chopped.	¼ lb. flour.
¼ teasp. baking powder.	½ teasp. chopped parsley.
Salt and pepper.	1½ oz. chopped suet.

Mix these ingredients well together, and mix with cold water to form a light dough.

Divide into 12 balls, flour each one, and add to the boiling liquid in which the meat is cooking.

To dish up, lift the meat on to a hot dish, put the dumplings and vegetables neatly round, together with a little of the stock.

BEEF, FILLET OF, BRAISED

Fillet of beef.	Larding bacon.
Vegetables. Stock.	Seasoning.
Herbs and spices.	2 slices ham or bacon.

Trim the fillet and tie it in an oval shape. Lard it thickly.

Place the vegetables, bacon, etc., in a deep stewpan, and just cover them with stock. Place the fillet on this, and cover it closely with greased paper.

Put a lid on the pan, and cook gently for two to three hours at least, basting frequently. When tender put the meat in a hot oven to crisp the lardoons. Strain the gravy; or boil it rapidly to a glaze. Pour this over the meat, serve it garnished with vegetables cut into fancy shapes, and pour a good brown sauce round.

OR, it may be finished off like hare, and be served with forcemeat balls and rolls of bacon, the sauce being flavoured with port wine and red currant jelly.

*BEEF OLIVES (6 or 7 people)

1½ lb. thick steak.	About 1 pt. stock.
2 oz. meat farce or veal forcemeat.	1 oz. dripping. ⎱ For brown ¾ oz. flour. ⎰ roux.

Cut the meat into slices ¼ inch thick, beat these, and cut them into oblong pieces about 3 inches by 2½.

Spread the farce on these, and roll them up, securing with a skewer or string. Heat the dripping and fry the olives until the meat is lightly browned. Braise them on a bed of vegetables, or stew gently in stock with the usual vegetable flavourings for about 1½ hours. Dish them on or inside a border. Skim the gravy in which they have been cooked, and thicken with the blended flour. Pour the sauce so made over the olives.

*BEEF, PRESSED

5 lb. pickled brisket of beef.	Water to cover the meat.
Bunch of herbs and spices.	2 carrots, 2 turnips, 2 onions.

Wash the meat. Put it into a saucepan with the vegetables, etc. Simmer gently for 4 hours, or until the bones slip out easily. Form into a good shape, and tie in a cloth. Place between two baking tins. Press with weights and leave till cold.

Trim, glaze, and serve garnished with forced butter, parsley, etc.

*BEEF AND RICE STEW (Economical)
(4 to 5 people)

½ lb. beefsteak.	1 onion, chopped.
1 oz. dripping.	1 pt. water or stock.
½ oz. flour.	2 oz. rice.

Salt and pepper.

Cut the meat into neat pieces. Fry the onion in the fat. Add the flour and brown this. Add the liquid. Boil the

mixture and season it. Cool slightly, and add the meat. Stew very gently for an hour. Add the washed rice and cook again carefully for another hour. Stir occasionally. Cook in the oven if possible.

*BEEF ROLL (4 to 5 people)

¾ lb. beefsteak.
¼ lb. forcemeat, sausage or quenelle meat.

This can be rolled exactly as in Beef Olives, but without cutting it into small pieces. The beef should be all in one piece, and not more than ½ inch thick. Beat well, season, and spread it with the forcemeat.

Braise it on a bed of vegetables for two or more hours. Glaze it, and serve it with a browned gravy made as for Beef Olives.

BEEF (SALTED), BOILED

Cook in the same way as Beef, Boiled, but the meat must be put into cold, *not* boiling water (this draws out some of the salt), and the timing must not commence until the water reaches boiling point. Then simmer very gently for the full time.

*BEEFSTEAK, FRIED

Put a little fat in a frying pan, and make it smoking hot. Put in the steak, which has been well beaten and seasoned. Brown one side, then turn, and brown the other. Then cook more gently for about 15 minutes.

Serve very hot with fried onions, fried potato, or tomatoes. Any sauce suitable for grilled beefsteak should be served with it.

Fried beefsteak is inferior to grilled, but as it is not always possible to grill, frying is very frequently required.

BEEFSTEAK, GRILLED

Well hung rump steak is the best for the purpose. For full directions see Grilling (page 53).

*BACON AND BEANS (5 or 6 people)

Bacon (2–2½ lb.).	1 oz. flour.
½ pk. broad beans, *or* ⅓ pt. cooked haricot beans.	¾ pt. milk and water.
	1 teasp. chopped parsley.
1 oz. fat.	Seasoning.

Soak the bacon for at least one hour in cold water. Put it

into fresh cold water after weighing, and allow for cooking about 25 minutes to the lb. and 25 minutes over. The water must boil before the timing begins. After the water has boiled simmer the bacon, carefully skimming it.

Shell the beans, and cook them with the bacon. Young beans take 20 minutes; old ones much longer.

Before serving, take the rind off the bacon and sprinkle it with browned breadcrumbs. Make a parsley sauce, and pour it over the beans.

BLANQUETTE OF VEAL or RABBIT (4 or 5 people)

1 lb. veal neatly cut up.	2 tablesp. cream.
	2 onions.
Bouquet garni.	2 egg yolks.
2½ oz. butter.	1 teasp. Liebig's extract.
2 oz. flour.	Juice of 1 lemon.

Garnish (chopped ham, lemon, and parsley).

Put the veal, herbs, Liebig and enough water or white stock to cover well in a stewpan. Simmer very gently till tender (1½ hours). Strain and keep the meat hot.

Make a sauce with the fat, flour and stock (coating consistency). Add the yolks beaten with cream and lemon juice. Re-heat. Pour over the veal and garnish with ham, etc.

*BRAWN (6 or 7 people)

½ a pig's head.	2 blades mace.
1 lb. fat pork.	20 peppercorns.
Bunch of herbs.	2 cloves.

Prepare the head by removing the brains, eyes and bristles. Wash it well in salt and water.

Pickle it and the pork for a week in any good brine. Wash it after the pickling and place in cold water. Bring to the boil, then add the herbs and spices. Cook gently till the meat begins to fall away from the bone (2 to 3 hours). Then cut the meat into dice. Put the bones and stock back in the pan and boil till they have reduced to 1 pt. or less. Season well. Put the meat into damped moulds, pour the stock over—it should quite cover the meat.

CALF'S BRAINS FRITTERS

To prepare the brains, wash them several times in salt and water. Remove the skin, then blanch them in stock or water for five minutes. Cool and dry them.

*c

Divide them into neat portions. Flour, season, and egg and crumb them. Fry in hot fat, and garnish with fried parsley.

OR, prepare the brains as above. Then dip them in a good coating batter. Fry and serve as above.

CALF'S BRAINS (or SHEEP'S BRAINS) À LA MAÎTRE D'HÔTEL

Prepare as in the preceding recipe. Then stew the brains in a good white sauce for 20 minutes. Before serving add 1 teasp. finely chopped parsley and a few drops of lemon juice.

CALF'S FEET

Two calf's feet. Blanch these, then cook in stock for 2 to 3 hours until the bones slip out easily.

The meat may then be:

(1) Cut up and served with good parsley or other sauce;

(2) Pressed between two plates till cold, then the pieces seasoned, egged, crumbed and fried;

(3) Pressed as before till cold, then dipped into frying batter and fried.

Pig's and sheep's trotters may be served in the same way.

CALF'S HEAD

Thoroughly clean half the head. Bone it and remove the brains. Roll it up and tie with tape. Place in buttered paper and then in a cloth. Boil for 3 or 4 hours. Dish it on a hot dish. Cut the ear with scissors to form a fringe. Skin the tongue and slice it round the dish. Cover the head with fried breadcrumbs, and serve with brain sauce.

To prepare the brains, wash them in salted water.

Skin them, and tie in buttered muslin. Place in cold water, and boil for ten minutes. Chop them and add them to ¾ pt. parsley sauce.

*CORNISH PASTIES (5 or 6 people)

½ lb. short crust.	½ small onion, grated
½ lb. meat (raw).	or finely chopped.
1 potato.	Seasoning.

Dice the meat and onion, slice the potato very finely. Mix these with the seasoning. Divide the pastry into 5 or 6 portions

and roll into rounds. Place some of the mixture on each, and, damping the edges of the pastry, press them together to form a frill on the top. Bake in a good oven for about 40 minutes. Brush with egg if convenient before baking.

Pasties can be made of cooked meat and cooked vegetables, and in this case moisten the filling with a little brown sauce and bake for 20 to 30 minutes only.

COW HEEL

Wash, scald, and scrape any hairs off the heel. Divide it into four sections after blanching it. Place the sections in cold water with an onion, herbs and seasoning. Cook for at least 4 hours. Serve with parsley, tomato or any good sauce. The sauce should be made partly from some of the stock in which the heel has been cooked.

CRÉPINETTES À LA FRANÇAISE (4 or 5 people)

6 oz. cooked poultry, game or pork.	¼ pt. good sauce. Lemon juice and nutmeg.
2 oz. lean cooked ham.	2 yolks of eggs.
6 mushrooms.	Calf's or pig's caul.

Mince the meat and mushrooms, and add sufficient panada to make a creamy mixture. Add the yolks, seasoning, lemon and nutmeg. Re-heat, and cook egg yolks, but do not boil. Turn on to a plate, cover with greased paper, and, when cold, cut into squares. Wrap these in caul, and brush with white of egg; then egg and crumb twice and fry. Garnish with fried parsley. Serve a sauce separately. Instead of frying, the crépinettes may be baked in a quick oven, and served in paper cases with fried parsley.

CURRIED MUTTON CUTLETS (4 or 5 people)

5 mutton cutlets (1½ lb.). | A little curry powder.

COATING. Egg and crumbs.

DISHING. Potato border. ½ pt. curry sauce. 1 oz. dry rice.

Prepare cutlets, dip in curry powder and coat with egg and crumbs. Fry in hot fat and drain well. Dish on potato border in a circle or semicircle, fill the centre with the cooked rice and pour the curry sauce round.

*CURRY (5 or 6 people)

(Of raw meat. Any meat is suitable. Example: 1 lb. beef, mutton or veal.)

1 lb. raw meat.	1 to 2 oz. coconut.
1 oz. dripping.	2 teasp. chutney.
1 oz. flour.	Pinch of sugar.
1 onion (chopped).	A teasp. red currant jelly
1 apple (chopped).	or gooseberry jam.
1 dessertsp. curry powder.	Lemon juice.
A few raisins or sultanas.	Seasoning.

3 gills stock for cooked meat; 4 gills stock for fresh meat.

Put the coconut to infuse in ¼ pt. boiling water. Cut the meat into dice; fry lightly in the fat, remove the pieces of meat, and in the same fat fry the chopped onion a little, add curry powder, stir well, add flour, and fry until a good brown, then add the chopped apple. Then add the stock, and the infusion, straining away the nut. Boil well. Add the squeeze of lemon juice, also the jam, chutney, etc. Put the pieces of meat into this and pour the whole into a casserole or stewpan and cook gently for one to two hours. Serve with 3-4 oz. carefully cooked dry rice. Garnish with lemon and parsley.

Any other vegetables may go into curry—tomato, marrow, etc. If carrots are added they should be semi-cooked first. Care should be taken to blend all flavourings well, as curry should have no outstanding taste, and it should be difficult to know what has been put into it. More curry powder may be added if wished, or a mixture of curry powder and curry paste.

DUTCH HARE (5 or 6 people)

1 lb. beefsteak.	2 oz. bread soaked in milk
½ teasp. ground cloves.	and squeezed dry.
Pinch mixed spice.	1 teasp. chopped onion.
1 yolk of egg.	½ oz. butter or dripping.

Salt and pepper.

Mince the meat and mix all the ingredients. Form into a roll or cake. Arrange strips of bacon on top to form a lattice. Bake 1 hour. Serve with a good brown gravy made in the tin after cooking. This dish is also good cold.

DUTCH STEW (7 or 8 people)

1 lb. neck of mutton (jointed).	1 cabbage.
	4 or 5 potatoes.
1 onion.	1 oz. dripping.
1 cup of water.	Salt and pepper.

Fry the joint in the dripping with the onion, then add the

water and simmer for 1 hour. Lift out the meat. Put in the cabbage and potatoes, cut up slightly, adding more liquid if necessary. Place the meat on top of the vegetables and braise till all are tender. Dish the meat on the cabbage and put the potatoes and gravy round.

FRICASSÉE OF VEAL or CHICKEN (5 or 6 people)

1 chicken or 1½ lb. raw veal.	Bunch of herbs.
White stock or water.	2 oz. butter.
Onion.	2 oz. flour.
Celery.	¼ pt. cream (optional).
Carrot.	Juice of ½ lemon.
	Salt and pepper.

Cut the meat into neat joints or pieces. Put them with the vegetables and herbs, and stock to cover them, into a lined pan or casserole, and cook till tender (1 to 2 hours).

Make a sauce of the butter, flour, and ¼ pt. of the stock. Boil well. Then add the cream, lemon and more seasoning if required. Do not re-boil, but re-heat. Then (1) mix half the sauce with meat, arrange on dish and coat with remaining sauce, OR (2) add all the meat to the sauce and dish neatly, garnishing with rolls of bacon, lemon butterflies, and parsley; or as desired.

Two eggs added to the cream and cooked in the sauce improves the dish.

*GALANTINE OF BEEF (I)
(8 to 10 people)

1 lb. beefsteak.	1 teasp. chopped parsley.
½ lb. (or less) of bacon or ham.	½ teasp. marjoram or thyme.
½ lb. of sausage or quenelle meat.	A dust of nutmeg.
¼ lb. breadcrumbs.	Salt and pepper.
	2 or 3 eggs.
	¼ pt. stock.

Mince the meat finely. Mix with the rest of the dry ingredients, then add the well-beaten eggs and stock if needed; the mixture should be rather moist or it will not be smooth. Form into a roll. Tie in a cloth. Boil in the stock pot for two hours. When cold, brush with glaze (melted) and decorate with butter put through a small forcing pipe, or coat with chaudfroid sauce.

*GALANTINE OF BEEF (II), Economical
(6 or 7 people)

1 lb. raw beefsteak.	¼ lb. boiled bacon or ham.
2 oz. breadcrumbs or minced bread.	2 oz. oatmeal.
	1 egg and ¼ pt. stock.
Salt, pepper, and nutmeg.	

Make as in the preceding recipe, and boil for at least 3 hours. When cold, glaze and decorate with leaves of aspic, etc.

GALANTINE OF VEAL (8 to 10 people)

Bone a breast or loin of veal. Prepare stuffing as for chicken galantine, but veal requires longer cooking. Boil for 3 to 4 hours.

GRENADINES DE VEAU (7 or 8 people)

2 lb. fillet of veal.	Stock for braising.
Larding bacon.	Cucumber.
Vegetables, herbs, and spices for braising.	Tomato or demi-glace sauce.

Trim the meat into round or oval fillets. Lard each thickly with the bacon. Braise for an hour or more.

Make a quenelle mixture with the veal trimmings. Peel the cucumber, and cut into rounds $\frac{1}{2}$ inch thick. Boil these in salted water for 10 minutes, then cool them by placing them in cold water. Remove the seeds, and fill the cavity with the quenelle mixture. Poach these for 10 to 15 minutes. Drain and glaze them.

When the grenadines are tender put them in a hot oven to crisp the lardoons. Glaze them and dish them on a potato (or other vegetable) border alternately with the cucumber rounds. Pour a good sauce round.

HAGGIS (10 to 12 people)

1 sheep's pluck.	1 teasp. chopped parsley.
1 sheep's paunch.	1 teasp. pounded mace.
1 lb. onion.	$\frac{1}{2}$ pt. good gravy or milk.
$\frac{3}{4}$ lb. suet.	2 teasp. salt.
1 lb. oatmeal.	1 teasp. pepper.

Wash the paunch well and soak it overnight. Then turn it inside out, and scald it. Scrape it. Leave it in cold water until wanted. Wash the pluck, especially the heart and liver. Boil it for $1\frac{1}{2}$ hours, then drain and mince it. Add the blanched and chopped onions, and all the other ingredients. Three-quarter fill the paunch with these. Tie it up and fasten it in a cloth. Boil it for 3 or 4 hours. Serve very hot without sauce or gravy.

HAM, BAKED

Soak it for 24 hours. Make a crust of 2 lb. flour and 1 pt. water, and in this wrap the whole ham entirely. Place on a baking tin, and allow 25 minutes to each lb. and 25 minutes over.

Boiled hams may be finished off by baking for an hour. If this is done they must be skinned, and covered with browned breadcrumbs before being baked.

HAM, BOILED

Soak the ham for 12 hours or more. Scrape and trim it. Allow for cooking 25 minutes to each lb. and 25 minutes over, putting the ham into fresh cold water, but not beginning to time it until the water boils. Simmer it gently. A pint of beer or cider if added to the water improves the flavour. If eaten cold, let the ham remain in the liquor, after cooking, for an hour or so. Ham so treated does not keep well.

Before serving remove the skin, and sprinkle the surface with browned breadcrumbs, or glaze the ham.

HAMBURG STEAK (5 or 6 people)

1 lb. good, well-hung steak, minced raw.	2 tablesp. mashed potato (optional).
1 tablesp. breadcrumbs.	1 beaten egg.
½ tablesp. finely chopped onion.	½ teasp. salt.
	¼ teasp. pepper.

Fry the onion lightly and mix it in a bowl with all the other ingredients. Shape to a steak about one or more inches thick. Place on a greased tin with a lump of butter or dripping on the top. Cook in a hot oven 15 to 20 minutes. Serve with gravy, chipped potatoes, and onion and tomato, if liked.

HARICOT BEANS AND BACON (4 people)

¼ pt. haricot beans and 5 slices bacon.

Wash the beans and soak them overnight. Cook till tender (2 hours or more). Drain. Fry the bacon and put it on a hot dish. Fry the beans in the bacon fat. Pile these, sprinkled with chopped parsley, in the centre of the dish.

*HARICOT OF MUTTON (5 or 6 people)

1½ lb. neck of mutton (best end).	1 pt. stock or water.
½ oz. dripping.	1 oz. flour.
2 carrots (small).	2 small onions.
1 turnip (small).	1 cup cooked haricot beans.
	Seasoning.

Divide the chined meat into neat cutlets. Trim these, removing most of the fat. Melt the fat, and fry the cutlets on both sides. Place these in a casserole or stewpan and proceed exactly as for Stew, Brown (p. 79), skimming off any fat that rises.

Arrange the meat in a circle on a hot dish and place the vegetables in the centre. Pour the sauce over the meat. Garnish if liked with little heaps of prettily cut vegetables that have been cooked separately.

*HOT POT

Follow the recipe for Irish Stew. Place the meat and vegetables alternately in a deep casserole, seasoning each layer well. The top should be formed of a layer of potato. This may be dealt with in two ways: (a) Place a lid on the casserole and bake for 1½ hours. Remove the lid and brush potatoes with fat, and return to oven for another hour without the lid, to brown the potatoes. (b) Cover the whole with grease-proof paper instead of the lid and bake for 2½ hours. This browns the potatoes without uncovering. Serve in the casserole.

*KIDNEYS, BROILED or GRILLED

Wash the kidneys. Skin them and remove the core. Cut them in half lengthways without dividing. Broil them *before* or grill them *over* a clear fire, turning frequently for 4 or 5 minutes. Serve very hot with a pat of maître d'hôtel butter on each and fried potatoes round.

*KIDNEYS, STEWED

Bullock's kidneys must be soaked for some hours before use in milk and water or in ½ pt. water mixed with 1 wineglass of vinegar.

Wash well. Soak for 15 minutes. Remove all core. Then proceed as for Stew, Brown (page 79). Dish with a border of piped potato.

*LIVER AND BACON (5 or 6 people)

1 lb. liver.	Flour.
½–½ lb. bacon.	½ pt. stock.

Cut the bacon into thin slices, removing the rind. Fry these till transparent on both sides, then remove the bacon and keep it hot. Fry the liver exactly as described in recipe for Liver, Fried, cooking it in the bacon fat which must be heated till it smokes freely. Arrange the liver on a hot dish, make a gravy by browning some flour in the pan in which the liver was cooked, and add boiling water or stock to this (the liver spoils if not served at once, hence the boiling stock for gravy to save delay). Pour the gravy round the liver and serve the bacon on the top.

LIVER À LA FRANÇAISE (4 or 5 people)

1 lb. tender liver.	1 very finely chopped onion.
½ lb. fat bacon.	¼ teasp. grated lemon rind.
2 tablesp. of breadcrumbs.	A little ketchup or Worces-
½ tablesp. of chopped parsley.	tershire sauce.
½ teasp. salt.	Stock to moisten.
¼ teasp. pepper.	A little beaten egg if possible.

Prepare liver for frying, lay the slices on a baking tin. Spread each with a layer of stuffing. Cover with slices of bacon. Pour on sufficient stock to cover the liver. Bake in a moderate oven for ¾ hour. Dish up and serve with gravy poured round.

* LIVER, FRIED

Lamb's or calf's liver is the best. Choose a fresh, plump one. Wash it well in tepid water, and place on a sieve or colander to drain until required. Then dry in a clean soft cloth. Cut into slices ½ in. thick, sprinkle with salt and a squeeze of lemon if convenient. Dust each piece lightly with flour. Make 1½ oz. lard or other fat very hot (smoking freely) and put in the slices. Fry carefully first on one side, then turn and cook on the other side. Liver should be thoroughly cooked. If the fat is really hot enough this will cook the liver right through, the outside being slightly crisp and the inside very tender. Serve at once.

LIVER, STEWED (4 or 5 people)

½ lb. liver.	1 pt. stock
¼ lb. bacon.	or water.
1 onion.	1 oz. flour.
Seasoning.	

Cut the bacon into dice and fry it lightly. Add the flour, and chopped onion, and fry. Add the liquid, stir and boil, then add the washed and sliced liver. Season and simmer for an hour. This is very nice with a garnish of beans.

Liver. Calf's liver may also be larded and braised.

*MEAT PORCUPINE

To 1 part of cooked or raw minced meat (include some ham or bacon if possible, for flavour) allow:
¼ breadcrumbs.   ¼ mashed potato.   Seasoning.

Mix these together, seasoning highly, and mix with beaten egg. Shape into the shape of a porcupine. Lard it thickly with fat

bacon to resemble a porcupine, and roast without basting for about 40 minutes (more or less according to size, and whether the meat is raw or cooked). Serve with good gravy. Do NOT BASTE or it may lose its shape.

*MINCED COLLOPS (Raw Meat)

(4 people)

½ lb. raw beef finely minced.	½ oz. butter.
	1½–2 teasp. flour.
1 small onion finely minced.	Seasoning.
	2 teasp. Worcestershire
Stock.	sauce (if wished).

(Particularly useful for invalids where raw meat must be used.)

Heat the butter, and in this fry the onion (if wished), then add the flour and fry lightly. Add the meat, and fry gently for 5 minutes, stirring and chopping the meat with the side of the wooden spoon while frying, to remove lumps and to mix the flour. Add just sufficient stock and the Worcestershire sauce to cover the meat. Cook very gently in a double saucepan or casserole, adding more stock if necessary to prevent it drying. Serve with sippets of toast, or a border of boiled rice (as for curry) or cooked macaroni.

*MOCK DUCK (8 or 10 people)

Bone a shoulder of mutton. Stuff the cavity with sage and onion forcemeat. Truss neatly. Allow 20 minutes to the lb. and 20 minutes over for roasting. Serve with a piquant brown sauce.

MOULDS

See under Veal below

*MUTTON

Three methods of cooking one leg for small family to avoid warming up meat constantly. Divide the leg into three: (1) the fillet—bone, stuff and roast this; (2) a slice cut (for the next piece) about 1 inch in thickness—to be grilled, stewed or fried and served with chipped potatoes; and (3) the knuckle end, which may be steamed or boiled with caper sauce, or treated as mock hare, etc.

*MUTTON, BOILED

See Beef, Boiled, page 62.

The savoury dumplings are usually omitted, and the meat is served covered with caper sauce, and vegetables are placed neatly around it.

*MUTTON, BRAISED LEG

1 leg of mutton.	Herbs. Spices.
½ lb. veal forcemeat or	Vegetables.
1 lb. sausage meat.	8 small tomatoes.
Stock.	Seasoning.

Bone the meat and stuff the cavity with forcemeat. Sew up neatly. Braise it (follow directions for Braising, page 59). Glaze it, garnish with baked and glazed tomatoes or any vegetables and serve with good brown sauce. The forcemeat may be made with bearded oysters, mushrooms, etc., if feasible.

*MUTTON CHOPS, BROILED or GRILLED

Loin chops are best. Trim them, removing most of the fat. Broil before or grill over a hot fire (see full directions for Grilling and Broiling, pages 53, 54) and serve with maître d'hôtel butter, baked tomatoes, or however wished.

Mutton Chops (Fried). Leave on rather more fat when trimming. Heat a frying pan. Place the chops in this. The heat will seal the surface albumen, and sufficient fat will flow in which to finish frying. Turn quickly when one side is sealed, then finish in more gentle heat. Serve with good brown gravy.

*MUTTON STEWED WITH RICE (about 6 people)

1 lb. middle neck of mutton.	6 onions (or more).
4 carrots (or more).	2 oz. washed rice.
2 turnips (or more).	Chopped parsley.
	1½ pt. water.
Seasoning to taste.	

Put the meat with the vegetables into boiling water. Add 1 teasp. salt. Cook slowly for one hour. Add the rice, and continue cooking for an hour or more or till tender. The rice will have absorbed the water. Place the meat and vegetables on a hot dish, and the rice round them to form a border. Sprinkle with chopped parsley. Barley may be used instead of rice, but it takes much longer to cook.

Rabbit or any meat can be used, and a tough old fowl is excellent for this dish.

*MUTTON PIE (7 or 8 people)

2 lb. lean mutton.	1 small onion. **Seasoning.**
1 lb. skinned tomatoes.	Water or stock.

Follow directions for Meat Pie (page 170). Less meat may be used and ¼ lb. cooked macaroni added instead if preferred.

*OX CHEEK, STEWED

1 ox cheek.	Celery.
1 large onion.	Bunch of herbs.
1 carrot.	Seasoning.
1 turnip.	1 teacup of vinegar.

Soak and wash the cheek well. Bone it (a butcher will often do this if requested to) and either cut it into pieces and season it, or roll it neatly, secure it with tape and stew it whole. Put it with the vegetables, herbs and seasoning into a saucepan. Stew gently till tender, about 4 hours. Lift out the meat and vegetables and thicken the gravy with flour mixed to a smooth cream with cold water, allowing 1 oz. flour to each pt. of liquid. Pour this sauce over the meat and put the vegetables neatly round.

OX PALATES (4 or 5 people)

A savoury stew can be made with these, following the recipe for Ox Cheek—3 or 4 palates make a dish. They must be soaked in warm salt and water, being rubbed well to remove any slimy substance. Drain and blanch without quite boiling them. Remove the hard skin. They look white and clear when ready for use.

*OX TAIL, STEWED (4 or 5 people)

1 ox tail.	1 oz. fat.
1 carrot.	1 qt. stock.
1 onion.	Bunch of herbs
1 stick celery.	and spices.
1 turnip.	1 oz. dripping.
1 oz. flour.	Seasoning to taste.

Divide the tail into pieces, coat them with flour and fry till golden. Place in a casserole or stewpan with the vegetables, herbs and spices. Cover with the stock. Cover pan closely and stew till tender (often 4 to 5 hours). Make a brown roux with the fat and flour. Add stock from the stew and make a good brown sauce, adding a glass of claret if wished. Skim

WHIPPED CUSTARD SAUCE (4 people)

½ pt. milk.   1 egg.   Sugar and flavouring.

Make a custard with the milk and yolk.   Add sugar and flavouring.   Whisk the white stiffly.   Add to custard and heat again till light and frothy, whisking all the time.   Serve at once.

SAUCES—Class IV
(Cold Sauces)

AGRO DOLCE SAUCE (6 or 7 people)

1 small jar red currant jelly.	10 lumps of sugar.
Juice of 2 lemons.	1 small glass port wine.
Cayenne.	Juice of 2 oranges.
	Small piece of butter.

Boil all together.   Strain.   Serve with cold ham, or suitable cold meats.

ASPIC MAYONNAISE
(Would coat about 2 lb. salmon)

½ pt. aspic jelly.   1 gill stiff mayonnaise.

Dissolve the aspic; then add it carefully to the mayonnaise and use it, just before it sets, for coating, etc.

BIGARADE SAUCE (4 people)

¼ pt. espagnole sauce.	Lemon juice.
1 glass port.	¼ pt. good gravy.
	1 Seville orange.

Cut the peel of half the orange into thin julienne strips. Just cover them with water, and boil 5 minutes.   Drain.   Boil the espagnole sauce, gravy, and half the juice of the orange till reduced to half.   Add the orange peel, 1 teasp. lemon juice, port; season well, and serve with roast wild duck and game.

CHAUDFROID SAUCE
(Would coat a chicken)

½ pt. good béchamel or other sauce.
½ pt. aspic jelly.

Heat both separately, and, when cool, mix them, and tammy. Use just before they set, for coating.

well and season. Lift the pieces of ox tail on to a hot dish, cover with the sauce and garnish with some of the vegetables stamped into rounds the size of a shilling.

OX TONGUE

This, if taken straight from the pickle, needs washing only. If it has been smoked and dried, soak it for 12 to 24 hours. A smoked tongue then goes into cold, and a pickled one into lukewarm water. Bring to the boil, then simmer gently for 3 to 4 hours. Then skin carefully. Shape it either by: (1) trussing it to a neat shape and fixing it on to a board with two forks; (2) while still hot, cut it in two lengthways and place it in a cake tin, letting the root overlap the tip. Fill up the tin with strong jellied stock. Place a small plate on the tongue and a heavy weight on the plate.

If served hot, re-heat it in stock and send to table covered with browned crumbs and with a good sauce. If served cold, glaze it and decorate it. If trussed, a frill is put round the root.

PIGEON CUTLETS (8 people)

| 4 pigeons. 1 egg. | ¼ lb. quenelle meat |
| Breadcrumbs. | or any good farce. |

Cut the pigeons in half. Remove all bones, except the drumstick. Beat, season and shape and trim each half-pigeon to resemble a cutlet. Fry these gently in 1 or 2 oz. clarified butter, then braise them till tender. Press them between two dishes, weighted, till cold. Cover the cut side neatly with the farce; flour, egg, crumb and fry them. Dish them on a purée of potato or green peas and serve.

Garnish with peas, cherries, etc., and hand salad with them, adding a few cherries to the salad.

PIG'S FRY or MOCK GOOSE (6 or 7 people)

1 lb. fry.	Salt and pepper.
2 lb. potatoes.	½ teasp. powdered sage.
½ lb. onions.	1 apple (if liked).

Peel the potatoes, chop the onion and apple. Cut the fry and potatoes in thick slices.

Put everything in layers in a deep casserole, sprinkling the seasoning between each layer. Add ½ pt. cold water.

Cover the whole with caul or greased paper.

Bake in a moderate oven for 2 hours.

PORK CHOPS

These may be fried, grilled, or broiled, but must be well cooked or they are most unwholesome.

Allow 15 minutes each, and serve with apple sauce. See Grilling, Broiling, and Frying, pages 53–54.

*SHEEP'S HEAD (4 or 5 people)

1 sheep's head.	Stick celery.
2 carrots, 2 turnips.	Bunch herbs.
2 onions.	1 teasp. chopped
1 tablesp. flour.	parsley.
2 oz. rice.	Seasoning.

Divide the head and remove the brains, placing them in cold salted water. Remove any small bones from the head and any hair. Wash well, using salt for the nose and eye sockets. Remove the tongue. Blanch, and throw away water. Place in a saucepan with the tongue, cover with hot water, add a dessertsp. salt, and, as the water boils, remove all scum. Cook 2½ to 3 hours. Add the vegetables. Cook for 1½ hours, add the rice and continue cooking for another ½ hour.

Wash the brains, tie them in muslin, and cook with the head for twenty minutes, then cover them with cold water.

Remove the meat from the bone, and pile it on a hot dish. Coat with brain sauce, i.e. white sauce, to which the cooked brains (chopped) and chopped parsley and seasoning have been added. Arrange the vegetables round.

Skin the tongue, cut it in four, and put it round the head. If liked the meat can be cut off the head. This makes a nicer-looking dish. The liquor is used for Sheep's Head Broth.

SHEEP'S HEART (Stuffed)

(2 or 3 people)

1 sheep's heart.   Fat.   Veal or onion stuffing.

Well wash the heart to free it from all blood. Dry well. Remove the ' deaf ears ' and cut through the division in the middle. Fill the cavity with the stuffing. Tie a greased paper over to keep this in. Flour the heart. Bake it for 40 minutes to 2 hours according to size—a sheep's heart takes about 40 minutes; a calf's 1 to 1½ hours; and a bullock's 1½ to 2 hours. Baste frequently and serve with a good gravy.

OR, boil the heart for 20 to 45 minutes before roasting it.

OR, stew or braise it.

SHEEP'S TROTTERS
See recipe for Calf's Feet.

STEW, BROWN (4 or 5 people)

1 lb. beefsteak.	¾ oz. dripping.
1 onion.	½ oz. flour.
1 carrot.	Salt and pepper.
1 small turnip.	½ pt. stock.

½ oz. seasoned flour.

Trim, wipe and beat meat. Dip in seasoned flour. Slice onion, melt dripping, and when hot fry meat and onion in stew-pan till browned. Meantime cut carrot and turnip into neat shapes and keep in water to cook later as a garnish. When meat is browned remove from pan, add flour and fry to a golden brown. Add stock and bring to boil. Add trimmings of vegetables, then replace meat and stew gently till tender—at least 1½ hours—stirring occasionally. Place meat on a hot dish, strain gravy over, and garnish with cooked carrot, turnip and a little finely-chopped parsley if liked.

N.B. For a simpler method, cut all vegetables into neat pieces, and serve in gravy without straining.

*STEW, IRISH (5 or 6 people)

1 lb. neck of mutton.	½ lb. or more onions.
1 to 2 lb. potatoes.	½ pt. water or stock.

Salt and pepper.

Peel the potatoes, and slice them thickly. Cut the onions into rings and divide the meat into neat joints. Put the vegetables and meat in layers into a saucepan—seasoning each layer. Pour in the water. Stew gently for 2 hours.

STEW, WHITE
See Fricassée, page 69.

SWEETBREADS

PREPARATION. Soak 15 minutes. Blanch, then cook for 5 minutes in boiling salted water. Put at once into cold water, to preserve the colour, for 20 minutes. Then dry and trim them. Lambs' sweetbreads being much smaller than calves', more of the former will be required for a dish.

SWEETBREADS, BRAISED (5 or 6 people)

2 calves' sweetbreads.	Carrot, turnip, and celery.
Larding bacon.	Herbs and spices.
Onion.	Good brown sauce.

Place the prepared (see previous recipe) sweetbreads between two plates, and press for an hour or more. Lard them. Place them on a bed of vegetables, cover with strong stock, place a buttered paper closely over, and braise for an hour. Finish them off by browning in the oven. Then glaze and dish them on fried croûtons of bread. Pour the sauce over and garnish with green peas, or with a chestnut, spinach or carrot purée.

SWEETBREADS, FRIED

Prepare as usual. Simmer them for an hour or more in stock until tender. When cold cut into slices 1 inch thick. Egg, crumb, and fry these.

Drain and dish on a folded napkin, and garnish with fried parsley.

Or, dish them on a purée of pea, spinach or potato, and pour a good sauce round.

TRIPE

In some parts of the country only undressed tripe is sold by the butchers. Where this is the case, the tripe should be washed and scraped in several waters, and all fat and discoloured parts removed. Put it then in a deep pan, cover with cold water, bring to the boil and throw this water away. Repeat 2 or 3 more times until the tripe smells quite sweet. Cover with water and simmer from 8 to 10 hours until it is tender. After that it can be used in any of the ways given below.

TRIPE, BRAISED

Prepare as before. Cut into slices, and on each put some forcemeat and a slice of thin bacon. Tie with string. Braise these on a bed of vegetables for 2½ to 3 hours or even more. Serve dished on a border of mashed potato, with brown gravy poured round, and garnished with some of the braised vegetables. (See detailed rules under Braising, page 59.)

TRIPE AND ONIONS (4 or 5 people)

1 lb. dressed tripe.	1 pt. milk or milk
2 onions.	and water.
1 tablesp. flour.	Seasoning.

Blanch the tripe and onions. Cut the tripe into neat slices, and the onions into quarters. Add milk and 1 teasp. salt. Simmer gently for 2 hours. Mix the flour to a smooth cream with ¼ pt. cold milk, and stir this to the contents of the saucepan. Boil for a few minutes, season and serve.

Tripe can also be cooked in brown or tomato sauce.

VEAL, BREAST OF, STEWED (6 or 7 people)

3 or 4 lb. breast	12 peppercorns.
of veal.	1 blade of mace.
1 carrot, turnip,	Celery.
onion.	2 cloves.
Bunch of herbs.	1 teasp. salt.

Put the meat in a pan with just enough water to cover it. Add the vegetables, spices and salt. Stew gently for 2½ hours, skimming well.

When cooked, remove the bones (these will slip out). Coat entirely with parsley sauce and serve hot.

*VEAL JELLY (5 or 6 people)

3 lb. knuckle of veal.	1 onion.
3 pt. stock or water.	The rind of a lemon.
20 peppercorns.	Bunch of herbs. Salt.

Divide the meat into several pieces; cover these with the liquid and cook gently for 3 hours or more. Add the rest of the ingredients, and cook again till the meat all comes away from the bone. Strain, cut the meat up small, and return all to the saucepan.

Stir over the fire till very little liquid remains, add a squeeze of lemon, and pour into a wetted mould. Turn out when set, and garnish with salad.

*VEAL, KNUCKLE OF, STEWED (I)

Stew gently in good stock, simmering until tender (3 hours or more). Serve with a white sauce made from the stock.

*VEAL, KNUCKLE OF, STEWED (II)

After cooking as above, remove the lower bone. Egg and breadcrumb the joint. Brown it in a quick oven and serve with forcemeat balls, fried bacon and a brown sauce.

VEAL MOULDS (5 or 6 people)

1 lb. veal.	1 pt. strong jellied stock.
¼ lb. bacon or ham.	¼ teasp. grated lemon
1 or 2 hard-boiled eggs.	rind.
1 teasp. chopped pars-	Salt and pepper.
ley.	1 oz. gelatine.

If no jellied stock is available, add extra gelatine.

Rinse a mould with cold water and decorate it with some of the egg and bacon. Cut up the veal, bacon and eggs into neat dice. Fill the mould with layers of these, seasoning each layer. Dissolve the gelatine in the stock and cover the meat with this. Place a greased paper over the top. Cook in a moderate oven for 2 to 3 hours.

Fill up when cooked with the rest of the stock. When cold, turn out and garnish with salad.

Rabbit Mould. This is made in the same way.

Beefsteak and Kidney Mould may be made in the same way.

*VEAL, ROASTED SHOULDER or FILLET

6 or 7 lb. fillet.   Forcemeat.

Bone the fillet and fill the cavity with forcemeat. Cover with caul or greased paper and roast, allowing 20 to 25 minutes to the lb. and 20 to 25 minutes over.

Baste well, and serve with brown gravy, to which a squeeze of lemon is added. Garnish with bacon and forcemeat balls.

COLD MEATS WARMED, or RÉCHAUFFÉS

For this branch of cookery it is important to remember certain points:

(1) As the meat has already been cooked, it really requires only to be RE-HEATED—NOT RE-COOKED. Therefore, any sauces, vegetables, etc., to be served with it must be thoroughly cooked before adding the meat to them.

(2) As meat really suffers by re-heating, it is better to divide it into small portions (mince, etc.), as these re-heat more rapidly than larger portions.

(3) The meat should be protected from direct action of heat by being encased in something, i.e. sauce, batter, pastry and potato, etc.

*BUBBLE AND SQUEAK

It should be noticed that in this recipe the meat is not usually encased, hence it is often very dry. An improvement would be to coat the meat in a frying batter. The usual ingredients are:

Slices of any meat.	(Cold cooked potato and
Cold cabbage (cooked).	onion may be used also.)
Seasoning.	

Season the meat. Fry it very lightly in dripping. Fry the cabbage (and other vegetables if used) in the same fat. Put this in the centre of a dish and arrange the meat round.

*CASSEROLE OF POTATO AND MEAT (5 or 6 people)

1 lb. mashed potato.	1 egg.
1 oz. fat.	½ lb. cooked meat.
¼ pt. good panada.	Browned breadcrumbs.

Add the egg and fat to the potato. Well grease a 4-in. cake tin, or make in a 1-lb. size casserole. Coat it with crumbs, then line it with potato, leaving a cavity in the centre. Fill with the meat mixture (see Croquettes), cover with greased paper, heat thoroughly in oven. Turn out and pour gravy round.

COTTAGE PIE (4 people)

This is an example of the minced class of réchauffés. Any cold meat will do, but a mixture of two gives a better flavour. Mince the meat finely with, if possible, any cooked tongue, bacon, liver, etc.

Make a 'panada'. For this, to each ½ lb. of minced meat allow ½ oz. fat. In this fry a small chopped onion. Add ½ oz. flour, and fry this till golden brown. Add gradually ½ pt. of stock or water, or rather less.

Boil well, then add the meat and season to taste. Put this

in a pie-dish and cover the top entirely with mashed potato. Smooth the surface, place small pieces of fat on it, and bake for 20 minutes until well browned.

*CROQUETTES (5 or 6 people)

 Rissoles

½ lb. cold minced meat.	¼ pt. good thick sauce
2 oz. minced ham (if convenient).	or panada.
	Salt and pepper.
1 teasp. chopped parsley.	A dust of nutmeg.

To these ingredients, for the sake of economy, ¼ lb. mashed potato may be added.

Make a panada with 1 oz. fat, 1 oz. flour, and about ¼ pt. good stock, or stock and milk. (For brown meat (beef, etc., and game) a brown panada must be made; for chicken, or white meat, a white one; in this case béchamel panada would be the nicest.) Boil this, cool slightly, then add the remaining ingredients, stir well and season. Turn the mixture on to a greased plate and cover with a greased paper, and leave till cold. Then divide into equal portions. Roll each into a round ball; flour each one, then dip it into beaten egg, then into crumbs, and for dark meat do this twice. Fry in hot deep fat, drain well, and garnish with fried parsley.

*CURRY OF COLD MEAT (6 or 7 people)

See Curry, page 68, and prepare the curry sauce in the same way. Then add the meat and thoroughly re-heat, but on no account must the meat boil, so that if any vegetables, etc., require cooking, see that they are done before the meat is added. Re-heat in a double saucepan, or in a casserole in a cool oven.

Serve as before with rice.

*CURRY CROQUETTES (5 or 6 people)

1 lb. mashed potatoes.	Breadcrumbs. 1 egg.
Remains of curry.	2 oz. butter. Seasoning.

Mix the melted butter and egg yolk to the potatoes. Roll this out on a floured board, and stamp into rounds about 2 inches in diameter. On one round put a little curry and cover with a second round, damping the edges. Trim egg and crumb the croquettes. Fry in hot fat. Garnish with cut lemon and parsley.

DARIOLES OF COLD MEAT (4 people)

½ lb. cold meat (minced).	½ small onion (chopped).
½ tablesp. of parsley (chopped).	½ oz. dripping. Seasoning.
¼ pt. of good stock.	Pinch of mace.
½ oz. of flour.	1 egg.

Fry the onion in the fat. Remove it from the fat, add the flour, cook for a few minutes and add the stock. Boil well. Put the meat, parsley, onion, and seasoning in a bowl and mix well. Add the sauce and egg.

Turn into 4 small darioles that have been well greased. Steam for 30 minutes. Turn out and coat with sauce and decorate with peas or any vegetables.

N.B. Raw meat can be used, and in that case steam 1 hour or longer. If white meat is used, coat with white sauce such as béchamel.

DRESDEN PATTIES (4 people)

Cut slices of bread 1½ inches thick. Cut these into rounds 2 inches in diameter. Remove the centres with a small cutter. Fry in hot fat till golden. (The bread may be dipped in milk before being fried if liked; this makes a softer croûte. They must next be egged and crumbed and then fried.) Fill the centres with a mixture of meat as for Croquettes. Place a small round of fried bread on the top to form a lid. Serve with fried parsley.

DURHAM CUTLETS (5 or 6 people)

½ lb. cooked meat.	1 teasp. chopped parsley.
1 oz. dripping.	1 teasp. ketchup or Worcestershire sauce.
1 oz. flour. } PANADA.	
1 gill stock.	Salt and pepper.

If meat is scarce, 2 oz. breadcrumbs may be added to 6 oz. cooked meat.

Make the panada, add the other ingredients, mix well and allow to cool. When cold form into 4 or 5 equal-sized portions. Shape into cutlets. Coat (twice if possible) with egg and crumb. Fry in deep fat. Dish on a potato border. Insert an inch of macaroni to represent the bone and on this put a frill. Pour a good sauce round.

The same mixture may be used for Rissoles, Dresden Patties, Croquettes, and, if made more liquid, for Cottage Pie.

GÂTEAU OF COLD MEAT (5 or 6 people)

1 lb. minced meat (or meats).	2 oz. breadcrumbs.
	1 gill good stock or gravy.
1 tablesp. tomato or other sauce.	2 eggs.
	Seasoning.

Mix the ingredients and put them in a well-greased cake tin coated with browned breadcrumbs. Bake or steam for 30 to 40 minutes. Turn out and serve with sauce, or serve cold with salad.

*HASH

Slices of cold mutton neatly cut.

OPTIONAL MARINADE.
- 1 wineglass stock.
- ½ wineglass white wine.
- 1 dessertsp. lemon juice or vinegar.
- 1 teasp. Harvey or Worcester sauce.
- 1 finely chopped shallot.
- 1 teasp. chopped parsley.

Mix the bracketed ingredients, and let the meat lie in them for at least 2 or 3 hours. If wished, this process may be omitted. Make a sauce as follows (4 people):

To each ½ lb. meat allow ½ oz. fat, in this fry a small onion; add ½ oz. flour, fry till golden brown; then add about 1½ gills stock, using with the stock any of the marinade left over.

Season well, adding, if wished, chopped capers, etc. Put the meat with this sauce, and stand it in a double saucepan or in a cool oven, where it cannot possibly boil.

When really hot through, serve with sippets of toast or macaroni, etc. The marinade may also be omitted.

MACARONI TIMBALE (5 or 6 people)

4 oz. pipe macaroni.	2 oz. breadcrumbs.
8 oz. cooked meat.	Seasoning. 2 eggs.
¼ pt. stock or gravy.	A dust of nutmeg.

Place the macaroni in boiling salted water and cook for about 20 minutes or longer. It must be quite tender. Drain it thoroughly and line a well-greased plain mould with it. Mince the meat, add the eggs beaten, breadcrumbs, seasoning and stock or gravy. The success of the timbale depends on its flavouring, and a little cooked ham or tongue is a great improvement. Place the mixture into the prepared mould, and cover with greased paper. Steam for 20 to 40 minutes till firm. Turn out the timbale on to a hot dish, and pour a good sauce (tomato, espagnol, etc.) around it. N.B. A meat timbale can be made by using browned crumbs instead of macaroni.

*MINCE

Prepare meat and sauce, exactly following the directions for Cottage Pie. If liked, the mince may be made slightly more liquid. Serve it with sippets of toast, cooked macaroni; or poached eggs may be served with mince.

MINCE EN COQUILLES

The same mixture may be put into greased shells. If so, sprinkle the top with breadcrumbs, pour a little clarified butter over, and bake in a hot oven till brown.

*RISSOLES

A slightly softer mixture than for Croquettes, and the mixture enclosed in pastry and then usually dipped in egg and crushed vermicelli.

Roll the pastry very thinly. Stamp out rounds about 4 inches in diameter. Put some meat mixture on one half, damp the edges and fold the other half over.

Trim off any surplus paste, then dip in egg, crushed vermicelli, or breadcrumbs, and fry.

Garnish with fried parsley.

*ROMAN PIE (4 or 5 people)

Rather more than ¼ lb. pastry.	1½ oz. macaroni.
¼ lb. meat (poultry, if possible).	¼ pt. good sauce.
	Salt and cayenne.
	1 oz. grated cheese.

Grease a pint cake tin. Line it with pastry and fill in with layers of the meat cut into dice, cooked macaroni cut into neat lengths, and cheese and sauce. Cover the top with a lid of pastry.

Bake for about 40 minutes. Turn out and serve with tomato, brown, or white sauce.

*RUSSIAN PIE (4 or 5 people)

Remains of curry and rice. 1 or 2 hard-boiled eggs.
6 oz. pastry.

Roll the pastry into an oblong sheet barely ¼ inch thick.

On this put the curry, rice, and eggs cut up. Damp the edges, and fold over. Decorate with strips of pastry. Bake ½ hour in a hot oven. Other fillings, fish, etc., may be used.

*SAVOURY MOULD (5 or 6 people)

1 lb. cooked veal.	1 teasp. chopped parsley.
¼ lb. cooked ham.	1 or 2 hard-boiled eggs.
1 oz. gelatine, dissolved in 1 pt. jellied stock.	Grated lemon rind.
	Seasoning.

Damp a mould and decorate it with egg and ham. Fill up with the meat cut into large dice, and the egg, flavouring, and stock. Cover with greased paper. Bake in a moderate oven for 1 hour. When cold turn out and serve with salad. Any other meat may replace veal.

*SAVOURY PANCAKES

Make a good pancake batter. Fry this, as usual, on both sides, and turn on to a plate.

Put a large spoonful of any good mixture (e.g. the one for Croquettes) on each pancake, roll it up, re-heat. Serve on a bed of spinach, or other vegetable, and pour sauce round.

These pancakes may be filled with a savoury vegetable filling, lentil, etc., if preferred.

SAVOURY POTATOES (5 or 6 people)

1½ to 2 lb. potatoes.	½ pt. stock or water.
3 large onions.	2 oz. bacon scraps
½ oz. fat.	Pepper, salt.

Cut up bacon and fry slightly. Add the fat. Cut up potatoes into fairly large pieces. Slice the onions. Toss the vegetables in the fat till it is absorbed. Add the stock and seasoning and simmer gently till vegetables are tender. Dish neatly and serve very hot with a garnish of chopped parsley.

STUFFED CABBAGE ROLLS
(5 or 6 people)

1 nice young cabbage.

½ lb. sausage meat.
1 oz. ham or bacon (chopped).
1 oz. breadcrumbs. ⎫ STUFFING.
1 oz. chopped suet.
Pinch herbs.
Egg to bind. Salt, pepper.

Wash and blanch the cabbage. Take nice leaves and roll up the stuffing inside to make neat sausage shapes. Tie up and braise till tender. Serve with a brown sauce poured over.

IV. POULTRY, GAME, AND RABBITS

Choice of Birds, etc. In young birds the legs and feet are smooth, and the breast bone, which is gristle, bends easily. Geese and ducks have pliable feet, and the body should be free from hairs.

Game birds should have soft beaks also.

Hares should have sharp claws and ears that tear easily.

Game and hares should be hung before cooking for several days, and, in frosty weather, even for 2 to 3 weeks without being plucked or skinned.

Rabbits and pigeons do not keep well and should be eaten quite fresh. Poultry should be hung for 2 or 3 days after plucking.

Method of preparing Poultry, etc.

(1) Pluck the birds. In the case of poultry this should be done, if possible, while still warm immediately after killing.

(2) Remove any remaining young feathers or hairs by singeing.

(3) Draw the sinews in the legs. To do this, make an incision between the two bones of the leg below the knee, cutting downwards and not across. Then with a skewer draw out the white sinews until they can be grasped with the hand and withdrawn. This should be done to all birds, as the sinews of the legs are very stringy.

(4) Clean the birds. This is a difficult process to explain, but any poulterer would be willing to show his customers. A short description may be of use. Turn the bird breast downwards, make an incision at the back of the neck, and slit this up the back of the neck. Cut the head off, leaving a long flap of skin in the front to fold over when trussing. Remove the crop and windpipe, and press a finger down into the bird and loosen all the internal organs that can be reached. Turn the bird on to its back and make a slit crossways just above its tail. Through this again loosen and then withdraw all the remaining interior. Wipe out the bird with a damp cloth. Keep the gizzard (cutting it to remove the bag of grit inside) and the liver. These, with the neck, are known as 'giblets', and are very useful for gravy, etc.

(5) Truss the bird. For BOILING, loosen the outside skin from the thighs by pressing upwards with the fingers until the whole leg can be slipped inside the skin. Place the bird on its back, draw the long flap of skin over the hole at the top and tuck it under the bird at the back, fixing it in place by crossing the lower joints of the wings over it. Then slip the legs inside the loosened skin, pass a needle through the thighs and body, and again through the wings and body, and tie the string firmly. For ROASTING, the only difference is that the legs are left outside the body.

Boning. Cut off the neck of the bird, leaving as before the long flap of skin in front. Cut off also the two top joints of the wing and the legs, breaking the bones and cutting the skin **above** the second joint. Draw back the skin slightly and begin at the neck, working with a sharp knife and separating the flesh from the bones. Cut through the wing joint (where the wing joins the body) from the inside and scrape down the bone, turning the wing inside out. Do both wings. When these are free repeat round and round the body, gradually turning the bird inside out. Cut through the joint of the leg from the inside, and turn this also inside out, scraping the bone cleanly as this is done. Continue boning right to the tail and then sever the skin. Turn the bird right side out, carefully placing the flesh, and fill the bird with various stuffings.

For this, if possible, take: Half an ox tongue, 1 lb. sausage or quenelle meat, 2 hard-boiled eggs, truffles, pistachio nuts, etc.

Cut the tongue in half to allow the round of it to replace the carcass that has been removed, place this in the bird and cover it evenly with the quenelle meat, eggs, etc. The bird must look more plump than usual.

Fold over the long flap of skin, sprinkle the bird with salt, pepper and lemon juice, wrap it in a greased paper, and bind or secure it carefully in a cloth, fixing or sewing it firmly to preserve the shape. Steam it on a bed of the bones and any vegetables for about 3 hours. Old birds are excellent for boning, and the time for steaming may be increased to 5 or 6 hours, if necessary, to make them tender. (See Chaudfroid of Chicken, page 106.)

Boning for a Galantine. This is a much more simple matter. Slit the bird down the back, cutting the skin from the back of the neck to the tail. Insert a knife under the cut edges and so work off the flesh from the bones. The legs and wings are boned as before by severing the joints, and turning them inside out. (For recipe see page 94.)

METHOD OF COOKING

All the methods of cooking meat can be applied to the cooking of poultry and game (see pages 52–60). The more usual method is to lard or bard them and then roast them. They are usually served in the following manner:

Blackcock, Teal, and Ptarmigan. Average time ½ hour. Stand the birds on rounds of buttered toast before cooking them. Serve them on the toast with gravy, browned crumbs, chipped potatoes and bread sauce.

Duck, Roast. Average time 1 hour. Stuff tail end with sage and onion stuffing. Serve with fried or roast potatoes, gravy, and apple sauce. Watercress or orange salad may be served with duck.

Fowl, Boiled. Wrap this in greased paper and simmer gently for at least 1 hour. STEAMING is better than boiling. Wrap the bird in greased paper and steam for 2 hours or more. Either steamed or boiled fowl can be coated with a good white sauce and decorated prettily.

Fowl, Roast. Average time 1 hour. Stuff, if wished, at the head end with any good forcemeat. Lard or bard (see page 53) the fowl. Baste well. If barded remove the bacon 10 minutes before serving and sprinkle the breast with sifted flour (this process is known as 'frothing'). Brown the flour. Serve the bird with gravy made from the giblets, bread sauce, and rolls of bacon. These are placed on a skewer and cooked in the oven for 10 to 15 minutes.

Goose, Roast. Stuff at the tail end with sage and onion forcemeat. Roast from 1½ hours. Serve with gravy, and gooseberry or apple sauce.

Grouse, Roast. Average time 40 minutes. Draw the bird, wipe but do not wash it. Place a small piece of butter and some salt and pepper inside the body. Truss it and place it on a round of toast. Bard it, and if possible wrap it in a vine leaf. Roast in a quick oven, basting well. 10 minutes before serving froth (see Fowl, Roast), remove the bacon and serve on the toast, with bread sauce, chipped potatoes, browned crumbs, and gravy. Garnish with watercress.

Hare, Roast. Average time 1 to 1½ hours or longer. Stuff it with forcemeat, to which the blanched and chopped liver has been added. Lard or bard it and baste frequently. 10 minutes before serving, remove the bard, froth (see Fowl, Roast), and brown, basting the frothing with cream if possible. Garnish with forcemeat balls, and serve with gravy (to which port wine has been added) and red currant jelly.

Ortolan. See Snipe.

Partridge. Average time 25 minutes. Cook and serve in the same manner as Pheasant.

Pheasant. Average time 45 minutes. Baste constantly with butter. Serve with gravy, bread sauce, browned crumbs, and chipped potatoes.

Pigeon, Roast. Average time 20 to 30 minutes. Lard or bard, place on toast and baste frequently. Serve with bacon, bread sauce, gravy, crumbs and chipped potatoes.

Plover. See Snipe.

Ptarmigan. See Blackcock.

Quail. See Snipe.

Snipe, Plover, Woodcock, Ortolans, Quail. Average time 15 minutes. These are not cleaned. The inside, known as the ' trail ', is left in. Place on rounds of toast, lard or bard, and roast in a quick oven. Serve with browned crumbs, chipped potatoes and gravy.

Teal. See Blackcock.

Turkey, Roast. Average time 15 minutes to the lb. and 15 minutes over. Hang the bird for a week or longer, drawing before hanging. Stuff at the neck with good forcemeat, usually made of chestnuts (see Forcemeats). Truss, lard or bard and froth (see Fowl, Roast) ten minutes before serving. Serve with gravy, potatoes and green vegetables. Fried sausages are placed round as a garnish. Boiled ham or bacon may be served with turkey, also oyster, mushroom, tomato, or celery sauce.

Venison, Roast. Average time 13 minutes to the lb. and 13 minutes over, weighed with paper and paste on.

Venison should be hung in a cool place 2 to 3 weeks. Wipe it with a clean cloth daily to keep it dry, and dust with pepper. The more fat there is—the fat should be bright and clear—the better the meat. The shank bone should be sawn off before cooking, any dark dry skin should be trimmed off, and the gristle and sinews removed. Wipe all over with a damp cloth and then dry. Place the joint in a thick fold of greased paper. Cover this with a crust made of flour and water, and wrap the whole in thick greased paper. Roast, basting at once and almost continually during the cooking.

Twenty or thirty minutes before dishing remove the paper and crust. Baste well with butter. Froth with flour or salt. Serve on a very hot dish, as the fat soon gets firm, with good gravy and red currant jelly (this may be dissolved in port wine). Decorate the haunch with a paper frill.

Wild Duck. Serve very underdone. Average time 15 minutes only. Roast in a VERY hot oven, baste frequently. Squeeze the juice of a lemon over the breast. Sprinkle with salt and cayenne. Before carving pour a glass of port wine over the breast. Serve with bigarade sauce, also, if possible, orange salad.

Woodcock. See Snipe.

CHICKEN À LA MARENGO (Poulet sauté à la Marengo)

(6 people)

1 chicken.	¼ pt. good brown sauce.
1 shallot.	½ pt. tomato sauce.
4 truffles.	Puff paste for garnishing.
6 mushrooms.	4 poached eggs (if
Salad oil, if convenient.	wished).

Cut the chicken into neat joints and skin these. Fry until golden in the salad oil, if possible; if not, in clean fat. Fry the shallot. Place both in a stewpan, adding the sauces, mushrooms and truffles. Cover securely and stew gently for an hour or more.

Dish the chicken high on an entrée dish. Skim the sauce free from fat and pour it over, and garnish with the truffles, mushrooms, etc., and with crescent or other shapes made from the puff paste.

Poached or fried eggs may be served as an additional garnish.

COMPOTE OF PIGEONS (4 people)

2 pigeons.	1 glass Madeira (optional).
¼ lb. bacon.	Salt and pepper.
12 button onions.	2 oz. butter.
12 button mushrooms.	1½ oz. flour. Stock.

Truss the pigeons for boiling. Cut them in halves. Cut the bacon in dice and fry it. Then fry the pigeons till well browned. Place in a casserole or stewpan, and cover with the stock and wine. Add the blanched onions, and cook till all is tender (1 hour or more).

Dish on a border of potato. Skim the stock free from fat, brown the flour in the butter, add about ¾ pt. of the stock, and boil. Pour this over the pigeons. Garnish with the onions and mushrooms, or green peas, etc.

Cherries are a good garnish for pigeon. If fresh, stone and boil them for 10 minutes in slightly salted water.

N.B. Pigeons may be stewed whole. If so, allow longer for cooking, and dish on a fried croûton of bread.

GALANTINE OF CHICKEN (8 to 10 people)

1 fowl (raw and boned and cut down the centre of the back).

1 lb. quenelle or sausage meat.	Truffles.
	Pistachio nuts.
2 or 3 hard-boiled eggs.	Salt and pepper.
	Glaze.
Strips of bacon or tongue.	Aspic.
	Salad.

Spread open the fowl and cover it evenly on the inside with the seasoned quenelle meat, spreading the eggs, etc., on this, arranged so that it will look nice when cut. Roll up securely. Wrap in greased paper, and then tie up firmly in a cloth. Boil for 2 or 3 hours.

Then untie and wrap in a clean cloth, and place between 2 baking tins weighted with a 2 lb. weight, and leave till next day. Then glaze, or coat with a chaudfroid sauce, and serve with salad.

HARE, JUGGED (10 to 12 people)

1 hare.	2 onions stuck with 4 cloves.
1 lb. beefsteak (optional).	Veal forcemeat.
¼ lb. bacon or ham.	3 oz. flour.
Rind of ½ lemon.	¼ pt. port wine.
Bunch of herbs.	Red currant jelly.

Seasoning.

Cut the hare (unwashed) into neat joints; flour, season and then fry them with the bacon cut into dice. Put them into a casserole with the onion, lemon, herbs, and the steak cut into neat pieces.

Cover with stock or water. Put on a lid and cook in a gentle oven for 3 hours, or until the meat is tender.

The liver should be parboiled, minced, and mixed with the forcemeat, which should be formed into little balls, egged, crumbed and fried.

Dish the hare. For gravy mix the rest of the flour to a smooth cream with water, stir to the gravy and boil; add the wine and seasoning, and lastly the blood of the hare, after which the sauce must not boil. Re-heat the meat and forcemeat balls in the gravy. Serve with red currant jelly.

RABBIT À LA TARTARE (Lapin à la Tartare)

(4 or 5 people)

1 young rabbit.	Tartare sauce.
3 oz. clarified fat.	Fried parsley.
Egg and breadcrumbs.	

Divide the rabbit into joints, sauté these till brown and nearly cooked. Add the rest of the fat to the beaten egg. Brush the joints with this, and coat with breadcrumbs.

Fry and garnish with fried parsley. Serve with tartare sauce.

*RABBIT, BOILED (4 or 5 people)

1 rabbit.	1 pt. onion or parsley
Veal forcemeat.	sauce.

Soak the rabbit and wash well in salt and water (warm). Remove liver, lungs, etc. Blanch the liver and chop it and mix it with the forcemeat. Stuff the rabbit inside and sew it up. Truss it, by drawing back the front legs and forward the back ones, making a cut at the thigh joints. Secure with string. Turn the head to one side and fix it by putting a skewer through the jaws.

Boil gently for one hour. Remove the string, pour the sauce over. Serve with bacon or pickled pork. For the pickled pork allow 20 minutes to the lb. and 20 minutes over. It improves the rabbit to cook it in the water with the pork.

*RABBIT, JUGGED (5 or 6 people)

Follow the recipe given above for Hare, Jugged. The following different points must be noted:

(1) Wash the rabbit, and, if convenient, soak it in milk overnight;

(2) After frying the rabbit and bacon, remove these to the jar, and make a brown gravy with the flour, some fat and some stock.

This latter obviates the thickening process at the end, and as jugged rabbit is often served in the casserole in which it has been stewed, no dishing will then be necessary. The forcemeat balls can be added at the last, the sauce skimmed, and the whole served very hot.

*RABBIT, RAGOÛT OF (5 or 6 people)

1 rabbit.	Rolls of bacon.
¼ lb. bacon.	Herbs, blade of mace.
Slice carrot, turnip, onion, celery.	2 cloves, 10 peppercorns.
Forcemeat balls.	¾ pt. stock.
	1 oz. flour.

Soak and wash the rabbit as usual.   Joint it.   Cut the bacon into large dice, fry them till transparent.   Fry also the vegetables and the floured joints of the rabbit.   Put all in a stewpan or casserole and stew gently for about 2 hours.

Mix the flour smoothly with some stock, and add this to the boiling liquid, OR, make a brown roux before stewing the rabbit and thin this down with the stock, stewing all together. In the latter case no after thickening is required, and a browner stew is obtained, which requires skimming before serving. Garnish the meat with forcemeat balls and rolls of bacon.

*RABBIT, ROAST or BAKED (4 or 5 people)

1 rabbit.   Bacon.   ½ lb. forcemeat, OR ½ lb. sausage meat.

Prepare as for boiled rabbit, but the head is fixed upright on to the back.   To do this, pass a skewer through the mouth and pass it down between the shoulders.   Bard the rabbit with bacon.   Roast for ¾ to 1 hour, according to age and size, basting frequently.

Serve with rolls of bacon or fried sausages and brown gravy.

*RABBIT, STEWED (5 or 6 people)

1 rabbit.	1 pt. stock or water.
2 onions.	1 gill milk.
3 slices bacon.	2 tablesp. flour.
Seasoning.	

Wash and joint the rabbit.   Place it in a saucepan with the vegetables and water.   Stew gently for 1½ hours.   Mix the flour to a smooth cream with the milk, and add it, stirring, and boil for three or four minutes.   Season and serve.

*BROWNED BREADCRUMBS
(brace of pheasants)

¼ oz. clarified butter.   ¼ pt. fresh breadcrumbs.

Fry the crumbs in the butter over gentle heat until they are a golden brown in colour.   Drain well on paper and serve.

V. ENTRÉES

THESE may be described as 'dressed' or 'made dishes' and are complete in themselves, i.e. the sauce and vegetables are served in the same dish as the meat.

Entrées are served after the fish course and before the remove or joint.

They may be divided into 2 classes, Hot and Cold. In elaborate dinners where 2 entrées are served, the hot precedes the cold.

Each class of entrée has also 2 divisions, i.e. light (e.g. soufflé) and solid (e.g. cutlet). Should two of these be served, the lighter precedes the heavier.

Before commencing to dish an entrée, everything should be prepared and must be kept very hot. The saucepans containing the sauces, potato borders, etc., should be stood in a 'bain-marie', i.e. a deep tin containing boiling water. An ordinary deep meat roasting tin may be improvised for this purpose.

While dishing an entrée, the entrée-dish itself should be stood in boiling water. To help the housekeeper whose daily duty it is to choose, or possibly to cook or to help to cook dinners, the following classes of entrées have been collected, and in glancing down the headings it should be easy to choose and adapt a large variety of dishes made either from fresh or from cooked meat.

Any recipe may be varied, by the alteration of flavours or by the substitution of more expensive ingredients or vice versa.

HOT ENTRÉES

These may roughly be divided into the following classes:

1. **Beignets or Fritters.** E.g. Chicken Fritters. Slices of cooked chicken (or any well-flavoured meat) are dipped in coating batter (see page 230) and fried in deep fat.

2. **Bouchées,** i.e. tiny puff paste cases filled with any good mixture. E.g. Bouchées de Volaille. Chicken cut in dice and mixed with good béchamel sauce and placed in the cases. Serve hot.

3. **Petits Caisses.** Small round cases of paper, china or pastry filled with any good mixture of cut-up or minced chicken, game, etc., in a good sauce.

4. **Coquilles.** A mixture similar to the above but served in shells or china cases shaped like shells.

5. **Cannelons.** Small rolls of puff paste filled with savoury mince and shaped like sausage rolls.

6. **Creams.** These somewhat resemble quenelles and soufflés.

7. **Croquettes.** Savoury mince shaped into rounds, floured, dipped in egg and crumb, and fried. These are usually known as Rissoles.

8. **Croustades** or **Cassolettes.** Cases made of fried paste, fried bread, rice, potato, butter, or other crusts. Fill with well-flavoured 'ragout' or 'hash' (meat cut up into small dice) of chicken, fillets, mushrooms, truffles, ham, tongue, etc., and sauce suprême.

9. **Cutlets.** Meat, if specially required for cutlets, should be carefully chosen or ordered. For mutton cutlets the meat should come from small well-fed mutton which should be free from any 'interleaving' of fat with lean. The best end of the neck of mutton is the only part that is suitable for neck cutlets, and, before buying it, the butcher should be asked to remove the chine bone by sawing it off. This 'chine' bone is composed of the heads of the vertebrae, and, if sawn off, the cutlets can be cut apart neatly with a sharp knife. On no account should the vertebrae be chopped or the cutlets cannot be really well shaped. Having removed the chine bone cut carefully with a sharp knife; keep the cuts exactly parallel to each other. If the mutton is large, cut closely outside the bone and then at each side of each bone in turn. This gives one cutlet with bone and one without. The latter can be reserved for haricot of mutton, stews, etc., or for household cutlets, while the ones with bone are kept for the special dish of cutlets. If the mutton or lamb is small, cut through the meat half-way between each bone, so obtaining one cutlet of medium thickness. Trimming should be done after all the cutlets have been cut. Before trimming beat the cutlets with a cutlet bat (wetted) or a wet rolling pin. Then trim off all superfluous fat and cut the cutlets to the correct shape, scraping any skin from the inside of the bone, and also freeing the end from all meat and skin to a depth of $\frac{1}{2}$ inch to allow a frill to be put on after cooking.

Cutlets so prepared may be grilled, or fried, or egged and crumbed and fried.

Loin Cutlets. For these the best end of loin is required, which in mutton corresponds to the sirloin in beef. Loin cutlets should have the bone removed and then they can be trimmed and neatly rolled, allowing a small margin of fat to surround them. If skewered thus in shape, after cooking the skewer can be removed and the cutlet will retain its shape.

10. Darioles. Fluted shaped tins well greased, filled with a light mixture of minced meat, egg, etc., poached in the oven or steamed, turned out and served with a rich sauce.

Petits Pains. The same as darioles but made in plain instead of fluted tins.

11. Épigrammes. These may be made in two ways: (*a*) Breast of mutton or lamb boned, stuffed and rolled tightly. This is then braised or steamed, then pressed until cold, when it is cut into rounds about ½ to ¾ inch thick. These rounds are dipped into good sauce, then egged, crumbed and fried. (*b*) Small cutlets may be boned and the boned part rolled round the ' noisette ' or ' fillet ' (see below). This is then skewered, braised or steamed, and pressed till cold. It can then be dipped into good sauce, egged and crumbed, and fried.

12. Fillets. Strictly speaking, the fillet of mutton, veal or pork is the top part of the leg, whereas the fillet of beef is the undercut of the sirloin. But fillets of mutton, for the purposes of entrées, are often obtained from the loin or neck, only the round part of the cutlet being used. These are also called ' Noisettes '. Fillets of beef, if obtained from the undercut, must be cut into slices about ¾ inch thick. If they are cut from good steak they are trimmed into rounds about the size of a small teacup.

13. Kromeskies. Well-flavoured mince, mixed with a good sauce, shaped when cold into cork-shaped rolls, and wrapped in very thin slices of bacon, then in coating batter (see Batter, page 230), and fried.

14. Mousse. This is really a very light and rather more soft-textured soufflé. To obtain this, follow exactly the directions given for a Soufflé (see page 236), but add one extra egg, i.e. 4 yolks and 4 stiffly beaten whites instead of 3 yolks and 3 stiffly beaten whites. Add also a tablesp. of whipped cream, which must be added just before the whites are ' folded in '. Any solid added to mousses must be sieved or pulped as finely as possible. The cooking also requires additional care, as owing to the extra egg a mousse will only stand the most gentle steaming. A mousse should be turned out, and served with a thinnish sauce poured round.

If the mousse is steamed in small greased tins, these are called ' MOUSSELINES '.

15. Noisettes. The round part of the cutlet, with the bone part cut away, is known as the Noisette.

16. Omeletes. See page 234.

17. Patties. See page 173.

18. Pies. See page 170.

19. Quenelles. See page 103.

20. Rissoles. Savoury mince encased in thin pastry, egged, crumbed and fried. These are frequently called Croquettes.

21. Salmi. A rich hash made of game, duck, etc.

22. Soufflé. See page 236.

23. Timbales. The word means a cup or bowl, and the name is given to entrées cooked in a ' timbale ' and turned out. These moulds are usually well greased and lined with macaroni, potato or other purée, or just the top may be decorated.

24. Vol-au-Vent. The same as Patties (see page 173), but the paste is cut with one large round or oval cutter.

CHICKEN CREAM (I)
(4 or 5 people)

½ lb. raw sieved chicken.	¼ pt. cream. 2 eggs.
½ pt. good béchamel or veloutée sauce.	Seasoning (salt, pepper, and lemon).

Make the sauce of 2 oz. fat, 2 oz. flour and ½ pt. liquid. Measure exactly ½ pt. of it. Mix the raw sieved meat thoroughly with the raw eggs, add the sauce and seasoning, and lastly the semi-whipped cream. Pour into a greased mould, stand this on and cover it with greased paper and steam gently for about 45 minutes to 1 hour.

Turn out and pour a thin creamy sauce round. If wished, this recipe may be varied by adding ½ pt. cream and by reducing the amount of sauce to ¼ pt.

*CHICKEN CREAM (II)
(Plain and economical. 4 or 5 people)

½ lb. raw chicken, rabbit, veal, etc. (cooked meat can be used, but is not so good).

½ pt. good sauce (made with 2 oz. fat, 2 oz. flour, ½ pt. flavoured liquid). 1 or 2 eggs. Seasoning (salt, pepper, and lemon).

Mix the raw sieved meat well with the unbeaten eggs. Add the sauce. Mix well and cook as in the above recipe for 45 minutes to 1 hour or until firm.

ÉPIGRAMMES D'AGNEAU À LA DAUPHINE

Lamb épigrammes, lightly cooked, then dipped into a mixture of oiled butter and yolk of egg. Egg and crumb and fry. Serve these on a purée of green peas, and pour a good sauce round.

FILLETS OF BEEF À LA BÉARNAISE (4 or 5 people)

1½ lb. fillet of beef.	Clarified butter or dripping.
Sauce béarnaise.	½ pt. brown sauce.
	Potato border.

Cut the fillet into even-sized rounds. Beat and trim them. Fry in the butter or dripping. Glaze the fillets and arrange them in a circle on the potato border. Fill the centre with thick béarnaise sauce and pour the other brown sauce round. Garnish in any suitable way. The following make good garnishes:

Cooked and glazed chestnuts. Prettily fried potato chips. Banana quarters floured, egged, crumbed and fried. Tomatoes sliced and heated, etc.

FILLETS OF BEEF À LA MAÎTRE D'HÔTEL (4 or 5 people)

1½ lb. fillet of beef.	Tomatoes.
Juice of ½ a lemon.	Seasoning.
½ oz. butter.	Potato border.
½ teasp. chopped parsley.	Sauce demi-glace or espagnol.

Fry the trimmed fillets in the butter, browning them on both sides. Time, about 4 minutes. Cut the tomatoes into rounds and put them on a baking tin with a small piece of fat on each. Bake in a slow oven. Cream the butter, adding the parsley, lemon juice, and seasoning. Flatten this mixture and stand till cold and firm, then stamp into rounds with a small hot cutter. Glaze the fillets, the rounds of fat, and the tomatoes. Arrange them alternately on a bed of potato purée. Pour the sauce round and at the last moment put the rounds of cold butter mixture (known as maître d'hôtel butter) on each fillet. Serve quickly.

FILLETS OF VEAL À LA TALLEYRAND (5 or 6 people)

2 lb. fillet of veal.	Mashed potato for border.
1-2 oz. clarified butter.	½ pt. béchamel sauce.
6 mushrooms.	2 egg yolks.
1 chopped shallot.	1 tablesp. cream.
1 teasp. chopped parsley.	¼ a lemon. Seasoning.

Cook the prepared fillets in the butter with the shallot and mushrooms for about 15 minutes, turning frequently. Lift them into a casserole and keep them hot. Pour the sauce into the pan in which the fillets, etc., were fried, and stir quickly, then add the yolks and cream and cook carefully to avoid curdling. Lastly, season and add the lemon juice. Dish the fillets on a potato border, and pour the sauce over them.

N.B. The fillets can be re-heated in the sauce if more convenient.

*FILLETS À LA VIENNOISE (4 people)

½ lb. beefsteak.	Glaze.
1 teasp. chopped parsley.	1 egg.
½ teasp. chopped marjoram and thyme.	2 onions.
	Salt, pepper, and nutmeg.

To lighten the above mixture a small proportion of mashed potato may be mixed with the meat.

As an example of a made-up Fillet, made from raw meat.

Mince the meat finely (to sieve it also is an improvement) and mix it with the parsley, herbs, seasoning, potato (if used), and the yolk of the egg. Turn this on to a plate, and when firm form into rounds exactly the shape of a fillet. Flour these and fry them in clarified butter or fat. Cut the onions into rings. Flour these, then coat them with white of egg, and again flour them. Fry them. Glaze the fillets. Dish them on a purée of onion mixed with mashed potato, pour brown sauce round them, and garnish with the fried onion rings.

To make the onion purée: Chop the pieces of onion left from the rings. Fry these and cook them in enough brown sauce to cover them, adding a little mashed potato.

LAMB CUTLETS À LA PRINCESSE (5 or 6 people)

6 prepared lamb cutlets.	Green peas. 2 oz. butter.
½ lb. chicken or other good farce (see p. 389).	2 teasp. mushrooms (chopped). Dust nutmeg.
1 teasp. chopped parsley.	Sauce, suprême, veloutée or
1 teasp. lemon juice.	any other.

Fry the cutlets lightly. Press them between 2 dishes till cold. Mix the parsley, chopped mushrooms, lemon and nutmeg with the farce. Spread one side of the cutlets neatly with this. Egg and crumb them and fry in deep fat. Dish on a potato and green pea purée. Garnish with green peas. Pour the sauce round.

MUTTON CUTLETS À LA MILANAISE (5 or 6 people)

2 lb. best end neck of mutton.	2 oz. cooked spaghetti.
¼ pt. tomato sauce.	¼ pt. espagnol sauce.
1 oz. grated cheese.	Mashed potatoes.
	Seasoning.

Trim the cutlets. Egg and crumb them. Fry them in deep fat. Dish on a potato border in a circle. In the centre put the spaghetti mixed with the tomato sauce; sprinkle the cheese over this. Pour the brown sauce round the cutlets.

MUTTON CUTLETS À LA RÉFORME

Egg and crumb some trimmed cutlets. Fry them. Dish them on a potato or green pea border. Pour a Réforme Sauce (see page 118) round, and garnish with strips 1 inch long and barely ¼ inch wide of each of the following: Gherkin, hard-boiled white of egg, truffles, mushrooms, tongue and cooked carrot. Heat these in a little stock with a small piece of butter and put in centre of dish.

*MUTTON CUTLETS À LA SOUBISE

Egg and crumb some trimmed cutlets. Fry them. Dish them in a circle on a potato border. Fill the centre with thick Sauce Soubise (see page 119) and pour a good brown sauce round.

NOISETTES À LA JARDINIÈRE

Noisettes trimmed and fried, or egged and crumbed and fried. Dish on a purée of potato, green peas or carrot. Pour round any good brown sauce and garnish with prettily cut heaps of any vegetable in season.

Noisettes de Mouton à la Maintenon. Fried noisettes, dressed on croûtons of bread garnished with artichoke bottoms, filled with green peas; sauce demi-glacé poured round.

QUENELLES

(A typical recipe for 6 or 7 people)

1 lb. raw white meat (Veal, etc.).	2 eggs. Lemon juice. Seasoning.

2 oz. butter.	
2 oz. flour.	PANADA, or 2 tablesp. cream.
¼ pt. stock.	

Mince the meat finely. Make the panada. Pound the meat, panada or cream, eggs, seasoning, doing half at a time. Sieve the mixture. Form the mixture into egg-like shapes with the aid of two dessertspoons dipped in hot water. Place these in a buttered sauté-pan, pour in enough water to cover them. Poach for 10 minutes. Drain on a hair sieve. Dish prettily on a potato border. Coat with sauce and garnish to taste.

COLD ENTRÉES

Under this heading come:

1. Aspics.
2. Chaudfroids and Mayonnaise Chaudfroids.
3. Creams and Mousses.
4. Galantines, Cold Pies, etc.

COLD ENTRÉES—Class I

ASPICS

The actual recipe for aspic jelly comes under the heading of Jellies, and the detailed recipe will be found on page 244.

To set meat in aspic:

Melt the aspic and line the mould with the jelly. To do this rinse the mould out with cold water. Then put in a small amount of the liquid (but quite cool) jelly, and let this set. Decorate it, when firm, with parsley, hard-boiled egg, vegetables cut into shapes, etc., and on the decoration pour a few drops of jelly to keep it in place. Let this set. Then just cover the decoration with jelly and let this also get quite solid. Now fill up the moulds with whatever is to be used, i.e. lobster, prawns, chicken, game, etc. Pack them lightly and fill all interstices with the liquid jelly. Leave this to set, and to turn out the moulds prepare a bowl of hot water, hold the mould in the hand and dip it quickly right under the water, give a sharp sideways shake, and the jelly should come out of the mould quite easily.

If the water is too hot, the jelly will be melted.

Dish the jellies on salad, etc., and send to table prettily decorated.

CHARTREUSE OF PHEASANT (Chartreuse de Faisan)
(4 or 5 people)

½ cooked pheasant.	¾ pt. good brown
1 hard-boiled egg.	sauce.
4 truffles.	¼ oz. gelatine.
Aspic jelly.	6 mushrooms.
1 glass sherry.	1 teasp. glaze.

Line a plain mould with aspic. Decorate with the egg and truffle. Boil the sherry and sauce till reduced to ½ pt. Add ¼ pt. aspic. When cold mask the mould with this.

Fill it with the cut game, etc., dissolve the glaze in a little aspic, and strain to the remainder of the reduced sauce. Season well and fill up the mould with this. When quite cold, turn out on to a bed of salad, etc., and garnish with chopped aspic.

CUTLETS À LA RUSSE

Braised neck of mutton or lamb.	A mixture of cooked vegetables.
Chaudfroid sauce.	Tartare sauce.
Aspic jelly.	

Divide the meat into neat cutlets. Trim these and coat with chaudfroid sauce. If white, decorate with truffle, carrots, etc.; if brown, with white of egg. Set the decoration with aspic; then mask with aspic. Dish on a bed of tomato mixed with chopped aspic, and decorate with tartare sauce mixed with the vegetables.

PLOVERS' EGGS IN ASPIC

Boil the eggs for 8 minutes. Shell and place them in cold water. Line dariole moulds with aspic jelly and decorate prettily. Place an egg in each mould and fill up with aspic. When firm, turn out and serve with sliced cucumber and chopped aspic.

QUENELLES IN ASPIC

Coat some good cooked Quenelles (see page 103) with chaudfroid sauce.

Decorate prettily. Set the decoration with liquid aspic. Then coat with aspic to give a bright surface.

COLD ENTRÉES—Class II

CHAUDFROIDS

This name is given to any pieces of game, poultry, fish, etc., coated with chaudfroid sauce.

Chaudfroid Sauce is really a sauce made of equal quantities of any good sauce and STRONG aspic jelly (2 oz. gelatine should be allowed to each qt. of stock).

For white meat or fish, a white chaudfroid is needed; the sauce used should be béchamel or veloutée.

For game a brown chaudfroid should be used; the sauce, therefore, should be espagnole, or any other sauce made from a brown roux.

A red chaudfroid requires tomato sauce, or a mixture of tomato and brown sauce.

A salmon pink one (for salmon) can be obtained by frying the roux for a béchamel to a straw colour, and tingeing the sauce when made with carmine.

For each of these the foundation sauce should be made with $2\frac{1}{2}$ oz. fat and $2\frac{1}{2}$ oz. flour to the pt. of liquid. When the sauce is made it must be carefully measured and an equal quantity of COOL aspic jelly added.

The sauce must then be put through a tammy cloth, and then add 1 tablesp. of cream to each pt. of the sauce. All chaudfroid sauces should be tammied before use.

If a larger proportion of aspic is used, the sauce will be more shiny but more difficult to manipulate.

To mask meat, etc., with chaudfroid, the right temperature must be ascertained, the sauce must flow sufficiently freely, but it must not be too thin or it will not coat sufficiently. Two coatings are usually given and the whole can then be covered with liquid aspic, quite cool but just not set. One layer of sauce must be quite set before the next is applied.

CHAUDFROID OF CHICKEN (I)
(Chaudfroid de Volaille. 6 people)

1 cooked chicken.	Aspic jelly.
Chaudfroid sauce	Chicken or ham.
(white).	Truffle.

Salad and dressing.

Divide the chicken into neat joints. Skin these, and coat each piece with chaudfroid sauce. Decorate with stars of ham or truffle. When quite set, mask with liquid aspic.

Cut up the rest of the chicken, and mix it with the salad and dressing. Place this on a large entrée dish, and arrange the coated chicken joints on it, and decorate with chopped aspic.

CHAUDFROID OF CHICKEN (II)
(8 or 9 people)

Coat a whole boned and stuffed cooked chicken with white chaudfroid sauce. Decorate it, and pour a little liquid aspic first to set the decoration and then to mask the whole. Dish on a bed of salad and garnish with tomato, etc.

MAYONNAISE CHAUDFROID OF CHICKEN

Exactly follow the first of the above recipes, using a stiff mayonnaise sauce instead of the chaudfroid.

COLD ENTRÉES—Class III

CREAMS

To each ½ lb. of meat purée (sieved, cooked and minced chicken, etc.) allow ¼ pt. aspic jelly (strong aspic made with 2 oz. gelatine to 1 qt. stock) and ¼ pt. half-whipped cream.

Mix the meat with the liquid but cool aspic, and just before this sets pour into the cream.

Plainer Creams may be made by the substitution of some thick sauce for a part of the cream.

CHICKEN CREAMS (4 or 5 people)

½ lb. cooked chicken.	½ gill béchamel sauce.
¼ lb. cooked ham or tongue (or a mixture of both).	1 gill semi-whipped cream. Seasoning.
1½ gills aspic jelly.	Salad.

Line some small moulds with liquid aspic. When set, decorate these and set the decoration.

Mince the chicken and ham and pound it with the sauce. Sieve this. Add it to the liquid aspic. Before setting fold the whipped cream in and fill the moulds.

When set, unmould them on to a bed of salad.

MOUSSES

These, with Cold Soufflés, should be spongy and very light. To obtain this, the cream must be whisked till points of it stand alone; and, also, the aspic jelly should be whisked till light and frothy.

MOUSSE DE JAMBON (Ham Mousse)
(5 or 6 people)

½ lb. lean cooked ham.	1½ gills cream.
½ pt. espagnole sauce, *or* tomato sauce.	½ oz. gelatine. 2 stiffly-beaten whites of
1 gill aspic jelly.	egg.

Seasoning.

Pound minced ham with the sauce, and sieve it. Whisk aspic till frothy and beat the white of egg stiffly. Half whip the cream and dissolve the gelatine in a little stock. Add ham purée, aspic, and gelatine and cream. Fold in white of egg. Colour slightly and pour into prepared soufflé case. When set remove paper band, decorate and serve.

MOUSSELINES DE CANARDS (Duck Mousselines)

(5 or 6 people)

1 small duckling.	2–3 tablesp. cream.
1 pt. cooked green peas.	½ gill béchamel sauce.
2 hard-boiled egg yolks.	2 oz. cooked ham.
1½ gills aspic.	Seasoning.

(Mousselines are small Mousses.)

Braise the duckling, and before it is cold, skin it and pound the best pieces with the ham. Add the yolks, cream and peas. Sieve these, then add the sauce and ½ gill of melted aspic.

Line 12 pea-pod moulds with aspic and decorate them with whole peas. Fill up with the mixture. Make a flat cornflour or semolina shape. Let it set, and turn it on to a dish. Turn out the little pea-pod moulds on to this, and serve with a good cold sauce. Decorate with parsley and cucumber.

For Mousses (Sweet) see page 238.

COLD ENTRÉES—Class IV

GALANTINES

For Galantines, Cold Pies, etc., see pages 69 and 70, also 172–175.

VI. SAUCES

THESE may be classified as follows:

1. **Plain White or Brown Sauces (with Roux)** made of fat, flour and liquid—the cooked flour being the thickening. These may be varied by the addition of flavourings, such as onion, capers, etc., but in each case the sauce itself is made as follows: The quantities of fat and flour should be equal, but they vary in proportion to the liquid, according to whether the sauce is needed as a coating sauce (e.g. the sauce needed to coat a chicken), or whether it is to be served as a GLAZE or GRAVY, when it will be considerably thinner. A coating sauce will need 1 oz. fat and 1 oz. flour to about $\frac{1}{2}$ pt. liquid. A glazing sauce will need $\frac{1}{2}$ oz. fat and $\frac{1}{2}$ oz. flour to the $\frac{1}{2}$ pt. liquid. Whereas a thick sauce, properly known as PANADA (used as a foundation for soufflés, etc.), will need 2 oz. fat and 2 oz. flour to the $\frac{1}{2}$ pt. The following recipe is for a good coating sauce.

Coating Sauce. 1 oz. fat. (Butter is the best fat, or margarine may be used, and for brown sauces, dripping.)

1 oz. flour.

$\frac{1}{2}$ pt. liquid. (The liquid for plain sauces should usually be $\frac{1}{2}$ milk and $\frac{1}{2}$ stock, flavoured with whatever the sauce is to be served with. The amount of liquid cannot be stated accurately, as flour varies so in quality, and good flour absorbs more liquid than bad flour; e.g. (i) fish sauce—liquid $\frac{1}{2}$ milk, $\frac{1}{2}$ fish stock, made from skins, heads, etc., boiled in water; (ii) cauliflower sauce —liquid $\frac{1}{2}$ milk, $\frac{1}{2}$ water in which cauliflower has been boiled.)

Seasoning, salt, pepper, etc.

METHOD:

(1) Melt the fat.

(2) Add the sifted flour, all at once. Stir briskly for a few minutes, when it will be seen that the mixture, from being solid, becomes more liquid, and looks honeycombed. This mixture is called a ' roux ' (a white roux).

N.B. Up to this point both brown and white sauces are made in the same way, but for brown sauces continue stirring, cooking the roux until the flour browns in the fat and the mixture becomes of a rich chestnut colour. Stirring must be constant during this process, and a metal (aluminium, etc.) pan should be used, as in this frying process great heat is needed and an enamel pan may crack. This browning of a roux takes a considerable time, and it will be found advisable periodically to take 1 lb. fat (dripping is admirable) and 1 lb. flour and brown these, cooling the mixture and storing it in a jar. When a brown sauce is needed, a spoonful of this brown roux may be taken, melted, and thinned down with stock, so saving much labour and time. This roux having been heated to a very high temperature will keep for a long time.

(3) If a white sauce is needed, as soon as the roux honeycombs add the liquid. As hot liquid mixes more quickly and with less stirring, add hot stock (cauliflower water, etc.) before adding the milk (where possible *heat* the milk for reason given above), and let the sauce be beaten and well stirred as the liquid is added. It must be allowed to boil up between the additions of liquid. When about half the liquid is added the 'Panada' stage is reached; and when the panada is thinned down the sauce is obtained. The difference between a high-class and a plain sauce is that the milk or stock for a high-class sauce is specially prepared as follows: Place it in a pan with the desired special flavourings. These are left to INFUSE, i.e. to flavour the milk. The pan must be covered and placed over gentle heat for 20 minutes, when the liquid is strained, and the milk or stock so flavoured is then added to the roux instead of in its plain form.

(For dish for 4 people)

Plain Sauce (for fish)	Béchamel Sauce (high-class)
About ½ pt. liquid. { 1 oz. fat. 1 oz. flour. ½ milk. ½ fish stock. Seasoning.	1 oz. fat. 1 oz. flour. ½ pt. milk flavoured with 1 sprig parsley, 1 sprig thyme, 1 bay leaf, 1 slice onion, 1 slice turnip, 1 slice celery. Seasoning.

Béchamel is one of the standard high-class sauces.

Veloutée is another, and is made with white stock (veal or chicken stock), infused as above instead of milk infused.

Melted Butter Sauce differs from both, as the proportion is 1 oz. flour to 2 oz. butter, water instead of milk or stock, and a few drops of lemon juice. If sauces are re-boiled they must always be skimmed, as long cooking makes the flour 'throw up' (as it is called) a portion of the fat that it has previously absorbed, and if this is left the sauce will be greasy.

To high-class brown sauces glaze is often added, but this must be done with great care, and the addition of Bovril is preferable. Many sauces require to be wrung through a tammy cloth or rubbed through a hair sieve. Some sauces need to be 'reduced,' i.e. to let a portion of the liquid evaporate by rapid boiling, and so concentrate the flavour.

II. **Sauces Thickened by the Addition of Egg.**

It is important only to cook the sauce enough to thicken the egg, but not to curdle it. The most usual sauce of this kind is Hollandaise (see recipe).

Plain Custard Sauces are a variation of the above. These are made by pouring milk, warmed to rather above blood heat, on to beaten eggs (2 eggs to 1 pt. milk). Re-heat carefully in a double pan till the mixture begins to thicken. Add flavouring (sugar, vanilla, etc.) to taste, and serve at once.

A simple method (but inferior) is to make a thin cornflour sauce. Cool this. Pour it on to 1 or 2 beaten eggs. Flavour, re-heat and serve. This will not curdle so easily. The variety of plain custards solely consists in the addition of different flavourings.

III. **Whipped Custard,** or 'Mousseline', **Sauces** are of the same class, but the egg and liquid are whipped over boiling water.

IV. **Cold Sauces.** Under this head comes 'Mayonnaise', composed chiefly of raw egg and oil. Salad dressings also come under this head. See recipes. The **Chaudfroid** sauce, made of cooked sauce (e.g. béchamel) and aspic jelly, is typical of the other class of cold sauces. The best chaudfroid sauces are made by mixing equal quantities of any good sauce and aspic jelly. This is then allowed to cool and used just before the sauce sets.

V. **Plain Sauces (without Roux)** can be made of starchy material (flour, cornflour, etc.) and liquid only, without any addition of fat. The proportions in this case must not exceed $\frac{1}{2}$ oz. starchy material to $\frac{1}{2}$ pt. liquid.

Mix the flour, etc., to a smooth cream, quite free from lumps, with a little cold liquid. Boil the remainder of the liquid and add it to the cold mixture. Return to the pan and boil, thoroughly stirring all the time. Season and serve. This will do admirably to serve with marrow, cauliflower, etc. In this case, mix the flour with $\frac{1}{4}$ pt. cold milk, and to this add $\frac{1}{4}$ pt. of the water in which the marrow is boiling. Pour into a small saucepan. Boil up well, stirring, and serve. The sole variety in these, as in custards, consists in adding different flavourings.

VI. **Jam Sauces.** See recipes.

VII. **Syrup Sauces.** (Fruit.) Add $\frac{1}{4}$ to $\frac{1}{2}$ pt. water to each lb. of fruit, cover closely and put in a double pan or in a casserole in the oven. When the juice runs freely, strain it. Add an equal amount of sugar ($\frac{1}{2}$ lb. to $\frac{1}{2}$ pt.). Boil and skim. The longer the mixture boils the thicker the syrup. From 5 to 7 minutes is usually enough.

VIII. **Miscellaneous Sauces.**

SAUCES—Class I

(Plain White or Brown Sauces made with Roux)

*ANCHOVY SAUCE (Sauce Anchois)
(4 to 6 people)

1 oz. fat.	$\frac{1}{4}$ pt. fish stock.
1 oz. flour.	1 dessertsp. anchovy
$\frac{1}{2}$ pt. milk.	essence.

Make a roux of the fat and flour, add the liquids by degrees. Stir and boil for ten minutes. Add the anchovy, re-boil and serve.

BÉCHAMEL SAUCE

See full directions on page 110.

BORDEAUX SAUCE (4 people)

2 shallots or 1 onion.	1 gill claret.
$\frac{1}{2}$ teasp. crushed pepper-corns.	Sprig of thyme. Parsley and marjoram.
1 gill brown or espagnole sauce.	1 teasp. anchovy essence.

Chop 2 shallots or 1 onion, and cook this with 1 gill claret, and $\frac{1}{2}$ teasp. crushed peppercorns, a sprig of thyme, parsley and marjoram. Reduce to half. Then add 1 gill espagnole sauce. Boil for 10 minutes. Add 1 teasp. anchovy essence, season and serve.

BRANDY SAUCE (4 people)

$\frac{1}{2}$ pt. sweet sauce. (See recipe.)	1 glass brandy. Mix and serve.

*BROWN SAUCE, PLAIN (about 6 people)

1 pt. stock.	1 small onion.
2 oz. dripping.	Piece of carrot, turnip
2 oz. flour.	or celery.
Bunch of herbs.	2 cloves.
6 peppercorns.	Blade of mace.

Seasoning.

Fry the vegetables, cut up, lightly in the fat. Add the flour and fry to a nut-brown colour. Add the herbs, spices, and stock by degrees. Simmer for 1 hour; skim; season and strain.

*CAPER SAUCE (7 or 8 people)

1 pt. white sauce and 2 tablesp. capers.

Add the capers to the sauce just before serving. They may be chopped if desired.

CARDINAL SAUCE (4 people)

½ pt. béchamel or velouté sauce. (See page 120.)	½ gill mushroom liquor.
½ oz. lobster coral.	Juice of ½ lemon.
1 oz. butter.	½ gill cream.
	Seasoning, nutmeg.

Reduce the sauce with the mushroom liquor, season, and add some grated nutmeg. Add the lemon juice and whisk in the butter and lobster coral. Tammy. Re-heat (do not re-boil) and serve.

*CELERY SAUCE (5 or 6 people)

3 heads of celery (white part only).	½ pt. water.
1 oz. butter.	¾ pt. velouté or white sauce.

2 tablesp. cream.

Cream may always be omitted if it is not procurable. Wash and cut the celery. Cook it with the butter and water for 30 minutes. Add the sauce, cook again for 15 minutes. Skim. Add the cream. Tammy and re-heat (not boil).

CHAMPAGNE SAUCE (4 or 5 people)

¼ pt. espagnole sauce.	1 glass champagne.
6 peppercorns.	1 bay leaf. 2 cloves.

Put the sauce, bay leaf, cloves and peppercorns in a pan. Slightly reduce them. Add the champagne and a little essence remaining from braised ham. Reduce for about 10 minutes, or longer if still too thin. Strain and serve with braised ham.

CHOCOLATE SAUCE (4 or 5 people)

½ oz. flour.	½ pt. milk.
½ oz. butter.	½ teasp. vanilla essence.

½ oz. grated chocolate (or more).

Dissolve the grated chocolate in the milk, add the vanilla essence and follow directions for Coffee Sauce.

COFFEE SAUCE (4 or 5 people)

½ oz. butter.   ½ oz. flour.   A few drops of vanilla.

1 gill milk.
1 gill good coffee. } OR { ½ pt. milk and 1 tablesp. of good coffee essence.

Melt the butter, add the flour and stir together. Add the milk and coffee and boil up, stirring well. Add the vanilla and serve.

*CURRY SAUCE (4 or 5 people)

½ pt. stock.	1 oz. fat.
1 onion.	½ oz. flour.
½ sour apple.	1 teasp. (more if wished) curry paste.
Lemon juice (a squeeze).	
1 teasp. (or more to taste) curry powder.	½ teasp. chutney.
	½ teasp. sugar.

Fry the onion. Add the curry powder and paste. Fry lightly. Add the flour. Fry that. Add the apple and fry. Add the stock (or water) and chutney. Simmer for an hour. Season and add the lemon juice, skimming as the fat rises. If served separately, strain.

The sauce is improved by the addition of many vegetables, tomato, carrot, celery, etc. Also a few raisins and sultanas can be added, and an infusion of coconut. (See Curry, p. 68).

DEMI-GLACÉ SAUCE (Half-Glaze Sauce)
(4 people)

¾ pt. espagnole sauce.   1½ gills good gravy.
Seasoning.

Reduce espagnole sauce by boiling it nearly to half the original amount (half-glaze). Add the gravy, strained and freed from fat; simmer 15 minutes; season and serve.

DEVILLED SAUCE (Sauce Diable)
(4 people)

½ pt. demi-glacé sauce.	1 tablesp. mixed mustard.
1 dessertsp. Worcester sauce.	½ oz. butter.
2 finely chopped onions or shallots.	Salt, cayenne, and finely chopped parsley.

Fry the onion till golden. Add all the ingredients, except the parsley. Boil, skim and strain. Add a teasp. chopped parsley and serve.

*EGG SAUCE (4 people)

1 hard-boiled egg. (Boil for 10 minutes, then place in cold water, and remove shell.)
½ pt. white sauce. Seasoning.

Chop the egg, add it to the boiling sauce. Season and serve.

ESPAGNOLE SAUCE (8 to 10 people). *See also* Appendix, p. 414

This is the chief standard Brown Sauce, and it is the foundation for most other high-class brown sauces.

2 oz. lean ham or bacon.	2 oz. fat. } Roux.
1 oz. fat.	2 oz. flour.
1 qt. stock.	6 peppercorns.
Bouquet garni.	½ glass sherry.
1 small onion.	½ carrot.
Stick celery.	6 mushrooms.
2 tomatoes.	2 cloves.
	1 teasp. lemon juice.

Fry the vegetables and ham (cut up) in 1 oz. fat. Add the herbs, spices, stock and wine. Cook gently for 1 hour in a covered pan.

Make a brown roux with 2 oz. fat and 2 oz. flour. Add the strained prepared stock. Stir till this boils. Cook gently for at least half an hour, skimming off any fat that rises. Add the lemon juice and strain through a tammy cloth.

*HORSERADISH SAUCE (I), Plain

Half pt. good white sauce, or béchamel sauce. Heat this. Grate 2 tablesp. horseradish, barely cover this with vinegar, and just before serving add this, with ½ teasp. castor sugar and a pinch of cayenne, to the sauce. Serve at once with roast beef.

HORSERADISH SAUCE (II), Rich
(4 people)

2 tablesp. grated horseradish soaked for 15 min. in 1 tablesp. white vinegar.
1 gill cream.   Seasoning.   1 teasp. sugar.

Stir horseradish into cream just before serving.
N.B. If cream is very thin it can be slightly whisked.

ITALIAN SAUCE (Sauce Italienne)
(4 people)

¼ pt. espagnole or brown sauce.	2 chopped onions or shallots.
1 oz. butter or salad oil.	6 chopped button mushrooms.
1 glass white wine.	2 tablesp. of stock.
1 bay leaf.	

Sauté the mushrooms, shallots and bay leaf in the fat.   Add the stock and wine.   Reduce to ⅓ by boiling.   Add the sauce. Boil, and skim all fat as it rises.   Remove the bay leaf and serve.

*LEMON SAUCE (Plain)
(4 or 5 people)

Infuse the thinly cut rind of a lemon in milk.   Do not boil. Make ½ pt. sweet sauce with this.   Boil the sauce.   Add the juice of half a lemon at once before serving.   Do this carefully, without re-heating, or the sauce will curdle.   A safer way is to make the sweet sauce with water and cornflour, instead of flour and milk.   In this case more lemon juice can be added as no curdling need be feared.

Serve with plain puddings, lemon puddings, etc.

LOBSTER SAUCE (6 or 7 people)

1 pt. white sauce made with fish stock and milk.	1 oz. lobster butter (see recipe).
1 small lobster.	Cayenne and lemon juice.

Cut the meat from the lobster into small pieces.   Add this to the sauce.   Colour with the butter.   Season and serve.

MADEIRA SAUCE (Sauce Madère)

Follow the recipe of Demi-glacé Sauce.   Add 1 glass of sherry or Marsala.   Reduce a little, add a small amount of meat glaze and use.

MAÎTRE D'HÔTEL SAUCE (Parsley and Lemon Sauce)
(4 people)

½ pt. béchamel or veloutée sauce.	1 teasp. chopped parsley.
1½ to 3 oz. butter.	½ lemon.
Seasoning.	

Put the sauce into a pan with a little water. Stir till boiling and reduce well. Whisk in the butter by degrees and tammy.

Re-heat (not boil), adding the parsley, lemon juice and seasoning.

*MELTED BUTTER (4 people)

2 oz. butter.	1 oz. flour.
½ pt. water.	Seasoning.

Make a white roux of 1 oz. of the fat and the flour. Add the water by degrees. Stir and boil well. Remove from the fire and add the seasoning and the rest of the butter and a squeeze of lemon. The sauce should be of the consistency of good cream, and if household flour is used, nearly double the amount of liquid given may have to be used.

*MUSTARD SAUCE (4 people)
(Served with Broiled Herrings and Mackerel)

½ oz. fat.	½ oz. flour.
¼ pt. fish stock or milk.	1 or 2 tablesp. vinegar.
1 teasp. mustard.	Seasoning.

Make a sauce of the fat, flour and stock. Boil well. Mix the mustard smoothly with the vinegar. Add the sauce and boil. Season. If possible, a little cream added is a great improvement.

*ONION SAUCE (5 or 6 people)

½ lb. onions. 1 pt. white sauce.

Blanch the onions, and put them with a little salt in cold water and cook till tender, about 1 hour. Chop them finely, and add to the white sauce. Season and serve.

OYSTER SAUCE (5 or 6 people)

1 doz. oysters.	Juice of ½ lemon.
1 pt. white sauce.	Salt and cayenne.

Blanch the oysters, using their own liquor for the purpose. Remove the beards. Cut them in halves. Reduce the oyster liquor. Strain it and add to the white sauce. Add the oysters and lemon juice. Season and serve.

*PARSLEY SAUCE (5 or 6 people)
(SERVED WITH BOILED FISH, POULTRY OR MEAT)

1 tablesp. finely-chopped parsley.
1 pt. white sauce.

Add the parsley to the hot sauce and serve.

POIVRADE SAUCE (5 or 6 people)

1 pt. espagnole sauce.	1 oz. raw ham.
1 oz. butter.	A slice of carrot, turnip, celery, onion.
1 bay leaf.	
Sprig of thyme and parsley.	1 blade mace.
20 crushed peppercorns.	1 glass sherry (if wished).

Cut the vegetables and ham into dice. Fry them in the butter 3 minutes. Add the herbs and spices. Pour in the sauce. Skim. Add salt and pepper, and tammy. If wine is used, reduce the sauce to one-half before using.

RÉFORME SAUCE (4 or 5 people)

½ pt. poivrade sauce.   1 glass port wine.
1 teasp. red currant jelly.

Boil for 10 minutes and strain.

ROBERT SAUCE (4 or 5 people)

½ pt. brown sauce.	1 small onion.
1 teasp. mustard.	½ glass white wine.
1 teasp. glaze.	

Fry the onion in butter. Add the wine and reduce a little. Stir in the mustard, glaze and sauce, and cook 10 minutes. Skim, strain, and serve.

SALMI SAUCE (4 or 5 people)

½ pt. brown sauce, made from game stock.	2 shallots (chopped).
Parsley and thyme.	1 bay leaf.
1 glass port wine.	1 oz. butter.
Trimmings of game.	1 dessertsp. red currant jelly.

Fry the shallots, herbs, and game in the butter. Add the wine and cook in a covered pan 10 minutes. Pour in the sauce, stir, and simmer 15 minutes. Skim and tammy. Re-heat with seasoning and red currant jelly.

*SHRIMP SAUCE (4 people)

¼ pt. shrimps (shelled).	1 teasp. anchovy sauce.
Lemon juice.	½ pt. white sauce.

Salt and pepper.

Use the shells by cooking them in milk with a bay leaf and a blade of mace and straining to make fish stock for the white sauce. To this add the shrimps; boil a few minutes, and season with the lemon juice and anchovy sauce.

*SOUBISE SAUCE (4 people)

½ pt. béchamel sauce. 3 onions, blanched.

Cook onions, sieve and add to sauce; reduce if necessary.
N.B. Onions may be finely chopped if liked.

*SUPRÊME SAUCE (5 or 6 people)

2 oz. fat.	2 oz. flour.
¾ pt. chicken stock.	¼ pt. cream.
1 shallot.	1 small bay leaf.
1 teasp. lemon juice.	Salt and pepper.

Make a roux of the fat and flour. Add the stock, whisk till it boils. Add the bay leaf and shallot. Simmer for 20 minutes. Skim, and add the lemon juice and cream, and the yolk of 1 egg if required. Tammy and serve. (The cream may be omitted.)

*SWEET SAUCE (4 people)

2 oz. butter.	1–2 oz. sugar.
½ oz. flour.	½ pt. milk.

Flavouring (½ teasp. vanilla to each ½ pt. of sauce).

Make a sauce of 1 oz. butter, the flour and milk. Add the rest of the butter and sweeten to taste.

TOMATO SAUCE (4 or 5 people)

½ lb. fresh tomatoes, or ¼ lb. tinned.	1 piece of carrot. A small piece of bacon.
1 small onion.	1 oz. butter.
1 bay leaf (small).	½ oz. flour.
1½ gills stock.	A pinch of castor sugar.

Salt and pepper.

Cut up the vegetables and sauté them in the butter. Add the tomatoes. Add the stock and simmer until tender. Strain carefully, or if a slight roughness is not objected to, the whole may be passed through a hair sieve. Season. Cream the flour with 1 tablesp. of milk or cream, add this to the liquor, boil up well and serve. If a thicker or thinner sauce is required, add more or less flour.

VELOUTÉE SAUCE (4 or 5 people)

2 oz. butter.	2 oz. flour.
1 pt. veal or chicken stock.	6 button mushrooms.
	Bouquet garni.
Juice of ½ lemon.	6 peppercorns.
¼ pt. cream.	Salt, a dust of nutmeg.

Make a white sauce of the flour, butter and stock. Add the mushrooms, herbs and peppercorns. Simmer ½ hour, skimming and stirring frequently. Tammy, and add the cream and lemon juice. Season with salt and nutmeg. Re-heat without boiling.

SAUCES—Class II

(Those Thickened with Egg)

BÉARNAISE SAUCE (4 or 5 people)

½ gill vinegar.	3 finely-chopped onions.
About 6 crushed peppercorns.	3 or 4 yolks of eggs.
	1 tablesp. white sauce.
1 or 2 oz. butter.	Meat glaze.
Squeeze of lemon.	Sprig of thyme.

Cover the onions, peppercorns and thyme with the vinegar. Boil and reduce well; remove the thyme and add a little meat glaze. Cool slightly, add the yolks, and work in the butter in small pieces. Heat carefully, stirring well. Strain, add a little chopped fresh tarragon and chervil, a squeeze of lemon, and serve.

HOLLANDAISE SAUCE

4 tablesp. vinegar.   4–6 peppercorns.   1 bay leaf.

Boil these till reduced to half. Strain this into a double saucepan and when about blood heat add 3 raw yolks of eggs and stir continually till the mixture begins to thicken. Then add, little by little, 1 to 2 oz. of butter, season, and serve at once. Great care must be taken not to over-heat the sauce, and only to add the butter by degrees, or the sauce will curdle. If preferred, omit some vinegar, replacing it with white stock.

A ' safe ' hollandaise sauce, but inferior to the real one, may be made as follows: Take ½ pt. béchamel sauce. Cool this,

SWEET CHAUDFROID SAUCE (4 or 5 people)

1 gill stiff sweet jelly. 1 gill half-whipped cream.
Flavouring and colouring.

Make as for preceding recipe.

CUMBERLAND SAUCE (A Cold Game Sauce)
(4 or 5 people)

2 chopped onions or shallot.	1 orange, 1 lemon.
½ glass port wine.	1 dessertsp. mustard.
2 tablesp. vinegar.	2 tablesp. red currant jelly.
Pinch of ground ginger.	Seasoning and cayenne.

Put the chopped onions with the orange and lemon rind (cut into very fine julienne strips) in ½ gill water and cook for 10 minutes. Strain and return to the pan with the wine, ginger, jelly, orange and lemon juice, vinegar and the mixed mustard. Season, boil, strain, and serve cold. A gill of sauce espagnole added improves the sauce.

KING OF OUDE'S SAUCE (7 or 8 people)

½ pt. red currant jelly. ¼ pt. white vinegar.
2 tablesp. each of Harvey sauce and port wine.

Melt the jelly and shake all the ingredients well together in a corked bottle. Serve as a relish with cold meat.

MAYONNAISE ASPIC

Mayonnaise sauce may be mixed into an equal part of liquid aspic and used instead of chaudfroid.

MAYONNAISE SAUCE (4 people)

This sauce is the foundation for the most high-class salad dressing. It requires careful making. The ingredients are as follows:

1 yolk of egg.	1 teasp. malt or white vinegar.
1 gill olive oil (or more).	
½ teasp. made mustard.	1 teasp. tarragon vinegar.
Salt, pepper, and sugar to taste.	

Put the raw egg in a soup plate, add the seasonings, then the oil drop by drop, stirring all the time quickly and evenly with a silver fork or wooden spoon. 1 egg yolk can incorporate as much as 1 pt. oil, but ½ pt., or much less, is usually sufficient. When all the required oil is added, add the vinegar by degrees, stirring well. If the sauce is too thick, add just a little cream, or cold water. The secret of success lies in adding the oil slowly, and stirring quickly, otherwise the oil and egg separate.

ORANGE SAUCE (4 or 5 people)
(To Serve with Duck, Game, etc.)

2 onions.	A little gravy.
Squeeze of lemon juice.	1 orange.
	Raw ham.
Cayenne.	1 glass port wine.

Chop the onions and ham, and mix these with the finely grated orange rind (no pith must be grated) and the pepper. Just cover these with the gravy, add the port wine, and simmer for 5 minutes. Then add the orange and lemon juice; sieve through a silk or very fine hair sieve and use.

PIQUANTE SAUCE (Sharp Sauce)
(4 or 5 people)

½ onion.	2 or 3 chopped gherkins.
1 tablesp. chopped capers.	1 bay leaf.
½ pt. sauce espagnole.	½ gill vinegar.
½ teasp. anchovy sauce.	Sprig of thyme.

Chop the onion, cover it with the vinegar, add the bay leaf and thyme. Put a lid on the pan, and simmer gently for ten minutes. Strain, and add the chopped gherkins, the sauce and anchovy. Boil and serve.

TARTARE SAUCE (7 or 8 people)

To every ½ pt. mayonnaise allow 2 teasp. chopped parsley, 1 tablesp. chopped capers, 1 tablesp. chopped gherkins, ½ tablesp. chopped chervil and tarragon, green colouring. Mix well and serve.

SAUCES—Class V
(Plain Sauces without Roux)

* SWEET SAUCE (Arrowroot)
(4 people)

¼ pt. milk.	1 oz. sugar.
½ oz. butter.	Flavouring.
1 teasp. arrowroot or cornflour.	

Mix the arrowroot to a smooth cream with water. Stir it into the boiling milk. Cook for 5 minutes. Add the sugar, flavouring and butter.

SAUCES—CLASS VI

(Jam Sauces)

*APRICOT SAUCE (4 or 5 people)

3 tablesp. apricot jam.	Sugar to taste (this can be
1 gill sherry or apricot juice.	omitted).
1 gill water.	1 teasp. cornflour, mixed to a
½ oz. butter.	smooth cream with water.

Boil the jam with the water and butter. Remove from the fire, add the cornflour liaison and re-boil. Add sugar, if necessary, and just before serving add the wine. (If juice replaces wine it can be added previously and can be boiled.)

*JAM SAUCE (I)

(4 or 5 people)

1 tablesp. jam.	1 heaped teasp. arrow-
A little lemon juice.	root blended with
1 gill water.	a little water.

Boil the first 3 ingredients, strain these and add the blended arrowroot. Re-boil, stirring, and serve.

JAM SAUCE (II)

(4 or 5 people)

½ gill jam.	Juice of ½ lemon.
½ gill sugar.	½ gill water.

Boil these together for a few minutes. Strain and serve.

*MARMALADE SAUCE (4 people)

1 tablesp. marmalade.	¼ pt. water.
½ oz. sugar.	Rind and juice of ½
½ teasp. cornflour.	lemon (optional).

Cut the rind of lemon thinly, and boil it with the water and marmalade. Mix the cornflour to a smooth cream with a little cold water. Add this, stirring, also the sugar and lemon juice. Boil 3 minutes. Strain, if wished, and serve. Wine or liqueur may be added, if wished.

*TREACLE SAUCE (5 or 6 people)

1 gill golden syrup.	Juice of ½ lemon.
½ gill of water.	½ teasp. cornflour.

Boil these and serve at once.

*A more economical way. Omit the lemon, take equal quantities syrup and water. Boil and serve.

SAUCES—CLASS VII

(Syrup Sauces)

BRANDY SAUCE (4 or 5 people)

¼ lb. loaf sugar.	½ pt. water.
¼ oz. cornflour.	Glass of brandy.

Boil the sugar and 1½ gills water for about 10 minutes, skimming. Mix the cornflour with the rest of the water. Add it, and stir and boil for a few minutes. Add the brandy and serve hot with Christmas pudding.

OR, omit cornflour. (See Rum Sauce (II).)

CARAMEL SAUCE (4 or 5 people)

1 oz. loaf sugar. Juice of ½ lemon.

Boil these till quite a light golden colour. Add ½ pt. sugar syrup (¼ pt. sugar boiled in ½ pt. water, and reduced to ½ pt.). Boil till smooth, add a dessertsp. cornflour mixed to a smooth cream with a little water. Add vanilla to taste, strain and serve.

RUM SAUCE (4 or 5 people)

(SERVE WITH BABA)

(I)

Make as for Brandy Sauce, but add rum instead of brandy.

(II)

The cornflour can be omitted and the syrup thickened by reducing a little, i.e. by boiling it until some of the water has evaporated. This method is the nicer.

SAUCES—CLASS VIII

(Miscellaneous Sauces)

*APPLE SAUCE

(TO SERVE WITH ONE DUCK)

1 lb. apples, peeled and cored and sliced.	Grated rind of ½ lemon.
½ oz. butter.	¼ gill water.
	1 clove or nutmeg.

Sugar to taste.

Put all the ingredients in a covered pan. Stew gently till tender. Cooking in an oven is the better way, but if cooked on the top of the range, stir occasionally to prevent burning. Sieve, or beat to a pulp, and serve with pork, roast duck, etc.

BREAD SAUCE (I)

(To serve with one Chicken)

½ pt. milk.	2 oz. breadcrumbs.
Small onion.	2 cloves (stuck into
Blade of mace.	onion).
1 tablesp. cream.	½ oz. butter.
Salt and pepper.	

Infuse the onion and spices in the milk in a double saucepan for ½ hour or more. Remove the onion and spices, add the other ingredients and heat for 15 minutes.

BREAD SAUCE (II)

(To serve with two Chickens)

½ oz. butter.	½ oz. flour.
1 pt. milk.	4 peppercorns.
1 onion, 1 clove.	Blade of mace.
¼ lb. breadcrumbs.	Salt, pepper.

Make a roux of ½ oz. butter and ½ oz. flour. Add by degrees 1 pt. milk. Stir. Boil well. Place this in a double saucepan. Add the onion, stuck with 1 clove, a small blade of mace, 4 peppercorns and ¼ lb. fresh breadcrumbs. Also salt and pepper to taste. Leave this to cook gently for at least an hour or more, adding more milk if required. Remove the onion, herbs, etc. (the latter should be tied up), and serve.

*GOOSEBERRY SAUCE (I)

(Serve with Goose or Duck)

1 pt. green goose-berries.	½ oz. butter.
½ pt. water.	2 to 4 oz. sugar (to taste).

Cook all together gently. Sieve, re-heat and serve.

*GOOSEBERRY SAUCE (II)

Equal quantities of gooseberry sauce (made as in previous recipe) and good béchamel sauce. Re-heat both separately. Mix together, and serve.

*MELTED (OILED) BUTTER (4 or 5 people)

(SERVE WITH ASPARAGUS, ETC.)

Melt one or two ounces butter over GENTLE heat. Do not let it brown at all. Skim if necessary. Add salt and pepper and serve.

MINT SAUCE (5 or 6 people)

2 tablesp. finely chopped mint.	3–4 teasp. sugar (more if liked).
½ gill boiling water.	1 gill vinegar.

Wash the mint and dry thoroughly. Chop finely, add the sugar and pour on the boiling water (this improves the colour and dissolves the sugar). Add vinegar and serve cold.

SENIOR WRANGLER SAUCE (5 or 6 people)

2 oz. butter.   2 oz. sugar.

Beat these together. Add a small glass of brandy or sherry, adding a little at a time till the whole is a cream. Add a few ground almonds and serve with plum puddings, etc.

VII. VEGETABLES

THE three main divisions of this chapter are Plain Vegetables, Dressed Vegetables, Salads.

PLAIN VEGETABLES

There are four distinct classes of vegetables;

    I. Roots, such as carrots, turnips, etc.

    II. Greens, such as cabbage, spinach, etc.

    III. Tubers, such as potatoes, artichokes.

    IV. Pulses, such as haricot beans, lentils.

I and III. **Roots and Tubers.** Buy these in season. They should be firm, of a good shape, and with no soft parts. Tubers should have no eyes or green patches. If sold by weight, note the amount of earth left on them.

PREPARATION FOR COOKING. (*a*) Scrub in cold water. (*b*) Peel or scrape thinly, except turnips, which have a hard outer skin that needs removing. In potatoes and most other roots and tubers the most valuable salts lie just below the skin. By thick peeling they are lost. (*c*) Cook in boiling water, except old potatoes, which may go into cold. (*d*) Simmer gently, covering the saucepan with a lid.

THE FRENCH METHOD of cooking vegetables retains all their goodness, but in appearance they will be brownish.

FRENCH METHOD FOR ROOTS AND TUBERS. Boil, steam or bake them in their skins. Average time, 2 hours. If the skins are very tender (parsnip, beetroot), wrap them in greased paper and bake them in the oven. Lastly, peel and serve them.

II. **Greens.** (*a*) Choose medium-sized ones. (*b*) The leaves should be fresh, green, and crisp. (*c*) Cauliflowers and cabbage should have compact hearts.

RULES FOR COOKING (English method), EXCEPT SPINACH. (*a*) Remove withered or soiled outer leaves, and any damaged tops of leaves. (*b*) Soak in salt and water to withdraw any grubs. (*c*) Wash well. (*d*) Cook in quickly boiling salted water, adding a pinch of bicarbonate of soda only if the greens are stale and old

*E   129

(as it is thought that Vitamin C is readily destroyed in extremely alkaline solutions). Boil rapidly, the greens being quite covered with the boiling water. No lid must be put on the pan. (e) To test when done, pierce thick part of stalk with fork or skewer. If tender, the cabbage, etc., is done. (f) Never throw water from greens down a sink, unless there is a perpetual flush of water. The greens water has a very strong and unpleasant smell, which it is hard to get rid of. Pour the water on to earth. (g) Drain the greens well, and serve free from moisture. The above method of cooking greens is the ENGLISH METHOD. The result is a very good appearance, but as greens contain potash and sulphur most of these escape into the water and are lost.

FRENCH METHOD FOR GREENS. Blanch these (except for very young vegetables blanching is essential). Place them, cut up a little, into a covered casserole, with a very little stock or water, butter, salt and pepper. Cook for about 2 hours and serve. As the whole contents of the casserole is eaten, no goodness whatever is lost and all the flavour is retained.

IV. **Pulses.** Soak these for 24 hours in cold soft water. OR, a second method is: For 1 lb. haricot beans (for instance) boil 1 pt. of water and pour this on the beans. Leave till next day, and use the water and beans, finishing in the usual way.

The following day cook the vegetables until tender in as much water as required.

Salted Vegetables (French Beans, etc.) must be washed in many waters to remove the salt. It is usually better to bring them to the boil (after the washing), and throw away the water, repeating this once or twice, or the vegetables are too salt to be nice.

STORAGE. Roots should be kept in a cool, dark place to prevent sprouting. Tubers should be covered with straw to exclude light. Pulses should not be stored in quantity; buy as required.

ARTICHOKE BOTTOMS

Boil these in salted water, adding lemon juice and a small piece of butter, for 15 to 20 minutes, or until tender. Drain and serve with a good sauce. Tinned artichoke bottoms can be bought more economically than fresh ones.

ARTICHOKE CHIPS (Fried)

These are delicious. Follow the recipe for Potatoes, Chipped, and serve either as a savoury or as a vegetable.

ARTICHOKES, GLOBE

These may be cut into quarters, but are better cooked whole. Wash carefully, cut off the stems, tops, and any outer leaves. Put them into boiling salted water, and cook for 40 minutes or more. When tender, the leaves pull out easily. Drain upside down. Serve on a folded napkin and hand melted (oiled) butter or any suitable sauce with them.

ARTICHOKES, JERUSALEM

Peel these quickly, or even under water, as they turn brown so quickly. When peeled keep them covered with water to which salt and lemon juice (or vinegar) have been added, and, when boiling, add salt and lemon to the water. Average time for boiling, 30 to 35 minutes. When tender, drain them well and serve, coated in white sauce.

ASPARAGUS

Scrape the white stalks well, and cut off any hard or woody ends. Wash the tops carefully. Cut the stalks to one length, tie up in small bundles, stand bundles up in water for 10 minutes. Cook under water till tender (15 minutes). Boil gently to prevent the tops from breaking. Drain well, and dish on a folded napkin. Hand melted (oiled) butter or any good hollandaise sauce with it.

BEANS, BROAD

Cook these in boiling salted water for 15 to 30 minutes or until tender. Drain and serve with parsley sauce poured over them.

Old Broad Beans. Parboil these, slip the beans out of their outer skins; finish cooking, and serve with good sauce, or they may be sieved and used as a bean purée.

BEANS, FRENCH

Remove the strings and slice the beans thinly, or cut them into diamond shapes. Boil in salted water for 15 to 20 minutes, skimming well. No lid must be put on the pan. Drain well when tender, and re-heat with a small piece of butter, salt and pepper. Very finely chopped parsley may be sprinkled over them if liked.

BEANS, HARICOT

See notes on Pulses (page 130). Having soaked the beans over-night, put them in a saucepan with cold water, adding a little salt, $\frac{1}{2}$ an onion, and a small piece of fat (this last softens the skins). Cook gently for from 2 to 4 hours, or until tender. Drain thoroughly and serve with any good sauce, or they may be sieved and used as a purée. These beans make a good curry or can be used with meat for a curry. Serve with boiled rice, garnished with cut lemons.

As a breakfast dish they are nice if, when quite tender, they are lightly fried in bacon fat, then sprinkled with parsley and served with bacon and tomato.

BEETROOT

Great care must be taken not to break the outer skin, or the vegetable 'bleeds' and is a bad colour. This may be done in the digging or in removing the small roots and leaves. This last must be done by twisting the leaves off with the hand rather than by cutting them with a knife.

Cook gently, either by baking (wrapped in greased paper; this gives the best colour), or by boiling. Average time, about 2 hours. Skin when cold. If wished for a hot dish, cut it into slices, pour a little vinegar over to keep the colour, and re-heat it gently in stock. Make a good sauce, using partly the stock in which the vegetables are re-heated, and dish the beet with this poured over it. The sauce will be of a bright pink colour.

For salads, cut the beet in thin slices, and pour a little vinegar over. Season well and serve.

BROCCOLI

See Cauliflower.

BRUSSELS SPROUTS

Wash these well in salt and water to remove insects, grit, etc. Cook in boiling salted water. Boil gently for 10 to 20 minutes (according to age). Drain thoroughly. Re-heat with a small piece of butter, salt and pepper.

CABBAGE

Follow the direction for Brussels Sprouts Quarter the cabbage, and cut the thick stalk in four to ensure its being tender. Time, 15 to 40 minutes (according to age). Drain thoroughly. Chop the cabbage and re-heat, with or without a small piece of butter.

N.B. If stale or old, see note about bicarbonate of soda under Greens, Rules for Cooking, p. 129.

CARROTS

Wash and scrape these lightly. Then wash them again. Large ones should be quartered. Cook gently in a covered saucepan until tender. Old ones may take from 1 to 2 hours or even more.

Carrots (Young). Wash these and cook them in salted water (to which a pinch of salt is added) in their skins for 20 to 30 minutes. Then drain, rub the skins off with a soft cloth; re-heat them with butter and serve with finely chopped parsley.

CARROTS, BRAISED (4 or 5 people)

1 lb. carrots.	1 oz. butter or
1 gill stock or	margarine.
water.	Seasoning.

Prepare carrots and cut into rounds (young ones can be left whole). Melt fat in casserole and put in carrots, tossing them in the fat. Cover and put in moderate oven for 10 minutes. Add the stock, salt, and pepper, and cook gently till tender. Dish neatly, with or without the liquor. Sprinkle with a little chopped parsley. For Celery, Onions, etc., thicken with flour or cornflour. Add a little glaze or browning.

CAULIFLOWER

Wash well in salt and water, and cut the thick stalk into 4. Cook in boiling salted water (no lid on the pan) for from 15 to 30 minutes; place them head downwards in the pan to prevent the scum from settling on the flower. Drain well and serve with white sauce.

CELERY

Wash well, and remove any outer leaves and keep them for flavouring soups, etc. Cut into even lengths and tie in bundles. Cook in boiling water, with 1 teasp. salt and a pinch of sugar added; cover the pan with a lid. Cook for about 1 hour. Drain well, and serve with good white or brown sauce. Lay the celery on toast and pour the sauce over.

Old celery should be blanched before cooking.

Celery, Braised. See Carrots, Braised.

CELERIAC

Follow rules for Celery.

CUCUMBER (4 or 5 people)

Peel and cut this into thick slices. Boil in salted water for about 20 minutes. Drain and serve with white sauce.

CURLY GREENS

Follow recipe for Cabbage. They are nicer if sieved after boiling. Average time, 30 minutes.

ENDIVE

Wash well and remove outer leaves. Cook as for Cabbage.

KOHLRABI

Cut into cubes 1 inch square. Cook until tender in a small amount of boiling salted water. Serve with white sauce.

LEEKS

Cut off the tops and bottoms and peel off any outer layers that may have dirt in them, wash very well, splitting if necessary.

Blanch them, and either boil or braise for about 35 to 45 minutes. Drain well, place on toast and pour white sauce over. If the leeks are to be boiled, cook them in boiling water with no lid on the pan; if to be braised, follow the rules for braising, but do not finish by browning in the oven.

Leeks, Braised. See Carrots, Braised.

LENTILS

Follow directions for Beans, Haricot, but lentils cook more quickly than beans.

LETTUCES

Cook as for Cabbage. When tender, drain well and sieve, and serve with fried croûtons or quarters of hard-boiled egg.

MUSHROOMS

These have a characteristic smell; they should have a white skin with the underside pink to brown according to their size. The skin should peel off easily. It is important to choose mushrooms carefully.

Peel them and remove the stalks. The skins and stalks can be dried and used for flavouring.

They may be cooked in a variety of ways: (1) Fry in a small amount of butter; season, and serve on fried croûtons. (2) Put them on a buttered tin or fireproof dish, season well, cover with a greased paper and cook in the oven for about 15 minutes. Serve on toast with the liquid poured over. (3) STEWED IN SAUCE. If large, cut the mushroom up a little. Make a sauce of $\frac{1}{2}$ oz. fat, $\frac{1}{2}$ oz. flour, and $\frac{1}{2}$ pt. milk. Boil and cool this. Add the mushrooms, and simmer for 20 minutes, or until tender. Dish them. If the sauce is too thin reduce it and pour over them.

NETTLES

Young nettles are very wholesome. Follow the directions for Spinach. Old nettles are too strong in flavour to use.

ONIONS

These only require to have the roots and tops cut off and the outer layers peeled off. Rinse if necessary, but they should not be left in water. They should be blanched before being cooked. Time, small onions about 30 minutes, if very large 45 minutes. They may be boiled, stewed or braised. After being cooked they should be served with a white or brown sauce, or the centres may be removed, and they may be filled with any good farce, re-heated and served with sauce.

Onions, Braised. See Carrots, Braised. If the onions are nicely browned in the fat first, they have a better flavour and colour.

ONIONS (Fried)

(1) Cut into rings and fry in hot shallow fat. (2) Cut into rings, flour these, dip them into white of egg and again into flour, and fry in shallow fat about half-inch deep. They could be fried in deep fat, but the casing being of flour might spoil a large quantity of fat (see notes on Frying, page 54). (3) Cut into rings, egg and crumb, and fry.

ONIONS, SPRING

These may be cut into equal lengths, tied in bundles, and cooked for about an hour. Serve on toast with white sauce. In this case cook with no lid on the pan to preserve the green colour.

PARSNIPS

Follow the directions for Carrots. They may be served plain or mashed. (See Potatoes, Mashed.)

PEAS, DRIED

Follow the directions for Beans, Haricot.

PEAS, GREEN

Cook these, if young, in quickly boiling salted water for 10 to 20 minutes, adding a lump of sugar and a small piece of mint to the water. Drain well and serve with a small piece of butter, a pinch of sugar and seasoning.

Old Peas will be nicer if stewed, or cooked in the French method, in a small amount of stock and water in a closely covered jar or pan. If the lid does not fit tightly, put a piece of buttered paper under it. When tender, serve in a good brown sauce.

POTATOES

These may be treated in many ways:

BAKED. Large potatoes bake best. Scrub and prick the skins. Bake in a hot oven for 1 to 2 hours according to size. Serve on a folded napkin, and hand butter with them.

OR, when cooked, they may be halved, some of the potato removed, and each half filled with a savoury mixture or with mashed potato, parsley, etc. Re-heat and serve.

BOILED AFTER PEELING. Follow the method below except that the potatoes are peeled after scrubbing and left covered in cold water till required (a little vinegar added helps the colour when potatoes are old). When cooked, they must be tender (test with a skewer) but entirely unbroken. Drain off all water: the easiest way is to tip the saucepan, holding the lid firmly so that while the potatoes are kept in, a small space is left between the lid and the pan for the liquid to escape. Replace the pan on the fire half covered with the lid and allow the potatoes to cook a little more in their own steam. Shake gently to make the surface floury. The potatoes themselves must be whole and unbroken.

BOILED IN THEIR SKINS. For this select even - sized potatoes; scrub them and boil them. They should be placed in cold water and brought to the boil, add salt, and cook gently for about 30 minutes or until tender. They may then be served in their skins, or peeled and served as desired.

FRIED, COTTAGE STYLE. Place 1 or 2 oz. dripping in a pan. Heat it. Add any remains of cooked potatoes. Cut and mash this in the fat. When quite soft and mashed let one side brown by leaving it unstirred for a few minutes (care must be taken to prevent burning). Fold in two and serve. This resembles an omelet in appearance. The taste is nicer if done also in bacon fat. It may be turned like a pancake and browned on both sides if preferred.

ROASTED TO SERVE WITH HOT JOINTS. Peel and dry the potatoes. Put them in the baking tin with the partly cooked meat, allowing them to lie in the dripping. Baste occasionally. Add them to the meat tin about 1 to $1\frac{1}{2}$ hours before they are required.

OR, semi-cook them by steaming and boiling; they may be peeled before or after this first process as desired. Put them into the dripping pan about $\frac{1}{2}$ hour before they are needed. This plan ensures their being cooked through.

SAUTÉD. Slice cold cooked but unbroken potatoes. Heat a little fat—a little bacon fat is the nicest—and when smoking, place the potatoes in the pan; fry by the English or shallow fat method, and when one side is brown, turn and fry the other. These are very nice for breakfast with bacon.

STEAMED. This is the better way for peeled potatoes. A steamer to fit a saucepan may be used, and as this is fitted with holes, all the liquid escapes and the draining is dispensed with. Time, 45 minutes to 1 hour. Dry the potatoes to make them floury as in Boiled after Peeling.

POTATO BORDER

Follow recipe for mashed potato, but to each pound allow $\frac{1}{2}$ to 1 oz. butter, 1 raw yolk of egg, and 1 tablesp. milk. If the egg is omitted 2 tablesp. milk will be needed.

Beat well, and when no longer sticky shape with the hand (lightly floured). Roll on a floured board and use as required.

POTATO CROQUETTES

Use the mixture as for Potato Border. Add seasoning as required, and, if liked, parsley, ham, etc. Form into balls, flour these, coat TWICE with egg and crumb, and fry. OR, flour and fry them in shallow fat.

Croquettes may be made in many shapes, e.g. small cottage

loaves, crescents, etc. These shapes should be brushed with milk and egg and browned in a hot oven.

POTATOES, CHIPPED (Fried)

Peel, and when raw, cut into various shapes: (*a*) very thin slices (these are called chips); (*b*) small match-like strips (about 2 inches long by $\frac{1}{4}$ inch square), these are called straws; (*c*) into half, longways, and divide into sections resembling portions of an orange (called orange quarters); (*d*) into 'ribbons' by cutting a slice of potato $\frac{1}{4}$ to $\frac{1}{2}$ inch thick and cutting round and round this until a coil is obtained; (*e*) by using any of the very pretty potato cutters that can be bought cheaply.

Whichever of the above methods is followed, place the pieces in cold water and remove and dry them on a cloth just before cooking.

To FRY. Put some of the pieces in a frying basket and plunge them into hot deep fat at a temperature of about 380° F. (smoking freely). Shake gently to separate them, and cook till tender, but not crisp. Turn them on to a paper. Continue so cooking all the prepared sections. Re-heat the fat to about 400°, and put all the sections in the frying basket and plunge them into the fat to crisp and brown them.

POTATOES, FRENCH (Fried Whole)

Choose even-sized, not too big, potatoes. Peel and dry them. Have a pan containing sufficient fat to cover three parts of the potatoes. Make this smoking hot. Add the potatoes. When one half is brown turn them once to brown the other half. These are delicious. Time, about 20 to 30 minutes. OR, cut in marble size, dry well and fry in deep fat; then called à la Parisienne.

POTATOES, MASHED

Sieve or mash some hot, freshly-cooked peeled potatoes. To each lb. allow a small piece of butter, 1 to 2 tablesp. milk, and seasoning.

Boil the milk and butter; add the mashed potato and seasoning. Mix well and beat till white with a wooden spoon.

POTATOES, NEW

Rub off the skin, or lightly scrape it off. Have some boiling water, and to it add a sprig of mint and salt (1 teasp. to each pt.).

Into this put the potatoes and boil gently till barely tender. Drain and leave to finish cooking in their own steam. When done, add some butter and shake gently to coat all the potatoes in this. Add some very finely chopped parsley and serve.

POTATOES, OLIVE or PEA

Special cutters are used to shape the potatoes into the olives or peas. Cook them in boiling salted water for 10 to 15 minutes. Test with a trussing needle or fine skewer. Drain when tender and toss them in butter and sprinkle with parsley finely chopped, or leave till cold, then flour, egg, crumb, and fry them; or serve them in a good sauce or use as a garnish.

POTATOES, SOUFFLÉ or PUFF

Trim the potatoes into even-sized ovals and cut them length-ways into slices less than $\frac{1}{4}$ inch thick. Leave these for 30 to 40 minutes in cold water. Heat some fat to 260° F. Dry the slices and fry them till tender, but not coloured. Drain them. Re-heat the fat till just beginning to smoke, and replace the potatoes in this. They should puff; any that do not must be removed. Drain them again and re-heat the fat to 400° (very plentiful smoke), and re-fry the potatoes to crisp and finish them. Drain, sprinkle with salt and serve.

SALSIFY

Scrub and scrape the roots. Place them at once in cold water, to which lemon or vinegar and salt is added. Cook them for about 2 hours. Serve with white sauce. Salsify is known as the 'vegetable oyster'. They are very nice scalloped. See Scallops (page 37). If possible, add a few oysters to scalloped salsify.

SEAKALE

Wash and trim to equal lengths. Tie in bundles and cook for $1-1\frac{1}{2}$ hours in boiling salted water, to which a little lemon or vinegar is added and a small lump of sugar. Keep the lid partly on the pan, half-covering it. Drain, serve on toast with good white sauce.

SEAKALE (Fried)

When cooked and cold split it into halves, quarters, or convenient lengths, and egg, crumb, and fry these, or dip into coating batter and fry.

SORREL

May be cooked in two ways. (1) Follow the directions for Spinach. (2) Wash the sorrel. Put 4 oz. butter in a gallon-size pan, and put the sorrel wet from the washing on to this, filling the saucepan with it. (If less sorrel is used, less butter proportionately will be required.) Cover with a lid and cook gently. When reduced and tender, add 1 oz. or more of flour, sprinkling this in to absorb the fat. Stir and cook well. Sieve, re-heat, seasoning to taste. Add a squeeze of lemon and a pinch of sugar.

Sorrel may be used raw in salads and is very useful for soups.

SPINACH

Wash this well to remove grit, and pull off stalks and coarse midribs. There are two ways of proceeding: (1) Pack it wet from washing into a pan, cover with a lid, and let it cook gently, stirring now and then, until tender. (2) Add a little boiling salted water; this method gives rather a prettier green colour. Time for cooking, about 20 to 30 minutes.

With either method, when tender, drain it very well, sieve and re-heat it with a small piece of butter, salt and pepper. Serve with croûtons of fried bread or with quarters of hard-boiled egg. Or spinach can be well chopped instead of sieving for a simple dish.

Spinach à la crème. Add 2 tablesp. cream or white sauce, just before serving, to 2 lb. spinach.

TOMATOES

BAKED. Place them on a greased baking tin, putting a small piece of butter on each. Season and cover them closely with a greased paper. Bake in a moderate oven for 15 minutes or until tender but unbroken.

STEWED. Place them in a very small amount of stock. Cover with a greased paper, then with a lid, and cook very gently in the oven or on the range for 15 to 20 minutes, basting them frequently

TURNIPS

Peel these thickly. Time for old ones, 30 to 60 minutes, or even longer. Young ones, 15 to 20 minutes. Follow directions for root vegetables (page 129).

If washed, they must be well-drained first, or they are very watery. When mashed or sieved, re-heat with a tiny piece of butter, salt and pepper.

Turnips, Braised. See Carrots, Braised.

TURNIP TOPS

These are delicious and very wholesome greens.   Cook as for Cabbage.   When tender, if liked, sieve and serve with fried croûtons, or chop as for cabbage, and re-heat.

VEGETABLE MARROW

These are nicest if cut when the size of a large apple and before the seeds have really formed.

If this is possible, cook them whole, without peeling them, in boiling salted water for 10 to 15 minutes.   Drain, cut in half lengthways, and serve with oiled (melted) butter, or white or hollandaise sauce.

If larger marrows are used, peel them and divide into convenient slices.   Cook them in boiling salted water for about 30 minutes. Drain well.   Serve on toast with white sauce poured over.

DRESSED VEGETABLES

In the full menu it will be seen that these form the first of a group of three dishes, called the 'Entremets'.   The term ' dressed vegetables ', as the name implies, means that some vegetable is so elaborately prepared that instead of merely accompanying a meat dish, it is served as a separate course, and even as an entrée at small luncheons or informal dinners.   If the methods of cooking vegetables are carefully read, many ideas for dressing vegetables will be suggested.

PRACTICALLY ALL VEGETABLES may be ' dressed ' in the following ways.   One or two uncommon instances of each will be given, and the recipes may be varied according to the vegetables obtainable.

ASPIC

(Peas in Aspic)

Line small dariole moulds with aspic jelly.   Fill the moulds prettily with cooked peas, adding a little ham, tongue or anything available to add to the taste and appearance of the moulds. Cover with liquid aspic and turn out on to a bed of shredded lettuce, mixed with mayonnaise or other dressing.

BASKETS
(Asparagus Tips in Baskets)

Line small greased basket moulds with short crust. Prick this and cover it with a greased paper, pressing the greased side downwards against the paste. Fill with rice or dried peas. Bake till set. Remove the paper and rice. Put the baskets back in the oven to dry and brown. Cook the asparagus tips and mix them with a creamy panada of béchamel or other sauce. Remove the baskets from the tins and fill them with this. Semicircles of paste may be baked separately to form handles.

Decorate with a little sieved yolk of egg, or finely chopped parsley.

BATTER.　In Batter Cases
(French Beans in Batter Cases)

See Batter Cases (page 230). Fill these with French beans cut into diamond shapes, and mixed with thick white sauce and grated cheese.

À LA BÉCHAMEL
(Salsify à la Béchamel)

Cooked salsify served with creamy béchamel sauce.

BOUCHÉES
(Celery Bouchées)

Tiny puff paste cases, filled with celery mixed with a good panada.

CORNETS
(Seakale Cornets)

Roll some puff paste thinly. Sprinkle it with grated cheese and fold into three. Roll again, and repeat this. Then roll thinly, cut into strips and wrap these round a cornet tin. See Cream Cornets. Bake, and when cooked remove the case from the tin. Fill with cooked seakale mixed with a good panada.

À LA CRÈME
(Spinach à la Crème)

Cook some spinach. Drain, press well and sieve it. Melt 2 oz. butter in a pan, add 1 oz. flour. Cook a little. Add

1 gill or more of cream. Stir till very hot, then put in a double saucepan. Add the spinach. Serve when wanted in a fireproof dish and garnish with croûtons of bread.

À LA DIABLE
(Devilled Mushrooms)

Peel 12 mushrooms and remove the stalks. Fry six other chopped mushrooms in 1 oz. fat, add a finely chopped onion, 1 tablesp. chopped ham, a pinch of cayenne, a tablesp. or less of curry paste, and a teasp. chopped parsley. Place the mushrooms stalk-side uppermost in a fireproof dish or each one separately in a small soufflé case. Put some of the mixture on each mushroom. Cover the surface with a little grated cheese and white breadcrumbs and a few drops of oiled butter. Bake in a hot oven for 10 minutes.

N.B. Slices of marrow and rounds of cucumber are especially suitable for this, if possible using a devilled mushroom filling.

FARCE
(Mushroom Farce)
(For Filling Tomatoes, Small Marrows, etc.)

½ oz. fat.	½ pt. mushrooms.
1 teasp. parsley.	½ gill breadcrumbs.
Seasoning.	A very little sauce,
1 small onion.	cream or stock.

Fry the mushrooms and onion in ½ oz. fat. Add the rest of the ingredients. The whole should be of a thick, creamy consistency. This makes a good filling for an omelet.

FRITTERS
(Artichoke Fritters)

Cook and drain some artichoke bottoms. Put a little chicken or veal farce on them, and when cold dip them in a good frying batter, preferably the one made with yeast. Fry in deep fat, and hand a good sauce with them.

AU GRATIN
(Cauliflower au Gratin)
(See Macaroni Cheese)

Is a favourite dish. Cheese should be allowed in the proportion of 2 oz. to each ½ pt. of sauce. Cook the cauliflower carefully without breaking it. Lift it on to a greased fireproof dish, coat it with the sauce, sprinkle the top with a little grated cheese and a few breadcrumbs, place small pieces of butter here and there, and bake till brown.

À L'INDIENNE

(Curried Haricot Beans)

See Beans, Haricot (page 132) and Curry (page 68).

AU JUS

(Leeks au Jus)

Braised leeks served in any very good brown gravy.

MOULDS

(Picnic Mould.   4 or 5 people)

4 oz. grated Brazil nuts.	1 teasp. grated lemon rind.
2 oz. washed and grated pine kernels.	1 teasp. marmite mixed with ½ cup of boiling water.
4 oz. fresh breadcrumbs.	1 raw egg.
1 tablesp. finely chopped onion.	2 hard-boiled eggs.
1 teasp. made mustard.	Pepper, salt, and nutmeg.

Grease a plain round mould and line it with the sliced hard-boiled eggs. Mix all the dry ingredients and the mustard. Beat the raw egg, add it to the cooled marmite gravy and stir into the dry ingredients. Season carefully, and press gently but firmly into the mould. Cover with greased paper and a plate. Put a weight on the top. Steam for about ¾ hour. When cold, turn out and serve with salad.

(Tomato and Egg Mould.   5 or 6 people)

½ tin or 4 tomatoes.	¼ teasp. mace.
1 tablesp. of brown breadcrumbs.	1 large tablesp. cornflour.
3 hard-boiled eggs.	1 oz. butter or margarine.
	Pepper and salt.

Sauté the tomatoes in the butter, and add the cornflour, previously blended with a little cream or tomato liquor. Cook for 5 minutes. Add the finely chopped eggs, then the breadcrumbs, and mould the mixture. Turn out when set and serve with a mayonnaise sauce, salad or cress.

OMELET

(Tomato Omelet)

Make a French or English Omelet. Place some slices of cooked tomato on one half. Fold the other over and serve with tomato sauce poured over.

PATTIES

(Chestnut Patties. 5 or 6 people)

1 lb. chestnuts (or any nice vegetable).	A clove.
	1 pt. stock.
1 small onion.	A blade of mace.
A stick of celery.	1 oz. fat and 1 oz. flour.

Make some patties, see Puff Paste (page 171). When baked, remove the soft portion and fill with the above mixture.

Slit the chestnuts. Bake them for 10 minutes. Remove the husks, and boil for 20 minutes. Drain and remove the inner skin. Simmer them with the stock and vegetables for 45 minutes or until tender. Drain them. Make a brown roux with 1 oz. fat and 1 oz. flour. Add enough of the chestnut stock to form a thick panada. Boil well and skim. Add the chestnuts and fill the patty cases. Serve hot.

*PIES

See Vegetable Pie (pages 163 and 170). These may be varied by making the crust of some good purée. See recipe for Potato Border (page 137). This mixture can be rolled out and used as a pie crust. A similarly made green pea or carrot purée is also a variety.

*SOUFFLÉ

(Baked Cauliflower Soufflé. 5 or 6 people)

1 cooked cauliflower.	2 tomatoes (optional).
2 oz. grated cheese.	1 oz. flour.
1 oz. fat.	¼ pt. milk.
2 or 3 eggs.	Seasoning.

Divide the cauliflower and place with the sliced tomatoes and the cheese in layers in a prepared soufflé case (see page 236). Make a panada of the fat, flour, and milk. Boil well. Cool slightly, and add the yolks. Beat well. Lastly add the stiffly beaten whites of eggs. Season and pour over the cauliflower mixture. Bake in a moderate oven for about 30 minutes. Serve at once.

Some vegetables are better sieved for soufflés, e.g. spinach, carrots, etc. In this case follow the recipe for Chicken Soufflé (page 236), adding ½ pt. of vegetable purée instead of the raw chicken.

STUFFED VEGETABLES (Stuffed Tomatoes. 3 people)

6 tomatoes.	2 tablesp. of breadcrumbs,
3 mushrooms.	pepper, and salt.
½ shallot. ½ oz. butter.	1 tablesp. raspings
1½ oz. cooked ham.	(browned breadcrumbs).
1 teasp. chopped parsley,	1 teasp. grated cheese.
a little nutmeg.	6 croûtons.

Remove the insides from the tomatoes. Rub this through a sieve. Chop the mushrooms, ham, shallot. Cook the shallot and mushrooms in the butter for a few minutes. Add the ham, parsley, nutmeg, breadcrumbs, pepper, salt and inside of tomatoes. Fill the tomatoes with this, letting the mixture come up above the top. Mix the cheese and raspings together and sprinkle over the top. Bake for 10 minutes, put on croûtons and serve. Tomatoes can also be stuffed with any cooked meat or fish, bound with suitable sauce or with scrambled egg or cheese mixture.

(Stuffed Vegetable Marrow)

1 vegetable marrow.   Scraps of cold meat of any kind.   Sauce.

If young, cut off one end and remove the seeds from the centre with a knife and spoon, or, if impossible, cut lengthwise in two and remove seeds. Peel. Make a well-flavoured filling with minced meat, etc., moistened with sauce or gravy, and fill the cavity. If cut, tie together. Bake in moderate oven till tender, basting well. Serve with gravy made as for roast joint.

N.B. If liked, sprinkle marrow with browned crumbs before baking. If old, partly boil the marrow before peeling.

TIMBALES

See Entrée Recipes (page 86), and substitute some vegetable for meat.

À LA VELOUTÉE

(Brussels Sprouts à la Veloutée)

Cooked Sprouts served in Veloutée Sauce.

VOL-AU-VENT

Fill a vol-au-vent case (see page 173) with a variety of neatly
cut cooked vegetables, re-heated in a good creamy thick sauce

(Mushroom.   4 or 5 people)
FILLING FOR PASTRY CASES
1 gill of hollandaise sauce made with stock, milk, flour, lemon juice,
seasoning, and the yolk of an egg.
½ lb. of mushrooms.   Nutmeg.   1 teasp. parsley.

Peel the mushrooms and cook them between two plates in the
oven for 20 minutes.   Chop them up, not too finely, and if they
are ' buttons ' they need not be chopped.   Add salt, pepper,
nutmeg to taste, and the parsley.   Re-heat gently in the sauce,
fill the pastry cases and serve hot.

SALADS

The various kinds of salads may be divided into 5 classes:

I. **The typical English Salad,** made of lettuce and other raw
vegetables, such as cucumber, tomato, mustard and cress.   The
dressing is usually composed of egg, mustard, oil, vinegar,
seasoning, sugar, and possibly cream.

II. **Salads composed of Cold Cooked Vegetables**—either one
vegetable served alone in some dressing, e.g. beetroot in vinegar;
potato salad, the potatoes being sliced and mixed with a good
dressing; or several vegetables, neatly cut up and mixed in the
dressing.

III. **Meat or Fish Salads,** distinguished by containing solid
pieces of meat (e.g. chicken) or fish (e.g. salmon).

IV. **Russian Salads,** which are mainly composed of tongue,
ham, olives, anchovies, capers, any pickles, and a few vegetables such as beetroot, celery, and mixed with a dressing of
oil and vinegar, mustard and seasoning.

V. **Fruit Salads or Macedoines.**

RULES FOR MAKING SALADS

Only young, good vegetables should be used, any inferior
portions must be removed.   If a salad is to be decorated, keep
back all the parts suitable for this.   Mix the rest with the
dressing, and decorate the top with the reserved portions.

Class I.   Raw vegetables, such as lettuce, must be very carefully washed. Place the lettuce in cold, slightly salted water and examine each leaf to see that it is free from grit or insects. Then place it on a clean cloth, and so on, till all has been examined.

Fold the cloth firmly over the lettuce and shake it hard, out of doors if possible, to remove all moisture. Open the cloth and leave it, with the lettuce leaves spread over it, in a draught for a few minutes, and let the leaves get dry and crisp. Care must be taken not to crush the leaves.

They are then torn into neat little pieces with the hands, or they may be shredded with a knife, though it slightly spoils the flavour, at the same time improving the appearance of the salad.

If the raw vegetables have to be kept before use, place the stalks in water to keep the leaves crisp.

Class II. Any cooked vegetables must be neatly cut up—they must not be over-cooked or at all mashed. For this reason, new potatoes, if possible, should be used in preference to old.

Class III. Divide meat and fish into neat pieces—mix some with the lettuce, etc. and dressing. Save nice-sized portions; coat these with mayonnaise and place them tastefully in the salad.

Class IV. As Class II.

Class V. In making fruit salads, large fruits must be cut into neat slices or divided into two according to their size, and small ones should be put in whole. Grapes should be divided in two, peeled and stoned, and then added.

Salad Dressings. For these it is important to have the best oil. 'Huile de Provence' is better than Lucca Oil, and is no dearer.

The best salad dressing is Mayonnaise, but this is expensive, and any given in the following recipes are excellent:

BANANA SALAD (with Mock Mayonnaise Dressing)

DRESSING
(For 6 bananas)

1 yolk of egg.	Pinch cayenne.
½ teasp. salt.	2 tablesp. salad oil.
1 teasp. sugar.	1 tablesp. tarragon vinegar.
½ gill unsweetened tinned milk or cream.	1 tablesp. chili vinegar, OR 2 teasp. lemon juice.

¼ teasp. mustard.

Place nice lettuce leaves on a small dish, peel a banana (small one) and lay on lettuce. Coat with the above dressing and sprinkle thickly with chopped walnuts. Garnish with slices of banana.

Mix all dry ingredients to the yolk, then add the salad oil very carefully, then the vinegar, lastly the milk. Stir till thick.

BOILED SALAD DRESSING, Thick (to keep)

($\frac{3}{4}$ pt. for 20 people)

1 teasp. flour.	$\frac{3}{4}$ gill tinned milk OR thin
1 tablesp. sugar.	cream.
1 teasp. mustard.	$\frac{1}{4}$ gill chili or tarragon
1$\frac{1}{2}$ tablesp. melted butter.	vinegar.
1 teasp. salt.	2 yolks of egg.

Mix dry ingredients. Add the melted butter, beaten yolks and milk carefully, stirring well, then add the vinegar. Cook gently in a double saucepan for 20 minutes, till thick, stirring all the time. Store in screw-top bottles.

*CHEAP SALAD DRESSING WITHOUT EGG

(7 or 8 people)

2 tablesp. mashed potato.	1 or 2 tablesp. vinegar.
	Seasoning.
4 tablesp. cream.	Sugar to taste.

Mix the potato and cream smoothly, and add the rest of the ingredients.

CHINESE SALAD (4 or 5 people)

1 apple. 1 banana.	A few walnuts.
1 slice pineapple.	1 cold potato.
1 thick slice of cucumber.	1 tablesp. whipped cream.
1 heart of celery.	1 tablesp. mayonnaise sauce.

Peel the apple, cucumber and banana and cut all the ingredients into neat dice. Mix lightly with the sauce and cream, adding salt and pepper to taste. Pile up in rocky heaps in small salad dishes. Garnish with chopped nuts or parsley or cress or a slice of tomato.

EGG SALAD (with Chiffonade Dressing)

3 hard-boiled eggs cut in 4 lengthwise. Watercress. 1 large carrot.

DRESSING

(For 6 individual salads)

1 sieved yolk of egg (hard-boiled).	1 tablesp. chopped capers.
1 white of egg (hard-boiled) chopped.	1 tablesp. chopped cooked beetroot.
1 tablesp. chopped chives.	$\frac{1}{2}$ onion, scraped. Red pepper. Salt.
1 tablesp. chopped parsley.	$\frac{1}{2}$ gill salad oil. $\frac{1}{4}$ gill vinegar.

Or any good thick salad dressing may be used.

Mix all together very thoroughly. Arrange the watercress round the dish. Put the egg carefully in the centre arranged crosswise, the yolk having been mixed with some of the dressing and replaced. Grate or scrape the carrot and place it round the egg. Serve the dressing separately if preferred.

*FRENCH SALAD DRESSING (4 people)

½ teasp. made mustard.	Salt, pepper, and 1 teasp. sugar.
2 tablesp. oil.	1 dessertsp. vinegar.

Rub the oil and vinegar well together till they thicken; add the other ingredients, and mix this thoroughly with the salad.

N.B. Instead of the vinegar, the juice of ½ a lemon and 1 additional teasp. sugar may be used.

*PLAIN SALAD DRESSING, ENGLISH (5 or 6 people)

1 raw yolk of egg.	1 to 1½ tablesp. vinegar (white
4 tablesp. oil, cream, or both.	wine or malt).
½ teasp. of made mustard.	1 teasp. tarragon vinegar, if liked.

Salt and sugar to taste, usually 1 small teasp. sugar.

Mix the yolk and mustard, and add the oil or cream slowly, mixing well. Then add the vinegar very carefully, then the seasoning.

POTATO SALAD

If possible cook the potatoes in good stock until tender but unbroken. Drain, cover with French salad dressing and leave till cold, cut into dice. Add a very little finely chopped onion; or some onion juice. Mix with mayonnaise or any good dressing. Sprinkle liberally with fine parsley and serve.

SALAD DRESSING WITHOUT OIL (5 or 6 people)

1 hard-boiled (or raw)	3 dessertsp. cream.
yolk of egg.	1 dessertsp. vinegar.
½ teasp. made mustard.	Pinch of sugar.

Pinch of salt and pepper.

Mix the yolk, mustard and seasoning. Add the cream by degrees, and when smooth and thick add the vinegar very gradually.

TOMATO SALAD

1 small tomato.	A little crisp lettuce.
Pretty pieces of potato	Parsley finely chopped.
or beet or cucumber.	Red pepper.

Skin the tomato, place on lettuce. Coat the tomato with thick mock mayonnaise. Garnish prettily with tomato skin, or red pepper, and the vegetable decoration. Serve just enough for one person.

*FRUIT SALADS

(1) SIMPLE, BUT EXCELLENT METHOD. Arrange as large a variety of fruit as is possible in a glass dish, sprinkle each layer with sugar (castor). Pour over these the juice of a lemon, add a glass of claret, sherry or Madeira. Leave for a short time for the juice to flow; if possible, for 2 hours on ice. Add a glass of liqueur and serve.

(2) Arrange the fruits as above in a glass dish. Make a syrup of ¼ lb. sugar and ½ pt. water. Boil these together, and when cold pour over the fruits. Lemon and orange juice may be added if wished, and wine or not, according to taste.

Orange Fruit Salad, Simple (4 people)

| 4 oranges. 1 gill water. | A piece of the rind and |
| 1 banana if liked. | the juice of 1 lemon. |

2 oz. sugar, less or more according to sweetness of oranges.

Dip the oranges into boiling water and remove the peel, pith, and pips. Slice across and lay in a glass dish. Boil the water, sugar, lemon rind and juice for 5 minutes. Cool, strain over the oranges, garnish with the sliced banana or angelica or desiccated coconut.

Orange Salad (I)

1 orange.	Chopped parsley (fine
1 tender cabbage	and dry).
leaf.	Chopped walnuts.
1 oz. cheese.	Celery, etc.

Put the cabbage on a dish. Skin the orange and remove the pips. Open it, but do not separate completely, making it like a rose. Place it in the centre of the cabbage leaf. Coat it with a good dressing and garnish with cheese made into balls and rolled alternately in nuts and parsley. Decorate with pretty salad plants, celery, cress, tomato, etc.

N.B. Any other vegetables or fruit may be used.

Orange Salad (II)
(For wild duck)

| 4 oranges. | French salad dressing |
| Little chopped parsley. | (p. 150). |

Dip oranges in boiling water and peel carefully. Remove pith, slice neatly and remove pips. Arrange in glass dish; pour dressing over. Sprinkle with finely chopped parsley, and, if liked, a little finely chopped fresh herbs.

VIII. VEGETARIAN COOKERY

So many excellent books on vegetarian cookery are to be found, and so much of the food of true vegetarians consists of dried and uncooked food, that it will only be necessary to give a limited number of recipes here.

There are two types of restricted diets: (*a*) Strict vegetarians, who take no animal product at all; (*b*) Vegetarians who take no meat, fish, poultry, or game. When catering for vegetarians use only vegetable fats such as butter, nutter, olive oil, etc. For stock substitutes use any vegetable water, tomato liquor, with the addition of marmite if liked.

Many vegetables of the pulse order — lentils, peas, haricot beans, also nuts, cheese, etc.—are actually weight for weight more nourishing than meat, but their bulk is much greater, and they are frequently less digestible. They must, therefore, be carefully prepared and well cooked.

Vegetables (except pulses) are lacking in protein and all lack fat. Care, therefore, must be taken to maintain the necessary balance of food-stuffs in vegetarian dishes, e.g. such foods as pulses, cheese, and eggs must supply the protein, and nuts the fat.

For vegetarians, no fats made from meat, no gelatine from bones, and so on, must be used.

Excellent nut butters and vegetarian fats are on the market (see price lists from any large stores, and more especially from Eustace Miles, or from Pitman's, Birmingham), and ' Agar Agar ' is a vegetarian gelatine.

MARMITE is a vegetable preparation, in flavour much resembling bovril. It is expensive if used largely, but half a teaspoon added to soups, vegetarian gravies, etc., greatly improves them. It is also useful for spreading lightly on thin bread and butter for sandwiches; or it may be used for these in conjunction with mustard and cress, tomatoes or lettuce. It is made from yeast and is rich in vitamins.

BEANS

(Haricot or Butter Beans)

These are a valuable source of second - class protein. Fat should be added to make up for the fat deficiency in the beans. They are more digestible if sieved after cooking.

They make good CURRIES. Follow the directions for Curry (page 68), using cooked and very tender beans instead of meat. (For the cooking of beans see Pulses, page 130.) Serve with boiled rice.

CHEESE

This is more than twice as nourishing as meat, and if mixed with starchy food (such as rice) it should be easily digested. Allow 1 to 1½ oz. cheese for each person.

MACARONI

This requires cooking as follows: Boil some water, add the macaroni and a little salt, and cook for from 20 minutes to 1 hour, according to kind. When quite tender, drain and use.

OATMEAL

The remains of cold very stiff porridge can be sliced, seasoned, dipped into coating batter and fried. Serve with fried onion rings and tomato sauce.

PEAS

See Pulses, page 130. Peas may replace lentils or haricot beans in any of the recipes given under those headings.

RICE

Unpolished rice is cheaper and more nutritious than polished. The two kinds of rice in general use are Carolina and Patna. The former is better for milk puddings and rice borders, and the latter for curry, as the grains are not so inclined to stick together. There is much difference of opinion as to the best method in which to boil rice for curry.

The following gives a good result: Wash ½ lb. Patna rice (more or less, as required) in several waters. To do this put the rice in a deep bowl or jug, and cover it with cold water. Stir; the grains will sink to the bottom, and the water can be poured

F

off. Repeat this until the water is clear and clean. Have
ready a large saucepan containing plenty of rapidly boiling
water, add salt (2 tablesp. to the gallon) and a squeeze of lemon.
Boil the rice in this for 10 to 12 minutes until the grains are
tender but not squashed. Invert a sieve and drain the rice
through this. The rice water should be kept for soup, sauces, or
laundry purposes. Wash the rice thoroughly in cold water,
drain well, and either (i) spread on a cloth, turn the edges of the
cloth over it and place on a plate over boiling water. Dry for
about 1 hour, turning the rice over frequently with a fork.
When ready it should be hot and every grain dry and separate;
or (ii) put a sheet of unprinted paper on a baking tin and turn
the rice on to this. Then put it in a cool oven to re-heat and
dry off. Shake it, or carefully turn it occasionally without
breaking the grains. This process will take at least ½ hour.

SWEET CORN

This, known as Bootas, Mealies, Maize, Indian Corn, can be
grown quite successfully in England. Boil the heads whole for
20 to 30 minutes, leaving one outer covering of leaf. Sprinkle
with butter, salt, and pepper, and hand oiled butter with them.

OR, after boiling roast them for a few moments before a
clear fire before serving.

For ordinary English use, sweet corn is bought in tins.

ARTICHOKES AU GRATIN (4 or 5 people)

1 lb. Jerusalem artichokes.　1 pt. good cheese sauce made with 1 pt. white
sauce and 3 oz. grated cheese.

Cook and strain artichokes. Put into au gratin dish and pour
sauce over. Sprinkle well with grated cheese and a few breadcrumbs and bake till brown. Serve hot.

N.B. Any kind of root vegetable or pulse or cauliflower or
vegetable marrow is nice served in this way.

BAKED BEANS (5 or 6 people)

½ pt. butter or haricot beans.	2 oz. fat.
3 or 4 tomatoes.	3 or 4 small onions.
	Salt, pepper.

Wash and soak the beans well. Stew till just tender. Put
into a casserole with alternate layers of the other ingredients,

and cook in the oven till all is tender, adding just enough stock to cover.

BEAN CUTLETS

Follow the recipe for Lentil Cutlets, substituting beans.

*BEAN TIMBALE (5 or 6 people)

1 lb. cooked beans.	1 teasp. chopped
2 oz. butter.	parsley.
2 eggs.	Seasoning.

Sieve the beans while hot. Add the butter, parsley, and seasoning, and lastly the beaten eggs. Put into a well-greased mould, cover with a greased paper, and steam for 1 hour. Turn out and serve with tomato sauce. This timbale may be baked for 40 minutes in a hot oven if preferred.

BURMESE CROUTONS

4 oz. of rice.	4 oz. of cheese, grated.
5 tomatoes.	1 oz. of butter.
1 teasp. of curry powder.	Salt and pepper to taste.

Boil the rice and strain it. Melt the butter in a saucepan, put in the tomatoes, scalded, peeled, and cut into slices. Then shake in the curry powder and cook gently ten to fifteen minutes. Add rice, cheese, and seasoning. Mix thoroughly, making the mixture very hot, stirring all the time. Heap the mixture on slices of toast, and serve on a fireproof dish with a little cheese sprinkled on the top. Grill or bake to a rich brown colour.

CHEESE BOMBS (4 people)

2 eggs.	Spinach.
2 oz. breadcrumbs.	1½ gills milk.
½ pt. white sauce	2 oz. grated cheese.
for coating.	Seasoning.

Beat the eggs well, add the milk, and pour these over the crumbs. Soak well, then add the cheese and seasoning. Pour into small greased moulds. Cover these with greased paper and steam for 30 minutes, or until firm on the top. Turn them out on to a bed of spinach. Pour the sauce over them and decorate to taste.

CHEESE D'ARTOIS (5 or 6 people)

¼ lb. of puff pastry.	1 oz. butter. 1 egg.
2 oz. Parmesan cheese.	Salt, pepper, and cayenne.

Roll the pastry thinly and divide equally. Beat the egg and

add to the cheese, salt, pepper, and cayenne. Add the butter (melted). Spread this mixture on one half of the pastry. Wet the edges and place the other half over it. Press the edges, brush over with a little beaten egg and mark across in figures. Bake in a quick oven and divide where it is marked.

CHEESE PATTIES (4 people)

Cheese Filling

1 gill of milk.	Cayenne and salt.
1 oz. of flour.	2 oz. grated cheese.
1 oz. of margarine.	1 egg.

Line about 8 patty tins with 4 oz. short or flaky paste. Make a thick white sauce with the margarine, flour, and milk. Add salt, pepper, and cheese, reserving a little cheese for decoration. Cook the mixture till the cheese is smooth. Allow it to cool, add the yolk of the egg, mix well together and put into the pastry. Bake till firm. Decorate with white of egg stiffly beaten, and sprinkle with cheese and salt. Bake in a moderate oven till a pale golden colour. Decorate with coraline pepper.

CHEESE PUDDING (I)
(4 people)

2 oz. breadcrumbs.	3 gills milk.
4 oz. grated cheese.	½ oz. butter.
1 egg.	Salt and pepper.

Heat the milk and pour it over the crumbs. Allow to soak, add beaten egg, cheese and seasoning and stir in the butter in small pieces. Sprinkle with cheese and bake till set and golden brown.

*CHEESE PUDDING (II)
(4 or 5 people)

1 or 2 eggs.	¾ pt. milk.
3 oz. grated cheese.	4 slices thin bread
Seasoning.	and butter.

Grease a pie-dish and put in a layer of bread and butter, add half the cheese, then the rest of the bread and butter and the last of the cheese. Beat the eggs, add the milk and seasoning. Pour this over the bread and cheese. Leave for 1 hour to stand, then bake in a slow oven for 1 hour till set. Turn out and serve with tomato sauce.

CHESTNUTS WITH SAUCE (4 people)

1 pt. of chestnuts. Cut off the tips and boil for 10 minutes. Then skim and re-cook in sufficient water to cover them until tender. Drain. Fry them in a little butter, and serve with any good sauce poured over, and a green vegetable purée put round them.

See also Chestnut Patties (page 145).

*CORNFLOUR GNOCCI (An Italian Dish)
(4 people)

2 oz. cornflour.	1 pt. milk.
1 oz. fat.	2 oz. cheese.
Seasoning.	

Boil ¾ pt. milk, and mix the cornflour to smooth cream with the remainder. Pour the boiling milk into this, and return to the pan, stirring and boiling gently for 10 minutes. Season and turn on to a wetted plate. When cold cut into squares and pile neatly on a dish. Melt the fat and pour this over, also the cheese, and bake in a quick oven until brown.

*GROUND RICE—MOCK FISH (4 people)

1½ oz. ground rice.	2 yolks of eggs (the
2 oz. grated cheese.	whites boiled hard).
½-2 oz. fat.	½ pt. of milk.
Seasoning.	A dust of nutmeg.

Boil the milk and butter. Stir in the rice and cook till thick. Cool slightly, add the cheese and yolks. Re-cook till the mixture leaves the sides of the pan clean. Cut the whites into flakes and add these. Turn on to a greased dish. When cold shape into cutlets or imitation fillets. Flour, egg, crumb, and fry these. Garnish with fried parsley.

N.B. Chopped parsley may replace cheese, if wished.

INDIAN DAHL (4 or 5 people)

4 oz. lentils.	1 gill thick curry
½ pt. water.	sauce.
2 oz. boiled rice.	1 or 2 hard-boiled
Seasoning.	eggs.

Cook lentils in water till soft and practically all water absorbed. Stir frequently to prevent burning. Mix lentils with curry sauce. Heat thoroughly and dish with border of carefully cooked rice. Garnish with prettily cut egg, lemon, parsley, and red pepper.

LENTILS

See haricot beans, under Pulses (page 130).

LENTIL CUTLETS (4 people)

4 oz. lentils.	1 teasp. ketchup.
½ pt. water.	Pinch ground mace.
1 small onion (chopped).	2 tablesp. ground rice.
¼ oz. fat.	Salt and pepper.

COATING. Egg and crumbs.

Wash lentils and soak overnight. Put in a pan with water, margarine, onion, and seasonings. Cook slowly with lid on for about 2 hours, or until quite soft. Add the ground rice and cook for about 10 minutes till the mixture is of a fairly stiff consistency. Turn on to a plate to cool. When firm divide into 6 pieces and form into cutlet shapes. Egg, crumb, and fry in deep fat till golden brown. Drain and serve very hot with a good sauce.

*LENTIL PATTIES (6 or 7 people)

½ lb. flaky crust.	½ pt. lentils.
2 onions.	Small piece of fat.
Seasoning.	1 teasp. marmite.

Cook the lentils till tender in about 1 pt. of water. Fry the chopped onions. Add this to the lentils with marmite and seasoning. Turn on to a plate. Use when cold. Line some patty pans with the thinly rolled pastry. Three-parts fill them with the lentil mixture. Cover with pastry, and bake 30 minutes.

*LENTIL ROAST (4 or 5 people)

Prepare mixture as for patties, adding 1 large cup of cooked rice or mashed potato, 1 cup of breadcrumbs, and 1 beaten egg. Mix well and season. Bake for 1 hour in a greased cake tin. Serve with marmite gravy, browned potatoes, stewed carrots or other vegetables. If more convenient this may be steamed instead of baked.

LENTIL STEW (4 people)

½ pt. lentils.	1 oz. fat.
4 tomatoes.	1 onion (chopped).
1 teasp. marmite.	1½ gills stock or water.

Salt and pepper.

Fry the chopped onion in the fat till golden brown. Wash and soak the lentils overnight. Add to the onion and toss for a few minutes. Add 3 sliced tomatoes and the stock, and simmer till tender. Dish up, garnish with the last tomato and chopped parsley.

*LENTIL TIMBALES (4 or 5 people)

Follow recipe for Lentil Cutlets. Bake or steam in a greased mould 1 hour. Turn out and pour sauce round.

MACARONI À LA MILANESE (4 people)

2 oz. macaroni boiled and cut in 1 in. lengths.	TOMATO PULP
½ oz. butter.	3 tomatoes.
1 oz. flour.	1 slice onion.
2 tablesp. grated cheese.	1 oz. butter.
1 gill milk.	Salt and pepper.
½ tablesp. cream.	Cook together and sieve when tender.

Make a sauce with the ½ oz. butter, flour, milk, and tomato pulp. Put macaroni into pan. Heat it with half the sauce. Put into au gratin dish, add the grated cheese and cream to the rest of the sauce and pour over. Serve very hot, garnished with parsley.

*MACARONI CHEESE (4 or 5 people)

3 oz. macaroni.	1 teasp. mustard.
2 oz. margarine.	¼ lb. cheese.
1 pt. milk.	2 oz. flour.
Seasoning.	

Cook the macaroni. Strain and rinse with cold water. Make a sauce with the margarine, flour and milk. Boil well. Add the cheese, reserving 1 or 2 tablesp. Season well. Put the macaroni in a greased dish, with alternate layers of sauce, OR, mix macaroni and sauce in pan, pour into dish. Cover the top with grated cheese and a few breadcrumbs. Place small pieces of butter here and there and bake till brown.

Cauliflower and artichokes are excellent treated in the same way.

MACARONI WITH TOMATOES AND CHEESE (4 or 5 people)

½ lb. macaroni.	1 oz. of butter or margarine.
½ lb. tomatoes.	
3 oz. of cheese.	Salt and pepper.

Cook the macaroni in 1-inch lengths. Slice the tomatoes after removing the stems. Grate the cheese, put these ingredients in layers in a gratin dish, adding seasoning. Sprinkle a little grated cheese over the top and add a few raspings and the butter or margarine. Bake in the dish for 10 minutes and serve at once.

NUT CUTLETS (4 people)

2 oz. nuts (any kind).	2 tablesp. tomato pulp or sauce.
1 slice onion.	
1½ oz. plasmon (optional).	1 oz. fat.
	1 teasp. marmite.
2 oz. bread.	Celery. Salt.

Fry the onion and nuts in the fat till brown. Pass these and the bread through a nut mill. Mix together. Add the plasmon. Dissolve the marmite in a little hot liquid and moisten the nuts and tomato pulp with this. Season to taste. Turn on to a plate and form into cutlets. Insert an inch of macaroni. Egg, crumb, and fry in vegetarian fat till brown. Drain, and arrange round a mound of potatoes. Serve with sauce poured round.

NUT AND FRUIT ROLL

¼ lb. nuts blanched and slightly browned in the oven.
1 lb. figs or dates, well washed and dried.
Juice of a lemon.

Chop the nuts and fruit. Mix with the lemon juice and form into a roll. Expose to the air till dry, then cut into slices, and serve with biscuits or for sandwiches.

NUT ROAST (6 or 7 people)

½ lb. ground nuts.	1 egg (optional).
1 onion.	2 breakfast cups bread, OR
1 tablesp. fat.	1 bread and 1 cooked rice or mashed potato.
3–4 tomatoes, skinned and chopped.	1 teasp. marmite mixed with ¼ pt. water.
Salt and pepper.	

Fry the onion, put it with the bread crust and crumb through the nut mill. Mix all the ingredients, adding sufficient liquid to moisten them well. Bake in a well-greased tin 1 hour till browned all over, or form into a round ball and bake 30 to 40 minutes, basting with butter. Serve with bread sauce, marmite gravy, fried potatoes and green vegetables.

*PEAS PUDDING (7 or 8 people)

½ lb. dried peas. | 2 oz. butter.
1–2 eggs. | Seasoning.

Wash the peas and soak them overnight. Tie them in a cloth, leaving room for them to swell. Cook 2 or 3 hours, till tender. Sieve them; add the butter, egg, and seasoning. Form into a ball and tie in a floured cloth. Cook in boiling water 45 minutes. Turn out and serve with a good sauce. This pudding is also a good accompaniment to boiled pork or beef.

*POTATO CHEESE

Bake some large potatoes in their skins. When done, halve them and remove the soft potato. Mash this with milk, seasoning. Replace a little in the half-potato, sprinkle a good layer of cheese over this, add more potato, more cheese, and so on till the skins are full. Put a few fine breadcrumbs and small pieces of butter on the top and bake in a quick oven till brown. Serve very hot. Tomato, cooked macaroni, may be added to this, or with sufficiently large potatoes a small egg may be dropped in raw and covered with cheese and potato and baked.

POTATO SAVOURY (5 or 6 people)

1½ to 2 lb. potatoes. | ½ pt. stock or water.
3 large onions. | 2 oz. nuttolene
½ oz. fat. | Pepper, salt.

Cut up nuttolene and fry slightly in fat. Cut up potatoes into fairly large pieces. Slice the onions. Toss the vegetables in the fat till it is absorbed. Add the stock and seasoning and simmer gently till vegetables are tender. Dish neatly and serve very hot with a garnish of chopped parsley.

POTATO SURPRISES (4 or 5 people)

2 oz. minced mushrooms, cooked chestnuts or cheese. | A little lemon rind.
| A little white sauce.
| Pinch of herbs.
Salt and pepper.

Form this mixture into balls.

Sieve 1 lb. potato, add salt and pepper, and ½ oz. butter and a little egg to bind. Cover each ball neatly with potato without any cracks. Coat with egg and crumb, and fry in hot fat. Garnish nicely. Serve with a good sauce if liked.

*F

RICH MOCK CRAB

¼ lb. cheese.	2 tablesp. vinegar.
4 tablesp. of milk.	1 egg. Salt and pepper.

Grate cheese and place in pie-dish, beat up egg, and add milk, vinegar, salt and pepper. Pour all on cheese. Bake in a very moderate oven until the mixture is of the consistency of thick cream. Spread on hot buttered toast, or pot and serve cold.

RICE BORDER (Hot)

Boil the rice as for curry till tender; drain, but do not dry it. Pack it tightly into a well-greased border mould. Cover with greased paper and stand in a pan with boiling water coming half-way up its sides. Simmer about ¾ hour. Then turn out hot.

*RICE AND CHEESE (4 or 5 people)

3 oz. rice.	2½ oz. grated
1 qt. milk.	cheese.
Seasoning.	

Cook the milk and rice gently in a double pan till thick and creamy. Add the cheese and seasoning. Put in a fireproof dish. Sprinkle with grated cheese, and brown in a quick oven.

*RISOTTO (Italian Recipe)
(4 people)

One onion, chop this finely; 1 oz. fresh butter; add 6 oz. Patna rice, and stir carefully 2 or 3 minutes over gentle heat. Add a pinch of saffron and 1 pt. of stock by degrees. Cover and cook slowly, stirring frequently to prevent burning. When quite soft remove from the fire and add 2 oz. grated cheese. Re-heat for 1 minute, adding a small piece of butter. Serve on a hot dish with grated Parmesan sprinkled over it.

SEMOLINA GNOCCI (4 people)

Follow the recipe for Cornflour Gnocci, allowing 2½ oz. semolina to the pt. of milk.

SUCCOTASH (4 or 5 people)

½ lb. cooked haricot	½ tin sweet corn.
or butter beans.	Seasoning.

Boil these for 20 minutes. Serve on a hot dish with sippets of toast.

*TOAD IN THE HOLE (5 or 6 people)

Place some vegetarian sausages on a greased Yorkshire-pudding tin. Make a pancake batter (see page 230). Pour this over them. Bake in a quick oven for ½ hour. Cut into squares and serve with gravy.

*VEGETABLE PIE (7 or 8 people)

Semi-cook as large a variety of vegetables (tomatoes, haricots, mushrooms, peas, beans, etc.) as possible in good stock. Place these in layers in a pie-dish, adding quarters of hard-boiled egg, etc., to taste, and putting the usual seasoning. Add ½ pt. vegetable gravy made with marmite. Follow the directions for Pies, page 170.

*VEGETARIAN SCOTCH EGGS (6 people)

4 hard-boiled eggs.	Seasoning.
2 oz. lentils.	1½ oz. butter.
1 teasp. chopped parsley.	2½ oz. breadcrumbs.
Grated lemon rind.	1 teasp. chopped thyme.

Cook the lentils with a little onion. Drain and sieve them. Mix them with the other ingredients. Shell the eggs and cover them with a thin layer of the mixture. Egg, crumb, and fry in deep fat. Cut them in half and serve on a border with sauce poured round.

WALNUTS AU GRATIN (5 or 6 people)

4 oz. shelled walnuts.	½ lb. tomatoes.
4 oz. cooked rice.	½ pt. good brown sauce.

Mince the walnuts. Put a layer of rice into an au gratin dish, then a layer of nuts, then a layer of sliced tomatoes. Pour the sauce over. Sprinkle with browned breadcrumbs and heat through. Garnish with slices of heated tomato sprinkled thickly with chopped parsley and put a half walnut on each slice.

YORKSHIRE CHEESE PUDDING (6 or 7 people)

½ lb. flour.	1 egg.
1 pt. milk.	3 oz. grated cheese.
Seasoning.	

Make and bake as for Yorkshire Pudding, page 234, and serve with gravy and vegetables.

IX. PASTRY AND PUDDINGS

Part I

PASTRY

A practical lesson in pastry making is of great value, but if this is not possible, successful results should be obtained by following out the instructions with great care:

There are six chief classes of pastry:

I. Suet crust, suitable for plain boiled puddings.
II. Short crust, suitable for fruit tarts.
III. Flaky paste or rough puff, suitable for meat pies.
IV. Puff paste, suitable for vol-au-vent, patties, etc.
V. Hot water crust, suitable for game or pork pies.
VI. Choux paste.

There are certain variations in pastry making, and not all good cooks agree as to methods, but the following ways are generally accepted and taught.

PASTRY—Class I

SUET CRUST

Beef suet is very much better than mutton suet for cooking purposes.

PREPARATION. Remove any thin or discoloured parts, shred and chop the suet very finely, using a little of the measured flour to prevent sticking. 3½ oz. prepared suet equal 4 oz. fresh suet.

The proportion of fat varies slightly according to the richness of the paste. Those who dislike the taste of suet, or who must study economy, will prefer the smaller amount; the larger gives a lighter and more nourishing result.

PROPORTION. To each pound of flour, allow ¼ to ½ lb. finely chopped suet (dripping may replace suet) and ½ teasp. of salt. Baking powder is allowed in the following proportion: ½ teasp. to the lb. if the ½ quantity suet is used; or 1 teasp. baking powder if the smaller proportion of suet is used, to each lb. of flour. This crust is very much lighter if breadcrumbs are added. Up to ¼ of the flour may be substituted by breadcrumbs. E.g.

| 1 lb. flour (*or* ¾ lb. and ¼ lb. breadcrumbs). | 1 teasp. baking powder. ½ teasp. salt.   4 oz. suet. |

OR

| 1 lb. flour (*or* ¾ lb. and ¼ lb. breadcrumbs). | ½ teasp. baking powder. ½ teasp. salt.   8 oz. suet. |

Cold water must be added for the purpose of mixing. As flour varies so in its absorbent qualities, it is impossible to give an exact amount, but the average is about ¾ gill water to every ½ lb. of flour. More or less must be used as required.

METHOD. (1) Sift the flour and salt into a bowl, adding the baking powder. Sifting serves two purposes: (*a*) removes possible lumps from the flour; (*b*) by separating the particles of flour allows the admission of more air. (The more air there is the lighter will be the pastry. Pastry of this class must be kept very cool. It is then cooked; the heat expands the cold air, thereby forcing the pastry to rise.)

(2) Add the finely chopped suet. If dripping replaces suet it must first be chopped a little, and then rubbed into the flour with the tips of the fingers, until the whole resembles breadcrumbs.

(3) Mix these ingredients thoroughly with a broad-bladed pliable knife (a palette knife, if possible).

(4) Make a well in the centre of the mixture.

(5) Pour practically all the liquid at once into the well, mixing in the flour by stirring rapidly with a knife. The paste must not stick either to the hands or the bowl; it should be light and elastic, and the dough is held lightly and the bowl wiped with it; the basin should look perfectly clean. Should the dough be sticky, dust with flour and knead lightly.

(6) Turn the dough on to a lightly floured board. Shape it with the hands into an oblong, if for a roly poly, or into a round if it is to line a pudding basin.

(7) Roll the pastry, by placing a rolling pin on it and roll with a sharp short stroke straight forwards and then straight backwards. Then lift the rolling pin. Repeat this constantly, flouring the rolling pin lightly as required to prevent the pin sticking to it. Always roll directly forwards and backwards, never obliquely, and always in short strokes, stopping short before reaching the edges. Lift the pastry occasionally to reflour the board and to alter the position of the paste for the

purpose of shaping it. Roll till the paste is rather less than ¼ inch in thickness. Then use, as required:

For **Boiled Beefsteak** or **Fruit Puddings** grease a pudding basin. Before shaping the dough cut off about one quarter of it. Keep this for the lid. Roll both portions into rounds. Line the basin with the larger round, fitting the pastry neatly and without creases to the sides. Quite fill the basin with meat or fruit and add water. If for meats, the basin must be three parts filled with water. Juicy fruits require very little, and for these sugar must be added to taste. Trim the pastry round the outer edge of the basin, damp the edge, and cover neatly with the lid, pressing the edges together. Flour a pudding cloth and tie it tightly over the pudding, keeping the string under the rim of the basin. Take the four corners of the cloth and knot each opposite pair together to act as a handle for lifting the basin in and out of the boiling water. Have ready a saucepan of quickly boiling water. Immerse the pudding in this. Fruit puddings require boiling for two hours; meat puddings take 4 or 5 hours. Steamed puddings are preferable to boiled ones.

For **Roly Poly** roll the paste into an oblong shape. Spread the centre with jam, treacle, etc., leaving the paste bare for ½ inch all round. Damp the bare space. Roll the pudding up, folding the ends as for a parcel. Scald and flour a cloth. Roll the pudding first in a greased paper (to prevent sticking) and then in the cloth. Tie the ends very tightly, quite close to the pudding. Fasten the edge of the cloth with 2 or 3 pins or stitches. Immerse the pudding in boiling water, and boil 1½ hours. When the cloth begins to wrinkle the pudding is cooked. If left longer it would become sodden.

A false bottom or enamel plate should be placed in the saucepan for the pudding to rest on, or the cloth may stick to the bottom and burn.

PASTRY—Class II

SHORT CRUST

The following ingredients will make two large tarts, each sufficient for 6 or 8 people:

½ lb. fat (the fat may be butter, margarine, lard, or dripping, or a mixture of any of these).
1 lb. flour. Cold water for mixing—about ¼ pt. A pinch of salt.

Rub the fat into the flour (see Suet Crust (2); dripping replaces suet), add the salt. Mix these ingredients well together, then add only sufficient cold water to mix the whole. Less water is needed for short crust than for suet crust, but for the reasons explained under the latter an exact amount of water cannot be given.

PLAINER SHORT CRUST

SUITABLE FOR APPLE DUMPLINGS, OPEN JAM TARTS, ETC.

Six ounces fat to the pound of flour; in this case 1 teasp. of baking powder must be added as for Suet Crust.

SWEET SHORT CRUST

Recipe (1) 4 oz. flour, 2 to 3 oz. fat, 1 teasp. castor sugar, a little beaten egg to mix.

Recipe (2) PÂTE FONCE. 4 oz. flour, 2 oz. butter (1 oz. may be used), 1 oz. castor sugar, 1 yolk of egg, 1 dessertsp. of orange flour water.

Recipe (3) SWISS TARTLETS or FLEUR PASTE. 6 oz. flour, 3½ oz. butter, ½ teasp. castor sugar, yolk of egg and dessertsp. of water, a few drops of lemon juice or rum.

METHOD FOR ALL. Rub the fat into the flour. Add the sugar, mix well. Bind the mixture with the egg and a little water beaten and added together, according to each recipe. Roll the paste once to the desired shape.

This paste can be used to line 'FLEUR' RINGS. These are shallow rings used for making flat open tarts, which, when baked, are covered with cooked fruit arranged in neat layers, and often covered with jelly.

A good variety of other suitable fillings are given. See page 193.

THE BAKING OF SHORT CRUST

The oven must be cooler than for puff paste. (See Puff Paste, Baking, page 171.) If the top shelf of the oven is right for puff paste, a lower, and therefore cooler, shelf will be right for a tart.

TO LINE A PIE-DISH WITH PASTRY

Damp the edge of the pie-dish and line the whole with pastry, then cut out the part that covers the bottom of the dish—this would become sodden in the cooking from the moisture in the mixture which is to fill the dish—and decorate the edge prettily.

TO LINE DEEP PATTY PANS, etc., WITH PASTRY

Fit the paste, thinly rolled, to the sides. Prick it here and there and press on greased paper, greasy side downwards, closely, all over the inside of the paste. Fill this up with rice, crusts of bread, etc. Bake the cases, and when done at the edges and firm, remove the greased paper and crusts and just re-cook the case to dry the centre. It is then ready to be filled. This is called ' Baking Blind'.

TO LINE TINS FOR TARTLETS

Roll either flaky or short crust to about one-eighth inch in thickness. Cut into rounds one size larger than the patty pans and line them. These may be filled at once with a suitable filling: jam, raw cheesecake mixtures, etc.; or if they are to be filled with cooked mixtures it is often better to cook them first, as the pastry will then be light all through and not sodden. In this case ' bake them blind ' (see previous paragraph).

FRUIT TART (SHORT CRUST)

(1) Fill a pie - dish well with fruit; if rhubarb, it must be washed, and cut into neat lengths; if gooseberry, the fruit is washed; if apple, peel, core and cut the fruit into neat slices, and so on.

(2) Add sugar to taste, and sufficient water to allow of some juice in the pie—juicy fruits require little or no water.

(3) Roll the crust to the shape of the pie-dish, but slightly larger. The crust must be about $\frac{1}{4}$ inch thick.

(4) Measure across with a knife to judge the size of the top and cut the crust to one size larger than this.

(5) From the remaining paste cut strips wide enough just to cover the rim of the pie-dish.

(6) Damp the rim and lay these strips on.

(7) Damp these strips.

(8) Cover the fruit with the crust, pressing the edge of the crust to the strips.

(9) Decorate the edge tastefully.

(10) Bake the tart in a moderately heated oven. The pastry will require 20 to 30 minutes' cooking, and at the end of this time it should be of a golden brown colour. If raw fruit is used it may require longer cooking—from 40 minutes to 1 hour. Should there be any danger of burning, cover the paste with a greased paper.

(11) Before taking the tart out of the oven slip knife between the pastry and dish and test the fruit and make sure it is tender. If the tart is to be eaten cold, raise the paste gently from the dish at both ends to let the steam escape.

(12) Serve with fine castor sugar sifted over the top.

Tarts may be made of raw fruits (strawberries, etc.) as follows: Fill a pie-dish closely with crumpled kitchen paper. Cover this with pastry, and bake it till the pastry is cooked. Remove this crust carefully, throw away the paper, fill the dish with fruit, and replace the cooked lid.

OPEN TARTS (See also other Recipes)

For these a shallow oval or round tin is required. Grease this, place a strip of paste round the edge, then cover the tin with a round of paste. Decorate the edges and fill with jam, treacle, and breadcrumbs, etc., as required.

SMALL TARTLETS or PATTY PANS

For these roll the paste to about one-eighth of an inch in thickness. Strips of paste are not put under the edges of patty pans. (See recipes of Tartlets, pages 188 and 193–196.)

PASTRY—Class III

FLAKY PASTRY

8 oz. sifted flour.	Pinch salt.
6 oz. lard and margarine together.	Not quite 1 gill cold water.

Divide fat into four, rub in quarter. Mix to elastic dough with cold water. Roll into oblong strip $\frac{1}{4}$ inch thick. 'Flake' on quarter fat in small pieces over two-thirds of the pastry. Dust lightly with flour. Fold in three, taking care to ensure alternate layers of pastry and fat. Seal edges and turn halfway round. Roll. Repeat till all fat is used. Repeat till pastry is perfectly mixed (five rollings at least). If possible set aside in a cold place between rollings, especially in hot weather and after last rolling. Use as required. This pastry needs a hot oven, 450° to 475° F. at first.

ROUGH PUFF PASTRY

½ lb. flour.	Pinch salt.
6 oz. fat.	½ teasp. lemon
Cold water.	juice.

Sieve flour and salt into bowl. Add fat cut in pieces in flour to the size of a walnut. Mix with lemon juice and cold water to elastic dough. Roll and fold 4 times as for flaky pastry. Use for meat pies, patties, etc.

N.B. Excellent pastry can also be obtained by using the above ingredients and following exactly the method given for Puff Paste.

FOR PIES

The success of a pie depends (1) on the crust (if for a hot pie this may be made of short crust, but if for a cold one, a good puff or flaky pastry should be made); (2) the contents, which must be judiciously blended; (3) the seasoning; (4) the jelly or gravy.

There are two kinds of pies: ORDINARY PIES; RAISED PIES. Raised Pies come under Class V. For Ordinary Pies use Flaky or Rough Puff Pastry.

(1) THE CRUST. About ½ lb. pastry should be allowed for a pie for 7 or 8 people. Roll the pastry about ⅜ inch thick, and cut it out rather larger in size than the top of the pie-dish to be used. From any paste left over, cut strips rather wider than the rim of the pie-dish, and lay these on the moistened rim.

When the pie is full of the meat, lay the crust on, pressing the edges to the paste which covers the rim, and trim off neatly.

Puff paste needs no decoration to the edges, as it should rise in its own flakes.

For flaky paste the edges of the crust should be tapped with the edge of a sharp knife to represent the leaves of a book—this is called 'flaking'. The pie may also be scalloped. This is done by holding the paste with the left thumb and, with a knife, drawing the edge at regular intervals towards the centre, so rounding the pastry. Decorate the top, making a hole in the centre, and brush the surface, but not the edges, with beaten egg. Bake at first in a hot oven to ensure the rising of the pastry, then decrease the heat (placing the pie on a lower shelf), and, if the pastry seems rather dark in colour, cover with a greased paper.

The minimum time for a small pie containing 1 lb. meat would be 1½ hours. To time correctly, allow an extra 30 minutes for each lb. of meat after this.

(2) THE CONTENTS OF THE PIE. Beef, mutton, poultry, game, rabbit, pigeons, and any vegetables; also oysters, hard-boiled egg, mushrooms, olives, sausages or quenelle meat may all go into pies, either mixed or separately, in the proportions desired to suit individual taste. If vegetables are put in, they should be partly cooked first. Game, rabbits, pigeons, etc., should be cut into neat joints, whereas solid meat, beef, mutton, etc., should be cut into little strips about 2 to 3 inches long, $\frac{1}{4}$ inch thick and 1 inch wide. These should be beaten, dipped into seasoned flour (if a thick gravy is required) and rolled up with a small piece of fat, and any special flavouring (e.g. kidney in beefsteak pie) put inside each roll.

If the pie is to be filled with a clear jelly, SEASON the rolls of meat with salt, pepper, and, if liked, a squeeze of lemon, but avoid the addition of any flour, which would cloud the jelly.

The meat must be lightly packed into the dish to allow plenty of space for the gravy or jelly.

(3) SEASONING. The usual proportion will be $\frac{1}{2}$ teasp. of salt and $\frac{1}{4}$ teasp. of pepper to each lb. of meat. If a thick gravy is required, the above quantities should be mixed with a dessertsp. of flour, and into this mixture each piece of meat is dipped before being rolled.

(4) GRAVY OR JELLY. After filling the pie with the meat add water until it can just be seen between the meat.

After the pie has been baked, more gravy must be added at once, through the hole in the centre. If a hot pie, add any well-seasoned stock or gravy; or, for a cold one, add any clear strong jellied stock, just melted and seasoned, or, if no jellied stock is available, add $\frac{1}{4}$ oz. gelatine to each $\frac{1}{2}$ pt. stock and dissolve this.

PASTRY—CLASS IV

PUFF PASTE

PROPORTIONS. Equal quantities of fat and flour (the fat in this case should be butter, if this is possible—Vienna or Hungarian flour should also be used). Cold water for mixing. A yolk of egg may be added if wished in hot weather, and a squeeze of lemon juice makes the paste more digestible But the paste is lighter if these are omitted.

A small quantity of puff paste goes a long way, and for patties for 4 to 6 people, 4 oz. fat and 4 oz. flour are sufficient.

THE BAKING IS IMPORTANT. The oven must be hot, about

450° to 475° F. To test heat without a thermometer, sprinkle some flour in a tin. If it is golden brown in three minutes the heat is right. If it browns more quickly it is too hot, and if more slowly, the puff paste would be tough and heavy, as the fat would melt out of it.

METHOD:

(1) Sift the flour and add a pinch of salt. Mix well.

(2) Make a well, and add sufficient cold water to obtain a paste as described in Suet Crust.

(3) Knead this slightly till the whole is smooth and even.

(4) Roll the paste into an oblong with straight, even ends.

(5) Press the butter in a cloth to remove any water it may contain, and make it into an oblong just less than half the size of the rolled paste.

(6) Place the butter on one half of the paste, and fold the other over, joining the edges carefully all round.

(7) Place the paste on the board, so that the fold comes to the left hand, and the open edges face one.

(8) Flour the board, using a brush if possible, lightly flour the paste, and with the rolling pin seal these open edges gently.

(9) Press the paste with the rolling pin in several places to divide the air that has been enclosed by folding the paste over the butter.

(10) Roll the paste to a long straight strip, following the method of rolling described for Suet Crust. $\frac{1}{4}$ lb. of flour, with $\frac{1}{4}$ lb. butter enclosed, should be rolled to about the length of an ordinary pastry board.

(11) Fold the paste exactly into three.

(12) Turn it to have the open ends facing one again, and again press the edges, divide the air by pressing the paste in several places, and roll thinly, once more keeping the paste a good oblong shape with even ends.

(13) Repeat this, folding the paste in three, pressing and rolling it until in all the process has been performed six times.

It is better not to do this all at once. Repeat the process three times; then leave the paste to cool and to get firm for at least 15 minutes, and preferably for 1 hour or more. Three more rolls may then be given, and the paste should be left before the final roll, as the colder the paste the more the air expands with heat, and the lighter will the result be.

(14) After the final roll the paste is ready for use and should then be shaped as required.

FOR PATTIES

Roll the paste to about ½ inch in thickness. Cut it into rounds with a 2 or 2½ inch cutter. Mark these again in the centre, cutting only half through the paste with a smaller cutter. Lay these rounds on a baking tin, and bake them in a good oven for about 15 minutes.

When done, carefully remove the centre portion. The patties are then ready to be filled with any good mixture. The top part of the centre may be kept as a lid and used, or separate ones may be baked from thin pastry cut into rounds with a cutter just a shade bigger than the small cutter used for marking the centres. If this is done, the lids will fit exactly, as the paste shrinks in cooking.

VOL-AU-VENTS

These are made exactly like patties, but the paste is rolled out to nearly ½ inch in thickness and cut into one large round or oval, the centre being marked with a smaller cutter, leaving a rim of about 1 inch wide.

If a very high vol-au-vent is needed, two ovals or rounds of pastry may be cut and the centre of one stamped right out. When both are baked, this one can be fixed on to the other, but this is not usually necessary.

For jam puffs, or for lining small patty pans, puff paste need not be rolled more than ⅛ inch thick, as it should rise so much.

PASTRY—Class V

HOT WATER CRUST

Pork and Game pies come under the description of Raised Pies, and a special crust made with hot fat is the usual one.

GAME PIE

For Game pies special moulds are advisable; these are high, circular or oval moulds and open on a hinge, and they are made of metal. For about 3 lb. meat, 1 lb. flour will be required for the paste. This must be rolled to about ¼ inch in thickness, and the paste is carefully lifted and lowered into the greased mould and then pressed to fit the mould exactly inside.

For the filling of game pies, about an equal quantity of solid meat (joints of game, etc.) and meat farce should be used. For the meat farce, any good quenelle meat, or minced meat, would do.

A layer of the farce must be pressed around the bottom and sides of the paste with the hand, which is constantly dipped in cold water.

Next add a layer of the solid meat, together with hard-boiled egg, truffle, oyster, etc., and then another layer of farce, and so on till the pie is filled.

No extra water or stock should be used except what drips from the hand during the filling process.

When the mould is full, cut the lining crust off neatly with scissors and cover the pie with a top crust, wetting the edges of both and pressing them together. Trim with scissors. Brush the crust with water, and then decorate ornately. No hole should be made.

TIME. 2 hours would bake a small pie containing 1 to 1½ lb. of meat, and for each lb. over this amount allow 50 minutes.

The pie should be covered with greased paper throughout the baking.

When quite cold cut off the top crust with a sharp knife and fill up with a strong, well-flavoured stock that will jelly. Allow this to set, and cover the surface with finely chopped aspic. Then replace the cover.

The pastry of game pies is not usually eaten.

*PORK PIE (7 or 8 people)

1 lb. flour.		1½ lb. pork trimmings.
4–6 oz. lard.		½ pt. strong stock.
1 teasp. salt.	PASTRY.	¼ oz. gelatine added to stock
1¼ gills milk or		if necessary.
water.		Seasoning.

1 yolk of egg, if liked (worked into paste after mixing).

PASTE. Boil the lard and milk. Add this to the mixed salt and flour. Knead well and keep warm.

Cut the meat into small dice, mixing it with ½ teasp. salt and ¼ teasp. pepper, or less to taste.

Work the paste with the hands, and knead it to the desired shape, moulding it to take the form of a straight-sided basin, and leaving sufficient paste to form a lid.

Fill with the seasoned meat, adding 3 tablesp. of stock. Cover with a lid, trim the edges with scissors and decorate neatly.

Make a hole in the centre of the pie. Bake for at least 2 hours, covering the pie with greased paper.

When cooked and cold, fill up the pie with a jellied stock (melted), pouring this in with a funnel through the hole in the centre.

N.B. A raised veal and ham pie can be made using filling given on page 199.

PASTRY—Class VI

CHOUX PASTE

For éclairs, cream buns, profiteroles, and for a certain class of 'beignet soufflés', i.e. a kind of fritter. The best known examples of the latter class are Cheese Aigrettes (page 281) and Austrian Fritters (page 177). Profiteroles are small cream buns, the choux paste being forced into neat heaps instead of into strips as for éclairs.

CHOUX PASTE (6 or 7 good-sized éclairs)

Recipes for this vary considerably, but the following is perfectly reliable if rightly made:

¼ pt. water.   1½ oz. butter.   2½ oz. flour.   1 or 2 eggs
(sometimes 1½ eggs suffice).

(1) Boil the water and butter in a saucepan.

(2) Sift some fine Hungarian or Vienna flour, and add it all at once to the water and butter.

(3) Stir these off the fire until quite smooth, then return to the fire and stir and cook gently till the mixture forms into a ball and leaves the sides of the pan clean. Care must be taken not to let the mixture burn at all.

(4) Remove the pan from the fire. Cool slightly, then add the eggs one by one, beating very thoroughly. If this is not done, the paste becomes too thin. Beat till the mixture is soft, very light, but not really liquid in any degree.

(5) To shape the paste, a forcing bag fitted with a plain or fluted nozzle will be required. These can be obtained at any good stores. The bags are often made of a waterproof material, and, if so, must be washed in cold water; otherwise bags of

thick stout close material serve the purpose admirably. These may be washed in the ordinary way, soaking them first in cold water.

(6) Fill the bag about one-third full, putting the mixture close to the nozzle. Gather the top in the right hand and twist it, so forcing the mixture out—the left hand meanwhile steadying the bag and holding the nozzle.

(7) Grease a tin. For éclairs force the paste out into straight strips about 3 inches long. Have a knife standing in hot water, and cut off the paste with this when the strip is sufficiently long.

(8) For profiteroles, cream buns, etc., hold the bag absolutely upright at right angles to the tin, and force a small heap on to the tin. To complete each heap, instead of cutting the paste, press the forcer slightly downwards, giving it a quick twist. This will free it.

(9) Bake choux paste in a moderate oven for about 20–30 minutes, until quite crisp and light in weight. Éclairs are usually iced (see Icings, page 342), but if a glaze is required on the paste, brush it with beaten egg or milk before baking it. For filling, 1 gill cream will be required.

FLAVOURINGS

These may be added if wished. Example, a few drops of vanilla essence. Very light little cakes for tea or sweets for dinner can be made if small buns or profiteroles are forced on to a deep meat tin, which is then covered with a smaller inverted tin, any cracks between the two being filled with a flour-and-water paste. These are delicious if eaten as soon as possible after cooking. If served as a sweet, dust icing sugar over the tops of them and hand cream with them instead of filling them.

TO FILL CHOUX PASTE

When the pastry is cold, make a small slit in it, remove any damp inside portions should any be there (but if this is so they are not quite perfect), and fill with whipped sweetened cream, etc.

FOR SAVOURIES

Add salt and pepper to the paste. See recipes in XIII, Hors d'Œuvres and Savouries, page 280.

AUSTRIAN FRITTERS (5 or 6 people)

Make some choux paste; place it in a forcing bag with a rose pipe at the end, and force the paste into 2-inch lengths, cut these with a hot knife, and drop them into hot fat. Fry till crisp and golden brown. Only a few must be done at a time, as they swell so much. Serve, sprinkled with sugar, flavoured with vanilla. When cooked, the fritters may, if liked, be brushed with a melted jam or red currant jelly, and rolled in brown chopped almonds, coconut, etc.

PART II

SUET PUDDINGS

These may be grouped into three classes:

    I. Meat puddings with suet crust.

    II. Sweet puddings with suet crust.

    III. Flavoured suet puddings (sweet).

SUET PUDDINGS—Class I

MEAT PUDDINGS WITH SUET CRUST

BEEFSTEAK PUDDING
(6 to 8 people)

1½ lb. beefsteak.	½ teasp. salt.
¼ lb. kidney. ½ lb. flour. SEASONED	¼ teasp. pepper.
2 to 4 oz. of suet. Water. FLOUR	1 dessertsp.
½ teasp. baking powder.	flour.

Prepare the meat and dip it in the seasoned flour (see Contents of Pie, page 171).

Chop the suet, and mix it with the flour, salt, and baking powder. Mix to a dough with cold water. Cut off ¼ for the lid. Roll out the crust. Line a greased quart pudding basin with it. Fill with the meat and half fill with cold water. Damp the edges and put on the cover. Cover with greased paper and steam for 4 to 5 hours.

Any meat pudding is made in the same way.

*Rabbit Pudding. Flavour the rabbit with ham, bacon, and chopped parsley, etc.

Poultry and Game Puddings are excellent.

*CHOPPED MEAT PUDDINGS

These can not only be made by lining a pudding basin with suet crust, filling it with meat, covering it with crust, tying up and boiling, but by the following useful and very economical method:

8 oz. suet crust.	6 oz. (or less) chopped
Sauce. Seasoning.	meat.

Roll the pastry to an oblong about ¼ inch thick. Season the meat, and moisten it with any good sauce. Spread this on the pastry. Moisten the edges, and roll up. Tie in a cloth (exactly like a Roly Poly, page 166) and boil for at least 2 hours. Any raw meat and any vegetables may be used, according to taste.

*SEA PIE (6 or 8 people)

1½ lb. beefsteak.	1 teasp. salt.
1 onion, carrot, turnip.	¼ teasp. pepper.
1 oz. flour.	About 1 pt. stock or water.

CRUST: 6 oz. flour, 1½ to 3 oz. chopped suet, pinch salt, water.

Cut the meat into pieces and the vegetables into dice. Put them in layers into a saucepan, sprinkling with the flour, salt, and pepper, and add the liquid.

Make the crust and roll it 1 inch smaller than the size of the saucepan.

Bring the meat to the boil, then place the crust on to it. Cover closely, and simmer gently for 2 hours. Serve in the saucepan, decorating the handle, and cut the crust into triangular pieces like slices of a cake, or if preferred serve as follows: Cut the crust into triangular pieces, lift on to a warm plate and keep hot. Place the meat and vegetables neatly on a dish, and arrange the crust on the top in its original shape.

THREE-DECKER SEA PIE

Follow the Sea Pie recipe, but cover the crust carefully with peeled potatoes.

Any meat may replace beef.

SUET PUDDINGS—Class II

SWEET PUDDINGS WITH SUET CRUST

*APPLE ROLL

Prepare a suet crust (see Pastry, page 164). Roll it out as if for a Roly Poly. Cover with chopped apples and the grated rind of a lemon; or, if preferred, put a few cloves (3 or 4), sprinkle with ½ cup sugar, damp the edges, and roll up. Tie in a cloth and boil for 2 hours.

OR, the pudding may be baked; if so, place it on a greased tin or fire-proof dish; cover with ½ pt. hot water, 1 tablesp. sugar and 1 oz. fat. Bake in a good oven for 1 hour. Serve with the liquid poured round. Treacle or honey may replace sugar. Other fillings may replace apple.

FRUIT PUDDINGS WITH SUET CRUSTS

See Suet Crust, page 164.

*JAM LAYER PUDDING (Substantial)
(5 or 6 people if made with ½ lb. flour)

Make a suet crust (see page 164). Line a greased pudding basin. Put in a good layer of jam, then a round of crust, more jam, more crust, etc., till the pudding is full. The top must be crust. Tie down, covering with a floured cloth, and boil for 3 hours.

Treacle, or chopped apple and lemon may replace jam.

LEMON CURD ROLL

Follow the recipe for Lemon Roll, spreading the paste with lemon curd.

*LEMON ROLL (5 or 6 people)

½ lb. suet crust.	Rind and juice of 1 lemon.
1 tablesp. flour or corn-flour.	Stoned raisins and dried lemon peel (if liked).
2 tablesp. sugar.	

Roll the paste as for Roly Poly. Mix the flour, sugar, rind, and juice, and spread it with this. Tie up and boil for 1½ hours.
Orange Roll may be made in the same way.

* MINCEMEAT ROLY-POLY

Follow the directions given for Roly-poly on page 166, substituting mincemeat for jam.

* ROLY-POLY

See page 166.

* TREACLE ROLY-POLY

Follow directions for Roly - poly, page 166, substituting treacle for jam and allowing 3 oz. breadcrumbs to mix with each ½ lb. treacle.

SUET PUDDINGS—Class III

FLAVOURED SUET PUDDINGS, SWEET

In making these the following points are of importance:

(1) The suet must be very finely chopped.

(2) Add baking powder; if ½ quantity suet to flour, then ½ teasp. to the lb. of flour; if less suet, 1 teasp. to the lb. of flour.

(3) If breadcrumbs are used instead of all flour—example, ¼ lb. flour, ¼ lb. breadcrumbs, instead of ½ lb. flour, or even 6 oz. flour, 2 oz. breadcrumbs, instead of ½ lb. flour—a lighter pudding results, and less baking powder can be used.

(4) The mixture must not be mixed either too wet or too dry; it should be sufficiently stiff to heap it on a wooden spoon, but it must not be wet and sticky to the touch.

On opposite page is a table of proportions which would give a large variety of puddings.

THE METHOD for making puddings of this sort is as follows:

(1) Mix the dry ingredients thoroughly (should dripping replace suet it must be lightly rubbed into the flour first until the two resemble fine breadcrumbs, and the other dry ingredients then added) in a good-sized bowl.

(2) Make a well in the centre, and into this pour the liquids. If several are added, e.g. eggs, treacle, and milk, add them simultaneously, working the sides gradually in to the centre, and adding more liquid as required. The whole should never be allowed to get lumpy-looking or hard and dry, nor yet too wet.

FLAVOURED SUET PUDDINGS, SWEET

INGREDIENTS	PUDDING			
	PLAIN SUET.	SULTANA PUDDING.	FIG PUDDING.	GINGER PUDDING.
Flour and Breadcrumbs mixed	½ lb. (¼ lb. of each).	5 oz. flour, 3 oz. crumbs.	4 oz. of each.	4 oz. of each.
Suet	3 to 8 oz.	4 oz.	3 oz.	4 oz.
Dried Fruit, etc.	None.	3 or 4 oz. sultanas.	3 or 4 oz. figs.	A few raisins.
Sugar or Treacle.	2 or 3 oz.	2 oz.	2–4 oz. treacle.	¼ pt. treacle.
Milk	To mix (about ½ pt.).	To mix.	To mix.	A little (if needed).
Egg	1 (optional).	1 (optional).	1 (optional).	1 (optional).
Special flavouring	None.	Spice (optional).	None.	—
Baking powder	1 teasp. if only 3 oz. suet is used. Otherwise none.	1 teasp. baking powder.	Bicarbonate of soda ½ teasp.	1 teasp. ground ginger. Bicarbonate of soda ½ teasp.

(3) When well mixed, put the mixture in a well-greased mould or pudding basin.

(4) Cover it with a greased paper.

(5) If the pudding is to be boiled, a floured cloth must cover the paper.

To Boil a Pudding. Place the pudding into rapidly boiling water and take care to keep the water actually boiling.

To Steam a Pudding. This may be done in two ways: (a) in a proper steamer over boiling water; (b) by standing a bowl in a saucepan with sufficient boiling water to come about half-way up the bowl. There must be no risk of the water splashing over the top of the pudding as it cooks. Water evaporates fast, so that a kettle of boiling water should be kept on the fire to refill the saucepan and to keep the water to the right level. It is important to keep the water boiling the whole time.

Points to Remember in Making the Puddings:

(1) The more suet, eggs and fruit used, the richer the pudding.

(2) The more treacle and eggs, the less milk required.

(3) Eggs, if added, must be well beaten.

(4) Baking powder, in the proportion of 1 teasp. to $\frac{1}{2}$ lb. mixed flour and breadcrumbs, must be added if the suet is less than half the weight of the mixed flour and breadcrumbs. Otherwise add $\frac{1}{2}$ teasp. baking powder.

(5) Flour alone may be used in case of need, but breadcrumbs lighten the result.

As will be seen by the table on page 181, any variety of steamed or boiled puddings can be made. For convenience sake, named recipes here follow, but so long as the proportions given in the table are accurately kept to, the recipes may be varied to any extent.

*APPLE PUDDINGS (Small)

(7 or 8 people)

4 oz. flour.	8 oz. finely chopped
4 oz. breadcrumbs.	apples.
4 to 6 oz. suet.	Lemon juice or milk for
2 oz. sugar. 1 or 2 eggs.	mixing, if needed.

Mix the flour, crumbs, apple, sugar, and suet. Add the beaten eggs and lemon or milk if needed. Steam in small dariole moulds covered with greased paper for 1$\frac{1}{2}$ hours. Serve with sweet sauce.

*COLLEGE PUDDINGS (6 or 7 people)

½ lb. flour and breadcrumbs mixed (6 oz. flour, 2 oz. breadcrumbs).

4 oz. chopped suet.	2 teasp. of caramel (if
2 or 3 oz. sugar.	wished).
Grated lemon rind to taste.	2 to 4 oz. cleaned currants.
Milk. 1 or 2 eggs.	½ teasp. baking powder.

Mix the dry ingredients, then add the beaten egg and milk. Steam in small greased dariole moulds, covered with buttered paper, for 1½ to 2 hours. Turn out and serve with sweet sauce.

*CURRANT DUMPLINGS (6 or 7 people)

½ lb. flour.	Pinch of salt.
3 oz. suet.	Milk or water to mix
Currants to taste (1	(about ¼ pt.).
to 4 oz.).	1 teasp. baking powder.

Mix the dry ingredients. Mix to a dough (like suet crust) with the liquid. Roll with floured hands into 16 balls. Drop into boiling water, and boil for 20 minutes in a covered saucepan. Serve with sugar or sweet sauce.

These may also be steamed.

*DATE PUDDING (6 or 7 people)

(I)	(II)
¼ lb. flour.	6 oz. flour.
¼ lb. breadcrumbs.	2 oz. breadcrumbs.
¼ lb. suet.	3 oz. suet.
¼ lb. stoned dates.	4 to 8 oz. stoned dates,
2 tablesp. treacle.	chopped.
1 egg, if liked.	2 tablesp. treacle.
Milk to mix.	Milk to mix.
½ teasp. bicarbonate soda.	½ teasp. bicarbonate soda.

With either recipe, mix the dry ingredients thoroughly. Add the liquid. Put into a greased basin, cover with a greased paper and steam for 4 hours, or cover with a floured cloth and boil for 3 hours.

EQUALITY PUDDING (5 or 6 people)

½ lb. flour.	1 small teasp. bicar-
2 oz. lard or margarine.	bonate of soda dis-
1 tablesp. sugar.	solved in ½ gill warm
1 tablesp. jam.	milk or water.

Rub the fat into the flour. Add all the other ingredients and pour at once into a well-greased basin. Steam 2 hours or longer. Serve with a jam sauce.

FIG PUDDING (5 or 6 people)

4 oz. wheatmeal flour.
2 oz. butter or margarine.
3 oz. breadcrumbs.
Grated rind of ½ lemon.

4 oz. washed and chopped figs.
½ teasp. bicarbonate soda.
1 gill of milk or water.

Rub the fat into the flour. Mix all the ingredients to a soft dough with the liquid. Pour into a greased basin, cover with a floured cloth. Boil for at least 3 hours.

Dates or **Raisins** may replace figs.

FRENCH RICE PUDDING (5 or 6 people)

3 oz. rice.
3 oz. castor sugar.
2 oz. chopped suet.

3 oz. raisins.
1 oz. chopped peel.
2 eggs. 1 pt. milk.

Cook the rice till soft in milk. Add all the other ingredients. Steam in a greased mould till firm (2 hours). Turn out and serve with a good sweet sauce (marmalade).

*GLOUCESTER PUDDING (6 or 7 people)

¼ lb. flour. ¼ lb. suet.
¼ lb. fruit (currants, etc.), or less.
About ¼ pt. milk.

2 oz. sugar.
1 teasp. baking powder.
1 egg (optional).
2 oz. ground rice.

Mix the dry ingredients, moisten with the egg and milk. Put into a greased mould, and boil or steam for 3 or 4 hours.

GOLDEN PUDDING (6 or 7 people)

8 oz. flour (or 6 oz. flour, 2 oz. crumbs).
4 oz. suet.
2 tablesp. golden syrup.
Pinch of salt.

2 oz. sugar.
2 eggs.
Rind and juice of 1 lemon.
½ teasp. bicarbonate soda.

Mix the dry ingredients well, add the beaten eggs and lemon juice. Steam in a greased mould, covered with a greased paper, for 2 to 3 hours. Serve with lemon sauce.

GRETNA PUDDING (5 or 6 people)

4 oz. breadcrumbs.
4 oz. grated suet.
4 oz. brown sugar.
4 oz. flour.

1 egg (well beaten).
½ teasp. bicarbonate soda.
1 tablesp. jam.
About 1 gill milk.

Flavouring to taste.

Mix the dry ingredients, add the egg and jam Steam in a greased mould 3 to 4 hours.

*LEMON PUDDINGS (6 or 7 people)

6 oz. breadcrumbs.	4 oz. sugar.
2 oz. flour.	Grated rind and juice
¼ lb. suet. 1 or 2 eggs.	of 1 lemon.
¼ teasp. bicarbonate soda.	1 gill milk.

Mix the dry ingredients, moisten with the beaten eggs and lemon juice. Boil in a greased mould for 3 hours. Serve with sauce.

*MARMALADE PUDDING (I)
(6 or 7 people)

¼ lb. breadcrumbs.	1 teasp. of baking
¼ lb. flour.	powder.
¼ lb. suet.	1 oz. sugar.
¼ to ½ lb. marmalade.	1 or 2 eggs.

Mix the dry ingredients, beat the egg, add the marmalade to it, and mix the pudding, if necessary adding a little milk. Put into a greased mould, and steam for 3 hours.

*MARMALADE PUDDING (II)
(6 or 7 people)

8 oz. breadcrumbs.	1 or 2 oz. sugar.
¼ lb. marmalade.	4 oz. suet.
2 or 3 eggs.	

Make as in the above recipe. Steam for 3 hours.

*MARMALADE PUDDING (III), Cheap

Follow the first recipe, using soaked bread instead of bread-crumbs (see scraps of bread for bread puddings, page 212), omitting the egg, and adding 1 good teasp. baking powder. Less marmalade may be added too, e.g. 3 oz.

*PLUM DUFF or SPOTTED DOG
(6 or 7 people)

½ lb. flour or flour and breadcrumbs.	½ teasp. baking powder. Milk or water to mix.
¼ lb. raisins or sultanas, figs or dates.	1 to 2 oz. sugar. ¼ lb. suet. Pinch of salt.

Mix the dry ingredients, add the liquid. Form into a roll, tie in a floured cloth and boil for 2 hours. Serve with sweet sauce.

G

PLUM PUDDING (Christmas Pudding)
Cheap Christmas Pudding (10 or 12 people)

½ lb. breadcrumbs.	1 grated nutmeg.
½ lb. flour.	½ teasp. salt.
¼ lb. moist sugar.	1 pt. milk or beer.
1 lb. raisins (stoned).	3 eggs (these may be
1 lb. currants and sul-   omitted).
tanas (cleaned).	Rind and juice of 1
1 lb. chopped suet.	lemon.
½ lb. mixed peel.	4 oz. chopped almonds.

Make as Ingoldsby, below.   Boil or steam for 10 hours.

Ingoldsby Plum Pudding (about 20 people)

1 lb. breadcrumbs.	16 eggs.
1 lb. flour.	½ lb. almonds, blanched and
2 lb. suet (finely chopped).	coarsely chopped.
2 lb. currants and sultanas	Grated rind of 2 lemons.
(mixed and cleaned).	1 whole grated nutmeg.
2 lb. raisins (stoned).	¼ oz. mixed spice.
½ lb. candied peel.	¼ teasp. salt.
1 lb. sugar.	4 wine-glasses of brandy.

(This quantity makes 3 large puddings or 5 or 6 small ones.)

Mix the dry ingredients very thoroughly, add the very well-beaten eggs and brandy.   Place in greased bowls, which must be filled without pressing the mixture down too much.   Cover with greased paper, then with a floured cloth.   Boil for 7 hours the first day.   Then store the puddings.   Before serving, boil each one again for 3 hours.   This is an excellent pudding and keeps splendidly.

(Fewer eggs may be used if necessary, in which case mix with beer.)

Scotch Plum Pudding (Cheap)
(7 or 8 people)

½ lb. suet, chopped.	½ grated raw carrot.
½ lb. mashed potato.	¼ lb. flour.
¼ lb. sugar.	1 lb. mixed raisins,
½ grated nutmeg.	currants, peel, etc.

Make as Ingoldsby, above.   Boil or steam for 7 hours.   This pudding does not keep well.

*PRUNE-CAPPED PUDDING (7 or 8 people)

10 oz. breadcrumbs.	1 tablesp. wine or brandy.
4 oz. finely chopped suet.	1 lemon (juice and grated
8 oz. castor sugar.	rind).
1 egg (well beaten).	

Mix the dry ingredients well, add the egg, wine and lemon juice. Mix and place in a greased basin, the top of which has been lined with stewed prunes. Steam for 2 to 3 hours.

*RICHER SUET PUDDING (5 or 6 people)

4 oz. breadcrumbs.	1 well-beaten egg.
2 oz. flour.	1 teasp. baking
3 oz. suet.	powder.

About ¼ pt. milk.

Mix the dry ingredients, and add the well-beaten egg and sufficient milk. Steam in a greased bowl for 2½ hours.
(Excellent. It should be as light as a sponge.)

*SIX CUP PUDDING (7 or 8 people)

1 cup of jam.	1 cup of raisins (these
1 „ breadcrumbs.	may be omitted).
1 „ flour.	½ teasp. bicarbonate of
1 „ chopped suet.	soda, dissolved in milk.
1 „ milk.	1 tablesp. sugar.

Mix the dry ingredients. Add the soda in the milk last. Mix thoroughly, and steam for 3 or 4 hours, placing the bowl in a saucepan with water coming half-way up its side.

OR, place the jam in the bowl first. Mix the other ingredients and pour them on to the jam. Cook as above.

SNOWDEN PUDDING (5 or 6 people)

3 oz. chopped suet.	2 tablesp. marmalade.
4 oz. breadcrumbs.	2 eggs.
1 oz. ground rice.	Pinch of salt.
4 oz. raisins.	Grated lemon rind.
2 oz. brown sugar.	A little milk.

Grease a 1 pt. mould. Decorate it with a few stoned raisins. Mix all the ingredients well to a dropping consistency. Steam for 2 hours or longer. Serve with marmalade sauce.

*SPONGE PUDDING (5 or 6 people)

½ lb. flour.	1 egg (optional).
2 oz. lard or dripping.	¼ pt. milk.
2 oz. margarine.	1 teasp. baking powder.

2 to 4 oz. brown sugar.

Rub the fat in the flour. Add the baking powder and sugar. Mix well. Add the milk, and either bake in a greased pie-dish for 40 minutes, or steam for 2½ hours.
Serve with jam or jam sauce.

SYRUP SPONGE PUDDING (5 or 6 people)

½ lb. flour.	½ teasp. bicarbonate
Pinch of salt.	of soda.
¼ lb. suet.	2 teasp. ground
1 egg (well beaten).	ginger.
1 gill syrup.	1 gill milk.

Follow usual method for suet puddings. Cook for 2 hours and serve with syrup sauce. This recipe is equally good if the egg is omitted.

PART III

SWEET PUDDINGS WITH SHORT CRUST

ALMOND TARTLETS (4 or 5 people)

2 oz. almonds.	½ teasp. lemon
1 oz. butter.	juice.
1 oz. sugar.	A little grated
½ egg.	lemon rind.

SHORT CRUST PASTRY. Made with 2 oz. flour, etc.

Blanch the almonds and chop them finely. Cream the butter and sugar and beat in the egg with the almonds, lemon juice and rind. Make pastry and roll it very thinly, and use to line about six greased patty tins. Half fill the tins with the mixture. Bake in a hot oven till the pastry is set, then reduce heat and cook more slowly for 30 to 40 minutes till firm and a pale brown colour.

APPLE AMBER (4 to 6 people)

2 lb. apples, peeled and sliced.	Grated rind and juice of lemon.
2 oz. sugar (or to taste).	½ oz. to 1 oz. butter (or
1 or 2 eggs.	more up to 3 oz.).

Line a pie-dish or flan-ring with 4 oz. short crust. (See directions, page 167.) Prepare the following:

Cook the apples with the rind and juice of lemon, then sugar and butter. If necessary add a VERY little water. When quite tender rub this through a hair sieve. Add the egg yolks and put the mixture into the lined pie-dish. Bake till the pastry is cooked and the mixture firm. Beat the whites to a stiff froth, fold in 1 tablesp. of castor sugar, and pile this on the pudding.

Sprinkle more castor sugar over the top and, if liked, put a few almonds here and there. Bake till crisp and of a fawn colour in a very cool oven. Serve hot or cold. N.B. Other fruits can be used when in season (watery fruit requires an extra egg yolk).

*APPLE DUMPLINGS (5 or 6 people)

Allow 1½ oz. short crust for each apple.	Cloves or nutmeg, if liked. Sugar to taste.

Core the apples, then peel them. Roll the pastry to ¼ inch in thickness, and cut into rounds. Place a little sugar and a clove inside each apple. Place one on each round of paste, damp the edges and cover neatly. Place on a greased tin and bake in a good oven for about ½ hour, or until the apple is quite soft.

BAKEWELL TART (5 or 6 people)

Line a plate or shallow pie-dish with pastry, put a little fresh fruit such as raspberries or jam on the tart. Cover the fruit or jam with a cake mixture. Bake for 30 minutes and turn out and ice with water icing. Decorate to taste. The cake mixture should be the weight of 1 egg in flour, sugar, and margarine, with ¼ teasp. of baking powder and 1 tablesp. of water added.

BLAKEMORE PUDDING (5 or 6 people)

3 sponge cakes.   Rind and juice of ½ lemon.   2 tablesp. jam.

PASTRY

2 oz. cornflour.	2 oz. castor sugar.
5 oz. flour.	1 yolk of egg.
3 oz. butter.	A little milk.

Rub the cakes through a wire sieve, then mix the crumbs with the jam, the grated lemon rind, and the strained juice.

Sieve flour and cornflour and rub the butter in till like fine breadcrumbs. Add the castor sugar. Mix the yolk with a little milk and with this mix the dry ingredients to a firm dough. Cut in two and knead and roll lightly into two rounds about ¼ of an inch in thickness. Line a greased plate with the pastry. Spread the mixture on this. Damp the edges with water and cover with the second round. Trim, flute, and decorate the edges of the pastry. Further decorate with 4 large leaves made from the trimmings. Brush with white of egg, sift with sugar, and bake in a quick oven about 30 minutes.

CHEESECAKES (6 or 7 people)

½ lb. sugar.	1 lemon.
2 eggs.	2 oz. butter.
Short crust.	½ oz. cake crumbs.

Beat the yolks and sugar till thick and light. Add the rind of lemon finely grated and the juice together with the melted butter. Place these in a bowl over boiling water, add the stiffly beaten whites of eggs, and whisk till all thickens.

Cool. Three-parts fill patty pans, lined with the rough puff paste, to which 1 teasp. of jam has been added. Bake about 20 minutes.

N.B. Use rough puff paste if preferred.

These are for immediate use.

CHEESECAKES, ALMOND

(4 or 5 people)

2 oz. ground almonds.	2 oz. castor sugar.
Whites of 2 eggs.	Jam.

Line some patty pans with pastry. Place on each 1 teasp. of raspberry jam. Beat the whites stiffly, add the almonds and sugar. Mix lightly. Cover the jam entirely with this, and bake 20 to 30 minutes in a moderate oven.

CHEESECAKES, APPLE

(6 to 8 people)

1 lb. apple pulp.	2 to 4 oz. butter.
½ lb. sugar (or less to taste).	3 eggs.
	Rind and juice of a lemon.

Mix the ingredients, and stir them over the fire till the eggs are cooked. Use to fill tartlets.

CHEESECAKES, CURD

(6 or 7 people)

1 pt. of firmly set junket.	½ oz. currants.
2 oz. margarine.	½ oz. cake crumbs.
2 yolks of eggs.	Grated rind of 1 lemon.
½ oz. sugar.	1 teasp. brandy.
	A little nutmeg or salt.

Cut the junket finely and drain very well to remove whey on hair sieve. Cream the butter and sugar. Add eggs, crumbs, and flavouring, then the curd. Fill into patty pans lined with short or fleur pastry and bake in moderate oven.

CHEESECAKES, LEMON

(about 2 lb.)

| ¼ lb. castor sugar. | ¼ lb. butter. |
| ¼ lb. lump sugar. | 4 lemons. 4 eggs. |

Wash and dry the lemons, then rub them with the lump sugar till the sugar is yellow. Squeeze them, and pour the strained juice on to the sugar. Beat the eggs well and put all together into a double saucepan over boiling water. Stir well till the mixture will just thinly coat the back of the spoon. Pour it at once into jars and tie down when cold. This recipe keeps well.

CHEESECAKES, WELSH

(about 12 small cakes)

Line small patty pans with short or puff paste. On this place a small spoonful of jam or marmalade and cover this with a good teaspoonful of Canary Pudding mixture (see page 214).

Dust fine sugar over the top and bake for 20 to 30 minutes in a moderate oven.

CHOCOLATE PIE (5 or 6 people)

¼ lb. breadcrumbs.	2 oz. sugar (or more
¾ oz. bar chocolate (or	to taste).
½ oz. cocoa).	½ teasp. vanilla essence.
½ pt. milk.	3 eggs (2 will do).

A few blanched almonds.

Dissolve the chocolate or cocoa in the milk; pour this over the breadcrumbs. Add the sugar, yolks, and flavouring. Put this into a pie-dish previously lined with short or puff paste. Bake for about 30 minutes, till the pastry is cooked and the mixture firm.

Beat the whites to a stiff froth, add 1 oz. castor sugar, and pile this on the pudding. This is called a meringue. Sprinkle with more sugar, stick the almonds here and there, and bake in a cool oven for about ½ hour or till crisp and golden.

CHOCOLATE TARTLETS (4 people)

½ stick chocolate (¾ oz.).	1 teasp. sugar.
½ gill milk.	1 yolk.
½ teasp. cornflour.	Vanilla essence.
½ teasp. butter.	Pinch of cinnamon.

SHORT CRUST PASTRY. With 1½ oz. flour, etc.
MERINGUE. 1 white, 2 oz. sugar.
DECORATION. Cherries, angelica.

Dissolve chocolate in half the milk, add the cornflour mixed with remainder of milk, and boil till thick. Cool, and stir in rest of ingredients. Line some tartlet tins with the pastry and half fill with the mixture. Place in a hot oven till the pastry is set and the mixture well risen and firm—15 minutes. Pile the meringue on top. Dust with sugar and decorate with cherries and angelica. Dry off in a very cool oven till crisp but not brown (¾ to 1 hour).

COCONUT PUDDING (4 or 5 people)

2 oz. coconut.	2 or 3 eggs.
1 or 2 oz. sugar.	1 to 2 oz. butter or
2 oz. cake or bread-crumbs.	margarine.
	½ pt. milk.

Vanilla to taste.

Infuse the coconut in the milk for ½ hour. Cream the butter and sugar. Add the yolks and cake crumbs. Lastly add the coconut and vanilla. Pour this into a pie-dish lined with pastry. Bake till the mixture is firm and the pastry cooked. Make a meringue (see previous recipe), putting a few cherries here and there if liked. Bake till the meringue is crisp and of a golden colour.

DAUPHINS AU CITRON (12 small cakes)

1½ oz. flour.	1 to 2 oz. butter.
2 oz. sugar.	¼ pt. milk.
1½ oz. citron peel cut into dice.	2 or 3 yolks of eggs.
	Grated rind of 1 lemon.

Line 12 deep patty pans with short crust. Boil the milk. Add the sugar and flour all at once off the fire. Stir till smooth and boil for 3 minutes. Cool, add the butter, and lastly the peel and rind. Three-quarter fill the patty pans and bake for ½ hour. Force a meringue on to the top, dust with sugar, and put in a slow oven till crisp and golden.

DEVONSHIRE TARTLETS (5 or 6 people)

3 oz. sponge-cake crumbs (sieved).	½ gill cream.
	¼ lb. chopped-up apples.
Dust of nutmeg.	2 oz. castor sugar.

Line some patty pans with short or puff paste. Mix the ingredients and place a spoonful on each tartlet, decorate with twisted strips of paste. Brush with egg or milk and sugar, and bake in a moderate oven for about 30 minutes.

FILLINGS FOR FLEUR AND TARTS

For Chocolate Fleur (4 or 5 people)

1½ oz. of margarine.	1½ oz. of cake crumbs.
1 oz. of flour.	
½ pt. of milk.	Yolks of 2 eggs.
1 oz. of almonds.	Vanilla essence.
A little sugar.	1 oz. grated chocolate.

Make a white sauce with the margarine, flour and milk. Stir in the almonds, blanched and chopped, or shredded. Dissolve the chocolate in ½ gill of water over the fire. Mix together the chocolate, white sauce, cake crumbs, sugar, vanilla essence, and yolks of eggs. Bake in a fleur ring lined with pastry. Ornament with meringue made from whites of eggs and 2 oz. of sugar.

For Coconut Fleur (4 or 5 people)

1 oz. of flour.	1 gill of milk.
1 oz. of margarine.	1 oz. of sugar.
2 oz. of coconut.	Vanilla essence.
1 or 2 eggs.	

Make a sauce of the margarine, milk and flour. Add the sugar, coconut, vanilla, and yolk of egg. Mix well and add the white of egg well beaten. Turn into a fleur or open tart and bake till brown (about 30 minutes). When baked glaze with apricot and decorate with pistachios.

N.B. A little apricot ham may be spread on the pastry before filling with the mixture.

For Orange Tart (4 or 5 people)

2 oz. of sugar.	2 eggs.
2 oz. of margarine.	1 tablesp. of sponge-cake crumbs.
2 oranges.	

Cream fat and sugar together. Add the yolks of the eggs.

*G

Mix well and add the grated rind of 1 orange and the juice; add the cake crumbs. Remove the peel from the other orange and divide it. Arrange the sections of orange round the tart and pour the orange mixture over. Bake in a steady oven for 30 minutes. Decorate with a little orange peel and angelica. This tart may also be iced with orange icing if wished, or it may be finished with the meringue made from 2 whites of eggs and 2 to 4 oz. of sugar.

*FRUIT AND MERINGUE TARTLETS

Bake some tartlets blind. Fill them with any nice fruit in season, or with a compote of fruit, well drained free from juice. Pour a little jelly over the fruit (¼ pt. fruit juice, well boiled and reduced, then 1 sheet of gelatine added and dissolved). Make a meringue with 1 white of egg and 2 oz. sugar. Force a rose of meringue (see page 260), or a lattice work of meringue on each tartlet, dust with sugar, and bake in a cool oven till crisp. Serve cold if gelatine is used.

FRUIT TARTS

See page 168.

GOOSEBERRY PUDDING (Baked)

(6 or 7 people)

1 qt. of goose-berries.	1 or 2 eggs.
	Sugar to taste.
½ oz. butter.	¼ pt. breadcrumbs.

Stew the gooseberries in as little water as possible until tender. Sieve them and add the rest of the ingredients. Bake for about 40 minutes in a pie-dish lined with short crust or puff paste.

*ISLE OF WIGHT PUDDING (4 or 5 people)

¾ lb. short crust (made with ½ lb. flour and ¼ lb. fat).	½ pt. treacle.
	2 oz. breadcrumbs.
½ pt. milk.	1 to 2 oz. cleaned currants.

Roll the paste as for Roly Poly (see page 166); spread it with the treacle, currants and crumbs. Roll it up. Place it in a greased pie-dish, pour the milk over, and bake for 1 to 1½ hours.

JAM PUDDING (Baked)

Make 1 lb. short crust. Roll this as for Roly Poly (page 166). Spread with jam. Place in a pie-dish and bake for 1¼ hours.

LEMON CURD (about 1 lb.)

3 lemons.	½ lb. loaf sugar.
¼ lb. butter.	4 yolks of eggs.

Rub sugar over the lemon rind to take off zest. Melt the butter, and add the other ingredients. Cook till the mixture thickens. Pour into small pots and cover like jam.

*LEMON or ORANGE OPEN TART (5 or 6 people)

1½ oz. butter.	1 egg.
1 oz. sugar.	Rind and juice of
1 oz. cake crumbs.	1 lemon.

Line a plate or shallow dish with pastry. Cream the butter and sugar, add the egg and crumbs, beat well, then add the lemon rind and juice. Spread this on the pastry and bake till the pastry is cooked and the mixture golden.

LEMON PIE (4 or 5 people)

3 eggs. 2 lemons.	SHORT PASTRY
¾ pt. milk.	4 oz. flour.
1½ oz. cornflour.	2 oz. fat.
6 oz. sugar.	Pinch of salt.
Pinch of cinnamon.	Cold water.

Line and decorate a pie-dish with pastry and brush it with egg. Cook the cornflour in the milk. Add lemon rind grated, juice, sugar, and beat in the yolks very well. Pour into a dish and bake till the pastry is browned. Whisk whites and pile on top with sifted sugar. Brown.

LEMON PUDDING (Rich)
(5 or 6 people)

4 oz. butter. 4 oz. sugar.	Rind and juice of 2
3 whites of egg and 4 yolks.	lemons.

Line a shallow pie-dish with pastry. Cream the butter and sugar, add the yolks, lemon rind and juice, and beat well. Put this in the pie-dish and bake till the pastry is cooked. Make a meringue of the whites (see page 259) and put this on the top.
Bake till golden in a cool oven.

MANCHESTER PUDDING (5 or 6 people)

½ pt. milk. 2 egg yolks.	3 oz. short or flaky pastry.
2 oz. breadcrumbs.	1 tablesp. raspberry jam.
1 oz. butter. 1 oz. sugar.	2–4 oz. fine sugar ⎱ MERINGUE.
Grated rind of ½ lemon.	2 whites of egg ⎰

Heat the milk, add butter, sugar (1 oz.), lemon rind and beaten yolks. Pour over breadcrumbs and soak. Line a pie-dish (right size) with pastry, decorate and glaze. Put in mixture and bake till pastry is brown and filling set. Spread thinly with jam. Whisk whites stiffly, fold in sugar (meringue). Pile on top, dredge with sugar, and bake till crisp.

*NEWCASTLE PUDDING (5 or 6 people)

Line a pie-dish with pastry. Place a layer of jam at the bottom. Make a mixture as for Canary Pudding (page 214). Add ½ gill milk and cover the jam with this. Bake in a moderate oven for 1½ hours.

RAISIN AND LEMON TARTLETS (4 or 5 people)

3 oz. biscuit crust made of 4 oz. flour, 2½ oz. fat and a little beaten egg.

1 oz. sugar. 1 egg.	Rind and juice of
1 oz. butter.	½ lemon.
1 oz. sultanas.	1 tablesp. sherry.

Cream the butter and sugar well. Add the other ingredients and half fill the prepared patty pans. Bake in moderate oven 20 to 30 minutes.

*SWISS TARTLETS or FLEUR PASTE (6 or 7 people)

6 oz. flour.	3½ oz. butter.
1 oz. sugar.	Yolk of egg.
1 dessertsp. water.	Few drops lemon or rum.

Cream the butter and sugar, work in the other ingredients. Roll the paste, and stamp into flat rounds. Cut narrow strips and roll these into rounds to edge the tartlets. Prick them, brush them with egg, and bake. When cold, cover them with fruit from some good compote, drained free from syrup. Arrange the fruit neatly. (Gooseberries are excellent.)

Reduce 1 gill of compote syrup in which 1½ to 2 leaves of gelatine have been dissolved, to one-half.

Cover the fruit with this, just before it sets. If liked, the paste may be brushed with jam and coated with browned almonds before the fruit is put on it.

The same mixture would make a ' Fleur ' if one of the bought Fleur Rings were used.

SWISS TART PINEAPPLE

Roll the paste and stamp it into one large round. Roll strips for the edge. When cooked cover it with overlapping rounds of pineapple, with banana and cream piled in the centre.

TURNOVERS

* Apple

Cut the paste into squares. Place some sliced apple, sweetened to taste, on one half, damp the edges and fold the other half over. Decorate the edge neatly and bake.

* Banana

Make as for Apple, above. The bananas may be sprinkled with lemon or strawberry jam first.

Gooseberry or other Fruit

Make as for Apple, above.

*UPWEY CAKE (4 or 5 people)

½ lb. flour.	1 heaped teasp. baking
2½ to 3 oz. dripping.	powder.
1 tablesp. brown sugar.	Milk to mix.

Rub the fat into the flour. Add the sugar and baking powder. Mix well. Add just sufficient milk to bind the mixture, which should be rocky. Shape it to a long thin roll, in texture like rock cake mixture. Bake in a quick oven for 20 minutes. It should double its bulk and be well browned in this time. Serve at once with jam, handed separately.

PART IV

FLAKY AND ROUGH PUFF PASTRY

These may be grouped into two classes:

I. Meat dishes with flaky pastry.
II. Sweet puddings with flaky pastry.

FLAKY AND ROUGH PUFF PASTRY—CLASS I

MEAT DISHES WITH FLAKY PASTRY

BEEFSTEAK AND KIDNEY PIE (6 or 7 people)

1½ lb. beefsteak.   ¼ lb. kidney.   ½ lb. flaky pastry.

SEASONED FLOUR
{ 1 dessertsp. flour.
½–1 teasp. salt.
¼–½ teasp. pepper.

Follow the directions given for Pies, page 170, cutting the meat into small strips as described and dipping each one into the seasoned flour. Place on this a small piece of kidney, a tiny piece of fat, and roll up.

GIBLET PIE (6 or 7 people)

2 sets giblets (each set consists of gizzard, liver, neck, and feet of a bird).
1 lb. beefsteak   ¼ lb. flaky pastry.

SEASONED FLOUR
{ 1 dessertsp. flour.
1 teasp. salt.
¼ to ½ teasp. pepper.

Follow the directions given for Pies, page 170.

*RABBIT PIE (6 to 8 people)

1 rabbit.	1 teasp. parsley.
¼ lb. bacon or fat pork.	¼ teasp. thyme.
½ lb. beefsteak (if wished).	¼ teasp. grated lemon
2 hard-boiled eggs.	rind.
½ pt. good stock.	1 teasp. salt.
½ lb. flaky crust.	½ teasp. pepper.

Cut the rabbit into small joints. These may be fried to improve the flavour. Cut the meat (bacon, beef, etc.) into small pieces, and lay these alternately in the pie-dish, sprinkling with the herbs and seasoning. Add the stock. Finish as usual, following the directions for Pies, page 170.

SAUSAGE ROLLS

Roll some puff or flaky pastry rather thinly. Cut this into strips about 3½ by 5 inches. Divide a raw sausage into 4 or 6 pieces and roll to the required shape. Place one of these pieces on to one half of the pastry, damp the edges, fold the other half over, seal the edges neatly.

If larger rolls are needed, the sausages may be semi-cooked (by pricking and baking), left till cold, and then placed whole on the pastry. Brush the tops with beaten egg and cook in a quick oven.

To semi-cook the Sausages. Prick them and fry them until nearly done; or prick them and cook them on a baking tin in the oven. Leave them until cold and then peel them.

N.B. If sausages are divided into 4 or 6 pieces and rolled to the required shape no previous cooking is necessary.

VEAL AND HAM PIES (6 to 8 people)

1½ lb. fillet of veal.	½ teasp. pepper.
½ lb. ham (or ½ lb. bacon).	¼ teasp. grated lemon rind.
2 hard-boiled eggs.	1 teasp. chopped parsley.
2 teasp. salt.	About ½ pt. stock.

Follow the directions for Pies, page 170, rolling the veal, cut as described, and placing dice of the ham in the centre of each roll.

OR, cut the veal into pieces the size of an oyster, cut the ham into dice, and fill the pie-dish with the layers of each, putting the seasoning and herbs between each layer.

FLAKY AND ROUGH PUFF PASTRY—CLASS II

SWEET PUDDINGS WITH FLAKY PASTRY

*BANBURY CAKES (7 or 8 people)

2 oz. cleaned currants.	½ teasp. cake crumbs, nutmeg, spice, lemon juice.
2 oz. stoned raisins.	
2 oz. candied peel.	1 dessertsp. brandy.
2 oz. sugar.	½ lb. puff paste or flaky pastry.
1½ oz. melted butter.	

Mince the currants, raisins, and peel, add the other ingredients and finish as for Eccles Cakes (page 200), but form the pastry into oval shapes.

CORNETS

Roll some puff pastry thinly. Cut it into strips and fold these round and round the cornet tins. Bake in a hot oven for about 10 to 15 minutes. Slip out the tins; brush the cases with melted jam and sprinkle with sugar, chopped nuts, etc. When cold fill with fruit and whipped cream, jam and whipped cream, etc.

*ECCLES CAKES (7 or 8 people)

½ lb. flaky or rough puff paste.	1 oz. chopped candied peel.
¼ lb. cleaned currants.	1 oz. sugar.
Nutmeg & spice to taste.	1 oz. butter.

Roll the paste to ⅓ inch thick and cut into rounds the size of the top of a teacup. Mix the other ingredients and place a spoonful in the centre of each round. Damp the edges and draw them together, forming a ball-like shape. Turn this smooth side uppermost, flatten into a round, cut lightly to mark the top into squares, and to let the currants show, brush with white of egg, sprinkle with sugar, and bake in a hot oven for about 20 minutes.

MINCE PIES

Line some patty pans with puff or rough puff paste. Make mincemeat (see page 392). Place a spoonful of this on the paste, damp the edges and cover with another round of paste. Press the edges together, decorate neatly and bake.

WATERLOO TART (4 to 6 people)

2 eggs.	2 oz. of sugar.
2 oz. butter or margarine.	2 oz. of candied peel.

Line a plate with rough puff pastry. Chop the peel finely, melt the sugar and butter in a small pan, but do not cook it. Add the peel and eggs well beaten, pour the mixture into the plate and bake in a quick oven.

PART V

PUDDINGS

(General, other than Pastries)

These may be divided into eight classes:

    I. Milk puddings.
    II. Milk moulds.
    III. Fruits, stewed, compotes, and moulds.
    IV. Bread puddings, charlottes, etc.
    V. Puddings made from cake mixtures.
    VI. Pudding of the custard variety.
    VII. Fools.
    VIII. Puddings made with yeast.

PUDDINGS (GENERAL)—CLASS I

MILK PUDDINGS

These are really very simple to make, and there is no reason for them ever to vary or fail if the following rules are observed:

(1) Always measure the milk accurately.
(2) Always weigh the grain accurately.
(3) Cook in gentle heat. Long slow cooking is a necessity to swell and soften the grain properly.

The GRAINS usual are: Rice, Sago, Tapioca, Barley, and Barley Kernels, Flaked Oats.

The PROPORTIONS for all milk puddings are the same, namely $1\frac{1}{2}$ oz. grain to 1 pt. milk. But see Methods (3).

The METHODS of making milk puddings are:

(1) Weigh and wash the grain well under several changes of cold water. Large, hard grains should be soaked. Measure the milk into a pie-dish, sweeten it to taste if wished. Add the grain and cook for at least 2 hours in a moderate oven (stir carefully 2 or 3 times after putting in the oven), when the grain should be quite tender, the whole pudding thick and creamy and covered with a golden brown skin.

(2) Place the weighed and washed grain into a double saucepan with the measured milk. Cook this (covered) over gentle heat

for about $1\frac{1}{2}$ to 2 hours, until the whole is thickish and creamy. Sweeten to taste, if wished, and turn it carefully out into a pie-dish and place in a moderate oven for about $\frac{1}{2}$ hour to let a golden brown skin form.

(3) For small grain such as sago, etc. Use $1\frac{1}{2}$ oz. grain to the pint of milk, and add sugar to taste. Bring the milk to the boil in a lined pan that has been rinsed out with cold water. Scatter in the grains, stirring briskly, and continue to stir for about 10 minutes until the grain is semi-cooked and is evenly suspended in the milk. Turn into a greased pie-dish, sweetening to taste, put small pieces of butter on the top and brown in a moderate oven.

SKIM MILK may replace whole milk, and if a small piece of butter is added to replace the cream, the food value is as good as if whole milk was used.

EGGS may be added if required. Follow the second method. Cool the mixture, add the beaten eggs, and bake in a quick oven just to brown the surface.

*Milk Pudding Moulds of Whole Grain. Any milk pudding may be made and moulded and served cold, without the addition of gelatine, as follows:

PROPORTIONS. $2\frac{1}{2}$ oz. grain to 1 pt. of milk. Cook as for second method, i.e. place the grain and milk in a covered double pan and cook for at least 2 hours until the milk is all absorbed and the whole is a thick creamy mass. Then boil fast for a few minutes, stirring. Sweeten to taste, and turn it into a mould rinsed out with cold water. When cold this should be quite set and able to be turned out.

Milk Puddings made of Powdered or Crushed Grain. Examples of these are Ground-Rice and Cornflour puddings (see recipes).

*CHOCOLATE MOULD (4 or 5 people)

$1\frac{1}{2}$ oz. cornflour. | 1 pt. of milk.
1 to 2 oz. sugar. | $\frac{1}{2}$ oz. chocolate.

Dissolve the chocolate in the milk. Then follow the recipe for Cornflour Mould. Cocoa may replace the chocolate; if so, $\frac{1}{4}$ oz. cocoa is sufficient. OR, mix cornflour and cocoa together and follow the same recipe.

*COCONUT MOULD

Follow the recipe for Cornflour Mould, first infusing the milk with 1 oz. coconut. Finish in the usual way. When cold and turned out, sprinkle the top with coconut.

*CORNFLOUR MOULD (4 or 5 people)

1½ oz. cornflour.	Sugar and flavouring
1 pt. milk.	to taste.

Follow the method given for Ground-Rice Pudding, i.e. mix the cornflour to a smooth cream with ¼ pt. milk. Boil the rest, pour part of this on to the cornflour mixture, return all to the pan and boil, stirring for 3 minutes. Pour into a wetted mould. Turn out when cold.

*GROUND-RICE MOULD (4 or 5 people)

PROPORTION. 2½ oz. ground rice to each pt. of milk. Follow the directions for Cornflour Mould, adding sweetening and flavouring to taste. Turn out and serve cold.

GROUND-RICE PUDDING (4 people)

1 pt. milk.	1½ oz. ground rice.
1 oz. sugar.	A strip of lemon rind
1 egg.	or other flavouring.
Small piece of butter.	

Heat 3 gills of the milk in a pan that has been rinsed out with cold water. Mix the grain with the rest of the milk carefully. When the milk is hot, but not quite boiling, pour in the ground rice. Stir and boil for a few minutes. Add butter and beaten egg, pour into pie-dish and brown in quick oven.

N.B. 1. This method applies for use with puddings that are boiled first and for moulds. For very small puddings and moulds mix the grain in the saucepan with a little milk. Add the rest and stir till cooked.

N.B. 2. The appearance is improved if white of egg is kept back, whisked and spread over the pudding, dredged with sugar and browned in a moderate oven.

*HASTY PUDDING (5 or 6 people)

¼ lb. flour.	1½ pt. milk.
Pinch of salt.	1 egg.
1½ oz. sugar.	Flavouring.

Follow the method for Ground-Rice Pudding. When the mixture is cooked and smooth, turn it into a greased pie-dish. Place small pieces of butter on the top, re-heat it in the oven for a moment, and send it to table hot but with no skin on it and not browned. Serve with sugar or jam.

*HASTY PUDDING (Superior)
(4 or 5 people)

Small piece of butter.	2 or 3 eggs.
¾ pt. milk.	Sugar to taste, about
1½ oz. flour.	1 oz.

Follow the recipe for Ground-Rice Pudding. When the mixture is smooth, boil it for 5 minutes. Cool it and add the beaten eggs and butter and sweeten to taste. Bake till brown and serve with fruit or with a fruit syrup or jam sauce.

*JUNKET (4 or 5 people)

Essence of Rennet is usually sold for this. Small quantities should be bought, as it gives a better result if fresh. Read the directions with the bottle or tablets, but the usual proportion is as follows:

1 pt. milk.	Sugar and flavouring
1 teasp. rennet.	to taste.

Warm the milk to blood heat (98° F.). Sweeten it and add any flavouring during this process. Add the rennet, stir to mix the rennet evenly (1 or 2 stirs only), and then leave absolutely unshaken and undisturbed to set.

After adding the rennet, if liked, the mixture may be poured at once into small bowls or custard glasses to allow one or more of these for each person.

*Coffee Junket

Add sufficient strong coffee to the milk to give a good flavour and proceed as above.

*Chocolate Junket

Dissolve 1 oz. chocolate in the milk. In doing this care must be taken not to heat the milk over 150° F. or the junket will not be satisfactory.

The milk, after dissolving the chocolate in it, must be allowed to cool to 98° before adding the rennet.

Devonshire Junket

When set, cover the surface with Devonshire cream and, if liked, with grated nutmeg or with equal quantities of sugar and cinnamon sifted together.

Rum or Brandy Junkets

1 or 2 tablesp. may be added to the milk if wished before adding the rennet.

LEMON RICE (4 people)

2 oz. rice	Juice and rind of 1 lemon.
1 pt. milk.	A little jam.
2 eggs.	Sugar to taste.

Cook the rice in milk with a strip of lemon rind till thick. Add sugar and yolks. Put some jam into a pie-dish, pour the rice over, and set in a moderate oven. Whisk the whites and pile them up on the top. Sprinkle with sugar and bake in a cool oven until crisp.

*MACARONI PUDDING (4 people)

2 oz. pipe macaroni.   1 pt. milk.   1 or 2 eggs.   Sugar to taste.

Break the macaroni into 2-inch lengths. Cook them in the milk in a double saucepan till tender. Cool. Add the eggs, sweeten, and put into a greased pie-dish. Bake in good moderate oven till golden brown. This pudding is greatly improved if the macaroni is soaked previously. For good finish see Ground-Rice Pudding, N.B. 2.

PUDDINGS (General)—Class II

MILK MOULDS

*MILK LEMON JELLY (Lemon Solid) (I)
(4 or 5 people)

1 pt. milk.   ½ oz. gelatine (1 oz. in hot weather).
1 or 2 lemons.   Sugar to taste.   ½ gill water.

Cut the rind from the lemons so thinly that no white is visible on the under side. Put these rinds in the milk and stand in a warm place to extract the lemon flavour. Dissolve the gelatine in ½ gill of water. Add this to the flavoured milk. Sweeten to taste, dissolving the sugar. When quite cold but just not set add the juice of lemon; if the juice measures ½ gill, that amount less milk must be used. Strain into a wetted mould. The lemon juice may be omitted if preferred, owing to the possibility of the milk curdling. If curdled, beat or whisk to make it smooth again.

*MILK LEMON JELLY (Lemon Solid) (II)
(4 or 5 people)

Just under 1 pt. milk.   ½ oz. gelatine.   1 or 2 lemons.   Sugar to taste.

Put the thinly cut lemon rinds, gelatine, milk and sugar into
a double saucepan.   When the gelatine and sugar are dissolved,
and the milk well flavoured, strain, and when almost cold add
the lemon juice if wished.   Pour into a wetted mould.

*Milk Jellies of Coffee and Chocolate

These are made in exactly the same way by dissolving chocolate
in, or adding coffee to, the milk before dissolving the gelatine in
it.   Either of the methods given above may be used.   The whole
amount of liquid, whether milk, or milk and coffee, must be
exactly 1 pt. to each ½ oz. gelatine.   In hot weather it is always
necessary to increase the proportion of gelatine to ¾–1 oz. to each
pint of liquid.   The proportion is also increased where there is a
very limited time available for the jelly to set.

MILK MOULDS (I)
(4 or 5 people)
(ALSO CALLED BLANCMANGE)

1 pt. milk.   Sugar and flavouring to taste.
¾ oz. gelatine (1 oz. in hot weather.)

Tear the gelatine into small pieces (if French leaf gelatine is
used).   Dissolve the gelatine in a little water, and add this to
the milk.

Flavour and sweeten to taste; strain into a wetted mould
and turn out when cold.   A pinch of bicarbonate of soda added
prevents curdling.

Sweeten and flavour the milk.   Dissolve the gelatine in ½ gill
wine or water, and add it to the milk.   Cool and strain into a
china mould that has been rinsed out with cold water.

MILK MOULDS (II)
(4 or 5 people)
(ALSO CALLED MILK JELLY)

1 pt. milk.   Sugar and flavouring to taste.
½ oz. Cox's instant powdered gelatine.

Place all the ingredients in a lined pan, previously rinsed out
with cold water.   Warm carefully to dissolve all the gelatine.   The
milk will curdle if at all overheated.   Cool and strain into a
china mould that has been rinsed out with cold water.

SUPERIOR BLANCMANGE (4 to 6 people)

3 gills milk.	1 oz. sugar.
1 gill cream.	¾ oz. gelatine.
½ teasp. vanilla.	Little carmine.

Dissolve the gelatine in ½ gill water. Add this to the milk and cream; which may be slightly whipped. Colour and pour into a wet mould. When set, turn out and decorate with whipped cream, etc.

N.B. Use rather more gelatine in hot weather.

PUDDINGS (General)—Class III

FRUITS (stewed, compotes, moulds)

Fresh or dried stewed fruit is a most useful form of ' pudding ' and it is often served as an accompaniment to milk puddings.

Fruit for stewing usually requires washing. Apples must be peeled, cored, and either left whole or cut into halves or into segments.

Rhubarb should be cut into 2-inch lengths, gooseberries must be topped and tailed, and currants must be stalked.

Notes and Rules on Stewing Fruit, Etc.

(Stew in Jar in Oven when possible)

(1) Apples, Plums, Apricots, Green Gooseberries, etc. Make a syrup of sugar and water: 4 oz. sugar to 2 gills water per lb. fruit. Boil sugar and water 10 minutes, skimming as necessary, prepare fruit, lay in syrup and *simmer* only till tender, but *not* broken.

(2) Very Juicy Fruit, e.g. Raspberries, Rhubarb, etc. Prepare as above, but use half quantity water and be particularly careful that the fruit does not break up.

(3) Hard Stewing Pears. Allow 3 gills of water to above quantity, as they require long cooking and the water evaporates.

(4) Dried Fruit, e.g. Prunes, Figs, etc. Wash and soak overnight in enough water to cover them. Pour off water and make up to ½ pt. per lb. and add to it 2 oz. sugar to 1 lb. fruit; add suitable flavouring and make syrup and stew as before.

To make a Fruit Compote. Lay the fruit in the cold syrup, made as above, for 12 hours. Drain, and, for all fresh fruit, bring the syrup in which the fruit has soaked to the boil. Place the drained fruit in this and simmer gently till the fruit is tender. The skins should remain unbroken.

The preliminary soaking in the syrup prevents the fruit from shrivelling in the cooking. It is particularly important for delicate fruits such as strawberries, raspberries, orange quarters, etc., and it improves every kind.

Dried Fruits, Prunes, Apricots, etc. Soak these in the syrup for 12 or 24 hours; then put them in a saucepan with the cold syrup, bring gently to the boil and simmer gently until tender.

To Stew Pears for Compote. Place them, peeled and halved, in a covered pan, just covering them with cold syrup. Bring this to the boil and simmer them gently for several hours (at least 4 or 5) or until tender. If liked, the syrup may be coloured by adding a few drops of carmine before cooking the fruit in it.

*Fruit Moulds (Fruit Blancmange), etc. These may be made with the juice of any fruit, following exactly the recipes given for Milk Jellies and Milk Moulds, but rather more gelatine is required, i.e. 1 pt. of fruit juice sweetened to taste and ¾ oz. gelatine (1 oz. in hot weather).

Dissolve the gelatine in the juice, cool this, and pour it into a wetted mould. The result will give a very nice-tasting simple jelly, but not, of course, a clear jelly.

*APPLE MOULD (5 or 6 people)

| 2 lb. apples. | Sugar to taste. |
| 1 lemon. | Gelatine. |

¼ pt. water (more or less, according to the juiciness of the apples).

Peel, core and cut up the apples. Stew them in a covered enamel pan or a jar with the lemon rind, sugar and water. When tender rub through a hair sieve. Measure this and to each pt. allow ½ oz. gelatine. Dissolve the gelatine in 2 or 3 tablesp. of water and add this to the fruit pulp.

The mixture may be coloured pink if wished. When cool, pour it into a wetted mould. Turn out when set.

*CANADIAN FRUIT MOULD (6 or 7 people)

1 lb. red currants, black- berries or any fruit. Water according to fruit.	3 oz. crushed tapioca or 2 oz. cornflour. Sugar to taste.

Wash the grain. Stew the fruit with the sugar and water; when soft, strain or sieve (this should measure 1 pt.). Add the grain to the prepared juice and cook until quite clear and transparent. Pour into a wetted mould and turn out when cold.

If the fruit is not strained allow less grain. Very acid fruits require rather more grain to ensure setting.

*CORNFLOUR FRUIT MOULDS (4 to 6 people)

1 pt. fruit juice.	1½ oz. cornflour.
Sugar to taste.	

Follow the recipe for Cornflour Mould.

LEMON MOULD (4 to 6 people)

1 pt. water. 2 eggs. 1½ oz. cornflour.	Sugar to taste. 2 lemons.

Wipe and peel the lemons very thinly. Infuse the peel in the water. When well flavoured, strain this. Mix the cornflour to a smooth cream with the lemon juice. Pour the strained juice into this. Boil and stir well for about 3 minutes. Add the sugar. Cool and add the well-beaten eggs, cook gently until eggs thicken, cool, and pour into a wetted mould and serve when cold.

*PRUNE MOULD (4 to 6 people)

1 lb. prunes. 1 pt. water. 1 lemon.	Sugar to taste (about 2 oz.). Gelatine.

Wash and soak the prunes. Put them in a covered jar with the sugar and water. Stew gently till tender. Sieve this. Crack some of the stones and blanch the kernels. Measure the sieved prune mixture, and to each pt. allow ½ oz. gelatine. Dissolve the gelatine in a little wine or water, and add this to the fruit mixture. Mix well, and, when cool, pour into a wetted mould.

(If wished, the prunes may be stewed in claret, and the mixture may be poured into a border mould that has been lined with clear jelly and decorated. When turned out, the centre can be piled up with whipped cream.)

RASPBERRY CAKE

Make a light sponge cake from any good sponge recipe. Bake it, and when cool cut out some of the centre portion. Ice the sides with any good water icing and decorate prettily. Fill the centre with layers of raspberries and whipped cream. The top should be finished off by cream piled high, and then entirely coated with rows of choice fruit.

Any other fruit may make a similar cake.

RICE WITH APPLE (about 6 people)

½ lb. rice. 6 apples. Sugar.

Wash and cook the rice in boiling water for 10 minutes. Drain it and spread it on small floured pudding cloths. Place a peeled and cored apple on each, adding sugar to taste. Tie up the cloths, boil for 30 to 40 minutes. Serve with a sweet sauce.

To SAVE TIME, the rice can be spread on one large cloth, and the apples peeled and sliced into this. Tie in a ball and boil for 1 hour. Serve with sweet sauce.

*RHUBARB MOULD (4 to 6 people)

1 lb. rhubarb.	½ pt. water.
Sugar to taste.	3 oz. crushed tapioca
Grated lemon rind.	or sago.
Pink colouring.	

Cut up the rhubarb and cook it in a covered jar or double saucepan with the water, lemon and sugar. When the fruit is quite tender and the sago clear, pour the whole into a wetted mould.

SYRUP MOULD (4 to 6 people)

3 oz. small sago.	1 pt. water.
Rind and juice of ½	2 small tablesp. golden
lemon.	syrup.
Sugar to taste.	

Infuse the thinly cut rind in the water. Bring the water to the boil, removing the lemon rind, sprinkle in the sago, stirring all the time. Stir and boil till the grain is clear and quite thick —about 10 to 15 minutes. Add sugar, syrup and lemon juice. Pour into a wet china mould and leave till set. Turn out and pour round ½ pt. of cold custard sauce.

PUDDINGS (General)—Class IV

BREAD PUDDINGS, CHARLOTTES, ETC.

*APPLE CHARLOTTE (4 to 6 people)

2 lb. apples, peeled, and cored and sliced.	Lemon juice, or finely grated rind.
Bread.	Sugar to taste.
A little water to cook.	2 yolks.

Grease a plain charlotte tin. Sugar it with fine white sugar if a glazed result is required. Cut a round of bread rather less than ½ inch thick, and about 1 inch less in diameter than the top of the mould. Cut strips of bread also of the same thickness, and exactly to the depth of the tin. Dip each of these and the round in clarified butter, or brush each side of them with butter. Place the round at the top of the tin, and the strips round it, pressing them against the sides to line it.

Cook the apples in the water, adding the lemon and sugar. When quite tender, sieve this and add yolks. The mixture should be quite thick, not at all liquid. Fill the mould with this and cover with another round of bread also brushed with butter.

Bake in a moderate oven until the whole is well browned. Turn out and serve.

*APPLE CHARLOTTE, SWISS

(4 to 6 people)

6 oz. breadcrumbs.	1½ lb. apples.
3 oz. sugar.	3 oz. chopped suet.
Rind and juice of a lemon.	

Mix the suet, breadcrumbs and half the sugar. Grease a pie-dish and cover the bottom and sides with some of the mixture. Slice the apples (a good cooking kind that cook quickly must be used), and put them with the remainder of the sugar and lemon until the dish is full. Cover with more breadcrumbs, suet and sugar, then with a greased paper. Cook in a good oven for 1 hour or rather more, until the whole is brown and the fruit tender.

Turn the pudding out, and serve hot.

BREAD PUDDINGS

To make these successfully, soak the bread overnight, if possible, in cold water. Then squeeze the bread well in a cloth or with the hands to free it from all moisture. It should then be sieved.

Bread scraps so treated may be used instead of breadcrumbs in any plain pudding recipes; but, if this is done, use less liquid than the recipe gives, so allowing for the moisture contained in the sieved scraps of bread.

To SAVE TIME the soaked bread may be wrung out and beaten with a fork to break up any lumps instead of sieving it.

*Scrap Bread Pudding (5 or 6 people)

3 oz. bread.	3 oz. of dried fruit, currants, raisins, etc.
Spice or nutmeg.	
1 oz. margarine or suet (chopped).	1 egg (if liked).
	3 oz. sugar. 1 pt. milk.

Melt the fat in the milk. Pour it over the sieved scraps of bread prepared as above, and mix with the fruit, spice, sugar, and egg. Pour into a greased pie-dish, and bake till well browned, putting small pieces of fat on the top.

N.B. This pudding is nicer steamed and served with a custard or jam sauce when an egg and 4 oz. bread are necessary.

*BREAD AND BUTTER PUDDING (4 people)

3 oz. very thin bread and butter.	1 pt. milk. 1 oz. sugar.
	1 or 2 eggs.
1 or 2 oz. currants, raisins, peel, etc. (or 1 tablesp. marmalade).	

Grease a pie-dish. Clean the currants, stone the raisins and slice the peel and arrange some at the bottom of the dish. Cut the bread and butter into neat three-corner pieces, and lay these on the fruit, sprinkling with the rest of the fruit. Beat the egg, add the milk and sugar and pour this over the bread. Leave for 1 hour to soak. Then bake in a cool oven for 1 hour, or until the custard sets.

BREADCRUMB PUDDING (4 or 5 people)

4 oz. breadcrumbs.	1 oz. sugar.
1 pt. milk.	2 eggs.
1 oz. margarine.	Vanilla essence.

Boil the milk and margarine in a saucepan, then pour the milk over the breadcrumbs; add the sugar. Break the eggs, add the yolks to the mixture and mix well. Add the flavouring, beat the whites of the eggs stiffly and fold lightly into the other ingredients. Turn the mixture into a greased pie-dish, soak for 20 minutes, and bake in a moderate oven from 20 to 30 minutes.

CONSERVATIVE PUDDING (4 people)

2½ oz. Savoy biscuits or ratafias.	1 tablesp. of brandy.
	½ pt. milk.
2 eggs and 1 yolk.	1 tablesp. of apricot jam.

Grease a soufflé tin. Put in the biscuits with a layer of jam between. Pour the brandy over. Beat the eggs and add the milk and pour over. Soak for ½ hour. Steam till firm. Serve with apricot jam sauce.

FRIAR'S OMELET (4 to 6 people)

2 lb. apples.	1 lemon.
2 eggs.	2 oz. sugar (more or
½ oz. to 2 oz. butter.	less to taste).

Stew the apples with the lemon rind, juice and sugar. Add the butter and well-beaten eggs. Put the mixture into a pie-dish well coated with crumbs. Cover with more crumbs and a well-greased paper. Bake 30 to 40 minutes. Turn out, and serve sprinkled with sugar.

LEMON PUDDING, BAKED
(4 or 5 people)

3 oz. crumbs.	Rind and juice
2 oz. sugar.	of 1 lemon.
½ pt. milk.	2 eggs.

Prepare as for Breadcrumb Pudding.

*SUMMER PUDDING

Line a pudding basin neatly with thinly cut strips of bread from which all crusts have been removed. Fill the basin with any hot freshly stewed and sweetened fruit, or with any hot compote of fruit, but without too much juice or syrup being added. When quite full cover with a round of bread; place a saucer or plate on this, and a weight, and leave for 12 to 24 hours. Turn out and serve, surrounded by any good custard, cream, or fruit juice.

Red currants and raspberries are particularly nice for this, and can be used uncooked.

PUDDINGS (General)—Class V

PUDDINGS MADE FROM CAKE MIXTURES

See rules for cake-making, Class II Method, page 314. Puddings are made in exactly the same way, but the mixture is usually mixed to a slightly softer consistency.

*CANARY PUDDING (5 or 6 people)

The weight of 2 eggs in each of the following: Butter or margarine, sugar, flour. Grated rind of 1 lemon. Good pinch baking powder. A little milk, if needed.

Beat the butter and sugar to a cream. Add 1 egg and 1 tablesp. of the flour. Beat well. Add the second egg and more flour, beat again, then the rest of the flour by degrees, beating well and adding the baking powder with the last tablesp. of flour. The mixture should drop easily from the spoon. If too stiff to do this, add a little milk.

Steam in a greased mould covered with greased paper for 2 hours. Turn out and serve with jam or wine sauce.

*CASTLE PUDDINGS (3 or 4 people)

Make as for Canary Pudding, using half quantity. The mixture is then put into small greased dariole moulds, which must only be half filled. Bake for 20 to 30 minutes. Serve with jam sauce.

CASTLE PUDDINGS (Steamed)

Make as above, but steam in the moulds, covered with greased paper, for 30 to 40 minutes.

CHERRY PUDDING

Follow the recipe for Jamaica Pudding, substituting cherries for ginger.

*CHOCOLATE PUDDING (I)

The same mixture as for Canary Pudding, adding either 1 oz. chocolate powder, or ½ oz. cocoa, or 1½ oz. bar chocolate (this last should be dissolved in 2 or 3 tablesp. milk). The chocolate

powder or cocoa should be mixed with the flour. Steam for
2 hours, using an aluminium or china mould, and serve with
custard or vanilla sauce.

CHOCOLATE PUDDING (II), Richer

The same mixture, but add 4 eggs instead of 2. This makes a
very light pudding indeed. Serve with a mousseline or custard
sauce.

CHOCOLATE PUDDINGS (III), Small

Steam the same mixture in small greased dariole moulds as
for Chocolate Pudding (I) 30 to 40 minutes, or bake them for
about 20 minutes.

*FRENCH PANCAKES (4 to 6 people)

| 2 oz. butter. 2 eggs. | 2 oz. flour. |
| 2 oz. sugar (castor). | ½ pt. milk. Jam. |

Beat the butter and sugar to a cream, add 1 egg and 1 tablesp.
flour, beat well, add the second egg, more flour, and beat again.
Work in the rest of the flour, beating well, and lastly stir in the
milk. Half fill six greased flat tins or saucers. Bake in a good
oven for 10 to 15 minutes. Turn out on to a sugared paper.
Place a spoonful of hot jam on each, fold in two like an omelette
and serve at once on a d'oyley.

To save time the mixture may be baked in two flat sponge
sandwich tins.

*FRUIT SPONGE (4 or 5 people)

Nearly fill a shallow dish with raw or cooked fruit. Spread a
half-quantity of Canary Pudding Mixture (i.e. weight of 1 egg in
butter, sugar, and flour, adding 1 tablesp. milk and ½ teasp. baking
powder) over the surface. Bake in a moderate oven for 45
minutes. Serve hot or cold.

N.B.   If stewed fruit is preferred, pour this while still at boiling-
point into the pie-dish and cover at once with the mixture, com-
pleting the recipe as above.

*JAM PUDDING (5 or 6 people)

(Also called Randall Pudding)

The weight of 2 eggs in butter and in flour and half their weight in
sugar. 1 tablesp. raspberry or strawberry jam. ¼ teasp. bicarbonate
of soda or ½ teasp. baking powder.

Make as for Canary Pudding and steam for 2 hours. Serve
with jam.

*JAMAICA PUDDING

Follow the recipe for Canary Pudding, adding 2 to 4 oz. preserved ginger cut into dice. This goes in last. Steam for 2 hours. Serve with ginger sauce.

NANTES PUDDING (6 or 7 people)

¼ lb. French plums or stewed prunes (stoned). A few kernels.	¼ lb. ratafias. 3 tablesp. of cream or milk. Canary Pudding mixture.

Line a greased mould with ratafias. Pour in the Canary Pudding mixture, to which, lastly, the cut-up prunes, kernels and cream have been added. Steam for 3 hours. Serve with a sauce made of the prune juice, 1 glass sherry and twelve kernels. Colour if wished.

PRINCESS PUDDING (5 or 6 people)

1 oz. candied peel, cut up. 6 oz. stoned raisins. 2 oz. currants (cleaned).	1 oz. almonds, chopped. Grated rind of a lemon. A little brandy, if liked.

Make the Canary Pudding mixture with 2 eggs, their weight in flour and butter, and half their weight in sugar. Add the above ingredients, ½ teasp. baking powder, and steam for 5 hours. Serve with a rich sauce.

*RAILWAY PUDDING (4 or 5 people)

6 oz. flour. 3 oz. margarine. 3 oz. castor sugar. Jam.	1 egg. 1 teasp. baking powder. Vanilla essence.
Enough milk to mix to a dropping consistency.	

Sieve flour and baking powder. Rub fat into flour until as fine as breadcrumbs, add sugar. Beat egg with a little milk and mix to right consistency. Flavour with few drops of vanilla essence. Pour into Yorkshire-pudding tin or shallow cake tin and bake at once in a moderate oven. When just firm and golden brown turn out carefully, split, and spread with warmed jam. Put the pieces together, cut into neat fingers or squares. Dredge with castor sugar and serve hot or cold.

SULTANA PUDDING

Follow the Canary Pudding mixture, omitting half the sugar, and adding ¼ lb. sultanas.

PUDDINGS (General)—Class VI

PUDDINGS OF THE CUSTARD VARIETY

These puddings depend for their thickening or setting on the use of eggs, therefore great care must be exercised to see that the egg is sufficiently cooked, at the same time avoiding any over-heating, which would either make it curdle or else make the mixture tough.

First among this class come the plain custards. For these, either whole eggs (yolk and white) or egg yolks only must be used, in which case each yolk would count as half an egg. If solid flavouring is added, thinly cut lemon rind, etc., infuse it in the milk first, then strain it away. Yolks only make the best custard.

CUSTARD (Baked)

(4 people)

1 pt. of milk.	Sugar and flavouring
2 large eggs.	to taste.

Warm the milk to blood heat; pour it on to the beaten eggs (these must be beaten till the yolks and whites are thoroughly mixed but no longer, as custards must not rise and so no lightness or froth is required). Strain this into a greased fireproof dish or pie-dish. Sweeten to taste. Place in a cool oven on a deep tin and bake carefully. When the custard begins to set, pour water into the surrounding tin. This prevents overheating at the critical time, allows of quicker cooking, and produces a browner surface than the old method of standing the custard in a tin of water from the first. If the custard is full of holes and broken, it is a sign that it has been overheated in the cooking.

Serve hot or cold, in the dish in which it is cooked, for a custard made of the proportion given—1 egg to $\frac{1}{2}$ pt. milk—would not be stiff enough to allow of its being turned out of the dish.

CUSTARD known as ' BOILED ' or CUP CUSTARD

(4 to 6 people)

1 pt. milk.   2–4 eggs.   Sugar and flavouring to taste.

Warm the milk to blood heat, pour it on to the eggs (just mixed as for baked custard, but not beaten for lightness).

H

Strain this into a jug, or into the top part of a double saucepan, surrounded with hot water, and stir gently over the fire. The custard must not be allowed to boil, but as the water in the under saucepan, or round the jug, simmers, it will be seen that the custard just begins to thicken. From being clear and milky a slight thickness is just visible, and if tasted the raw egg taste can no longer be detected. Sweeten to taste, and pour the custard into a cold bowl, as the thickening continues during the cooling and if left in a hot pan it might still curdle. Stir occasionally until cold, to prevent a skin from forming, then carefully pour into small custard glasses. The custard, when cold, should be of the consistency of good cream.

CUSTARD (Steamed)

Same as Caramel Custard but omit the caramel.

CABINET PUDDING (4 to 6 people)

6 small sponge cakes, OR 3–4 oz. sponge cake.	1 oz. citron peel.
	2 oz. cherries or raisins, etc. (if liked).
6 macaroons.	Sugar to taste (very little
¾ pt. milk.	is needed).
2 or 3 eggs.	Flavouring to taste.

Grease a mould and decorate it prettily. Line the sides with strips of the sponge cake, and place the rest with the macaroons in the centre. Warm the milk to 98° F., pour this over the beaten eggs, add the sugar and flavouring, and pour over the sponge cakes. Leave it for fifteen minutes to soak, then cover with a greased paper and steam for 1 hour. Turn out and serve with jam sauce.

*CABINET PUDDING (Cheap)

(4 people)

Decorate a greased mould with raisins, peel, etc. In it place 3 oz. bread, either:

(1) Dice of bread that have browned in the oven (or toast).
(2) Slices of thin bread and butter.
(3) Dice of stale bread.

Beat 1 egg and pour on to it ½ pt. milk at blood heat. Strain this, sweetened and flavoured to taste, over the bread. Leave to soak for 1 hour. Cover with greased paper and steam for about 1 hour. Serve with sweet sauce.

CABINET PUDDING, COFFEE (4 or 5 people)

4 oz. bread or cake cut into dice.	1 oz. almonds, if wished.
¼ pt. milk.	Sugar to taste.
¼ pt. strong coffee.	2 eggs (1 white may be omitted).

Proceed as for Cabinet Pudding, Cheap.

Chocolate Cabinet Pudding may be made in the same way, dissolving 1 oz. chocolate in ½ pt. milk and omitting the coffee.

CARAMEL CUSTARD (3 or 4 people)

CARAMEL

2 oz. loaf sugar. Juice of lemon, or about 2 tablesp. water.

Place the sugar and water (or strained lemon juice) in the tin that is to be caramelled. Place this on the hottest part of the stove, and SHAKE very occasionally until it browns evenly to a rich golden brown colour.

Lift the tin with a cloth and carefully run the mixture all over the bottom and sides. This will set like toffee. The tin is then ready. Or, the caramel may be made in a small, strong saucepan, and then poured into a hot tin.

FOR SMALL TINS, 2 or 3 lumps of sugar should be put into each, and 1 teasp. of water or lemon juice.

(If the sugar seems inclined to crystallize instead of to melt and brown, add more water, and put the tin on to a hotter place.)

CUSTARD

½ pt. milk.	3 whole eggs (or 2
Sugar and flavouring to taste.	whole eggs and 2 extra yolks).

Make the milk blood heat, pour it on to the beaten (see Custard, Baked) eggs. Sweeten and flavour to taste, and strain this into the mould ready coated with caramel.

Cover with a greased paper, and place the tin in a pan of water at simmering point—the water must not boil and must only come half-way up the tin. Cover with a lid and simmer gently for rather less than 1 hour, until just firm in the centre. Turn out at once, and serve hot or cold.

If large moulds are needed it is wise to strengthen the custard. If it is to be served cold, dissolve ¼ oz. gelatine to each pint of milk before pouring it on to the eggs. If it is to be served hot, add ½ oz. cornflour to the milk. (Do this in the correct way: Mix some of the cornflour to a smooth cream with cold milk. Boil the remainder. Add this, and re-boil the whole for 5 minutes.) Cool the milk, after it has been boiled with the cornflour, to blood heat, and then proceed exactly as in the recipe.

*CARAMEL RICE (4 to 6 people)

2 oz. rice. 2 eggs.	Rind of lemon, grated.
1 pt. milk.	Caramel (as for Caramel
Sugar to taste.	Custard).

Wash and cook the rice in a double saucepan with the milk and grated lemon rind, or it may be cooked the day before in a hay box. When it has absorbed the milk add the beaten eggs and sugar to taste. Put the mixture into the mould ready coated with caramel, cover with a greased paper, and steam gently for about 45 minutes.

*CARAMEL TAPIOCA or SAGO
(4 to 6 people)

3 oz. small tapioca or sago.	1 egg.
1 pt. milk.	1 small handful of bread
Sugar and flavouring to	or cake crumbs or crushed
taste.	macaroons.

Wash and cook the tapioca in the milk until it is thick and creamy. Add the sugar, flavouring and crumbs. Cool it a little. Then add the beaten egg. Steam for 1 hour in a mould lined with caramel. (See Caramel Custard.)

COCONUT PUDDING (4 or 5 people)

2 oz. coconut.	1 oz. sugar.
2 eggs.	1 oz. butter.
1½ gills milk.	½ teasp. vanilla.
1 oz. cake crumbs.	1 oz. breadcrumbs.

Simmer the coconut in the milk for a few minutes. Add the other ingredients, the stiffly whisked whites last. Steam in a greased mould till set. Turn out and serve with sweet sauce.

CRÈME FRITE (4 to 6 people)

¼ pt. milk.	Cake crumbs.
¼ pt. cream.	1 tablesp. flour.
3 egg yolks and 1 white.	1 tablesp. sugar. Flavouring to taste.

Mix the flour to a smooth cream with the milk. Boil this well till cooked and smooth, cool, and add the beaten eggs, cream, and sugar. Strain into a double saucepan and stir until the mixture thickens and leaves the sides of the pan clean. Flavour and turn on to a greased dish. When quite cold cut into neat shapes. Dip these in beaten egg, and then into cake crumbs. Fry in very hot fat.

Drain and sprinkle with sugar.

*CUSTARD (Cheap)

(4 to 6 people)

1 tablesp. flour or cornflour.	1 or 2 eggs. Sugar and flavouring
1 pt. milk.	to taste.

Mix the flour to a smooth cream with some cold milk. Boil the rest and add to it. Re-boil the whole, stirring for 5 minutes Cool, add the sugar, flavouring, and beaten (to mix) egg. Reheat carefully to cook the egg (do not boil), and serve cold.

CUSTARD, CHOCOLATE

Dissolve 1 oz. chocolate (or ¼ oz. cocoa) in each ½ pt. of milk, then proceed as under Custard, Baked, page 217.

CUSTARD, COFFEE

Make some strong coffee. Add it to milk till 1 pt. of both mixed is obtained. Follow recipes for Custard, Baked, Boiled, or Steamed, pages 217–18.

CUSTARD, CONFECTIONER'S (nearly 1 pt.)

¾ pt. milk.	Sugar to taste.
2 yolks or 1 whole egg.	½ oz. cornflour.
3 sheets of gelatine.	Vanilla, etc., to taste.

This custard is used for fillings for cold cooked cases such as puff paste, choux paste, etc., when whipped cream is not available.

The custard has, therefore, to be strengthened by the addition of gelatine.

Beat the egg to mix it. Mix the cornflour to a smooth cream with a little cold milk. Boil the rest and pour on to it. Cook this for 5 minutes. Cool, and add the egg, sugar and flavouring. Carefully re-cook, but do not boil; then add the gelatine dissolved in a very little wine or water. Strain and use when cold.

CUSTARD, MACAROON (or RATAFIA)

Prepare a custard (see Custard, Baked, page 217). Put it in a pie-dish and entirely cover with macaroons. Stand for ½ hour, then bake as usual.

GENERAL FAVOURITE PUDDING (3 or 4 people)

2 sponge cakes or dry Swiss roll.	A little jam.
2 eggs.	½ pt. milk.
	Vanilla.

Arrange the cake to lie flat in a pie-dish. Beat the yolks, add the milk and flavouring and pour over the cake. Soak, then bake till set. Whisk the whites stiffly, add 2 tablesp. of fine sugar, pile on the top, dredge with sugar, and crisp in a cool oven.

MARMALADE AND VERMICELLI PUDDING (4 or 5 people)

3 oz. vermicelli.	1 tablesp. of
3 gills milk.	marmalade.
1 oz. raisins.	1 oz. sugar.
2 eggs.	

Simmer the vermicelli in milk (after breaking it into short lengths) for 20 minutes. Add all the other ingredients. Steam in well-greased mould till firm. Turn out and serve with marmalade sauce.

QUEEN OF PUDDINGS (4 people)

½ pt. milk.	1 tablesp. sugar for
1 or 2 eggs.	meringue.
2 oz. breadcrumbs.	Grated lemon rind or
1 tablesp. jam.	other flavouring.
½ oz. sugar for mixture.	

Boil the milk, pour it on to the crumbs and soak for 10

minutes. Add the sugar, yolks of eggs and flavouring. Pour the mixture into a small greased pie-dish. Bake it in a moderate oven until set (20 to 30 minutes). Place a very thin layer of jam on, and lastly the stiffly beaten whites of eggs to which the sugar is quickly added. Pile this meringue on the pudding. Sprinkle it with more sugar, and bake till crisp and just golden in parts.

*RICE CROQUETTES (5 or 6 people)

4 oz. Carolina rice.	1 oz. butter.
1 pt. milk.	1½ oz. sugar.
2 yolks of eggs.	Lemon rind.
Beaten egg.	Breadcrumbs.
Angelica.	

Wash the rice and cook it in the milk till soft or, if possible, cook in a hay box overnight. Add the sugar, butter, lemon, and yolks. Cook without boiling, turn on to a wetted plate. When cold form into six or seven balls. Egg and crumb these, fry in hot fat.

Drain and serve with a little piece of angelica in each. Serve with lemon sauce.

TIPSY CAKE (6 or 7 people)

1 large sponge cake.	1 pt. 'boiled' custard
¼ to ½ pt. cream.	(see page 217).
Sherry.	Almonds, cherries, etc.

Cut the cake crosswise into thin slices. Soak them in wine, then put them together again and re-form the cake. Coat it entirely with the custard and decorate it with whipped cream, almonds, cherries, etc.

TRIFLE (5 or 6 people)

6 or 7 small sponge cakes.	¼ to ½ pt. whipped cream.
1 pt. 'boiled' custard	Sherry. Jam.
(see page 217).	6 macaroons, almonds, etc.

Slice the cakes, soak them in wine and spread them with jam. Place these with the macaroons in a deep glass dish. Cover with the custard, then with the whipped cream, and decorate to taste. The wine may be replaced by fruit juice.

TRIFLE, APPLE (5 or 6 people)

2 lb. apples, cooked and sieved.	2 or 3 sponge cakes.
	Fruit juice or wine.
2 yolks or whole eggs.	1 gill cream.
Sugar and flavouring.	

Add the eggs to the apple and cook till thickened.

Put sponge cakes into a rather deep dish and soak with the juice or wine. Spread the apple over smoothly and when cold pour over the cream partly whipped. Decorate with a little apple, etc.

TRIFLE, CHOCOLATE (5 or 6 people)

8 sponge cakes.	3 oz. chocolate.
3 oz. bread or cake crumbs.	1 gill cream (whipped).
1 pt. milk.	Almonds.

Dissolve the chocolate in the milk. Pour this over the cake and crumbs. Cover and leave till cold. Serve in a glass dish, entirely covering the surface with whipped cream, and decorate to taste.

Coffee Trifle may be made in the same way, using 1 pt. good coffee.

TRIFLE, FRUIT (Fresh)

Place the fresh fruit in a deep dish alternately with sliced sponge cake; if banana is used, slice it and spread the cake with jam. Soak with wine or fruit syrup. Cover the whole with custard and decorate with cream, almonds, etc.

TRIFLE, FRUIT (Stewed)

Place 6 sponge cakes in a dish. Cover them with any hot compote of fruit, adding wine to taste. When cold cover with custard, then with whipped cream, and decorate to taste.

TRIFLE, JELLIED (5 or 6 people)

6 sponge cakes (small).	1 pt. any good jelly.
Whipped cream.	Almonds, etc.

Put the sponge cakes in a glass dish. Cover them with the melted jelly. Leave till cold. Cover the surface with whipped cream and decorate to taste.

OR, place the sponge cakes in a damped mould. Pour the jelly over. Turn out when set; mask entirely with cream and decorate to taste.

VIENNOISE PUDDING (Hot)

(5 or 6 people)

4 oz. stale bread, freed from crust and cut into dice.	1 tablesp. sherry or cream.
2 or 3 oz. castor sugar.	3 oz. sultanas.
2 whole eggs and 1 extra yolk.	2 oz. candied peel.
	Grated lemon rind.
	½ pt. milk.

Make a Caramel (see above) of 6 lumps of sugar and 1 tablesp. water. When dark brown add the milk and boil it. Strain this on to the dice of bread. Leave for 20 minutes.

Add the rest of the ingredients, mix carefully, so as not to mash the bread, and steam in a greased mould for 2 hours. Serve with German egg sauce or any good sweet sauce.

PUDDINGS (General)—Class VII

FOOLS

These may be made of any fruit, though gooseberry is the best known example. If made of fruit that requires no cooking, such as raspberry, strawberry, etc., sieve the fruit and add sugar to taste. If made of harder fruits, cook, and in either case finish off as for Gooseberry Fool.

CHEAP FRUIT FOOLS

The custard for these may be made with any good custard powder, such as Bird's.

CHESTNUT FOOL

Cook and peel the chestnuts in the usual way. Sieve them and mix 1 pt. custard to 1 lb. sieved chestnuts. When cold add from ½ to 1 pt. whipped cream. Add liqueur, etc. to taste.

*H

FRUIT FOOL

1 lb. fruit.	1 gill cream
3–4 oz. sugar.	(half-whipped).
½–1 gill water.	

Cook the fruit, sugar and water till tender. Sieve these and stand aside to get quite cold (if possible on ice). Just before serving semi-whip the cream and add it to the fruit pulp. Serve at once, either in one large glass dish or in small custard glasses.

Some custard may be used to make a more economical sweet.

The following fruits also make excellent fools: Apples, Bananas, Blackberries, Loganberries, Raspberries, Red and Black Currants, Rhubarb, Strawberries, etc.

If banana is used, mix about 8 bananas, 1 pt. of cold custard, and sieve these together. Add ½ pt. whipped cream, and serve at once, as bananas lose their colour. (Banana Fool is nice if half cup of strawberry jam is sieved with it.)

PUDDINGS (General)—Class VIII

PUDDINGS MADE WITH YEAST

BABA (6 to 8 people)

½ lb. flour (warmed).	¼ gill warm water
½ oz. yeast.	(98° F.).
½ oz. castor sugar.	4 or 5 oz. butter.
3 large eggs.	

Baba is a high-class hot or cold sweet, or very light yeast cake, and is sometimes classed under ' Pastries '.

Cream the yeast with the sugar, add the water to it, and mix this to a ¼ of the flour. Set this to rise (see Bread, rules for making, page 297). Sift the rest of the flour into a bowl, and with the hands beat the raw eggs into it, and then the creamed butter. Beat till the whole is smooth. Then take the risen dough and beat this into the mixture, which will leave the hands clean when sufficiently beaten.

Grease a large Baba ring (a round tin with a hole in it) and flour it, or prepare several small Baba rings in the same way. Barely half fill them with the mixture. Put them to rise. When they have doubled their bulk, bake them in a quick oven for 10 to 15 minutes. Turn out, split and soak them in Rum Syrup Sauce (see page 126). If served cold they may also be decorated with cream, almonds, cherries, etc.

*DAMPFNUDELN PUDDING (8 or 9 people)

½ lb. flour (warmed).	1 oz. sugar.
½ oz. yeast.	Barely ¼ pt. milk at
1 egg (optional).	blood heat.
1½ oz. fat.	Pinch of salt.

Cream the yeast with 1 teasp. sugar, add the warmed milk. Work this into a little of the flour (see Setting the Sponge, page 298). Cover and leave this to rise for 20 minutes, then work in the rest of the flour, the fat and egg (if used), and beat till the mixture leaves the hands clean. Form into 12 balls, kneading each. Place these on a greased baking tin, and set to rise until they have doubled their bulk.

Melt 1 oz. butter in ½ pt. milk, add 1 oz. sugar. When boiling pour this round the dumplings. Cover them with a lid and bake in a slow oven till the milk is absorbed and the dumplings golden. Serve with jam sauce.

*YEAST 'KLOESZE' (12 to 14 people)

1 lb. flour (warmed).	About ¼ pt. milk
1 or 2 eggs.	(warmed).
½ oz. yeast.	½ cup melted butter.
Pinch salt.	Sugar (1 tablesp.).

Cream the yeast with the sugar. Add some of the milk, and work this into a part of the flour (see Setting the Sponge, page 298). Leave for 20 minutes, then work this and the rest of the ingredients into all the flour. Beat well. Set to rise. When well risen cook as follows:

(1) Grease a large mould, and coat it with flour, sugar and almonds (browned and chopped). Fill it only one-third full, cover with a greased paper, and set to rise till three-quarters full. Then steam for 2 to 3 hours. Turn out and serve with good stewed fruit or fruit compote or fruit syrup.

(2) Form into small balls. Set these to rise. When well risen drop into boiling milk or water, and boil for ½ hour gently with the lid on. Serve with fruit, etc.

(3) Form into small balls. Set these to rise, and when well

risen fry in deep fat. Sift sugar over them before serving with stewed fruit.

This recipe with fruit, etc., added makes nice buns, or, with jam enclosed, is excellent for doughnuts. The same mixture may be made with balls, as in (3), and these may be boiled for 30 to 40 minutes, and served with boiled mutton. If so, cook them in the pot with the mutton.

X. BATTERS, OMELETS, AND SOUFFLÉS

PART I

BATTER

IN culinary language a 'batter' often means a thinnish mixture, rather like a thin cream, but strictly speaking a batter should be a mixture of flour, egg, and milk (with possibly other ingredients such as oil added), and as the name implies, this mixture must be well beaten.

Batters are made in the following way:

Sift the flour and salt into a bowl. Make a well in the centre. Add the egg or eggs unbeaten, and a little of the milk. Stir with a wooden spoon, adding milk as required (the mixture must never get dry or hard, but at the same time it must be thick enough to allow any lumps to be rubbed out with the spoon). Keep a pool of liquid in the centre, surrounded by dry flour, and as more liquid is added, work in the dry flour gradually.

When half the liquid is added BEAT the mixture for 5 to 10 minutes until it is full of air bubbles. If possible stand it aside for 1 hour or for as long as possible, adding the remainder of the milk, and then use as required.

The proportions of flour, milk, and egg vary in accordance with the richness of the desired batter, e.g.:

*Plain	Richer (4 to 6 people)
For Yorkshire Pudding and Pancakes.	For steamed Batter and richer Pancakes.
¼ lb. flour.	¼ lb. flour.
1 egg.	2 eggs.
½ pt. milk.	Just under ½ pt. milk.

Both are made in exactly the same way, following the directions given above.

Cheap (4 or 5 people)

¼ lb. flour.	½ teasp. baking powder added just before frying.
1½ gills milk or water.	
¼ teasp. salt.	

229

*Cheapest Batter for Frying Fish (8 people)

½ lb. flour.	½ to ¾ pt. water or
½ teasp. salt.	milk (or both).

Mix as usual. Beat very well and stand all night if possible. Dip fish in this and fry in deep fat.

A Superior Batter for Pancakes, etc. (3 or 4 people)

2 oz. flour.	4 large tablesp.
2 eggs.	milk.

Pinch of salt.

Make in the usual way.

*TO COOK PANCAKES

Melt 2 oz. lard in a small pan. Pour a little of it into a frying pan, heat, and when smoking, pour back any surplus fat. Pour in just enough batter to cover the surface of the pan. Let one side brown. Turn or toss the pancake and brown the second side. Roll up and serve with cut lemon and brown sugar. A little fresh fat must be poured from the small pan for each pancake.

A COATING BATTER (for Kromeskies, etc.)
(4 to 6 people)

2 oz. flour. Pinch of salt.	1 egg (yolk optional [1]).
1 dessertsp. salad oil.	About ½ gill warm water.

Mix the salt and flour. Make a well and into that put the oil and egg yolk. Mix to a batter with the warm water. Stir till smooth, beat till light. Stand aside in a cold place. Just before use add the very stiffly beaten white of egg. Dip the kromeskies, rounds of apple, etc., into this and fry in hot deep fat.

This quantity coats sufficient for a dish for 4 or 5 people.

BATTER FOR BATTER CASES (8 to 10 people)

¼ lb. flour.	2 whites and 1 yolk
½ tablesp. oil or oiled butter.	of egg.
	½ gill warm water.
1 tablesp. cream.	Pinch of salt.

Mix the flour and salt. Make a well. Add the yolk and oil and mix with the warm water. Beat well and add the cream.

[1] Some authorities think that by omitting the yolk a lighter batter is obtained.

Stand aside. Immediately before use add the stiffly beaten whites.

To MAKE THE BATTER CASES. Special moulds, like small dariole moulds on a long handle, must be bought.

Have ready a large pan of deep fat, just smoking. Dip the moulds into this (to grease them) and then into the batter. Hold them in the fat until crisp and brown.

Remove them with a knife or by shaking gently and drain them. Fill as required, i.e.:

(1) If for meats, with a good salpicon of chicken or game and serve as an entrée.

(2) If for sweets, with jam and cream, or a purée of fruit, and decorate prettily.

(3) If for dressed vegetables, filled with any nice vegetable in a good cream sauce, etc.

YEAST BATTER FOR FRITTERS (8 to 10 people)

½ oz. yeast creamed with 1 teasp. sugar. Pinch of salt.	½ lb. flour (warmed). 1 oz. butter. ¾ pt. milk.

Mix the flour and salt. Make a well and add the creamed yeast mixed with ½ the warm milk (98° F.). Mix to a 'sponge' (see Breads, page 298). Cover and set this to rise for 20 minutes. Work in the rest of the flour and the butter, melted, and the remainder of the milk. Beat well. Set to rise for about 1 hour and use for orange, banana, etc., fritters.

*BAKED BATTER (4 or 5 people)

¼ lb. flour. 2 eggs. ½ pt. milk.

Make a batter with these ingredients. Pour into a pie-dish and bake for about 30 minutes. Serve with brown sugar and butter, or with golden syrup.

*BAKED BATTER, PLAIN

Follow the recipe for Yorkshire Pudding, and add 3 oz. finely chopped suet.

*BAKED BATTER WITH FRUIT (4 or 5 people)

Grease a pie-dish or soufflé case, and into this put ½ lb. apples, peeled and sliced, gooseberries, or any fruit in season. Cover this with the batter (Baked Batter, Plain recipe), and bake for 40 minutes.

*Very light Baked Batter Puddings may be made by adding 1 tablesp. finely chopped suet to the above recipe.

*BLACK CAP PUDDING (4 or 5 people)

The same as Boiled Batter, except that 2 oz. currants are added. These fall to the bottom, and when the pudding is turned out, the top is black. Steam if possible, instead of boiling.

Cherries, etc., may be added to make the top red.

*BOILED BATTER PUDDING (4 or 5 people)

¼ lb. flour. ½ pt. milk. 2 eggs.

Make a batter of these ingredients. Beat well and stand aside for 1 hour. Beat again, sweeten slightly to taste, and put this into a greased basin which must be only two-thirds full. Cover with a greased paper, and steam for about 1½ hours, or cover with a floured cloth, and boil for 1 hour. Turn out and serve with jam sauce.

*BOILED BATTER WITH FRUIT (5 or 6 people)

¼ lb. flour. ½ pt. milk. 2 eggs.

Make a batter with these ingredients, then follow method for Baked Batter with Fruit, but cut the apples up into small pieces. Two-thirds fill a greased pudding basin, cover it with a greased paper and steam for 1½ to 2 hours, or cover with a floured cloth and boil for 1¼ hours.

*FLAP JACKS (4 people)

2 oz. flour. | ½ teasp. baking
½ oz. currants. | powder.
½ gill water.

Mix the flour and baking powder to a batter with cold water. Add the currants. Fry in hot fat on both sides. Serve hot with sifted sugar.

*FRITTERS, APPLE

Peel some large cooking apples. Stamp the core out with a column cutter and cut into rings about ¼ inch thick. Prepare some Coating Batter (see page 230), and into this drop each apple ring.   Coat it entirely, lift it out, putting a skewer through the centre hole where the core was; and drop gently into fat that is just smoking.   When one side is brown, turn it to brown the other.   Drain well on paper, and serve on a paper with castor sugar sifted over.

FRITTERS, BANANA

Peel and cut bananas into 4, lengthways and across.   Dip each of these sections into coating batter, and fry in just smoking fat till the batter is golden brown and crisp.

*FRITTERS, ORANGE

Divide the oranges into segments, or cut them into slices. Dip each of these into batter and fry.

*Gooseberries, Cherries, Pineapples, etc., may all be dipped into frying batter, and fried in the same way.

*PANCAKES

See To Cook Pancakes, page 230.

*SNOW PANCAKES

Follow the usual recipe, but instead of using all milk, use half snow.   Follow the recipe exactly until half the milk is added. Then stand aside and when ready to fry stir in lightly $\frac{1}{4}$ pt. freshly fallen, clean snow.   These are excellent.

*TOAD-IN-THE-HOLE (5 or 6 people)

BATTER
$\begin{cases} \frac{1}{2} \text{ lb. flour.} & \frac{3}{4} \text{ lb. very tender} \\ 1 \text{ egg.} & \text{steak.} \\ \frac{1}{2} \text{ pt. milk.} & \text{Salt and pepper.} \end{cases}$

Make a batter of the flour, egg, and milk.   Beat well and season.   Grease a fireproof dish very thoroughly.   Place the steak on this, and pour the batter over.   Bake in a hot oven for $\frac{1}{2}$ hour.

OR, heat 1 or 2 tablesp. dripping in a tin.   Make this smoking hot.   Pour the batter in and lay carefully on it the steak, etc. Bake for 20 minutes in a hot oven.   Cut into squares and serve.

N.B.   Only *very* tender steak is satisfactory.   Sausage, kidney, or any underdone meat makes excellent Toad-in-the-hole.

YORKSHIRE CHEESE PUDDING (5 or 6 people)

½ lb. flour.	3 oz. grated
1 pt. milk.	cheese.
1 egg.	Seasoning.

Make and bake as for Yorkshire Pudding and serve with gravy and vegetables.

YORKSHIRE PUDDING (4 to 6 people)

¼ lb. flour. ½ pt. milk. 1 egg.

Method as detailed under Batter, Plain, page 229.

To Bake. Put 2 or 3 tablesp. of dripping from the hot, roasting meat into a tin. Pour the batter on to this and bake in a HOT oven for about 20 minutes. The dripping gives the required meaty taste to the Yorkshire Pudding.

PART II

OMELETS

There are two kinds of omelets: ENGLISH or SOUFFLÉ, and FRENCH.

The number of eggs used must be in accordance with the size of the pan, i.e. not less than 2 or 3 eggs in the usual sized omelet pan. To each egg allow 1 teasp. of water (this is the lightest), milk (more nourishing than water), or cream (for high-class omelets). It is usual to allow 1 egg at least to each person.

To CLARIFY BUTTER. Omelets must be made with clarified butter. Melt the butter in a small pan. Heat until it smokes slightly. Leave and cool until all bubbling ceases. Remove the scum and pour off carefully the liquid butter, leaving any sediment at the bottom of the pan. The liquid butter is now clarified and ready for use. Throw away the sediment; rub pan with paper till bright, and proceed.

ENGLISH or SOUFFLÉ OMELET

(6-inch omelet pan)

2 eggs.	½ oz. butter.
1 teasp. sugar.	½ teasp. vanilla.
½ tablesp. jam.	

Separate yolks from whites of eggs. Lightly beat yolks with sugar and flavouring. Fold in stiffly beaten whites. Heat butter in 6-inch omelet pan until just smoking, pour in mixture.

Cook over gentle heat until golden brown and set underneath. Cook top surface under hot grill until golden brown (2 minutes). Turn on to a sugared paper, mark across centre with the back of a knife, spread with hot jam. Fold in two and dish immediately. A good sauce, such as lemon or jam can be served with this omelet.

N.B. 1. This omelet could be completely cooked in the oven. Time 5–6 minutes.

N.B. 2. Savoury omelet. Chopped ham, etc. can be added before folding in the whites.

FRENCH OMELET

Melt clarified butter in a frying or omelet pan. When this is hot and just smoking, add the eggs, which have been beaten a little with the water, milk, or cream. The eggs must be beaten till the whites and yolks are well mixed, but not to a froth. Add salt and pepper. Place the pan over moderate heat and, as the egg commences to set, make small slits with a knife and let the liquid part run through until the whole is nearly set. Carefully turn half the omelet on to the other half. If a meat omelet is to be made, before doing this, place, on one half, some good mixture of meat cut into dice, and mixed with a good panada, to which is added cooked vegetables, mushrooms, etc., cut into dice, and then fold the other half over this filling. Make it into a good shape. Re-heat to brown the under surface slightly and turn right over on to a hot dish. It may be marked with a hot skewer two or three times as a decoration. Serve at once.

FRENCH OMELET, SAVOURY (1 or 2 people)

2 eggs. ½ oz. butter.	Pepper and salt.
½ teasp. chopped parsley.	Small piece of finely chopped
Pinch of powdered herbs.	onion (if liked).

1 tablesp. water *or* 2 teasps. cream.

Beat eggs slightly, add parsley, herbs, pepper and salt. Heat clarified butter in omelet pan and fry. Pour in eggs and proceed as above.

SWEET OMELETS

Follow either of the previous recipes, adding a little sugar to the omelet. Before folding over, lay some hot jam, etc., on one half, and then fold. A jam sauce may also be poured round.

Rum Omelet. Sweeten the omelet and pour a well-flavoured rum sauce round. Any liqueur may replace rum.

Part III

SOUFFLÉS

A soufflé is composed of three distinct parts:

(1) A foundation of thick sauce;
(2) Eggs in the proportion of 3 or 4 to each ¼ pt. liquid used to make the sauce;
(3) A distinct flavouring.

To Cook a Soufflé there are two methods:

(a) Bake in a moderate oven for about ½ hour.

(b) Steam very gently for 35 to 40 minutes. (If the soufflés are cooked in small cases allow 10 to 15 minutes.) Steamed soufflés are turned out and served with sauce poured round.

CHEESE SOUFFLÉ (4 to 6 people)

3 oz. grated Par-
mesan cheese.
Cayenne, salt.
3 yolks and four
whites of egg.

PANADA
1 oz. butter.
½ oz. flour.
¼ pt. milk.

Melt the butter, add the flour, then the milk by degrees, and boil well. Remove from the fire, and add the cheese and the yolks one by one. Beat well. Season. Lastly, fold in the stiffly beaten whites. Bake in a prepared soufflé case for 20 to 30 minutes, or bake in small prepared ramequin cases for about 10 minutes. Serve immediately.

CHICKEN SOUFFLÉ (4 or 5 people)
(A Typical Example)

1 oz. butter.
1 oz. flour.
¼ pt. milk or stock. } Make these into a panada. (See p. 109.)

Flavouring. ¼ lb. raw or cooked (preferably raw) chicken, which has been minced, pounded, and sieved. 3 or 4 eggs (if possible 3 yolks and 4 whites).

Add the sieved chicken to the panada, season to taste, cool a little, add the yolks of the eggs, one by one, beating well. Lastly, stir in the stiffly beaten whites very lightly, and put the mixture into a case prepared as follows: Grease a case or tin thoroughly, tie a band of buttered greased paper firmly round the case, projecting 3 or 4 inches above its top. The case must not be more than half filled with the mixture. Grease a round of paper big enough to rest on the paper band.   In baking, this prevents burning, and in steaming it prevents the drops of moisture, which condense on the lid, from dropping into the soufflé and making it sodden.   Baked soufflés are served in the case, the paper band being removed.

The same recipe may be used for any kind of meat or fish.

TABLE FOR HOT SWEET SOUFFLÉS

(Each soufflé is sufficient for 4 or 5 people)

GINGER.	CHOCOLATE.	COFFEE.	VANILLA.
1 oz. butter.	1 oz. butter.	1 oz. butter.	1 oz. butter.
1 oz. flour.	1 oz. flour.	1 oz. flour.	1 oz. flour.
¼ pt. milk.	¼ pt. milk.	¼ pt. milk and coffee mixed.	¼ pt. milk.
[1] 3 eggs.	[1] 3 eggs.	[1] 3 eggs	[1] 3 eggs.
1 oz. sugar.	Sugar to taste.	Sugar to taste.	1 oz. sugar
2 oz. ginger cut into dice.	1 oz. chocolate dissolved in the milk.		½ teasp. vanilla essence.

N.B. To make PINEAPPLE SOUFFLÉ follow recipe for GINGER, substituting 2 oz. pineapple.

To make CHESTNUT SOUFFLÉ follow recipe for GINGER, substituting 2 oz. chestnuts cooked in syrup; also add a few drops liqueur.

METHODS FOR ALL:

(1) Prepare a soufflé case.   (See Chicken Soufflé, above.)

(2) Make a thick sauce or ' panada ' of the fat, flour and milk. Stir and boil this till it leaves the sides of the saucepan clean.

(3) Add the sugar; cool, then beat in the yolks one by one, beating well.

(4) Add the flavourings.

(5) Beat the whites very stiffly, and add these last very quickly and lightly.

(6) Put the mixture in the prepared case (see Chicken Soufflé), and bake for about 30 minutes, or steam for about 40 minutes or longer, *very* gently.

[1] The addition of an extra white of egg improves the soufflé.

MOUSSES

Mousses are light sweets suitable for high-class dinners. The texture much resembles that of a soufflé, therefore recipes for Mousses (Sweet) are given here. They are delicate, rather difficult, but very delicious sweets, and need care and practice in making. For Mousses (Meat) see Entrées, page 107.

Lemon Mousse

Make as for Orange Mousse, using lemon instead of orange.

Orange Mousse (Hot)
(4 to 6 people)

2 oz. castor sugar.	2 oz. butter.
½ an orange.	3 eggs. ½ oz. flour.

Cream the butter and sugar, then add gradually the yolks and orange juice. Whisk this over a saucepan of boiling water until thick and creamy. Fold in the flour lightly and the stiffly beaten whites of egg.

Grease thoroughly a charlotte mould and coat it with flour. Half fill it with the mousse and place the mould in a tin, half full of hot water. Cover with a greased paper and put in a moderate oven for about ½ hour.

Turn out and serve with a good mousseline sauce.

Raspberry or Strawberry Mousse (4 to 6 people)

2 oz. castor sugar. 4 eggs. 2 oz. butter. 1 oz. flour.

¼ gill of raspberry or strawberry juice, and 5 or 6 slightly divided strawberries, or about 20 whole raspberries.

Make as for Orange Mousse.

SWEET SOUFFLÉS, COLD

These are really not soufflés, properly so called, but a very light cream in which there is enough gelatine to support the mixture, but not enough to enable it to be turned out.

TO PREPARE CHINA CASES FOR COLD SOUFFLÉS. The case must be dry and clean. Tie a stiff band of kitchen paper round the outside of the case to project 2 or 3 inches above the case.

In filling the case the mixture should be piled on to it, so that it comes 1½ to 2 inches above the top, where it is supported by the paper. When the soufflé is set, the paper can be carefully removed by drawing it off by unrolling it from the soufflé, easing it off with a silver knife dipped in cold water. This piled-up effect gives the false idea that the soufflé has risen.

Chocolate Soufflé (Cold)

(6 or more people)

3 eggs.	½ oz. gelatine dissolved
2 oz. chocolate.	in ½ gill wine.
¼ to ½ pt. cream.	3 oz. castor sugar.
Vanilla.	1 gill milk.

(2 oz. pounded French almond rock—not essential.)

Dissolve the chocolate in the milk. Whisk the yolks, sugar, and dissolved chocolate over boiling water till thick and light. Pound the rock and add this, also the vanilla and the gelatine dissolved in the wine.

Then add the whipped cream, and, lastly, the stiffly beaten whites of egg.

Pour into the prepared case, and, when cold, decorate tastefully.

Coffee Soufflé (Cold)

Follow the recipe for Chocolate Soufflé (Cold), putting 1 gill strong coffee instead of milk, and leaving out the French almond rock.

Orange Soufflé (Cold)

Follow the recipe for 'Soufflé au Sabayon,' using orange instead of lemon.

Raspberry and Strawberry Soufflés (Cold)

Follow the recipe for Chocolate Soufflé (Cold), leaving out the chocolate and rock, and adding ¼ pt. fruit juice to the egg yolks and sugar, and putting in, lastly, 2 oz. raspberries or strawberries cut into dice and soaked in maraschino.

Soufflé au Sabayon (Lemon Milanese Soufflé)

(6 or more people)

3 eggs.	3 oz. castor sugar.
The juice of 2 and rind	½ pt. cream.
of 1 lemon.	½ oz. gelatine dissolved
Vanilla, etc., to taste.	in ½ gill wine or water.

(1 gill stiff wine jelly may replace the wine and gelatine.)

Whisk the yolks, castor sugar, and lemon juice over boiling water till thick and light. Add the grated rind and let this cool.

Whisk the cream. Dissolve the gelatine in the wine (OR, melt the jelly and whisk it till nearly cold). Lastly, whip the whites of egg very stiffly.

Add the gelatine mixture (or jelly) to the cooled yolks; fold this into the cream, then fold in the whites. The mixture should set almost at once. Just before it sets, fill the case as described.

When set, decorate tastefully. Roses of cream forced round the so-called ' risen ' sides look well, and a rim of crushed violets, etc., at the top.

Vanilla Soufflé (Cold)

Follow the recipe for Chocolate Soufflé, Cold, omitting the chocolate, and adding vanilla to taste. This may be varied by omitting the almond rock, and by adding 2 oz. cherries, or pineapple cut into small dice, and soaked in brandy before being put into the soufflé.

They must go in last of all, and the soufflé requires stirring till it just begins to set, or the fruits all fall to the bottom.

XI. JELLIES, CREAMS, MERINGUES, AND ICES

JELLIES

EXCEPT for calf's foot jellies, the use of gelatine (or isinglass) is necessary. The most satisfactory is probably Cox's instant powdered gelatine; Marshall's is also very good. If 'French leaf gelatine' is used the leaf should be as fine as possible.

Nelson's packets of gelatine require previous soaking. If Marshall's is used, rather less gelatine than the proportions given here will be required. The same proportions will always make plain jellies of fruit juice, etc., and if not wanted cleared the clearing process can be omitted.

Recipes have already been given for milk jellies. The ones particularly dealt with here are those which are cleared; and the method of clearing a jelly is very similar to that employed for clearing a soup.

IF A GOOD ELECTRIC REFRIGERATOR IS AVAILABLE, AND COX'S GELATINE IS USED, IT WILL BE FOUND THAT UNDER ONE AND A HALF OUNCES OF GELATINE WILL SET ONE QUART OF LIQUID.

METHOD:

(1) Put all the ingredients into a large lined pan at one time.

(2) Whisk briskly over the fire until the top is covered with a thick foam.

(3) Stop whisking well before boiling point when a good froth has been formed.

(4) Let the whole boil right up in the pan. Care must be taken not to allow it to boil over. Then simmer it very gently for ½ hour.

(5) Stand the jelly in a perfectly undisturbed place for five minutes, to 'settle'.

(6) Strain it either through a jelly bag or through a cloth; in either case see that this is perfectly clean, and to further ensure this pour a kettle full of boiling water through it before straining the jelly, and after the cloth has been fixed on to the stand or tied to the legs of a chair. Remove the bowl containing the

PROPORTIONS FOR JELLY-MAKING
(Enough for 6 or 7 people)

Ingredients	Lemon Jelly	Orange Jelly	Wine Jelly	Claret Jelly
Gelatine (Cox's or French Leaf)	2 oz.	2 oz.	2 oz.	2 oz.
Liquid, 1 qt.	The juice of 3 or 4 lemons. 1½ pt. water.	1 pt. orange juice. 1 pt. water.	1 pt. sherry 3 gills water. 1 gill lemon juice.	1½ pt. claret ½ pt. water.
Sugar	6 or 8 oz. lump sugar.	6 or 8 oz. lump sugar.	6 oz. lump sugar.	6 oz. lump sugar.
Flavourings	The rind, thinly cut, of 2 lemons. 4 cloves and 1 in. cinnamon stick.	Thinly cut rind of two oranges.	4 cloves, 2 in. of stick cinnamon.	Rind of four lemons.
For clearing	The crushed shells and two whites of eggs.	The crushed shells and two whites of eggs.	The crushed shells and two whites of eggs.	The crushed shells and two whites of eggs.

In very cold weather, or where ice is available, use 1½ oz. gelatine to the qt. Similarly in exceptionally hot weather, more gelatine may be needed.

water that has run through the bag, put a fresh one underneath to catch the jelly, and the bag is then both clean and hot for the straining purposes.

(7) Strain the jelly very carefully without shaking it, and if the first part is slightly cloudy, put it through the bag again, slipping a fresh bowl underneath as the first one is removed.

The straining is really only to keep back the particles; the real clearing takes place in the pan.

(8) Keep the jelly warm while straining it. To do this, stand it out of the draught, and cover the top of the bag with a cloth. In cold weather a jar of boiling water may be carefully lowered into the bag to dissolve any jelly that seems to be setting in the bag.

IMPORTANT POINT. The success of jelly-making depends on the accurate weighing and measuring of the ingredients, as well as on the straining.

ONE OUNCE OF GELATINE is required for exactly ONE PINT OF LIQUID. The LIQUID may be mixed in any proportion, e.g.: water $\frac{1}{2}$ pt., lemon juice $\frac{1}{4}$ pt., wine $\frac{1}{4}$ pt.; or water $2\frac{1}{2}$ gills, lemon juice $\frac{1}{2}$ gill, wine I gill, and so on—but so long as the whole amount equals I pt. the jelly will set and turn out.

TO MOULD A JELLY. The mould must be perfectly clean and absolutely free from grease. Keep it lying in cold water while making the jelly.

Jelly must be cold to the touch before it is moulded; all perceptible warmth must have gone, but of course it must still be in a liquid state.

The cold water must then be poured out of the mould, and the jelly poured in while the mould is still damp.

TO LINE A MOULD with jelly. This is often required when the mould is to be filled with cream, etc.

Rinse the mould out with cold water, then pour in jelly in small spoonfuls until the bottom is coated to a depth of between $\frac{1}{8}$ and $\frac{1}{4}$ of an inch. Leave the mould standing in cold salt and water (salt reduces the temperature of water) or on ice until this sets firmly. Decorate tastefully with pistachio nut, cherries, etc., being careful not to over-decorate but to carry out some clear design. Place a spot of jelly on each of the decorations, and let this set to keep them in place. Then add a few more spoonfuls to make them secure. When this is absolutely set, the mould may be filled up with any prepared fruit cream, chocolate cream, etc., or with a layer of overlapping or prettily arranged fruit. In the latter case each layer must be set with a few drops of jelly, then covered with jelly, and one layer must be allowed to set before the next can be added.

THE CREAM, if added, must be cold, but not set. If at all warm it will melt the jelly and quite spoil the effect.

VERY PRETTY SWEETS may be made by lining the mould with jelly and placing a layer of raspberries, etc., on this; cover them with jelly and let this set. Then add a layer about ½ or ¾ inch in thickness of prepared raspberry cream. Let this set. Add another layer of raspberries, cover these in jelly, and repeat till the mould is full. Each must be quite set before the next is added.

TO LINE THE SIDES OF A MOULD WITH JELLY. To do this well, ice is required. Line the bottom with jelly as described. When this is set decorate the bottom and set the decoration. Then place a few spoonfuls of jelly on the side and let this lie on ice; as it sets turn the mould and add more, and continue to do this until all is evenly coated.

If a bomb mould, or one with a rounded top is used, the same method must be used to line the top.

TO TURN OUT A JELLY. Dip the mould into water that is quite hot, but not hot enough to scald. Shake it firmly sideways after dipping it right under the water, and it should slip out easily. If not, dip it under once more.

ASPIC JELLY

7 gills good first stock,

1 gill acid
$\begin{cases} \text{½ gill sherry.} \\ \text{1 tablesp. malt vinegar.} \\ \text{1 dessertsp. tarragon vinegar.} \\ \text{1 teasp. chilli vinegar.} \\ \text{Rind and juice of 1 lemon.} \end{cases}$

1 onion.　1 carrot.	½ teasp. salt.
1 stick celery.	Whites and shells of 2 eggs.
8 white peppercorns.	2–2½ oz. gelatine.

Put all ingredients into a large, lined pan, scalded. Stir over a clear fire till gelatine is dissolved. Whisk briskly till a good froth is formed, remove the whisk and allow the jelly to boil up with force; then draw to one side of the fire and leave to settle for 20 minutes. Strain through a jelly cloth till clear.

CALF'S FOOT JELLY (about 3 pt.)

2 calf's feet.	Rinds cut thinly of
2 qt. water.	3 lemons.
½ pt. sherry.	Whites and shells of
¼ pt. lemon juice.	4 eggs.
6 oz. sugar (loaf).	

Cut the feet into 8 pieces, blanch them, then wash them well again, and put them into a pan with the 2 qt. of water. Simmer gently for 6 hours, skimming whenever necessary. Strain. Next day remove all fat.[1] Follow the recipe for making jelly, omitting, of course, all gelatine and just melting the stock and sugar with the rinds and adding to these the whites, beaten, and mixed with the crushed shells, wine and lemon juice.

CHARTREUSE OF BANANA (4 or 5 people)

1 pt. wine or lemon jelly.	Pistachio nuts, etc., for decoration.
3 bananas.	A few cherries.

Line a border mould with clear jelly to ¼ inch in depth. When set, decorate with cherries and chopped nuts. Set this decoration with a few drops of jelly. On this place a layer of slices of banana overlapping each other; add a few drops of jelly to set these in place. When quite set add sufficient jelly to cover the fruit. Let this set, and so proceed until the mould is full. When the mould is set, turn it out and fill the centre with whipped cream and decorate with chopped pistachio nuts.

CHARTREUSE OF GRAPES

This is made in the same way. The grapes must be skinned, halved, and the stones removed. Any fruit may replace the grapes.

COW HEEL JELLY

Follow exactly the recipe for Calf's Foot Jelly.

EGG JELLY (4 or 5 people)

½ pt. water.	1½ oz. sugar.
Rind and juice of 1 large lemon.	¼ oz. gelatine.
	1 tablesp. sherry.
2 eggs or 3 yolks.	

Heat the lemon rind, sugar, and gelatine in the water for

[1] Note the consistency of the jellied stock and add gelatine if required.

10 minutes, without boiling. Add the lemon juice and beaten eggs, and heat carefully, stirring all the time, until of a creamy consistency. Strain (through muslin, if wished), add the wine and pour into the prepared mould.

MACEDOINE OF FRUIT

This is made in the same way as Chartreuse. A stiffer jelly is required, viz. 1 oz. gelatine to 1 pt. liquid, and in this as large a variety of fruits as possible should be set.

PRUNE GÂTEAU (5 or 6 people)

6 oz. loaf sugar.	½ pt. water.
½ pt. claret.	The peel of 1 lemon,
½ in. stick cinnamon.	thinly cut.

Place these together in a pan. Dissolve the sugar, and boil for 1 or 2 minutes, add 1 lb. French plums, and stew till tender. Then strain the syrup and sieve the plums. Measure this, and to each pt. allow ½ oz. gelatine. Dissolve the gelatine in the syrup. Add 1 glass of sherry, the juice of an orange, and carmine to colour. Mix this with the sieved plums. When cool pour into a mould which has previously been lined with clear jelly and decorated with strips of blanched almond. If liked, serve with custard poured round.

RAINBOW JELLY (6 or more people)

1 qt. lemon jelly.   Colourings and flavourings.

Line a mould with clear jelly, and decorate it to taste (see page 243). Divide the jelly into three parts, leave one plain, and colour another pink, and another pale green. Flavour to taste. Whisk both separately until stiff and spongy. Put in pieces of the sponge and cover with jelly. Repeat till the mould is full.

SPONGES

Lemon Sponge (4 to 6 people)

½ oz. gelatine.	2 whites of egg.
2 small lemons.	3 oz. sugar.
½ pt. water.	

Cut the rinds of the lemons very thinly and put these into a saucepan with the water and gelatine. Leave in a warm place to extract the flavour and to dissolve the gelatine. Add the sugar and lemon juice.

When quite cool strain to the whites, and whisk till white and spongy. This may then either be moulded or piled on to a dish. If moulded, serve a lemon custard poured round it.

Orange Sponge

Follow the directions for Lemon Sponge, using orange instead of lemon.

Pineapple Sponge (4 to 6 people)

1 small tin pine-apple chunks.	½ oz. gelatine.
¼ pt. water.	Juice of a lemon.
1 glass of wine.	2 oz. sugar.
	3 whites of egg.

Cut the fruit into dice; cook for 15 minutes with the sugar, lemon juice, and pineapple syrup. Dissolve the gelatine in the water, add the wine. Pour these ingredients into a large basin, and when quite cold add the stiffly beaten whites and whisk till all is spongy. Pile on a glass dish, serve with pieces of pine-apple, and decorate with pistachio nuts, etc.

Raspberry Sponge

Follow the directions given for Lemon Sponge, using ½ pt. raspberry juice instead of water. Colouring also will be needed to improve the colour.

Semolina Sponge (4 to 6 people)

2 oz. semolina.	Fruit and sponge cake, if liked.
Sugar to taste.	
Juice of 2 lemons } 1 pt.	
Water }	

Boil the water in a well-lined pan and sprinkle in the semolina, stirring carefully all the time. Continue stirring and cooking till the grain is clear and quite thick. Add the lemon juice and sweeten to taste. Turn into a large, cold basin and whisk briskly till white, and thick, and frothy. Pour into a glass dish and, when set enough, decorate to taste.

This dish is improved by putting fresh or tinned fruit, sponge cake, etc., into the bottom of a dish and making it into a trifle. In this case decorate with some of the fruit.

Fruit juice may be used instead of water as, for example, when tinned fruit is put into the bottom of the dish.

Unless the mixture is quite thick after boiling, the sponge will not be frothy and light.

WHISKED JELLIES

Jellies may be whisked until cold, when they become a sponge, resembling lemon sponge.

CREAMS—Moulded

These may be divided into three classes:

    I. Those composed of cream alone sweetened and flavoured (probably with wine), and sufficient gelatine added.

    II. Fruit creams, composed of fruit purée, cream, and gelatine.

    III. Custard creams, composed of flavoured custard, cream, and gelatine.

I. Cream Only. This is very rich, and, when used, should be the filling for a 'charlotte russe' (a tin lined with sponge fingers), or else it may be put in a mould with alternate layers of jelly.

PROPORTION. 1 pt. cream, $\frac{1}{2}$ oz. gelatine dissolved in 2 or 3 tablesp. of wine or water, liqueur, and sugar added to taste.

METHOD. Dissolve the gelatine in the wine or water. Add this to HALF-whipped cream, sweeten to taste, and mould when on the point of setting.

ALLOW MORE GELATINE IN VERY HOT WEATHER FOR ALL CREAMS.

    II. **Fruit Creams.**

PLAIN (4 to 6 people)

RICH (5 or 6 people)

3 gills fruit purée (1$\frac{1}{2}$ lb. apples gives this amount) (sweetened to taste).

1 gill half-whipped cream.

$\frac{1}{2}$ oz. gelatine dissolved in $\frac{1}{2}$ gill liquid (fruit juice, hot water, or wine).

$\frac{1}{2}$ pt. fruit purée (sweetened to taste).

$\frac{1}{2}$ pt. half-whipped cream.

$\frac{1}{2}$ oz. gelatine dissolved in $\frac{1}{4}$ gill liquid (fruit juice, hot water, or wine).

In either case sieve the fruit and sweeten to taste. Add to the whipped cream; then add the dissolved gelatine. Stir gently on ice, or stand the bowl in cold salt and water until the mixture just begins to set, then mould at once. If moulded too soon, the cream will separate, and the appearance be spoilt.

OR, dissolve the gelatine. Pour this into the fruit purée, stirring briskly. When the mixture shows faint signs of setting, fold in the cream and mould at once.

IN MAKING FRUIT CREAMS, if fruit is plentiful and cream scarce, the fruit purée and cream may be combined in any proportion, so long as the two together equal exactly 1 pt. to each ½ oz. gelatine.

In hot weather 1 or 2 extra sheets of gelatine must always be allowed.

III. **Custard Creams.** These are suitable for chocolate and coffee, and also for ginger or such fruits that would be too solid if sieved—banana, pineapple, etc.

PLAIN (4 to 6 people)	RICH (5 or 6 people)
½ pt. half-whipped cream.	½ pt. half-whipped cream.
¾ pt. custard.	½ pt. custard.
Sugar and flavouring to taste.	Sugar and flavouring to taste.
½ oz. gelatine dissolved in ½ gill liquid (fruit juice, hot water or wine).	½ oz. gelatine dissolved in ½ gill liquid (fruit juice, hot water or wine).

In either case make a ' boiled ' custard, if coffee, with milk and coffee mixed to taste; if chocolate, with 1 oz. chocolate dissolved in the milk. (See Custards, page 217.) When the custard is quite cold, add it to the half-whipped cream and sweeten to taste. If fruits are added (ginger, cherries, etc.), cut 2 oz. of these into dice and mix lightly in. Add the dissolved gelatine. Stir over ice or in cold water until setting commences, then mould.

OR, make a boiled custard and prepare fruits as for above. Add the dissolved gelatine to the cold custard, add the fruits lightly, sweeten to taste, and when the mixture shows *faint* signs of setting, fold in the half-whipped cream. Mould when sufficiently thickened for the fruits to be evenly suspended in the mixture.

APRICOTS WITH GOOSEBERRY CREAM (6 to 8 people)

Clear jelly. Apricots (stewed).
1 pt. gooseberry cream (see recipe Fruit Cream, p. 248).

Line a plain charlotte mould with clear jelly. When set, coat the bottom and sides entirely with halves of apricot. Set these

I

with a little more jelly. Fill up the centre with a good goose-berry cream ($\frac{1}{2}$ pt. gooseberry purée, $\frac{1}{2}$ pt. cream, $\frac{1}{2}$ oz. gelatine). Turn out when cold, and decorate with whipped cream and finely chopped pistachio nuts.

BAVAROISE AU CHOCOLAT (5 or 6 people)

$\frac{1}{2}$ pt. milk.	2 oz. chocolate.
3 yolks of egg.	$\frac{1}{4}$ pt. cream.
2 oz. sugar.	$\frac{1}{4}$ oz. gelatine.

Dissolve the chocolate in the milk. Make a custard with the eggs, sugar, and milk. Cool, and add it to the semi-whipped cream. Dissolve the gelatine in $\frac{1}{2}$ gill of wine or water. Stir this into the mixture. Mould when almost cold.

N.B. The mould may be masked first if liked.

BROWN BREAD CREAM (6 or more people)

3 oz. brown breadcrumbs.	$\frac{1}{2}$ oz. gelatine dissolved
$\frac{1}{2}$ pt. ' boiled ' custard.	in $\frac{1}{2}$ gill hot water or
$\frac{1}{2}$ pt. cream.	wine.
Sugar to taste.	Vanilla.

Line a mould with clear jelly or with jelly in which 1 oz. chocolate has been dissolved. Decorate this. Pour the custard (hot) on to the crumbs. Cool this and add dissolved gelatine, vanilla, and sugar. When quite cool add the whipped cream. Stir till setting, then mould. This may be served with a good chocolate sauce.

CHARLOTTE RUSSE (4 to 5 people)

Line a plain 4-inch charlotte tin with 12 to 14 sponge fingers. Split them and fit them closely to the tin, the bottom of which should be lined with an oiled paper. Both bottoms and sides should be covered with the biscuits. Fill the mould with a rich, moulded cream (Class I, see page 248). When set, turn out, remove the oiled paper, and decorate tastefully with glacé cherries, and a few roses of whipped cream, etc.

The bottom of the tin may be lined with clear jelly and decorated. The mould may be filled with any fruit creams or the following:

CHARLOTTE RUSSE, APRICOT (4 to 6 people)

1 gill apricot purée.	Little carmine.
1 gill cream.	1 tablesp. sugar.
¼ oz. gelatine.	1 teasp. lemon juice.

Decorate and line mould with savoy fingers. Sieve the apricots and sweeten. Dissolve the gelatine in lemon juice and 2 tablesp. of water. Partly whisk the cream. Add the apricots to the cream and the hot dissolved gelatine. Pour in a mould when just setting. Turn out and decorate with whipped cream, chopped jelly, etc.

CHARLOTTE RUSSE, CHESTNUT

Line a plain charlotte mould with clear jelly. When this is set, cover the bottom and sides with split marrons glacés, and set these in a little more jelly. Fill the centre with chestnut cream. See recipe, page 252.

CHARLOTTE RUSSE, Economical (4 to 6 people)

About 1 doz. savoy fingers.	¼ oz. gelatine.
1 gill fruit pulp of any kind.	1 gill cream.
	A little clear jelly, if liked.
Sugar to taste.	

Set the jelly in the bottom of a straight mould (tin). Decorate as liked. Trim the biscuits evenly and fix carefully round the tin. Sieve the fruit and add it to the lightly whipped cream. Dissolve the gelatine in 2 tablespoons fruit juice or water and add. Stir till just setting, pour into mould. Turn out when set. Decorate with chopped jelly.

CHARLOTTE RUSSE, ORANGE (4 to 6 people)

¾ gill orange juice.	¼ oz. gelatine (more in hot weather).
1 gill cream.	
Sugar to taste.	

Line the top of a charlotte tin with clear orange jelly, decorate it with quarters of tangerine orange.

Make the orange cream in the usual way, using a little of the orange juice for dissolving the gelatine. Line the sides of the tin with sponge fingers and when the cream is just on the point of setting pour it into the decorated tin.

CHESTNUT CREAM (I)
(5 or 6 people)

Boil 1 lb. skinned chestnuts till tender. Make a rich custard with 2 eggs and ½ pt. milk, and pour this on to the chestnut purée. Add ½ oz. gelatine dissolved in ½ gill wine or hot water. When cool, add this to ½ pt. whipped cream. When it is on the point of setting, mould it.

CHESTNUT CREAM (II)
(6 or 7 people)

¾ pt. milk.	½ oz. gelatine dissolved
1 lb. chestnuts.	in ½ gill wine or hot
½ pt. cream.	water.
Sugar to taste (about	½ pt. clear jelly.
2 oz.).	1 oz. chocolate.

Vanilla.

Dissolve the chocolate in the jelly and line a mould with this. Boil the skinned chestnuts in the milk until tender. Sieve this, measure and use ½ pt. of the purée. Add the dissolved gelatine, whipped cream, vanilla and sugar to taste. Mould this. Turn out, and decorate with marrons glacés, and pour the rest of the purée round.

For Unmoulded Chestnut Cream, see page 258.

CHOCOLATE CREAM (Cheap)
(4 to 6 people)

¾ pt. milk.	Sugar to taste.
¼ pt. cream.	1 to 2 oz. cho-
½ oz. gelatine.	colate (or
Vanilla.	½ oz. cocoa).

Use a china mould and brush it with oil.

Dissolve the chocolate and gelatine in the milk without boiling it (If cocoa is used it must be mixed and boiled with a very little of the milk to dissolve it properly; this is then cooled and added to the rest of the milk and gelatine.) Sweeten to taste, and when cool, strain this to the whipped cream.

COFFEE CREAM (Cheap)

Use a china or good aluminium mould.

Make as for cheap chocolate cream, but add 1 tablesp. coffee essence (Allenbury's Café Vierge is excellent) instead of the chocolate.

COFFEE JELLY CREAM (4 to 6 people)

½ pt. strong coffee.   ½ oz. gelatine.
1½ gills new milk } or Ideal milk.
½ gill cream

Strain the coffee through fine muslin. Dissolve the gelatine carefully in it. Sweeten and add to the milk and cream. Set in a china mould, which should be lightly brushed with salad oil. Turn out when set. Decorate with whipped cream and cherries.

EVERLASTING CREAM (5 or 6 people)

1 pt. cream.   1 gill sherry. | Juice and finely grated rind
½ lb. finest castor sugar. | of 2 lemons.

Whisk all together for 20 minutes; put into custard glasses, and this will keep for four or five days.

FAIRY CREAM

See under Creams, Unmoulded, page 258.

GÂTEAU DE FRUITS

Line a plain charlotte mould or small cake tin with puff paste. Prick the bottom and sides and ' bake it blind ' (see page 168). Bake also a small round of paste to form a lid to the mould.

When cooked, remove the ' blind ' centre, and re-bake it for a few moments to cook the pastry in the middle, which might otherwise be damp. Turn the case carefully on to a sieve.

When quite cold fill it with any good fruit cream (on the point of setting) and fresh fruit—example, 2 inches of strawberry cream, then a layer of sweetened whole strawberries, and so on. The top layer should be of fruit still on the stems, artistically arranged so that the fruit hangs naturally over the edge. Pile this up at one side, filling any spaces with whipped cream, and put the lid on, resting it on one edge of the paste, and giving it the effect of a half-opened basket.

OR, the case may simply be filled with any fruit cream— example, apple cream—and the lid placed as before, the opening being filled with unbroken pieces of cooked apple and whipped cream.

GINGER CREAMS

See Class III, Custard Creams, page 249.

HONEYCOMB CREAM (4 to 6 people)

1 pt. milk. 2 large eggs.	Sugar and flavouring to
½ oz. gelatine.	taste.

Make a custard with the milk, yolks, sugar, and gelatine (this must not boil). Take it from the fire, and add the stiffly-beaten whites, stirring as little as possible. When cold, pour into a wetted mould.

LEMON CREAM (4 to 6 people)

¾ pt. cream. ½ pt. water.	4 to 6 oz. loaf sugar.
¼ pt. lemon juice.	¾ oz. gelatine.

Peel 2 lemons thinly, and rub the sugar on them to extract the flavour. Put the lemon rinds and water with the gelatine over gentle heat to melt the gelatine; when dissolved add the sugar, melt this, and when cool strain it to the cream which has been whipped with the lemon juice until stiff.

Pour into a wetted mould.

OR, pour into a flat meat dish, and, when cold, cut into strips and serve these piled high on a dish.

MOSAIC CREAM (4 to 6 people)

Clear jelly.	¼ pt. cream.
¼ pt. milk.	½ oz. gelatine.
	Sugar to taste.

Dissolve the gelatine in the milk and cream over very gentle heat. Add the sugar and divide into three portions. Leave one plain, and colour the other two to taste. Pour each third on to a damp dinner plate. Leave to set. Line a plain mould with clear jelly. Stamp the gelatine mixtures on the plates into fancy shapes with small cutters and arrange these all over the clear jelly that lines the mould to form a mosaic design. Add more jelly to set these. If ice is obtainable the sides also can be covered with mosaic. When the decoration is quite set fill the mould with any good cream, which must be on the point of setting before it is put into the prepared mould.

ORANGE CREAM (4 to 6 people)

DECORATION
Wine jelly.   Pistachio nuts.

FILLING

1 gill cream.	Lemon juice.
1 gill orange juice.	Colouring.
1 gill custard.	½ oz. gelatine.
Sugar.	½ gill water.

Line and decorate a mould.   Whip the cream and add the other ingredients, the dissolved gelatine last.   Mould when setting.   Turn out and decorate with chopped jelly.

NOTE. Infuse the milk used in the preparation of the custard with the rind of two lemons.

PINEAPPLE CREAM (4 to 6 people)

½ pt. cream.	½ pt. pineapple
½ oz. gelatine.	juice.
2 or 3 oz. small dice of pineapple.	

Follow the recipe for Fruit Creams on page 248, except that the gelatine should be dissolved in the fruit juice.

PLAIN ORANGE CREAM (4 to 6 people)

1½ oz. fine sago or semolina.	1 pt. water.
Juice and grated rind of a large orange.	2 eggs, OR 1 tablesp. marmalade and the juice of ½ lemon.
Sugar to taste.	

Boil the sago in the water till clear.   Add the sugar, orange, and beaten eggs (the whites may be left out).   Cook again slightly.   Pour into a glass dish and decorate with a little orange rind and angelica.

RICE À L'IMPÉRATRICE (4 to 6 people)

2 oz. Carolina rice.	½ pt. cream.
½ oz. gelatine.	Sugar and flavouring
1 pt. milk.	to taste.

Cook the washed rice in the milk till soft.   Add the sugar, flavouring, and the gelatine dissolved in ½ gill wine or hot water. Cool this, then add it to the whipped cream.   Pour into a prettily decorated mould or into small moulds. Turn out when set, and decorate with whipped cream. Serve with compote of fruit. The mixture may also be put into a border mould, and, when turned out, the centre can be piled up with fruit and whipped cream.

SAGO CREAM (4 to 6 people)

2 oz. fine sago or ground tapioca.	1 gill cream.
1 pt. milk.	A few ratafias.
½ gill sherry.	Few drops almond essence.
	Pistachio nuts.

Simmer the sago in milk in a double pan till cooked. Sweeten, flavour, and cool. Whisk the cream slightly, add the sago. Cover the bottom of a glass dish with ratafias, soak with sherry. Pour the mixture over. Decorate with ratafias, pistachios, etc.

STONE CREAM (4 to 6 people)

12 macaroons.	½ oz. gelatine.
1 pt. milk. Sugar ½ oz.	Flavouring and colouring
Apricot jam.	to taste.

Add more gelatine in hot weather.

Put 1 large tablesp. of jam at the bottom of a glass dish, and cover this with a layer of macaroons. Dissolve the gelatine in ½ gill liquid (fruit juice, wine or hot water), and add this to the milk, add the sugar, flavouring, and colouring. When cool pour some of this over the macaroons. Let this set, then pour in the rest, and, when firm, decorate with almonds, etc.

STRAWBERRY CREAM

See Fruit Creams, page 248.

STRAWBERRY MOUSSE (6 or more people)

1 lb. strawberries.	1½ pt. clear jelly.
⅓ pt. cream.	½ oz. gelatine.
2 eggs.	2 oz. sugar.

Whisk the yolks and sugar over boiling water till thick and light. Add the gelatine dissolved in ½ gill wine or hot water. Add the dissolved jelly and whisk again. Sieve the strawberries and add these. Lastly, add the whipped cream and stiffly

beaten whites of eggs. Mould just before the mixture sets.
Turn out and decorate with whole strawberries and whipped
cream.

TAPIOCA CREAM (4 to 6 people)

2 oz. crushed tapioca.	Sugar and flavouring
2 eggs. 1 pt. milk.	to taste.

Cook the tapioca in the milk. When thick and creamy
remove it from the fire. Add the yolks, sugar and flavouring,
also the stiffly beaten whites. Serve cold, piled on a dish.
Decorate to taste.

TIVOLI OF ANY FRUIT

Line a plain mould with clear jelly. Decorate—set the
decoration. Put in the following in layers: Fruit cream (see
page 248), custard cream, flavoured with vanilla, whole fruit just
covered in jelly. Each layer must be absolutely set before the
next can be added. Turn out. Decorate with whole fruit and
cream, or chopped jelly.

VELVET CREAM (6 or more people)

¾ oz. gelatine.	1 pt. cream.
2 lemons.	½ pt. sherry.
4 oz. loaf sugar.	

Soak the gelatine in the wine for 1 or 2 hours; then dissolve
it, stirring. Rub the rinds of 2 lemons with the lump sugar.
Add these with the lemon juice to the mixture. When melted,
but not too hot, pour this gently into 1 pt. cream. Stir this
gently till quite cold. Then mould it.

A cheaper Velvet Cream may be made by pouring the same
mixture into 1 pt. of milk and cream mixed in any proportion.

VOL-AU-VENT DE FRUITS

Make a vol-au-vent (see page 173). When cold fill it with
layers of any cream when set, and fruit. Rice à l'Impératrice
is one of the best creams to use for this.

Patties may be made and filled in the same way.

*I

CREAMS—Unmoulded

These are cold sweet dishes, in which little or no gelatine is used.

APPLE SNOW (4 or 5 people)

½ lb. apple pulp, weighed after cooking and sieving.	3 whites of eggs. The juice of ½ a lemon, strained.

Sugar to taste.

Beat the pulp, lemon juice, and sugar well, also, separately, the three whites together. These must be fairly thick but not solid. Mix the two together, and beat till the whole is thick and spongy.

Apple snow makes a useful substance for cream for decorating trifles, etc. It should be served soon after being made, as, owing to the absence of gelatine, it subsides a little by standing.

Orange, Lemon, Pineapple, etc., can replace the apple, but only ¼ pt. of these must be allowed for 3 whites of egg.

CHESTNUT CREAM (5 or 6 people)

Boil 20 skinned chestnuts in 1 pt. milk and ¼ pt. water till tender. Make a syrup of 4 oz. sugar and 1 gill water and reduce this well. Sieve and pound the chestnuts with the syrup to obtain a smooth paste. Whip ½ pt. cream and put it into the centre of a glass dish. Sieve the chestnut paste through a coarse sieve, piling it high on to the centre of the cream. Decorate with crystallized violets, etc.

FAIRY CREAM (5 or 6 people)

½ lb. macaroons.	2 or 3 oz. castor sugar.
1 tablesp. maraschino.	2 hard-boiled yolks of
¼ pt. sherry and fruit juice or water.	eggs (sieved).
¼ lb. ground almonds.	3 oz. fresh butter.
1 gill cream.	Vanilla and colouring to taste.

Put the macaroons in a deep glass dish and soak them in the wine and liqueur. Cream the butter and sugar, and the almonds and sieved yolks. Cover the macaroons with this mixture. Whip the cream and divide it into two portions, colouring one pink. Force roses of the alternate colours over the whole, and decorate with rose leaves and silver balls.

RASPBERRIES, STRAWBERRIES, Etc.

These make excellent unmoulded creams.

Thoroughly sweeten some fruit juice. Add sufficient of this to some cream to flavour and colour it. Whisk the two together until thick and light. If the fruit juice is too acid the cream will curdle.

These creams may be allowed to stand, and will become more firmly set owing to the gradual curdling of the cream due to the acid in the fruit. If, however, this takes place before the whipping, the dish is spoilt.

OR, first whip the cream, then add sufficient very well sweetened fruit pulp to flavour it. Serve in custard glasses.

RASPBERRY AND BANANA MOUSSE—Unmoulded

(6 or more people)

4 eggs.	4 bananas (sieved).
6 or 8 oz. castor sugar.	½ pt. fresh raspberry
½ pt. cream (whipped).	juice (strained through
½ oz. gelatine.	muslin).

Whisk the yolks, sugar and 1½ gills of raspberry juice over boiling water till thick and creamy. Cool, then add the gelatine dissolved in ½ gill raspberry juice, and whisk till nearly cold. Add the four sieved bananas, then the whipped cream, and, lastly, the stiffly beaten whites of eggs. Stir on ice till nearly setting. Then pour into a glass bowl, piling it up, and decorate with whole raspberries and chopped pistachio nuts.

MERINGUES

These are made with whites of egg and sugar.

To each white of egg allow 2 oz. of fine castor sugar. Whip the whites of eggs till, on lifting a portion with the whisk and turning it upwards, the points of whipped egg will stand upright. Add half the sugar very gradually, whisking thoroughly between each addition. Fold in the rest. Shape the meringues in a dessert-spoon into shapes resembling half an egg, smoothing them with a knife. Slip these by means of a second spoon on to oiled foolscap paper, which should, if possible, be placed on a small board or else on a baking tin, which must be heated and then rubbed with white wax. Dust the tops with icing sugar, and bake them in a very cool oven till crisp (2 or 3 hours). Remove them carefully from the paper. Reverse them, press down the centres, which will be slightly soft. Sugar these and bake them again bottom upwards till quite dry. Meringues, so made, will keep in tins.

To dish them, whip some cream, place a dessertspoonful on one half and cover with the second. Any cream projecting at the edge may be coated with finely chopped pistachio nut, ground almonds, or coloured sugar.

To COLOUR SUGAR. Put a small quantity of white sugar in an egg cup. To this add one drop of colouring. Rub with a salt-spoon until of the desired colour.

Meringues may also be moulded by putting the mixture into a forcing bag, and forcing fancy shapes on to the paper. They may be filled with sieved banana flavoured with strawberry jam, if cream is unobtainable.

APPLE MERINGUES (5 to 6 people)

Core and peel 6 even-sized apples. Place a few sultanas in each. Stew them carefully in syrup till just tender. Lift them on to a baking tin. Cover them with a meringue made in the usual way but with 2 whites of egg and 1 oz. of sugar. Dredge them with sugar, stick them with shreds of almonds and brown them in a very moderate oven. Decorate. Reduce the syrup, flavour and colour it and pour it round the apples, which if possible should be stood on a rice border.

FRUIT MERINGUE

Meringue mixture may also be spread over the top of a pie-dish filled with any fruit, which, if cooked, must be quite cold. Smooth the meringue with a damped knife. Quickly decorate the edges to resemble a tart, dust the top with icing sugar, and bake in a very cool oven till crisp and just golden brown (about 2 hours). Serve hot or cold.

ICES

These may be divided into two classes: simple, such as plain water and cream ices; and compound, such as mousse, sorbets and iced puddings.

SORBETS are served before the roast; ICED PUDDINGS may be served instead of sweets in the sweet course following the roast; DESSERT ICES are handed round as soon as the dessert is put on the table.

To make ices a special machine is required. Tin ones can be bought quite cheaply, and they are as effective, but not so durable as the more expensive ones. Each machine consists of two receptacles: the outer one to contain the ice and salt, the inner to contain the mixture to be iced. Care must be taken in filling or handling the machine not to let any of the salt get into the inner receptacle. Salt is as essential as ice for the making of ices, and freezing salt (a cheap coarse variety) should be obtained if possible. 4 lb. of salt should be allowed to 12 lb. of ice, this quantity being sufficient to make 1 or 2 qt. of simple ice.

TO FILL THE FREEZING MACHINE. With an ice pick or strong skewer, chip the ice into small pieces. Fill the outer receptacle with alternate layers of these and dry salt. During the process of freezing, as this melts, let the water away through the holes provided in the machine, and refill as required.

For compound ices, soufflés, etc., an ice cave is necessary, though ice puddings can be made without. An ice cave is a specially constructed cupboard with a space between the outside and inner lining. This space must be filled with ice and salt in the proportions given. This is called ' charging ' the ice cave, and the dishes when prepared are placed in the cave for the final freezing, which usually takes 2 hours.

For ice puddings, special moulds are required. These are usually made in three portions, and fit together closely so that the whole of the pudding is encased. If no ice cave is available, ice puddings may be made by wrapping the mould in greased paper (as a further protection from salt) and entirely immersing it in a bucket containing salt and ice. The bucket should be covered with sacking, felt, etc., and the whole left for 2 hours or longer till the freezing is complete.

Ice pudding can also be finished in a refrigerator, which must be kept below freezing point during the process.

ICES—Simple

For these the mixture is put into a freezing machine, the handle of which is then turned until the contents become sufficiently stiff and frozen. Remove spatula and leave to 'ripen' before serving. To SERVE, place rocky spoonfuls on small ice plates. Wafers should be handed with simple ices. It is correct, when possible, to sweeten with syrup instead of with sugar. ALLOW ONE PINT OF ICE TO EIGHT PEOPLE.

Syrup for Ices. To each lb. of sugar allow 2 pt. of water. Boil and skim. Reduce to half the quantity. Strain and bottle. 4 tablesp. are usually allowed to $\frac{1}{2}$ pt. of cream, etc., but the ices, when tasted, should be slightly over-sweet, as the freezing process detracts from the sweetness. If, however, ices are over-sweetened, the mixture will not freeze properly. If under-sweetened, ices are rough and flavourless.

ALGERIAN ICE

6 tangerine oranges.	10 cooked chestnuts.
$\frac{1}{2}$ small tin apricots.	Juice of 1 lemon.
$\frac{1}{2}$ wine-glass maraschino.	A few drops of carmine.
A few lumps of sugar.	$\frac{1}{4}$ pt. whipped cream.

Custard $\begin{cases} \frac{1}{2} \text{ pt. milk.} \\ 3 \text{ yolks of eggs.} \end{cases}$

Rub the rinds of the oranges on the lump sugar. Dissolve this in their juice. Sieve the chestnuts and apricots, add the lemon juice, the orange juice, and liqueur. Make a custard, and when quite cold add it to the mixture. Lastly add the whipped cream, sweetened if necessary. Colour to taste and freeze.

BANANA ICE

1 pt. sieved banana, flavoured with lemon, and added to the recipe for New York Ice Cream, would make an excellent Banana Ice Cream.

Any other fruit pulp may be added in the same way.

BLACK CURRANT ICE

Follow recipe for Strawberry Ice.

CHOCOLATE ICE

½ pt. chocolate custard cold, (see p. 221).	Vanilla. ½ pt. cream. Sugar syrup to taste.

Put the custard, sugar, and vanilla (to taste) into the freezer. Stir till semi-frozen. Add the stiffly whipped cream and freeze.

CRÈME DE FRUITS À LA MONACO

4 sticks of rhubarb cooked in a little water with white sugar. 4 bananas.	3 oranges. 1 lemon. 4 apricots. The pulp of 3 baked apples.

Sieve all these together. Add 1 pt. cold custard, also three sheets of gelatine dissolved in a little wine or fruit juice. Sweeten and colour. Freeze. When firm, turn on to a dish and cover the surface with blanched, chopped, and slightly browned almonds.

LEMON WATER ICE

1 pt. water. Rinds of 2 lemons. 6 oz. loaf sugar.	Stiffly beaten whites of 2 eggs. Juice of 4 lemons.

Put the water, thinly cut lemon rinds and sugar into a saucepan and boil for ten minutes—if tested with a sweet-making thermometer, 220° F. When quite cold add the lemon juice. Strain. Add the stiffly beaten whites and freeze till firm and dry.

MELON ICE

1 melon.   1 gill cream.   Sugar syrup to taste.

Cut off the top of a melon to make a lid. Scoop out as much of the pulp as the weight of the cream. Sieve this. Sweeten. Add the whipped cream. Mix well and freeze.

Serve melon piled up in melon case.

NEW YORK ICE CREAM

1 pt. cream very well sweetened.
2 yolks of eggs well beaten, and 2 whites stiffly frothed.
Vanilla to taste.

Mix the yolks thoroughly with the cream. Fold in the whites lightly and freeze.

ORANGE WATER ICE

2 oranges. 2 lemons. ¾ pt. sugar syrup.

Peel the fruit thinly. Boil the syrup. Pour it over the rinds and add the juice. When quite cold, strain. Add liqueur to taste and freeze.

PÊCHE MELBA

2 oz. sugar.	Vanilla ice.
1 tin peaches.	1 lemon.
Raspberry syrup.	

Drain the peaches. Add 2 oz. sugar and the rind of the lemon cut thinly to the peach syrup. Boil this for 10 minutes. Flavour with vanilla. Cool and pour this over the peaches. Leave them to soak one to two hours. Drain and serve as follows: (1) FOR SEPARATE PORTIONS. Pile the centre of each half-peach with vanilla ice. Sprinkle the top with browned chopped almonds and pour raspberry syrup round. (2) AS A DISH. Put a mound of vanilla ice in the centre of a dish. Coat it with peaches. Brush them with sieved raspberry jam and sprinkle them with browned chopped almonds. Pour raspberry syrup round. Or, the mound of vanilla may be placed if wished on a hollow round of sponge cake.

If possible, the peaches and syrup should beforehand be kept in a refrigerator.

STRAWBERRY CREAM ICE

1 pt. strawberries.	1 pt. cream.
Juice of ½ lemon.	4 oz. castor sugar.

Sprinkle some of the sugar over the fruit. Sieve this through a hair sieve. Add the lemon juice, sugar, and sugar syrup to taste, also the whipped cream. Colour with carmine and freeze.

STRAWBERRY WATER ICE

¾ lb. strawberries.	Juice of 1 lemon.
¾ pt. sugar syrup.	¼ pt. cream.

Sieve the fruit. Boil the syrup. Add it to the fruit pulp with the lemon juice. Cool, add the cream, and freeze.

VANILLA ICE CREAM

½ pt. milk.	3 yolks of eggs.
½ pt. cream.	Vanilla.
Sugar syrup to taste.	

Make a custard of the eggs and milk. Add the vanilla and sugar syrup. Cool, add the whipped cream, and freeze.

ICES—Compound

ICED MOUSSES

These are very light mixtures made of custard, fruit, eggs, and cream; the mixture is afterwards placed in an ice cave and frozen.

Apricot Mousse

¼ lb. castor sugar.	½ pt. cream (whipped).
3 eggs.	1 gill sieved apricots.
Rinds and juice of 2 lemons (rinds finely grated).	½ oz. gelatine.
	1 glass wine.

Whisk the yolks, grated lemon rinds, strained lemon juice and sugar over boiling water until thick and light. Cool this, add the gelatine dissolved in the wine (or in fruit juice), and the sieved apricot. When this is again quite cool add the whipped cream and stiffly beaten whites of eggs. Mix carefully, and add liqueur to taste. Pour the mixture into small cups or into a soufflé case, round which a band of paper has been tied, and place in a charged ice cave for 2 hours. Serve sprinkled with browned chopped almonds.

Any other fruit pulp may replace the apricot.

Coffee Mousse

1 oz. ground coffee.	½ pt. cream (whipped).
3 yolks, 2 whites of eggs.	2 oz. castor sugar.

Make a very strong cup of coffee, using 1 oz. ground coffee. Whisk 3 yolks of eggs and 2 oz. castor sugar over boiling water till thick and light. Cool, and add the cold strained coffee gradually. Add ½ pt. whipped cream and 2 stiffly beaten whites of eggs. Mix all lightly together, place the mixture in mousse cups, and put these in a charged ice cave for at least 2 hours,

ICE PUDDINGS

For these the mixture is semi-frozen until very thick. It is then packed into the ice pudding mould, which must be quite dry and cold, having been placed on ice. The mould must then be put together securely, and if it is to be immersed in salt and ice, a greased paper should be put at the bottom where the mould joins, and also the whole should be securely wrapped in greased or wax paper.

To Turn Out. Dip the mould quickly into cold water. Shake firmly sideways, and the pudding should slip out.

Brown Bread Ice Pudding

½ pt. good custard.	4 oz. breadcrumbs.
½ pt. whipped cream.	Sugar syrup to taste.
Flavouring of liqueur or vanilla or both.	

Sweeten and flavour the custard. When quite cold add the cream, put it into the freezer, and when partly frozen add the crumbs. Freeze again till of the consistency of thick batter. Then put it into an ice pudding mould. Cover very securely with greased paper, and immerse in a bucket of salt and ice for 2 hours or more. Turn out, pour a hot custard chocolate sauce over, and serve instantly.

Chocolate and Vanilla Ice Pudding

Line a mould with semi-frozen chocolate ice cream, and fill the centre with semi-frozen vanilla ice. Wrap the mould securely in greased paper and immerse in a pail of salt and ice for 3 hours.

Ice Pudding

(Glacé Tutti Frutti)

1 pt. good custard.	½ pt. whipped cream.
Liqueur and sugar syrup to taste.	Pistachio nuts.
Preserved ginger.	Glacé cherries.
2 whites of eggs.	Mixed candied fruits, etc., 4 oz. in all.

Cut the nuts in thin shreds, and the fruit into small dice. Soak these in brandy. Put the custard, sweetened and flavoured, into the freezer. When semi-frozen add the fruits, cream, and

2 whites of eggs stiffly beaten. Freeze till sufficiently frozen to mould. Fill an ice pudding mould. Wrap securely and freeze for about 3 hours in a pail of salt and ice.

La Dame Blanche

Line a freezing mould with white paper and stand it in a charged ice cave. Whisk ½ pt. cream; also, separately, 2 whites of eggs. Add 2 oz. castor sugar, vanilla essence, and Kirsch liqueur. Mix together the eggs and cream. Add a tablespoon of finely shredded and blanched almonds. Pour this into the mould, and freeze for 5 or 6 hours.

Turn out. Remove the paper. Cut into squares or fingers, and serve with wafers.

ICED SORBETS AND PUNCHES

These are iced drinks served separately immediately before the roast and preceding the entremets, but when served they are not mentioned on the menu.

They are served in goblets or glasses.

Lemon or Orange Sorbet

4 oranges, 1 lemon (for Orange Sorbet), or 4 lemons, 1 orange (for Lemon Sorbet).

1 glass Marsala or other wine.	1 oz. sugar.
	1½ pt. water.
5 oz. loaf sugar.	1 large white of egg.

Put the loaf sugar in a pan with 1½ pt. water, dissolve, then boil and reduce it slightly, skimming. Add the very finely grated rinds of 1 orange (or of 1 lemon), and the juice of all. Boil this. Strain and cool. Semi-freeze the mixture; whisk white stiffly, add the sugar to it, and add these and the wine to the semi-frozen mixture. Freeze until sufficiently thick (they must be semi-liquid), and serve in glasses.

Rum Punch

6 oz. loaf sugar.	2 oz. castor sugar.
3 small lemons.	1 white of egg.
1 glass of rum.	1 gill of water.

Rub the loaf sugar on the lemon rinds to extract their flavour. Put this in a pan with 1¼ pt. water and the strained lemon juice.

Dissolve, then boil up and reduce a little. Cool and strain when cold into a freezing machine and semi-freeze. Whip the white of egg stiffly. Dissolve the castor sugar in 1 tablesp. water, then pour this on to the white and beat well. Add the rum and mix this well with the semi-frozen mixture. Serve in cups or glasses.

PUNCH made as above may be varied in many ways. It may be flavoured with raspberry or strawberry pulp, and port wine may replace rum; or it may be flavoured with any liqueur or champagne.

ICED SOUFFLÉS

For these the cases must be prepared by tying a band of strong paper round the outside. This supports the soufflé during the freezing process. It is then removed and the soufflé is served in the case in which it was made.

Chocolate Soufflé (about 10 people)

3 eggs.	¼ pt. lemon jelly.
½ pt. cream (whipped).	Vanilla to taste.
2 oz. chocolate.	1½ oz. castor sugar.

Whisk the yolks and sugar over hot water till thick. Add the chocolate dissolved in a little milk or water. Cool this, then add the cool but liquid jelly and whipped cream. Add the vanilla and the stiffly whipped whites, and pour into a prepared soufflé case. Place in the ice cave for at least 2 hours. Remove the paper band, decorate tastefully and serve.

Coffee Soufflé (about 10 people)

6 yolks of eggs.	2 tablesp. sugar syrup.
3 whites of eggs.	2 tablesp. strong coffee.
½ pt. cream (whipped).	

Whisk the eggs, syrup, and coffee over boiling water until thick. Remove from the heat and whisk on ice till quite cold. Add the cream, and pour at once into the soufflé case. Put this into the charged ice cave and freeze for at least 2 hours.

TO SERVE, remove the paper band from the case, sprinkle chopped nuts, etc., on the top for decoration, and serve at once.

This recipe may be flavoured in any number of ways to give variety.

Lemon Soufflé (about 10 people)

½ gill fruit pulp.	3 eggs.
¼ oz. leaf gelatine.	½ pt. cream (whipped).
6 oz. sugar.	2 lemons.

Whisk the yolks, sugar, and lemon juice over boiling water till thick and light. Dissolve the gelatine in wine or water and add this. Cool, add carefully the whipped cream and the whites of 2 eggs stiffly whisked. Place the mixture in a prepared ice cave and freeze for 2 hours.

The top of this may be decorated in the following way: ½ hour before serving pour over the top 1 tablesp. of red currant jelly dissolved in ½ gill wine jelly.

This must be cool, but not set, when poured on to the soufflé, which is then replaced in the ice cave for ½ hour.

XII. EGG COOKERY

To Boil an Egg Lightly is the most digestible form of cooking it. There are several ways: (1) Place the egg in boiling water, and boil for 3½ to 4 minutes according to its size. (2) Place the egg in sufficient boiling water to cover it. Put a lid on the pan, remove the pan from the fire, and leave for 10 minutes. The egg will be soft boiled. (3) Place the egg in cold water. Bring slowly to the boil and boil for 1 minute.

To Boil an Egg Hard. Put it into cold water and bring to the boil. Boil for 15 minutes. Keep in cold water till shelled.

BAKED EGGS (I)

These are nicer if cooked in tiny fireproof casseroles, allowing one to each person. Butter the casseroles. Break 1 raw egg into each. Sprinkle with salt and pepper. Add 1 teasp. milk or cream. Cover with a lid and bake till just set, or steam in a saucepan containing enough boiling water to come half-way up the little dishes.

BAKED EGGS (II)

(2 or 3 people)

3 eggs.	1 onion stuck with
2 oz. breadcrumbs.	cloves.
1 oz. butter.	1 blade mace.

Salt and pepper.

Proceed just as for Bread Sauce (see page 127). When just the consistency of cream, pour into au gratin or 'Pyrex' dish. Break the eggs carefully into the sauce, keeping them whole and apart. Heat in moderate oven till the eggs are set. A little grated cheese may be sprinkled over and a small piece of butter put on each egg.

BUTTERED or SCRAMBLED EGGS

Allow one egg to each person. To each egg add ¼ to ½ oz. butter, and 1 or 2 tablesp. of milk.[1] Melt the butter, add the

[1] Less butter may be added and all milk omitted if preferred.

eggs, milk, salt, and pepper. Stir till the mixture thickens. If overcooked, it becomes tough and watery. Serve on buttered toast. This dish may be varied by adding minced ham or tongue, mushrooms, etc. The toast should be prepared beforehand, as even when the egg is removed from the fire it will thicken and cook further, owing to the heat of the saucepan, and therefore it should be turned out at once while still of a soft, creamy consistency.

BUTTERED or SCRAMBLED EGGS (Economical)

(1 or 2 people)

1 egg.	1 tablesp. milk.
1 teasp. white bread-crumbs or cooked rice.	¼ oz. (or less) butter. Salt and pepper.

Make as above.

CURRIED EGGS

Hard boil the required number of eggs. Make a good Curry Sauce (see page 114). Shell the eggs, place them in the sauce, sliced, and leave in sauce for 5 minutes. OR, put the eggs in whole, and to dish cut them in half lengthways. Place them on a dish with the sauce poured round, or over, and serve with boiled rice (1 oz. for each egg).

DEVILLED EGGS (I)

Fry some eggs, sprinkle well with cayenne, add a few drops of chili vinegar, a pinch of curry, and coat with black butter.

DEVILLED EGGS (II)

Hard boil some eggs. Shell and cut these in half. Remove the yolks and pound them with 1 oz. butter to 4 yolks, salt, cayenne, 1 tablesp. breadcrumbs, pinch of curry powder.

Refill the whites with this, and serve on a bed of watercress, or mustard and cress.

DUCKS' EGGS

Ducks' eggs are larger and richer than hens' eggs. They must be cooked at a sufficiently high temperature to destroy any harmful bacteria which may be present when the ducks have been in contact with dirty water.

FRIED EGGS (I)

These are usually served with bacon. Remove the cooked bacon and keep it hot, and fry the egg (breaking it into a cup and putting it gently into the hot fat) in the bacon fat. Baste it, and keep it a good shape with a spoon. Serve each egg on a rasher of bacon.

FRIED EGGS (II)

Break each egg of the required number of new-laid eggs into a cup separately. Season them and drop them very gently into a pan of hot fat. Keep them in shape and turn them frequently with a wooden spoon. When of a golden colour, drain them well on paper. Serve at once. These may be sprinkled with grated cheese before and after frying, if liked, or served with anchovy or other good butter.

FRIED EGGS (III)

(Fried in Butter)

Melt 1½ oz. clarified butter in a pan. When hot drop each egg carefully into it. Keep them a neat shape with a spoon. When golden, place them on toast. Reduce the butter till it browns, add ½ teasp. finely chopped parsley and ½ teasp. vinegar; reduce a little, and pour this over the eggs.

POACHED EGGS

Boil enough water in a shallow pan to cover the eggs well. Into this drop carefully the required number of new-laid eggs, each being broken into a cup and put in separately. Cook gently. Drain on a slice and serve as desired, i.e. on buttered toast, on spinach, etc.

EGGS MAY BE POACHED in the same way in MILK.

POACHED EGGS IN TOMATO SAUCE

Drop the eggs into tomato sauce and cook carefully in the same way. Serve them on toast with the sauce poured over.

POACHED EGGS IN SAUCE

Poached eggs may be placed on toast and coated with any good sauce as desired.

POACHED EGGS WITH CHEESE

Coat the poached eggs with a good Welsh Rarebit mixture (see page 289). Serve them on toast, or on a purée of peas, spinach, potato, as desired.

PLOVER'S EGGS

These are usually served hard boiled. Cook them from 8 to 10 minutes.

TURKEY'S EGGS

These are as delicate in flavour as a hen's egg, and may be used in any of the ways given.

To soft boil they will take about 7 minutes.

EGG DISHES

These may be termed Egg Entrées, and can be served as a first course for luncheons, or as light entrées for informal dinners. Many of them will be useful also for breakfast and supper dishes. Some can also be served as savouries.

CHAUDFROID OF EGGS

Poach some eggs carefully; trim them neatly. Dish each on a round of tomato, or on a mixture of ham, tongue, etc., mixed with chaudfroid sauce. Leave to set, then stamp into rounds the size of the eggs. Stand these on a wire tray. Place the eggs on them carefully, and coat them with chaudfroid sauce. Coat each one twice. Dish on salad.

EGGS IN ASPIC

Line some small moulds with aspic jelly. Decorate tastefully. Fill them with chopped or sliced hard-boiled egg. Cover with aspic. Turn out when set on to a good salad.

EGGS À LA CRÈME

Boil a sufficient number of eggs hard. Cut them in half.
Remove the yolks. Cut small pieces from the ends to make
the whites stand firmly. Mix the yolks with minced chicken,
ham or tongue, or with flakes of lobster, salmon, etc. Add a
little cream or sauce to soften the mixture. Refill the whites,
piling the centres high. Pour a creamy sauce round.

EGG CUTLETS or CROQUETTES (3 or 4 people)

| ½ oz. margarine. | 3 eggs (hard-boiled). |
| ½ oz. flour. ⅛ gill milk. | Salt and cayenne. |

Optional, a little chopped ham.

Make a panada with the butter, flour, and milk. Sieve or chop
the eggs. Add the chopped eggs. Spread on a plate till cool.
Shape as follows: 1 (for croquettes), into even-sized balls or
sausage-shaped rolls; 2 (for cutlets), into cutlet shapes. Flour,
egg, and crumb these. Fry in deep fat, and garnish with fried
parsley. If possible, serve with spinach.

N.B. If possible, coat twice with egg and crumb.

EGG FRITTERS

Cut 2 or more hard-boiled eggs in half lengthways. Brush the
cut side with beaten egg, and to this press a thin slice of ham.
Trim to the size of the egg. Dip this into coating batter and
fry. Serve with baked tomatoes.

EGG KROMESKIES (4 or 5 people)

Take even portions of the mixture for egg cutlets. Form
these into the shape of corks. Wrap them in slices of thin bacon.
Dip in a good coating batter and fry.

EGG PATTIES

Hard boil 4 eggs. Chop these. Make ½ pt. good thick
Béchamel Sauce (page 110). Add the eggs, season to taste.
Fill prepared patty cases (page 173) and serve hot or cold.
Any patties may be made in this way, using chicken, oyster, etc.

EGGS OF THE RISING SUN (4 or 5 people)

4 hard-boiled eggs.	Clarified butter.
Chopped parsley (if liked).	1 pt. well-flavoured white sauce.

Slice the eggs. Place them, sprinkled with the parsley, on a hot dish. Coat with the sauce. Pass 1 yolk through a sieve. Arrange in lines to represent rays on the top of the sauce. Make quite hot before serving, OR, pour a little clarified butter over, and brown in an oven or under a grill.

FARCED EGG

Cut rounds of bread ½ inch thick. Dip these quickly into milk which has been infused with onion, mace, and cloves. Drain, egg, crumb, and fry. Cover each piece of bread with a light farce, e.g. chicken, veal, or a stiff purée of spinach, pea, etc. Hollow this and slip a poached egg into the hollow. Pour a rich brown or tomato sauce round, and serve with vegetables.

FRICASSÉE OF EGG (4 or 5 people)

4 hard-boiled eggs and 1 pt. thick béchamel or good white sauce. Shell the eggs and heat them in the sauce. Cut them in two lengthways, and serve with the sauce poured over them. Garnish with fried croûtons.

GAME or CHICKEN CUSTARDS (5 or 6 people)

Butter 6 small soufflé cases, or dariole moulds. Fill each loosely with cold, chopped game, 1 teasp. breadcrumbs, ½ teasp. finely chopped parsley, a little chopped ham, tongue, etc., to taste. Beat 3 eggs with ½ pt. milk and fill up the cases with this. Steam gently, or bake, standing the cases in water. When firm, turn out and serve with good sauce.

GÂTEAU OF EGG (3 or 4 people)

2 hard-boiled eggs (finely chopped).	¼ pt. good white sauce.
2 raw eggs.	2 oz. breadcrumbs.
	Seasoning.

Mix these ingredients. Pour into a greased mould. Cover with a greased paper and steam for ½ hour until firm. Turn out.

Pour ¼ pt. good tomato sauce round and garnish with 1 oz. cooked macaroni cut into rings and sprinkled with grated cheese.

SCALLOPED EGGS (4 people)

Cook and sieve 1 lb. spinach. Grease 4 scallop shells. Cover them with a layer of spinach. On this place a neatly poached egg. Cover with a good white sauce. Sprinkle with grated cheese. Brown in a quick oven and serve at once.

* SCOTCH EGGS (5 or 6 people)

3 hard-boiled eggs, shelled.	½ pt. tomato or brown sauce.
Beaten egg for coating.	
Breadcrumbs.	2 raw sausages, or some
6 croûtons fried bread.	quenelle meat.

Cover the eggs completely with the sausage meat, flattening the ends. Egg, crumb, and fry in hot fat a few minutes till golden brown, then drain on soft paper. Cut in two with a sharp knife. Place each half on a croûton. Pour the sauce round and serve hot.

If served cold, omit the sauce, and garnish with salad instead.

SUPRÊME OF EGGS

1 egg per person and 1 over.

Boil the required number of new-laid eggs 3½ minutes. Shell them carefully and put them in boiling water to re-heat. Dish them on a purée of green peas. Pour a good suprême sauce (veloutée sauce in which a few mushrooms have been simmered) over them and garnish with heaps of freshly boiled green peas.

This dish may be varied by pouring Welsh Rarebit (see page 289) mixture over and browning it under a salamander or gas grill.

STUFFED EGGS

These may be made in many ways, of which a few instances will be given. The ingredients may be varied to taste.

ANCHOVY EGGS

To each hard-boiled egg allow ½ oz. butter (or 1 dessertsp. to 1 tablesp. cream), 1 anchovy, cayenne to taste. If preferred, allow 1 oz. butter to each egg and add ½ teasp. of tarragon vinegar.

Cut the eggs in halves, remove the yolks and pound them with the wiped and boned anchovies (or with essence of anchovy to taste) and the butter. Season with cayenne. Sieve this mixture, and fill the whites (if possible using a forcer). Cut a small piece off the bottoms to make the halves stand firmly, and serve dished on slices of tomato, cucumber, or salad. Decorate to taste.

COLD STUFFED EGGS (3 or 4 people)

Halve 3 hard-boiled eggs. Remove the yolks, and pound them with 3 boned anchovies, 1½ oz. watercress, ½ oz. butter, 1 teasp. cream, and a pinch of cayenne. Sieve and fill the whites with the mixture. Dish on salad mixed with good dressing.

EGGS À LA MANDOLIN

3 hard-boiled eggs.	½ tablesp. anchovy
½ tablesp. cream.	sauce.
6 prawns, shelled.	Angelica, mustard
3 oz. butter (or less).	and cress.
Cayenne.	

Divide the eggs lengthways. Take out the yolks and pound with the fat, anchovy, prawns, and cream. Season. Pass through a hair sieve. Re-fill the whites smoothly, using a hot knife. Form the strings of the mandolin with the fine stalks of cress, and the handle with a piece of angelica which has been soaked in warm water and thoroughly dried. Dish on a bed of cress.

EGGS STUFFED WITH PRAWNS (4 or 5 people)

Follow the recipe for Cold Stuffed Eggs, sieving 12 prawns instead of anchovies and cress. Dish on salad, decorating with prawns' heads.

HOT STUFFED EGGS (6 people)

Hard boil 6 eggs. Halve them, remove the yolks. Make the whites stand. Pound ¼ lb. white fish with ½ oz. butter and white sauce till a soft paste is obtained. Add the yolks. Season and sieve. Heat the mixture. Warm the whites and fill with the mixture. Place on croûtons. Decorate with sieved yolk of egg. Re-heat in a quick oven and serve.

XIII. HORS D'ŒUVRES AND SAVOURIES

THERE are two classes of Hors d'Œuvres, viz. Plain and Dressed. Examples of the first are:

Oysters, served in their shells. See raw Oysters (page 36).

Caviare. This should be iced, if possible, but it may be mixed with some finely chopped shallot and lemon juice, mixing with a wooden fork, as caviare should not be touched with any metal.

Other plain examples are: Olives, Sardines, Lax, Prawns, Smoked or Pickled Meat and Fish, such as Brunswick Sausages, Herring Fillets, Roes, etc., also Radishes, Sliced Tomato and Cucumber, Mixed Pickles, and various Salads, such as potato, melon, etc. As soon as any of these are served more elaborately they must be classed as Dressed Hors d'Œuvres. As Dressed Hors d'Œuvres and Savouries are interchangeable, the two may be combined under one heading.

DRESSED HORS D'ŒUVRES AND SAVOURIES

These should be made in very small portions, and daintily served. Many of the classes already given for entrées may be varied and adapted to give a large number of savouries and dressed hors d'œuvres, but the fillings should include oysters, caviare, lobster, cheese, sardines, etc., and they must have a piquant flavour. Hors d'Œuvres are served cold. Cheese recipes belong to Savouries.

Dressed Hors d'Œuvres and Savouries are here grouped under eight heads:

I. BATTERS

OYSTERS IN BATTER

Beard and drain a sufficient number of oysters. Poach them. Drain, and sprinkle them with salt, cayenne, and a squeeze of lemon. Dip them in good coating batter and fry in deep fat.

The following may also be fried in the same way: Sardines, anchovies, and pieces of tongue or ham cut into rounds and spread with any good forcemeat, with another round pressed on to this to form a sandwich, also cheese. The cheese must be cut into slices about ½ inch thick, and cut into neat shapes. Dip these into coating batter, and fry in very hot fat or the cheese will burst through the case.

SAVOURY PANCAKES

Make a pancake batter. Fry some very thin pancakes. Cut these into squares. Spread them with any very savoury filling, such as caviare, foie gras, chicken liver, bloater or other paste, a curried mixture, prawns, or a filling made of any vegetable and cheese. Roll these up, and serve very hot; or roll them, seal the edges, and egg, crumb, and fry them.

II. BOUCHÉES

These resemble very small patties, and are made of puff paste. When cooked, remove the soft centres and fill with any suitable filling, which must be mixed with a thick creamy panada.

III. CASSOLETTES

See Entrées (page 98).

BUTTER CASSOLETTES

Smooth some fresh butter into a cake about 1 inch thick. When quite cold stamp into rounds 1½ inches in diameter or less. Put these on ice for some time. Then egg and crumb them twice. Fry them in very hot deep fat till golden. Drain them. With a small cutter remove a round from the crust and drain off the liquid butter, which may be put aside for other purposes. Keep the removed portion of crust for a lid. Fill the cases so made with a good salpicon of prawns, chicken, etc., mixed with good sauce. Replace the lids, garnish with fried parsley and serve.

The cassolettes may also be made into the shape of small cylinders or balls.

IV. CHOUX PASTE

See page 175. Force the mixture into SMALL éclairs, using a small fancy forcer, or into small ' choux ' (cream bun shapes). Brush these lightly with a little egg, and bake them. When cooked remove the soft centres, if any, and fill with any of the following:

For Hot Savouries. Sardines, anchovy, haddock, salmon, prawns, etc., blended with a little sauce. Re-heat and serve.

For Cold Savouries. Sardines, anchovy, tongue, salmon, shrimps, foie gras, etc., mixed with mayonnaise, or sauce tartare, etc. Brush with aspic. Decorate prettily. For éclairs, small bunches of mustard and cress may project from each end.

Under this heading come also:

CHEESE AIGRETTES (10 to 12 people)

¼ pt. water.	1½ or 2 eggs.
2 oz. grated cheese.	1 oz. butter. 2½ oz. flour.

Salt, pepper, and cayenne.

Boil the butter and water. Add the flour and beat well till the mixture is smooth and leaves the sides of the pan clean. Cool. Add the eggs by degrees, beating thoroughly. Then add the cheese and seasoning. Drop small rough teaspoonfuls into fat that is just smoking. They should take 10 to 15 minutes to cook. If sufficiently brown too soon, the insides will not be cooked. When done, they should be golden and crisp. Serve sprinkled with grated cheese and red pepper.

V. CROÛTES, CROUSTADES, CANAPÉS

(Hot Savouries)

These are all names given to a large class of savoury which is made by spreading some savoury mixture on a fried or toasted round (croûton) of bread. The bread should be stale and must not exceed ½ inch in thickness, and the croûtes should not be quite 2 inches in diameter.

Sometimes fancy-shaped croûtons are preferred, or the bread may be cut into very neat fingers. The following are examples of this class, and as may be seen, the variety that may be made for these is infinite.

* ANCHOVY AND CREAM

Curl a washed and boned anchovy in the centre of a fried croûton of bread. Make this very hot in the oven, then force a rose of whipped cream on each, dust this with cayenne, and serve at once.

K

ANGELS ON HORSEBACK

Remove the beards from the desired number of oysters. Sprinkle them with salt, pepper, cayenne, and lemon. Roll each one in a very thin piece of bacon, place it on a fried croûte, and put it in a very hot oven till the bacon is cooked. Serve at once.

ARTICHOKE AND OYSTER

Put a cooked artichoke bottom on a round of fried bread. Grate some cheese on the artichoke, and on this place a poached oyster. Cover this with a spoonful of sauce. When very hot serve with a small pat of cold maître d'hôtel butter at the top.

BOMBAY TOAST (4 or 5 people)

Pound 1 oz. boned anchovies with 1 oz. butter. Melt this in a saucepan, and add 2 beaten yolks of egg. Stir till creamy, season, and spread on croûtons. Serve very hot.

CHEESE MUFF (4 or 5 people)

| ½ oz. butter. | 2 oz. cheese. |
| 2 eggs. | Seasoning. |

Dissolve the cheese and butter, add the beaten eggs and seasoning. When the mixture resembles scrambled eggs, spread it on hot fried croûtons and serve at once.

* COD'S ROE TOAST (4 or 5 people)

For preparation of roe, see page 32. Brush the roe with butter, then fry it in a little butter. Add 1 egg yolk and 1 tablesp. cream to ¼ pt. good sauce. Season, and add lemon and chopped parsley. Chop the roe, mix it with the sauce, and re-heat it. Place some fried fingers of bread on a dish, and put the mixture neatly on each. Serve very hot, decorated with parsley and dusted with cayenne.

* CREAMED HADDOCK (about 4 people)

Bone a small dried haddock, and sieve the meat from it. Mix this purée with 1 gill cream, 2 oz. Parmesan cheese (grated), and cayenne. Spread the mixture on toast, sprinkle it with cheese, place a small piece of butter in the centre, and bake for 6 minutes in a good oven.

* CROÛTES DE COBURG (4 or 5 people)

Fry some round croûtons of bread. Pound ¼ lb. cooked dried haddock with ½ gill of good sauce. Spread this thickly on the croûtes. Cover the haddock mixture with a round of tomato, and on this place a slice of pickled walnut. Heat in the oven and garnish with mustard and cress.

* CROÛTES À LA MIDAS (4 or 5 people)

Sieve some cooked kipper or bloater, and mix this with a small piece of butter, some pepper and chopped parsley. Form the mixture into very small cork-shaped pieces. Wrap thin bacon round each, and place them on a fried croûton. Cook in a quick oven, or under a gas grill, till the bacon is cooked. Serve very hot.

* CROÛTONS OF HADDOCK (3 or 4 people)

Fry some croûtons (oblong). Mix 2 tablesp. of cooked dried haddock with ½ tablesp. cream or white sauce. Add cayenne to taste, and place this mixture on the fried croûtons. Decorate with hard-boiled egg, gherkin, capers, etc.

* DEVILLED CHICKEN LIVERS (I)
(8 to 10 people)

5 or 6 livers. Wash and dry these. Season well with salt, pepper, and cayenne. Wrap each half liver in a thin slice of bacon. Place on fried croûtons, and bake till the bacon is cooked. Glaze and serve hot, garnished with fried parsley.

* DEVILLED CHICKEN LIVERS (II)
(4 or 5 people)

Wash and blanch 3 or 4 livers for 5 minutes. Pound them with 1 teasp. made mustard, ½ teasp. anchovy essence, ½ oz. butter, salt, and cayenne. Spread some croûtons thickly with this mixture and heat in a quick oven. Garnish with watercress or parsley.

* DEVILS ON HORSEBACK

(1 per head and 1 or 2 over)

Stone sufficient French plums. Fill them with chutney and
1 browned salted almond. Wrap a thin slice of fat bacon round
each. Place them on croûtons and cook in a quick oven till the
bacon is crisp. Decorate with parsley.

HUÎTRES (OYSTER) CROÛTES or BONNE BOUCHES (I)

(about 6 people)

Beard and chop 20 oysters, and pound 1 anchovy. Mix these
and put them in a saucepan, adding cream, and make the whole
of a thick creamy consistency. Add cayenne, and when very
hot spread the mixture on fried croûtons.

HUÎTRES (OYSTER) CROÛTES or BONNE BOUCHES (II)

(about 6 people)

6 small fried croûtons.	6 bearded oysters.
6 thin slices of lemon.	4 oz. cooked chicken.
4 boned anchovies.	1 or 2 oz. butter.
Lobster coral and	Chopped parsley.
cress.	Seasoning.

Pound the chicken with the butter and anchovies. Season
with cayenne and sieve this. Spread it smoothly on the croûtons.
Cover with a round of lemon and place an oyster on the top.
Decorate with chopped parsley, lobster coral or coralline pepper.
Serve garnished with cress (cold).

LOBSTER CANAPÉS (6 people)

Mix 2 tablesp. of chopped lobster meat with 4 tablesp. whipped
cream. Season and pile this lightly on the croûtons. Decorate
and serve cold.

* SARDINES À LA NOISETTE (16 to 18 people)

Bone and pound a small tin of sardines. Sieve these and
mix them with ½ oz. to 1 oz. butter; season well. Form the
mixture into the shape of filberts. Place a little of the sardine

mixture on a croûton; on this lay a slightly smaller round of beetroot, and on this place a sardine filbert. Decorate with a touch of parsley, and serve cold.

*SARDINES AUX PIEDMONTAISES (8 to 10 people)

Fry 8 or 10 fingers of bread lightly in butter. On each piece place a sardine. Heat these in the oven and prepare the following:

2 yolks.	$\frac{1}{4}$ teasp. made
$\frac{1}{2}$ teasp. **tarragon**	mustard.
vinegar.	$\frac{1}{2}$ teasp. malt
$\frac{1}{2}$ oz. butter.	vinegar.

Salt and pepper.

Heat these in a small pan until thick. Then coat the sardines and serve hot or cold.

SARDINES AND OYSTERS (about 6 people)

Skin and bone some sardines. Mix these with $\frac{1}{2}$ dozen bearded and chopped oysters; add a small piece of butter, and spread this on fried croûtons. Sprinkle with lemon and cayenne, and heat in a hot oven.

* SAVOURY CROÛTES (Economical)

(allow about 1 croûton per head)

These can often be made from the remains of breakfast. Chopped bacon mixed with any remnant of omelet, scrambled or fried egg, may be mixed with a dessertsp. of cream and sauce, capers, chopped parsley, curry, chutney added to taste, and the whole spread on a croûton, heated, and sent neatly decorated to table.

SAVOURY OYSTERS

Allow $\frac{1}{2}$ the soft roe of a bloater and 1 oyster for each person. Remove the beards and fry the oysters with the roes in a little butter. Place a piece of roe on each croûton and an oyster on this. Sprinkle with lemon and cayenne.

VI. PASTRY CROÛTES

These are made of Cheese Straw Paste, as a rule, or from remnants of puff paste, sprinkled with cheese, folded into three and rolled out; and most of the mixtures given for Croûtes may be served on small cheese biscuits if preferred. The pastry may also be used for small savoury tartlets, etc.

* CHEESE STRAW PASTRY (4 or 5 people)

½ to 1 oz. butter.	1 yolk of egg.
1 oz. Parmesan cheese (grated).	1 oz. flour.
	½ oz. Cheddar cheese.

Cayenne and salt.

Rub the fat in the flour (or chop the fat and flour finely together on a board), add the rest of the ingredients, mix thoroughly, and bind with the egg. Finish as in following recipes.

* Cheese Biscuits

Stamp the paste into small rounds, prick these, and bake in a cool oven till golden brown.

*For Cheese Straws

Roll the paste to less than ¼ inch in thickness. Cut it into match-like strips, about the size of the largest matches. Place these on an ungreased tin and bake in a very moderate oven till crisp and golden. Rings to put the straws through should be stamped out of the paste; they must not be more than ¾ inch in diameter. When cooked, leave to cool on the tin, then carefully pass through each ring as many straws as it will hold.

Fancy Shapes

Cheese straw paste may be used to line fancy tins, e.g. small boat-shaped tins, etc. In this case the pastry must be pricked and ' baked blind ' (see page 168).

It can then afterwards be filled with any savoury preparation.

*ANCHOVY BISCUITS (4 or 5 people)

Make a cheese straw paste, mixing it with essence of anchovy. Cut this into biscuits and bake. Spread with the following mixture: 2 or 3 pounded anchovies, some chopped capers, curry paste, grated cheese, and seasoning to taste. Re-heat and serve.

* ANCHOVY CREAMS, COLD (10 to 12 people)

Add anchovy essence and cayenne to ½ gill cream to taste. Then whip the cream stiffly. Pile this on to small cheese biscuits (or on to plain crisp water biscuits), and serve cold, decorated with strips of anchovy.

* CELERY CREAMS (10 to 12 people)

4 tablesp. whipped cream.	2 tablesp. grated cheese.
1 tablesp. chopped celery.	Salt, cayenne.

Mix the ingredients and pile them in the form of a rocky pyramid on cheese biscuits. Decorate with pale green celery tops and coralline pepper. Serve cold.

* CHEESE PYRAMIDS (10 to 12 people)

The same mixture as for Celery Creams, but omit the celery and add 3 oz. of cheese, and a few drops of tarragon vinegar, if liked. If convenient, 1 oz. butter and 2 teasp. cream may be used instead of 4 tablesp. whipped cream. In this case, cream the butter.

CROÛTES À LA ROYALE (10 to 12 people)

3 oz. minced chicken.	½ oz. minced tongue.
2 tablesp. sauce tartare, cayenne.	2 anchovies, wiped and boned.
½ oz. minced ham.	

Mix the ingredients, place on cheese biscuits, and garnish with egg, parsley, etc. Serve cold.

FARCED OLIVES (1 olive per head)

Pipe some cheese biscuits with anchovy or other butter. Stone (this is called TURNING) some olives. Stuff the cavity with the same kind of butter. Place one on each biscuit and curl an anchovy fillet round the base and decorate tastefully.

TARTINES DE CAVIARE (10 to 12 people)

Cut ¼ lb. cheese paste, rolled ⅛ inch thick, into oblong fingers, 3 inches by 1 inch. Bake till golden. When cold spread some caviare mixed with lemon juice and cayenne on half the fingers. Form into sandwiches with the other half. Decorate with forced roses of anchovy butter and fancy shapes of hard-boiled egg.

* TARTLETS (1 tartlet per head)

Line very small patty pans with cheese paste. Prick and bake this blind. When cooked fill with any mixture, e.g. spaghetti cooked in small lengths and mixed with grated cheese and a little cream. Sprinkle with grated cheese. Re-heat in a quick oven, and serve hot. Tartlets may also have a spoonful of cheese soufflé mixture placed on them. They are then re-cooked a few moments till the soufflé has risen and become golden brown.

* SAVOURY BOATS (1 boat per head)

Line some small boat-shaped tins with cheese paste. Bake these blind. When cooked, fill with lax, made hot in its own oil and seasoned with pepper and chopped parsley. Serve hot. If served cold, mix the lax with 1 tablesp. of mayonnaise. Decorate with sieved white of egg, strips of chili, etc. Small sails may be cut out of rice paper, and stood upright on the boats at the last moment; if put in place long before serving, the sails become sodden and fall over.

Any other savoury filling may replace the lax.

VII. ASPICS

Any very small moulds may be lined with aspic jelly, and in these olives, prawns, shrimps, etc. may be set. Line the moulds with a little jelly. When set, decorate the top with tiny sprigs of parsley, fancy shapes of hard-boiled egg, etc.

OLIVES IN ASPIC

Wipe some olives. Stone and stuff them. Place one in each mould. Set it with a spoonful of jelly. When quite set, cover entirely with jelly. Turn each on to a round of tomato, cucumber, etc., and garnish with salad.

VIII. MISCELLANEOUS

OYSTER RAREBIT (7 or 8 people)

4 oz. Cheddar cheese.	½ gill milk or cream.
1 well-beaten egg.	1 saltsp. mustard.

Salt, pepper.

Melt these, and add 6 chopped oysters, which have previously been heated in the liquor. Re-heat till thick and creamy. Pour on to hot croûtons or toast.

N.B. In making rarebit, if the cheese is over-heated it becomes tough and stringy. This may sometimes be remedied by mixing a dessertspoon of cornflour to a smooth cream with a little cold milk, adding this to the cheese mixture and boiling the whole.

SCOTCH WOODCOCK (about 4 people)

Hot buttered toast.	½ oz. to 1 oz. butter.
¼ pt. cream or ½ gill milk.	Anchovy paste.
	2 yolks of eggs.

Cayenne.

Spread some oblong fingers of buttered toast with anchovy paste. Stir the cream, eggs and butter over the fire till the mixture thickens (it must not boil). Season, and pour over the toast. Sprinkle with parsley and serve quickly.

* WELSH RAREBIT (about ½ oz. cheese per head)

Grate some cheese. Add a little mustard, cayenne and salt, and just enough milk or cream to moisten it. Melt this till it resembles a thick sauce, then pour at once over croûtons or hot toast. A little yolk of egg added is an improvement.

XIV. BREAKFAST DISHES

THE majority of dishes suitable for this meal will be found under their respective headings, e.g. fish in II. Fish, and in III. Meats, can be found ham or tongue, galantine, cold game, etc.

BACON FOR BOILING OR FRYING

The prime cut is the thick streaky, but for small quantities the flank is good and much cheaper. The middle of the back without the bone is also an economical piece. Rashers should be cut by machine—a grocer will do this, and it saves much waste. The thinnest rashers should be asked for.

BACON, BROILED

Cut the rind off each rasher, and broil it before a clear fire until the fat is transparent. This may be done in a Dutch oven. If crisp bacon is preferred, continue the cooking.

BACON, FRIED

Warm this slowly in a frying pan, then cook till transparent or crisp as required. No additional fat is required.

BACON AND EGG

Fry the bacon slowly, and when partly cooked drop raw eggs gently into the fat. Cook gently till the eggs are done—they require basting. By this time also the bacon will be done. Place each egg on a rasher of bacon and serve.

BACON AND HARICOT BEANS

Fry the bacon and keep it hot. Heat the cooked beans in the bacon fat. Sprinkle them with parsley and serve round the bacon.

BACON AND KIDNEY

Fry the bacon, remove it, and keep warm. Wash kidneys, remove core, and fry them in part of the hot bacon fat. Turn them once, and when the red gravy runs freely they are done. Place them on a hot dish with the bacon. Put 1 teasp. flour into the frying pan, and brown it; add a little stock and boil. Season, and pour this gravy over the kidneys.

BACON AND MUSHROOMS

Follow the recipe for Bacon and Tomatoes, cooking the mushrooms till tender.

BACON AND POTATO

Fry the bacon, remove, and keep it hot. Cut cooked cold potato into pieces resembling quarters of an orange and fry these in the smoking hot bacon fat. Sprinkle with parsley, and serve round the bacon.

BACON AND TOMATOES

Fry the bacon as above; then add the skinned and sliced tomatoes, and cook them until hot through in the bacon fat. Arrange them on a hot dish, with the bacon put round. Sprinkle with salt and pepper, and serve.

BATH CHAPS or PIG'S CHEEK

If straight from the pickle this will only require washing before cooking, but, if smoked, soak overnight. Put in lukewarm water. Cook gently, about 3 hours or longer, according to size. Remove the rind, and cover with raspings. Serve cold.

BLOATERS, FRIED

To prepare bloaters, make a small incision and draw out any gut. Then wash and dry.

Flour lightly, and fry in a small quantity of fat. When one side is brown, turn and fry the other.

BLOATERS, GRILLED

Brush them with melted butter, flour lightly, and grill.

HOMINY (3 or 4 people)

1 cup hominy.   1 pt. water.   Pinch of salt.

Wash and soak the hominy in water overnight.   Boil gently for $\frac{1}{2}$ hour or more.   Stir frequently, and serve as oatmeal porridge.

KIPPERS, FILLETED AND FRIED

Fillet the kippers, divide into neat pieces.   Dip each into frying batter and fry in deep fat until crisp and brown.   The same method is excellent for fillets of bloater or haddock.

KIPPERS, FRIED

Dip these in boiling water first, then wipe them, and fry in a small quantity of fat, covering the pan with a lid so that the fish is thoroughly cooked.

MARROW BONES

The marrow may be cooked in the bones.   If so, these are served on toast, with a napkin round them.   Garnish with parsley.

NORMAN PIE (7 to 9 people)

1 lb. calf's liver cooked (cooked tongue may replace this).

$\frac{1}{2}$ lb. fat bacon.	Seasoning to taste, including cayenne.
$\frac{1}{2}$ lb. cooked poultry or veal.	1 pt. stock.
1 dessertsp. meat extract.	1 oz. gelatine.
1 finely chopped shallot.	

Mince the liver, and cut the meat into dice.   Line a china mould with fat bacon in small slices, add the rest of the ingredients.   Melt the gelatine in the stock and fill up the mould with this, placing the rest of the slices of bacon on the top.   Cook in a moderate oven for 2 hours.   Add more stock, and when cold turn out.

PORRIDGE

This may be made of coarse, medium, or fine oatmeal, or with any of the varieties of flaked oats.   If coarse oatmeal is used, long cooking is required.   The method for making is the same for all except fine oatmeal.

PORRIDGE (Coarse Oatmeal)
(6 to 8 people)

PROPORTIONS. 1 qt. water, 2 gills oatmeal.

Boil the water rapidly, then stir in the oatmeal, with one hand sprinkling it in, and with the other stirring quickly. Boil and stir frequently for at least 2 hours. Make in a double saucepan to save the risk of burning. Add more water if too thick. The longer it is cooked the more digestible it becomes. It can be made overnight and heated next day, or boiled and finished off in a Hay Box. Salt is almost always added in the proportion of 1 teasp. to the above amount of water, but as a few dislike salted porridge, individual taste should be consulted.

Serve with milk or cream, salt or sugar.

PORRIDGE (Fine Oatmeal)

If porridge is made with fine oatmeal, this should be mixed to a smooth cream with a little cold water, and then added to the boiling water. It is otherwise likely to be lumpy.

Stir and boil well for 20 minutes.

PORRIDGE (Scotch Recipe)
(1 or 2 people)

1 tablesp. medium oatmeal. ½ pt. water. Salt.

Have the water freshly boiled in a deep pan, and add to it the salt. Sprinkle in the oatmeal, stirring carefully with a stick or a wooden spoon to prevent lumps. Boil and stir for the first 5 or 6 minutes till the meal is well swollen, then simmer for at least ½ hour, stirring up frequently. If necessary, add more boiling water, as porridge should be of a good pouring consistency.

SARDINES, CURRIED

Heat the sardines in a good curry sauce, and serve with boiled rice.

SAUSAGES, BAKED

Place on a greased baking tin, and cook in a moderate oven till browned. Serve on fried bread with gravy.

SAUSAGES (Economical)

Parboil and skin them. Divide into two lengthways. Roll each half, and coat it in mashed potato. Egg, crumb, and fry these. Serve on toast with gravy.

SAUSAGES, FRIED (I)

Prick these, flour them lightly and cook in a little hot fat till evenly browned. They must be cooked gently, or the skins will burst. Serve on toasted or fried bread.

SAUSAGES, FRIED (II)

Parboil the sausages. Skin them, egg and crumb, and fry them in hot deep fat.

SPATCHCOCK

Game and young chicken are excellent prepared in this way: Remove the head, neck, and feet at the first joint. Cut in half, through the backbone. Flatten each half, using skewers for the purpose. Brush with oil or butter; season; sprinkle with flour, and place between the gridiron. Cook in front of or over a clear fire for 20 minutes. Turn and baste with butter while cooking. The spatchcock may be sprinkled with browned breadcrumbs 10 minutes before finishing cooking. Serve very hot. It may also be served as an entrée with tomato or other piquant sauce.

TOAST, BUTTERED

Cut stale bread into slices about ½ inch thick. Toast quickly, cut off the crust, and butter immediately, taking care not to scrape the toast. Serve hot, on a hot-water plate.

TOAST, DRY

For this purpose use stale bread cut into thin slices. Toast slowly in front of a bright fire. As soon as ready cut off the crust and place in a rack. If laid on a plate the steam condenses on the under side, rendering it flabby and damp. The crisper the toast, the slower must be the toasting. It may also be further dried by standing the rack in a cool oven.

TOAST, HAM (1 person)

1 slice buttered toast.	Cayenne pepper.
A little milk, cream, or stock.	1 tablesp. minced ham.
1 anchovy, if liked.	1 tablesp. breadcrumbs.

Mix all together. Make thoroughly hot, and spread on the toast.

TOAST, MARROW

Cut the marrow into neat pieces. Cook in salted water for a minute or two. Drain and sprinkle with salt, pepper, and lemon. Serve very hot on the toast.

TOAST, SARDINE

Lay 2 sardines on a small piece of neatly cut toast. Heat in a hot oven, and serve garnished with parsley.

OR, skin and bone half a tin of sardines. Mix these with 1 oz. of butter (or less). Add cayenne to taste. Form into rolls, wrap these in thin bacon, place on toast, and cook in the oven till the bacon is done. Serve on the toast garnished with parsley.

XV. BREAD, SCONES, CAKES PLAIN AND RICH

THE methods of making these differ very much according to the raising agents used. All recipes where yeast is the raising agent will be placed in Part I, Classes I and II. Parts II and III will deal with cakes where the raising agents are egg, baking powder, or both.

PART I

BREAD, BUNS, TEACAKES, AND CAKES MADE WITH YEAST

The making of these may be divided into two main classes, viz.: Class I dealing with plain breads, and Class II with richer forms of breads, buns, and cakes where the raising agent is yeast.

Baking Yeast consists of microscopic plants which are capable of living on sugar and starch, and of converting these into the gas, carbon dioxide. The yeast plant is only really active in warm surroundings; if kept in the cold it ceases to be active, and if overheated it is destroyed altogether. Therefore in bread-making it is desirable to maintain an evenly warm temperature, so that the yeast plant may grow and reproduce rapidly and enough gas be generated to raise the dough. When this is done, the plants must be destroyed or the bread will be spoilt. The heat of baking destroys the yeast, and prevents any further action taking place.

Bread and Yeast Doughs. All materials should be kept warm, about blood heat (98° F.), during the whole process of making. Unless a machine is used, the mixing should be done by hand, as this helps to keep the right temperature. Roughly speaking, there are two kinds of doughs to consider; they may be grouped in two classes:

    i. The dough for household breads and rolls.

    ii. The mixture for richer breads, teacakes, plain buns, and dough cakes.

CLASS I

THE DOUGH FOR HOUSEHOLD BREADS AND ROLLS

If small quantities of bread are made, more yeast in proportion to the flour is required than if a big batch were made.

Yeast. The best for the purpose is German yeast. This has rather the appearance of putty. It should have a fresh, quite pleasant smell, and, on being broken, should look moist. It should be used as fresh as possible, but will keep for a few days in a cool place.

Brewer's Barm or Yeast. If this is used instead of German yeast it requires careful washing before use, but even so, may give a bitter taste to the bread. 2 tablesp. of this barm is equal to 1 oz. of German yeast.

Rising. The dough must be put to rise in a warm, not a hot, place, and the bowl containing it should be covered to protect it from draughts. A half-quartern (1¾ lb.) loaf should take about 1 hour to rise, but the better rule is that when the dough has doubled its bulk it is ready to be shaped. If a large batch of bread is made, it is usually put to rise overnight.

Baking. Bread should be put at first into a HOT oven to set the outside and to keep it a good shape. Then reduce the heat and allow the bread to cook all through. A half-quartern loaf will take rather over 1 hour to bake. When done, if the loaf is tapped it SHOULD SOUND HOLLOW.

The proportions for the ingredients are as follows: To each lb. of flour, about half its weight in water (at blood heat, 98° F.) will be required, also 1 teasp. of salt to each lb.

N.B. If no thermometer is available, it will be helpful to a beginner to note that 1 part of boiling water added to 2 parts of cold water will give the desired lukewarm temperature.

The term ' quartern ' really means quarter of a stone, i.e. 3½ lb. The half-quartern is, therefore, 1¾ lb.

RECIPE FOR A QUARTERN OF HOUSEHOLD BREAD

3½ lb. flour.	About 1¾ pt. luke-
3½ teasp. salt.	warm water.
1 oz. German yeast.	1 teasp. castor sugar.

If a large amount of bread were to be made, such as 1 stone (14 lb.), 1½ to 2 oz. yeast would be sufficient to raise the 14 lb. of flour.

METHOD:

(1) Sift the flour and salt together. Place them in a cool oven to warm them to the desired temperature.

(2) ' Cream ' the yeast with the sugar, i.e. rub them together in a cup with a teaspoon till the yeast becomes liquid.

(3) To the creamed yeast add about half the given amount of lukewarm water.

(4) Make a well in the centre of the warmed bowl of flour and into this well pour the creamed yeast and water, stirring with the right hand. Keep a pool of liquid in the centre, surrounded by the flour, and gradually work in some of the flour until the centre mixture is of the consistency of batter or cream.

(5) Put the bowl, after covering the top with a cloth, in a warm place, i.e. on the rack or before the fire, and in 10 to 15 minutes the centre mixture will be seen to be full of bubbles. This mixture is called ' THE SPONGE', and the process is called ' SETTING THE SPONGE'.

(6) Take the bowl again and work in the flour from the sides, adding, by degrees, the rest of the liquid, and so gradually mixing the whole until a rather soft dough is obtained.

(7) KNEAD again lightly. This term means a kind of pommelling, which can easily be shown, but which is difficult to describe. The edges of the dough are lifted and pressed into the centre, so enclosing air and mixing the whole dough. This quantity will require 5 to 10 minutes' kneading. When it is sufficiently kneaded the dough will leave the sides of the basin quite cleanly, and will also cease sticking to the hands. It becomes firm as it is kneaded.

(8) Remove the dough from the bowl, grease the bowl, put the dough back, and cut it right across in four. Sprinkle it with flour, and return it to a warm place to rise, covered with a plate or baking-tray, for an hour or more, until it has doubled its bulk.

(9) Turn the dough on to a floured board, and knead it again. This second kneading has the effect of dividing the bubbles of gas formed in the rising. If this is not done the bread will be too close in some parts, and full of large holes in others.

(10) Form into loaves, as follows:

Tin Loaves. Either grease a tin or grease and flour it. Cut the dough into 2 or 3 portions. Knead each, and form it into a neat shape, and put in the tin.

Cottage Loaves. Cut the dough into 2 or 3 portions. Knead each. Cut a quarter off each. Knead the larger portions into large rounds and the smaller into small round balls. Place the smaller on the larger ones. Press them together by pushing a finger down the centre. Cut the surface here and there with a knife. Stand on a greased and floured tin. Bake at once.

(11) Put loaves (except cottage) to rise again (this last rising is called 'PROVING') for about 15 minutes.

(12) Bake as described on page 297.

CURRANT BREAD, PLAIN

Put some currants and 1 oz. butter into 1 lb. risen dough. Knead, and put it into a tin. Prove, then bake as usual.

*CURRANT LOAF, PLAIN
(2 lb. bread tin)

1 lb. flour (warmed).	1 oz. yeast.
¼ pt. milk (about).	1½ oz. castor sugar.
2 oz. sultanas.	2 oz. melted butter.
1 egg (can be omitted).	

Cream the yeast and add to it some of the warmed milk. Make a well in the centre of the warmed flour, pour in the yeast and milk, and put in a warm place to 'set the sponge'. When full of bubbles (about 15 minutes) add the rest of the milk, the melted butter, the fruit, and the sugar, working in all the flour and adding a beaten egg, if liked. Mix to a light dough. Knead well and put to rise for an hour or more till the bulk is doubled. Then knead slightly, divide into two, knead each and put into two greased and floured bread tins. Set to 'prove' (about 40 minutes), then bake for 1 hour.

MILK BREAD

1 lb. household flour.	1 oz. butter.	½ oz. yeast.
½ pt. warm milk.	1 teasp. salt.	

Rub the fat in the flour. Follow the directions given for Household Bread. When baked, brush over with a sweet glaze, or butter if more convenient.

WHOLEMEAL AND WHEATMEAL BREAD

This is made from wholemeal and wheatmeal flour, and the recipe for Household Bread must be followed, but make rather a softer dough. It can be lightened by mixing one-third household flour with two-thirds wholemeal, and milk and water can be used instead of all water, adding, if liked, 1 oz. fat to each lb. of flour.

The process of setting the sponge may be carried out:

(1) In a well in the centre of the bowl of flour.

(2) In a small basin in which the yeast and sugar are creamed.

(3) By making a separate ferment, using part of the measured flour mixed with the liquid to make a batter-like consistency. This is only used for very rich mixtures.

Class II

THE MIXTURE FOR RICHER BREADS, TEACAKES, PLAIN BUNS, AND DOUGH CAKES

VIENNA BREAD DOUGH

| ½ lb. flour. | ½ teasp. salt. |
| 1 oz. margarine. | 1 egg (optional). |

Sponge { ½ oz. yeast.
½ teasp. sugar.
1 gill tepid liquid (milk or milk and water: if an egg is used include this as part of the liquid).

METHOD:

(1) Add salt to flour, rub margarine into flour. Warm these ingredients.

(2) Cream yeast with sugar, add tepid liquid.

(3) Make a well in the centre of the flour, and pour in the sponge (OR follow method 2).

(4) Scatter a little of the flour to lightly cover the sponge. Cover with a plate.

(5) Stand in a warm place for 15 minutes, when the sponge should have broken through the flour.

(6) Mix to form an elastic dough.

(7) Beat until smooth and glossy and the dough leaves the sides of the bowl.

(If the bowl is lighly greased at this stage the dough will not stick after the rising process.)

(8) Cover the bowl with a plate, stand in a warm place to rise for about 1 hour until the dough is twice the original size.

(9) Turn on to lightly floured board and knead.

To Make a Plait

(1) Divide the dough into 3 pieces.

(2) Knead lightly and roll to make 3 equal strips.

(3) Damp the ends, join together, plait, damp the other ends, and join.

(4) Place on a warm greased baking tin.

(5) Cover, prove in a warm place 20–30 minutes.

(6) Bake in a hot oven 30 minutes. When cooked rub the surface with a margarine paper.

To Make Bridge Rolls

(1) Divide the dough into 12–16 pieces.

(2) Knead lightly. Roll between the palms of the hands to make 'finger' rolls.

(3) Place, almost touching each other, on a warm greased baking tray.

(4) Cover, prove in a warm place 15–20 minutes.

(5) Bake in a hot oven 10–15 minutes.

To Make Fancy Shapes

Scrolls, twists, knots may be made after forming the dough into finger rolls.

TEACAKES

½ lb. flour.	½ teasp. salt.
1 oz. margarine.	1 egg (optional).

Sponge
- ½ oz. yeast.
- ½ teasp. sugar.
- 1 gill tepid liquid (milk or milk and water: if an egg is used include this as part of the liquid).

1 oz. sugar.	1½ oz. dried fruit.

Method: Follow the method for Vienna Bread, add the sugar and cleaned fruit before mixing.

The time taken for rising and proving this dough will need to be a little longer than the Vienna Bread dough as it is a richer mixture.

To Shape

(1) After the dough has risen, knead lightly and divide into 8 pieces.

(2) Knead each piece lightly and form into a round.

(3) Place on warmed greased baking tray. Cover, prove 20–30 minutes.

(4) Bake in a fairly hot oven 15–20 minutes.

(5) Rub the surface with a margarine paper.

TEACAKES (Quick Method)

Follow the recipe for Teacakes using a short gill of liquid.

METHOD:

(1) Proceed as for Teacakes. Omit the rising process.

(2) After shaping prove 60–70 minutes.

This length of time is essential as the 'rising' and 'proving' processes are both combined in this method.

HOT CROSS BUNS

Follow the recipe for Teacakes. Add ½ oz. candied peel, ½ teasp. mixed spice.

METHOD:

(1) Proceed as for Teacakes, dividing the dough into 10 or 12 pieces.

(2) When the buns have proved for 15 minutes make a cross with a knife on top.

OR

(3) Make a cross with narrow strips of pastry, damp the top of buns when half-proved in the form of a cross, and place the strips of pastry over it.

(4) After baking brush with sugar glaze, and return to the oven for a few minutes to set the glaze.

Sugar Glaze

1 dessertspoonful sugar.
1 dessertspoonful milk.

Boil until slightly thickened.

CHELSEA BUNS

Make the Vienna Bread dough and after rising have:

1 oz. margarine softened for spreading.
1 oz. sugar.
2 oz. cleaned dried fruit.

METHOD:

(1) Knead the dough lightly and roll out to make an oblong approximately 9 inches by 12 inches.

(2) Spread with margarine, sprinkle with fruit and sugar.

(3) Roll firmly, from the long side, to make a neat compact roll. Press together tightly.

(4) Cut the roll in ½-inch-thick slices, approximately 12 pieces.

(5) Place in a warm greased tin, the buns almost touching each other.

(6) Cover, prove 20–30 minutes until the buns touch each other.

(7) Bake in a hot oven 15–20 minutes.

(8) Rub with margarine paper or brush with sugar glaze.

SWEDISH TEA RING

Follow the instructions for Chelsea Buns, add 1 oz. chopped walnuts with the dried fruit.

METHOD:

(1) After forming the dough into a roll, damp one end and form the roll into a ring.

(2) Press join firmly.

(3) Transfer the ring to a warm greased baking tray.

(4) Using long scissors cut the ring around the edge only at ½-inch intervals, leaving the inner edge intact.

(5) Turn each slice to lie almost flat on the baking tray.

(6) Cover.

(7) Prove 20–30 minutes.

(8) Bake in a moderate oven 30 minutes.

HONEY TWIST

| ½ lb. Vienna dough. | ½ oz. margarine. | Cream |
| Honey topping. | 1 tablesp. honey. | together. |

METHOD:

(1) Warm and grease 2 sandwich tins 6 inches diameter.

(2) After rising divide the dough into 2 pieces. Form into 2 thin rolls.

(3) Coil the rolls into each tin, allow room for the dough to expand during proving.

(4) Cover and prove 20–30 minutes.

When half-proved spread the surface with the honey topping.

(5) Bake in a moderately hot oven 20–25 minutes.

DOUGH NUTS

Use the recipe for Vienna Dough, add 1 oz. sugar, and after rising include a little jam.

METHOD:

(1) Knead the dough lightly and roll out to $\frac{1}{4}$ inch thickness.

(2) Cut into rounds $1\frac{3}{4}$ inches diameter.

(3) Place a little jam on each.

(4) Form into balls enclosing the jam.

(5) Cover and prove on a warm greased baking tray, 20–30 minutes.

(6) Fry in deep fat—just smoking—if too hot the centres will not be sufficiently cooked.

(7) Reverse the position of the dough nut when transferring from the baking tray to the fat.

(8) Fry 5–7 minutes.

(9) Drain, sprinkle with castor sugar.

SALLY LUNN

Use the recipe for Vienna Dough, add 1 oz. sugar and use 1 egg.

METHOD:

(1) Grease and lightly flour 2 cake tins, $4\frac{1}{2}$ inches diameter.

(2) After mixing the dough beat well until smooth and glossy.

(3) Divide into 2 pieces, shape into rounds.

(4) Press lightly into tins.

(5) Cover, prove 30 minutes until the dough almost reaches the top of the tin.

(6) Bake in a moderate oven 25–30 minutes.

BATH BUNS (12 to 20 buns)

1 lb. flour (warmed).	1 oz. yeast.
6–8 oz. butter.	4 oz. sugar.
4 or 5 eggs.	About $\frac{1}{2}$ gill milk.
Candied peel.	Grated rind of 1 lemon.

Rub half the butter into the flour. Cream the yeast, and add the warm milk. Mix this into a little of the flour (this forms the sponge). Leave this to rise for $\frac{1}{2}$ hour. Then add the eggs unbeaten one by one, and mix these gradually to the rest of the flour, beating well. Put this to rise for 2 hours or more, till it doubles its bulk. Then beat in the sugar, peel, and grated lemon, and the rest of the butter in small pieces. When sufficiently firm form into buns. Brush these with egg. Rub some loaf sugar lightly over the lemon. Break this coarsely and sprinkle the buns with it. Set them to prove, then bake in a quick oven 20 to 30 minutes.

CRUMPETS or PIKELETS

1 lb. flour (warmed).	2 teasp. salt.
1 pt. milk.	2 oz. yeast.
	2 eggs. 2 oz. butter.

Cream the yeast and salt. To this add ¼ pt. warm water. Make a sponge with this and part of the flour. Set to rise. Add the melted butter and warmed milk, and gradually mix in the rest of the flour, adding the beaten eggs. Beat well. Set to rise for about 2 hours. Grease a girdle and some crumpet rings. Pour half a cup of the batter into each ring. When sufficiently cooked and firm enough, remove the rings and turn the crumpets to cook on the other side. The girdle must not be too hot, or the crumpets will burn before they have finished rising.

BABA AND BRIOCHE

For **Baba** see page 226, and for **Brioche** (4 medium-sized ones) as follows:

PLAIN	RICH
1 lb. Vienna or household flour (warmed).	1 lb. Vienna or household flour (warmed).
4 oz. butter.	8 oz. butter.
3 or 4 eggs.	6 or 7 eggs.
½ oz. yeast.	1 oz. yeast.
¼ gill milk.	About ½ pt. milk.
1 teasp. castor sugar.	1–4 oz. sugar.
A pinch of salt.	A pinch of salt.

Cream the yeast. Add the warmed milk. Pour this into part of the flour to make a sponge. Set to rise till it has doubled its bulk (about 20 minutes). Add the unbeaten eggs, one at a time, beating with the hands and gradually working in the flour from the sides, also the butter in small pieces. Beat till the mixture leaves the hands clean. Cover and set to rise for 3 or 4 hours, or all night. Form into rolls or put into tins for baking. Set to prove. Brush the tops with egg, and bake in a good oven. A large brioche will take over 1 hour to bake.

SAVARIN

Make and bake as for Baba and Brioche. They are generally served cold with fruit salad and decorated with whipped cream.

DOUGH CAKE (2 lb. bread tin)

12 oz. flour.	½ oz. yeast.
½ lb. butter.	½ teasp. spice.
¼ lb. currants.	¼ lb. sugar.
¼ lb. sultanas.	1–1½ gills warm milk.
2 eggs.	

Rub the butter into flour. Cream the yeast, add ¼ pt. warm liquid and set to sponge in warm place for 15 minutes. Warm the flour, add the yeast, eggs and the rest of the liquid, beat very well and put to rise for 1½ to 2 hours. Add the fruit, beat again with the hand, put into well-greased tin and prove for ½ hour. Bake in moderate oven for 1½ to 2 hours.

SIMNEL CAKE (7-inch cake tin)

½ lb. flour (warmed).	1 lb. almond paste, made
¼ lb. sugar.	with whites of eggs.
¼ lb. candied peel (sliced).	¼ lb. sultanas (picked).
3 yolks of eggs.	¼ lb. currants, cleaned.
¼ pt. milk.	Spice to taste.
¼ lb. butter.	½ oz. (good weight) yeast.

Cream the yeast. Add the warm milk. Pour this into the flour, working in sufficient to form a sponge. Set this to rise for ½ hour. Mix it with the rest of the flour, the creamed butter, and the rest of the ingredients, except the almond paste. Beat well; set to rise 1 to 2 hours. Put half in a greased and floured tin. On this place one-third of the almond paste formed into a flat round cake. Cover this with the rest of the risen dough. Prove this; then bake in a good oven for 1 to 1½ hours. When cold, cover the top and half the side with the rest of the almond paste. Mark this with a fork, and, if liked, place small round balls of almond paste round the top of the cake. Put in the oven a few minutes to give it a pale brown tinge.

N.B. Any good fruit cake mixture can be used.

LARDY CAKE

1 lb. flour.	3 oz. sugar.
4 oz. fat.	3–6 oz. fruit (if liked).
1 teasp. salt.	3 teasp. spice.
1 oz. yeast.	½ pt. milk.

(1) Rub in 1 oz. fat to warmed flour and salt.

(2) Cream yeast with 1 teaspoonful sugar, add tepid milk.

(3) Mix to an elastic dough, set to rise for 1 hour.

(4) Roll out 3 times as long as it is broad.

(5) Flake on 1 oz. fat, sprinkle with ⅓ sugar, spice, and fruit. Fold in as for flaky pastry. Repeat twice.

(6) Set to rise 20 minutes.

(7) Brush over with egg. Bake in a hot oven 20–30 minutes, reducing heat.

PART II

SCONES AND BAKING POWDER BREADS

These are a form of bread, the raising agent for which is baking powder, or bicarbonate of soda and cream of tartar.

Recipes for **Baking Powder** are:

(I)

Cream of tartar	.	.	.	4 oz.
Bicarbonate of soda		.	.	2 oz.
Ground rice	.	.	.	6 oz.

At least 2 teasp. of this baking powder is required to each lb. of flour.

(II)

Tartaric acid (an acid)	.	.	.	3 oz.
Bicarbonate of soda (a carbonate)		.	.	4 oz.
Ground rice	.	.	.	.	4 oz.

At least 1 teasp. of this baking powder is required to each lb. of flour.

With either mix the soda and rice, add the acid, sieve two or three times, and keep in tins.

Both, when mixed and moistened, give off carbon dioxide gas as always happens when an acid is added to a carbonate. This gas causes the scones, etc., to rise; but in so plain a mixture a taste of soda is apt to remain, due to the slight excess of bicarbonate which is present. If sour milk is used in making the scones the acid in the milk will help to use up the extra bicarbonate of soda.

It is important to remember that the carbonic acid bubbles begin to rise as soon as the baking powder is damped. Therefore, scones must be mixed very quickly and baked immediately.

Instead of baking powder, bicarbonate of soda is given in many recipes. It will always need cream of tartar (tartrate of potash) or some other acid with it.

The exact quantity of liquid needed for making scones, etc., cannot be stated, as good flour absorbs more than inferior flour. The consistency is the only accurate test for the amount needed.

For **Soda Scones**, etc.:

½ teasp. bicarbonate of soda,
1 teasp. cream of tartar,   } to each ½ lb. flour.
Fresh milk,

Rules for Making Scones

(1) Sieve the flour, salt, sugar (if used) and baking powder, and mix these thoroughly together. If this is omitted, scones are close in one place and have large holes in another.

(2) Rub fat, if any, into the above.

(3) Make a well; add three-quarters of the required liquid. Mix with a knife to a soft, but not sticky, dough, using rest of liquid as required. Average amount of liquid 1 gill to ½ lb. flour.

N.B. Where egg is used, add beaten egg and ¾ gill of milk.

Proceed as above.

(4) Turn this on to a floured board. Roll quickly to about ½ inch in thickness.

(5) Stamp into rounds, or cut into triangles.

(6) Place these on a greased tin, and bake at once in a very hot oven. In 5 minutes small scones should be quite brown and cooked.

Baking Powder Breads are made in the same way, but, being larger, they require longer cooking, and therefore rather less heat, or the tops would be burnt.

* BAKING POWDER ROLLS (12 to 16 rolls)

1 lb. flour.	½ pt. milk or milk and water.
1 or 2 oz. butter (optional).	2 heaped teasp. baking powder.
1 teasp. salt.	

See Rules for Making Scones. Form into small loaves. When cooked, brush with melted butter while still hot. OR, cut into 20 small rounds, for scones.

* BALMORAL SCONES (10 to 12 scones)

½ lb. flour. 1 egg.	1 oz. butter.
½ teasp. salt.	1 dessertsp. baking powder.
Milk to mix.	

Follow the Rules for Making Scones. These should be cut into triangles with a floured knife, and the oven should be sufficiently hot to bake them in 3 minutes.

BUTTER SCONES WITH CURRANTS (10 to 12 scones)

½ lb. flour.
1 oz. sugar.
Currants. 1 egg.

¼ lb. butter.
1 teasp. baking powder.

A small cup of milk, buttermilk, or sour milk. If sweet milk is used, use double the baking powder.

Mix the dry ingredients thoroughly. Rub in the butter. Whip the egg well, and add this with the milk. Mix to a light dough. Cut into rounds. Bake these or cook them on an ungreased girdle, which must not be too hot.

CREAM SCONES (10 to 12 scones)

½ lb. flour. 1 egg.
Pinch of salt.
1 gill cream.

1 oz. butter.
1 teasp. baking powder.

Follow the Rules for Making Scones, mixing with the beaten egg and cream to a stiffish dough. Bake at once in a quick oven.

DROPPED SCONES or SCOTS PANCAKES (I)

½ lb. flour.
½ teasp. bicarbonate of soda.
½ tablesp. sugar.

½ teasp. cream of tartar.
1 teasp. syrup.
1 oz. melted fat.

Follow the method given for recipe (II).

DROPPED SCONES or SCOTS PANCAKES (II)
(10 to 12 scones)

½ lb. flour.
½ teasp. bicarbonate of soda.
½ teasp. cream of tartar.

1 tablesp. of castor sugar.
1 egg (well beaten).
2 gills buttermilk.

(Or sweet milk with double the above quantity of cream of tartar.)

Sieve dry ingredients TWICE into a basin. Make a well in the centre and drop in the egg and a little buttermilk. STIR with the back of a spoon till perfectly smooth, then add enough milk to make a thick creamy batter. Grease a hot girdle and drop on the mixture in small rounds. When the surface rises in bubbles, turn the scones over and brown on the other side. When cooked, place in a cloth as for following recipe.

DROPPED SCONES or SCOTS PANCAKES (III)
(10 to 12 scones)

The same ingredients, but 2 well-beaten eggs are required.

Mix to a thin batter, and pour 1 spoonful on to a girdle. This should spread to a round 4 to 5 inches in diameter. Turn when one side is cooked. When cooked, place in a cloth on a sieve and cover with the cloth. When cold, spread with butter and roll up.

GIRDLE SODA SCONES (10 to 12 scones)

½ lb. flour.	½ teasp. cream of tartar.
½ teasp. bicarbonate of soda.	½ teasp. salt.
	About 1 gill buttermilk.

Sieve the flour, soda, cream of tartar, and salt; add enough milk to mix to a soft dough. Turn on to a floured board; knead lightly and roll out quickly to ¼ inch in thickness. Cut across in four or in rounds. Place on a hot girdle and bake steadily till well risen and of a light brown colour underneath. Turn and bake on the second side till quite dry in the centre. If sweet milk is used, double the quantity of cream of tartar.

NOTE. If baked in the oven, 1½ oz. margarine should be rubbed into the dry ingredients. The oven should be hot enough to bake the scones in about 7 minutes. In either case no time should be lost between adding the milk to the dry ingredients and the baking.

* POTATO SCONES (I)
(3 doz. scones)

10 oz. sieved floury potatoes.	6 oz. flour.
	½ teasp. salt.

Mix these with 3 oz. melted butter. Roll into cakes ¼ inch thick. Bake in a moderate oven or on a girdle about 15 minutes. Split, spread with butter, and serve at once.

POTATO SCONES (II)
(16 to 18 scones)

½ lb. cold potato.	About ½ gill milk (sweet).
About 2 oz. flour.	Pinch of salt.

Mash the potatoes and add the salt; knead as much flour into this as it will take up, and add enough milk to make a stiff dough. Roll out very thinly on a floured board. Cut into rounds and prick with a fork. Bake on a hot girdle for about 5 minutes, turning when half done. When baked, butter the scones and serve very hot.

These scones may be cut in rounds the size of a breakfast cup or rolled to wafer thinness and made into rounds the size of a small plate.

* RAISLEY SCONES (10 to 12 scones)

8 oz. flour.	Milk. 1 egg.
3 oz. fat.	1 oz. Raisley flour
½ teasp. salt or	or 1 heaped teasp.
1 oz. sugar.	baking powder.

Follow the Rules for Making Scones, mixing with the beaten egg and milk.   Reserve some beaten egg for brushing the tops before baking.

* SULTANA SCONES (8 scones)

½ lb. flour. 1 or 2 oz. fat.	Small ½ teasp. bicarbonate
1 oz. picked sultanas.	of soda.
1 oz. sugar.	About ¼ pt. milk.

1 small teasp. cream of tartar (or instead of the soda and tartar 2 teasp. baking powder may be used).

Follow the Rules for Making Scones.   Mix to a damp dough. Turn on to a floured board.   Form into two round cakes ½ inch thick.   Cut each quickly into four, place on a greased tin, brush with egg, and bake in a quick oven 15 to 20 minutes.

TEA SCONES (Hot)
(8 cakes)

½ lb. flour.	1 egg, well beaten.
2 oz. beef dripping.	1 dessertsp. baking
Milk to mix.	powder.
Pinch of salt.	

Follow the Rules for Making Scones, not making mixture too wet.   Cut into fairly large rounds, brush with egg, and bake 10 to 15 minutes.   Serve split, buttered, and quartered.

TREACLE SCONES (8 scones)

½ lb. flour. Pinch salt.	2 teasp. of sugar.
Small ½ teasp. bicar-	½ teasp. spice.
bonate of soda.	1 oz. margarine.
Small ½ teasp. cream	Large tablesp.
of tartar.	treacle.

Buttermilk or sour milk.   If sweet milk is used, double the quantity of cream of tartar.

Mix all dry ingredients, rub in the margarine.   Add treacle and enough milk to make a stiff dough.   Turn on to a floured board, knead, and roll out quickly and lightly. Cut in pieces and bake in a steady oven 15 to 20 minutes.

* WHOLEMEAL SCONES (6 to 8 scones)

¼ lb. wholemeal flour.	2 oz. fine flour.
1 heaped teasp. baking powder.	1 oz. fat. Salt.
	Milk and water to mix.

Follow the Rules for Making Scones. Bake 10 to 15 minutes, reducing the heat after the first few minutes.

The wholemeal flour may be omitted and the scones made with ½ lb. white flour and 2 oz. fine oatmeal.

Part III

CAKES MADE WITHOUT YEAST

To make good and wholesome cakes the following points should be noted:

Flour. Good household flour is the best to use for ordinary cakes, though Vienna or fine Hungarian should be procured for very light sponges, etc. Some self-raising flours are good, but as baking powder in excess is not really wholesome, it is difficult to tell in what proportion it has been added to the self-raising flour; also, rich cakes, if well beaten, rise, from the butter, eggs, and air that they contain, and the use of baking powder is then unnecessary, indeed it causes the cakes to be dry. When self-raising flours are used, omit any baking powder.

Whatever flour is used, it should be thoroughly dry and free from lumps.

Currants and Sultanas. These should preferably be washed, and dried in a cool place. OR, they may be rubbed in flour and any stalks, etc., removed.

Raisins. Stone these, and divide them into smaller pieces.

Fat. Fresh butter is the best fat to use; if salt, wash it; if rancid, it will spoil the flavour of the cake. Margarine is the best substitute for butter, but lard, clarified fat or dripping (or a mixture of these) may be used, provided that whatever fat is used is perfectly fresh and sweet.

Both lard and dripping should be used sparingly, or mixed with butter and margarine, as their flavour is too strong. They are only suitable for plain cakes.

Eggs must be perfectly good, and the ' speck ' or germ should be removed.

There are three chief Classes of cakes, determined by the method employed; a fourth class is appended, composed of cakes or biscuits in which the method of making is irregular and does not conform to any cake-making rule.

Class I

Under this heading come Plain Cakes, and the method given below should be used when the fat does not exceed half the weight of the flour.

Standard Recipe for a Plain Cake (6-inch tin)

½ lb. flour. 1 egg.	Milk to mix.
3 to 4 oz. fat.	1 teasp. baking powder.
2 to 4 oz. sugar.	2 to 6 oz. candied peel
Spice to taste.	and dried fruits mixed.

If soda is used instead of baking powder, sieve the soda with the flour and mix it with sour milk or other acid (a little lemon juice or vinegar mixed with the milk). If soda (alkali) and cream of tartar (acid) are used with sweet milk, sieve them thoroughly with the flour.

This ensures the soda being well mixed. It is otherwise apt to taste very strongly in the cake, and, sometimes, can be seen in the form of yellow patches.

METHOD:

(1) Prepare a cake tin by greasing it all over. Then line the bottom and sides with greased paper; at the sides this should project 2 inches above the edge of the tin. The tins need not be lined with paper for very plain cakes.

(2) Sift the flour and baking powder into a bowl. Mix well.

(3) Rub the fat into these until no lumps can be seen.

(4) Add the rest of the dry ingredients, and mix well.

(5) Make a well in the centre of these.

(6) Beat the egg (if any), and add it quickly with sufficient milk, and make a very stiff batter (mixing with a wooden spoon), one that is much too stiff to pour and is at the same time sticky and impossible to handle.

L

(7) Put the mixture into the prepared tin, which must not be more than two-thirds full.

(8) Bake in a fairly hot oven, reducing the heat after the first. Should the cake become too brown, cover it with a greased paper. A cake should be disturbed as little as possible, and the oven door must never be banged.

(9) TO TEST WHEN DONE. Time carefully, and if the centre feels firm to the touch, and if bubbling round the inside has ceased, the cake should be done. It should be firm to the touch and nicely browned when taken from the oven.

(10) Turn the cake out on to a sieve, and after a few moments remove the papers from the bottom and sides.

(11) Keep in a warm place to cool gradually.

CLASS II

Under this class come richer cakes, and all kinds of really rich ones, also small light cakes.

The method given below is applied when the quantities of fat, flour and sugar are equal, or nearly so; and, in any case, the fat will be half the weight of the flour or more. Eggs are an essential ingredient, and little or no baking powder is required, and the eggs usually supply enough liquid for the mixing process.

Standard Recipe for a Rich Cake (6-inch tin)

Two eggs, their weight in each of the following: fat, sugar, and flour. One good pinch of baking powder. Fruit may be added for rich cakes up to 4 oz. for the above mixture, whereas for small queen cakes 1 oz. will probably suffice.

This recipe can be varied to any extent. If half the flour is omitted and an equal amount of ground rice added to replace this, it becomes a **Rice Cake**; 1½ oz. desiccated coconut added gives a **Coconut Cake**; 1½ oz. glacé cherries added gives a **Cherry Cake**. It can also be baked on a flat tin, and when cold cut into fancy shapes—these are then iced.

METHOD:

(1) Prepare a cake tin as described for Class I Method, page 313.

(2) Cream the butter by beating it until soft with a wooden spoon.

(3) Add the sugar and continue to beat or cream the two together until white and rocky, rather resembling whipped cream.

(4) Add 1 egg, unbeaten, and beat thoroughly for 5 minutes.

(5) Add a second egg, and beat again for 5 minutes.

If more eggs are required they must be added in the same way.

(6) Sieve flour and raising agent and fold in these lightly.

(7) Add any fruits, and, lastly, the baking powder.

(8) Mix these thoroughly in.

(9) Drop the mixture, which should be of dropping consistency, into the prepared tin.

(10) Bake in a moderate oven until done. Test as for plain cakes (page 314).

(11) Turn on to a sieve. Very rich cakes are too soft to be turned out for ½ hour or so. The bottom paper can then be removed to let the steam escape. The side ones can remain till the cake is firm. Keep in a warm place to cool gradually.

Tins for cakes of this type, Wedding Cakes, etc., require several layers of greased paper to protect the cake during the long cooking.

CLASS III

Under this heading come sponge cakes, and the method given below should be applied to a recipe when the proportion of sugar exceeds, or is equal to, that of the flour; when there is a large amount of egg, little or no fat, and, as a rule, no raising agent. Sponge cakes are dependent on the beating of the mixture for their lightness.

Standard Recipe for a Sponge Cake (5 or 6-inch tin)

3 eggs. The weight of these 3 eggs, weighed in their shells, in fine castor sugar. The weight of 2 eggs only in fine (Hungarian or Vienna) flour.

METHOD:

This varies somewhat according to different recipes, but many of the elaborate methods give no better result than that detailed below, which may therefore be accepted as the standard and should be followed unless any special rules are given with a reliable recipe.

(1) Prepare the cake tin. For sponge cakes, to give their distinguishing crust of sugar, the preparation of the tin needs great care.

Brush the inside of the tin or mould carefully all over with just warm melted clarified butter. If the butter is too hot it will not coat the tin sufficiently thickly.

Sift together 1 teasp. fine castor sugar and 1 teasp. fine flour; put these through a hair sieve, and mix them well. Coat the whole of the inside of the tin with this mixture. It will adhere to the melted butter, and the whole should look evenly covered.

Any flour and sugar should be lightly shaken out of the tin. Grease a band of paper and tie this outside the tin (as for a soufflé), and when the inside coating is set the tin is ready for use.

(2) Beat the eggs whole, add the sugar and beat again over hot water till thick. Then beat till cold.

(3) Fold in the slightly warmed flour. No further beating must be done. The mixture is just 'folded' together till evenly mixed.

(4) Put the mixture into the prepared tin or mould.

(5) Stand the tin on another one on which is spread a thick layer of salt or sand. Put the whole into a very moderate oven, and bake for about ¾ hour. If there is any chance of the top burning when it has risen well, cover it with greased paper. Test with a bright skewer, and see if the cake is done.

(6) Leave the cake in the tin for a few moments, when the sides will shrink from the edges of the tin, and the cake will then turn out easily.

(7) Turn it on to a sieve.

(8) Stand it on the rack or in a warm place to cool gradually, or it will become damp and heavy.

CAKES—Class I

PLAIN CAKES

* BOODLE CLUB CAKES (7-inch tin)

1 lb. flour.	¼ lb. raisins.
½ lb. butter.	1 teasp. baking
½ lb. sugar.	powder.
3 eggs.	A little milk.
½ lb. sultanas.	1 teasp. mixed
¼ lb. currants.	spice.

Follow rules for cake-making, Class I Method, page 313. This makes an excellent large lunch cake.

* BRETZELS (about 20 bretzels)

½ lb. flour. | 2 or 3 oz. sugar.
4 oz. fat. | 1 yolk of egg.

Rub the fat into the flour, add the sugar, then mix with the yolk. Knead a little. Roll out to ¼ inch thick. Cut into strips ¼ inch wide and 12 inches long. Roll these between the board and fingers to round off the square edges, and form into bretzel shape or fancy knots. Brush these with white of egg, and sprinkle them with coarsely chopped almonds or nuts. Bake in a moderate oven for about 20 minutes.

* CORNISH CAKE (7-inch tin)

1 lb. flour. | 2 oz. candied peel (sliced).
6–8 oz. fat. | ½–1 lb. sultanas.
4–8 oz. sugar. | ¼ teasp. nutmeg or
1 or 2 eggs. ½ pt. milk. | cinnamon.
½ teasp. bicarbonate of | 1 teasp. cream of tartar.
soda. | 2 oz. loaf sugar.

Put the 2 oz. loaf sugar in a small metal saucepan with 2 tablesp. of water. Make a caramel of this (see page 219). Add the milk, and stir till the whole is mixed and the colour of coffee. Rub the fat in the flour—add the rest of the dry ingredients except the soda. Make a well in the centre of these. Dissolve the soda in a little of the caramel milk. Pour this, with the beaten egg, into the well, adding the rest of the caramel milk to form a damp dough. Bake in a moderate oven 2½ hours, or more.

CUMBERLAND BUN LOAF (2 lb. bread tin)

1 lb. flour. ¼ lb. fat. | ½ nutmeg, grated.
6 oz. sugar. | 1 teasp. bicarbonate of
4 oz. currants. | soda.
2 oz. peel. | 1 tablesp. vinegar.
1 tablesp. golden syrup. | ½ pt. milk.

Rub in fat. Mix all dry ingredients. Add soda dissolved in a little milk. Mix quickly and bake in moderate oven for 2½ to 3 hours.

* DEVON CAKE (6-inch tin)

½ lb. flour.
¼ lb. fat. 1 egg.
2 oz. moist sugar.
1 teasp. caraway seeds (optional).
⅛ teasp. bicarbonate of soda.

2 oz. French plums (cut up).
¼ lb. treacle (short weight).
1 oz. candied peel.
½ glass brandy, port, or milk.
1 teasp. ground ginger.

Dissolve the soda in brandy, port, or milk. Warm the treacle, and add it to the soda mixture. Follow the rules for cake-making, Class I Method, mixing the dry ingredients with the soda mixture.

* OATMEAL BISCUITS (12 biscuits)

5 oz. oatmeal.
3 oz. fat.
1 egg.
A pinch of salt.

3 oz. flour.
1–3 oz. sugar.
½ teasp. baking powder.

Mix the oatmeal, flour, baking powder, and salt. Rub in the fat. Add the sugar. Mix to a stiffish dough with the beaten egg, adding water if necessary. Roll on a floured board to ¼ inch. Cut into rounds or squares. Bake on greased tins in a moderate oven 10 to 15 minutes.

*PARKIN (6-inch square tin)

½ lb. flour.
1 gill oatmeal.
2 oz. fat.
¾ lb. (6 tablesp.) golden syrup.

¼ teasp. ginger.

¼ teasp. bicarb. soda (dissolved in ½ gill milk).

Melt the fat, add the syrup and allow to cool. Mix the flour, oatmeal, and ginger. To these add quickly the cooled mixture and milk mixture. Pour into a well-greased tin and bake for ¾ hour in a moderate oven.

* RAISIN CAKE (7-inch tin)
(WITHOUT EGGS)

1 lb. flour, OR 12 oz. flour and 4 oz. ground rice.	1 dessertsp. vinegar or lemon juice.
4–8 oz. sugar.	6–8 oz. fat.
2 oz. almonds, chopped and blanched (optional).	4–8 oz. stoned raisins.
	1–2 oz. sultanas.
½ pt. sour milk.	Nutmeg.
	¼ teasp. bicarbonate of soda.

Dissolve the soda in the vinegar, and add this to the milk.

Follow the rules for cake-making, Class I Method, page 313. Bake 2 hours, or more.

* RASPBERRY BUNS (12 buns)

¾ lb. flour.	Raspberry jam.
¼ lb. fat.	1 tablesp. milk.
2–4 oz. sugar.	1 teasp. baking powder.
1 egg.	

Follow the rules for cake-making, Class I Method, page 313, forming a paste. Roll this to ¼ inch thickness. Cut it into rounds. Put a spoonful of jam in the centre and draw the edges of the paste together to enclose the jam. Put the smooth side uppermost on to a greased tin. Flatten the cakes. Brush the tops with white of egg and sprinkle them with coarse sugar. Then make 2 or 3 incisions across the top, not quite cutting through to the jam. Bake in a good oven 20 minutes.

OR, make like Rock Cakes. Insert a little jam in the centre and draw the edges together.

* ROCK CAKES (12 to 16 cakes)

Plain	Richer
8 oz. flour.	8 oz. flour.
2–3 oz. fat.	3–4 oz. fat.
3 oz. sugar.	3 oz. sugar.
1 oz. currants.	1 large teasp. baking powder.
1 heaped teasp. baking powder.	1 *well* beaten egg.
Spice to taste, and milk to mix.	2 oz. fruit (currants and sultanas).
1 well-beaten egg if liked.	1 oz. finely chopped candied peel.
	Spice if liked.

In either case follow rules for cake-making, Class I Method (page 313), mixing to a stiff dough. Make into rocky heaps and bake 10 to 15 minutes in a very hot oven.

*SEED CAKE
(6-inch tin)

10 oz. flour.	3 teasp. caraway-seeds.
4 oz. fat.	
3 oz. sugar.	2 teasp. baking powder.
1 egg.	
About ¾ gill milk.	Pinch of salt.

Follow the rules for cake-making, Class I Method, page 313.
Bake for about 1 hour.

*SEED LUNCH CAKE (7-inch tin)
(FRUIT MAY REPLACE SEEDS)

1 lb. flour.	1 oz. caraway seeds.
¼ lb. fat.	¼ lb. sultanas.
¼ lb. moist sugar.	1 teasp. baking powder.
3 eggs.	

Milk to mix, about 1 breakfast cup.

Follow the rules for cake-making, Class I Method, page 313.

CAKES—CLASS II

RICH CAKES

ALMOND RINGS (24 rings)

Make a mixture for Shrewsbury Biscuits (page 329). Roll it
out and stamp it into rounds. On each round force some almond
mixture (see Almond Cakes (II), page 334) to form a circle.
Bake in a good oven for 15 minutes. When cold put some red
currant jelly in the centre of each. Sprinkle with chopped
pistachio nuts or browned chopped almonds.

CHERRY CAKE (7-inch tin)
(I)

¼ lb. flour.	¼ lb. ground rice (or rice flour).
½ lb. fat.	
¼ lb. castor sugar.	½ lb. cherries (cut up a little).
4 large eggs.	
2 oz. citron peel (cut up).	½ teasp. baking powder.
Rind of 1 lemon, grated.	

(II)

½ lb. flour.	4–6 oz. crystallized
½ lb. fat. 3 eggs.	cherries.
6 oz. castor sugar.	½ teasp. baking
1 teasp. vanilla.	powder.

In either case follow rules for cake-making, Class II Method, page 314.

CHOCOLATE CAKE (I)

(5-inch tin)

6 oz. flour.	3 eggs.
5 oz. fat.	½ teasp. vanilla.
5 oz. sugar.	1½ teasp. baking powder.

1½ oz. chocolate powder *or* chocolate dissolved in
a little milk.

Follow the rules for cake-making, Class II Method, page 314. Bake in a moderate oven for 1¼ hours.

* CHOCOLATE CAKE (II)

(6-inch tin)

8 oz. flour. 6 oz. fat.	1 oz. chocolate powder
6 oz. sugar. 3 eggs.	(or ½ oz. cocoa).
1 heaped teasp. baking	1 teasp. vanilla essence.
powder.	Little milk if necessary.

Follow rules for cake-making, Class II Method, page 314, but mix flour and chocolate powder together.

* CHOCOLATE CAKES, SMALL (12 to 16 cakes)

4 oz. flour. 4 oz. fat.	4 oz. sugar. 2 eggs.
1 pinch of salt and	1 oz. chocolate (or ½
baking powder.	oz. cocoa).

Vanilla to taste.

Follow rules for cake-making, Class II Method, page 314. Bake in small greased tins 15 to 20 minutes. Ice when cold.

*L

* CHOCOLATE KISSES (18 to 24 cakes)

½ lb. flour.	1 yolk of egg.
¼ lb. fat.	½ teasp. baking
3 oz. sugar.	powder.
2 oz. grated chocolate, or 1 oz. cocoa.	

Follow the method for cake-making, Class II Method, page 314, adding the egg yolk and the chocolate or cocoa dissolved in as little milk or water as possible, making a dry firm mixture. Place this in small teaspoons on a greased baking tin. Bake for 10 minutes in a quick oven till firm.

When cold stick two together with icing.

CHOCOLATE MARBLE CAKE (7 or 8-inch tin)

2½ cups of flour.	1 teasp. vanilla essence.
1 cup of butter.	1 cup milk.
1½ cups castor sugar.	1 oz. chocolate, melted
6 whites of eggs.	in a little milk or
2 teasp. baking powder.	water.

Cream the butter and sugar, add the milk (lukewarm), then the stiffly beaten whites. Sift the flour and baking powder together, and add these with the vanilla. Divide the mixture in two. Add the chocolate to one half. Put alternate spoonfuls of light and dark mixture into the tin to give the effect of marble. Bake in a moderate oven.

CHOCOLATE ROLL
See page 330.

CHOCOLATE SANDWICH CAKE
(pair of 7½-inch sandwich tins)

4 oz. flour.	1 oz. chocolate powder.
4 oz. fat.	1 teasp. baking powder.
4 oz. castor sugar.	2 large eggs.

N.B. Bar chocolate, dissolved in milk, can be used with smaller eggs.

Follow the rules for cake-making, Class II Method, p. 314. Bake in sandwich tins in good moderate oven for about 20 minutes.

CHRISTMAS CAKE (6–7-inch tin)

5 oz. flour. 5 oz. butter.	A little grated lemon rind
5 oz. castor sugar.	and caramel if liked.
3 oz. currants. 3 oz. sultanas.	1 oz. glacé cherries.
3 oz. seedless raisins.	1 oz. chopped peel. 3 eggs.

Follow the rules for cake-making, Class II Method, page 314.
Bake in well-lined tin in a very moderate oven for about 3 hours.

* COCONUT CAKE (5 or 6-inch tin)

6 oz. flour.	1 teasp. baking powder.
¼ lb. fat. 2 eggs.	1 oz. coconut.
¼ lb. sugar.	¼ pt. milk.

Follow the rules for cake-making, Class II Method, page 314.
Bake in a shallow prepared tin, 6 inches in diameter, for nearly
1 hour.   Ice when cold.

* COFFEE CAKE (5 or 6-inch tin)

6 oz. flour. 4 oz. butter.	4 oz. sugar. 2 eggs.
1 teasp. baking powder	1 tablesp. coffee
(or less).	essence.

Follow the rules for cake-making, Class II Method, page 314.
Bake in a shallow tin, 6 inches in diameter, for about ½ hour.
Ice when cold.

* COFFEE KISSES

See Chocolate Kisses.   Substitute 1 teasp. coffee essence
for chocolate.

* CORNFLOUR CAKE (Fluffy Cake)
(4-inch tin or small tins)

2 oz. cornflour.	½ teasp. baking
2 oz. butter.	powder.
2 oz. sugar.	½ teasp. vanilla
2 eggs.	essence or grated
½ oz. flour.	lemon rind.

Follow the rules for cake-making, Class II Method, page 314.
Bake 40 to 60 minutes in a moderate oven.

* CORNFLOUR CAKES, SMALL

Grease some small tins. Sprinkle them with ground rice. Half fill them with the above mixture (page 323). Sprinkle them with castor sugar and bake in a moderate oven 20 to 30 minutes.

* DUNDEE CAKE (8-inch tin)

14 oz. flour.	10 oz. sultanas.
8 oz. fat. 3 eggs.	3 oz. candied peel.
8 oz. sugar.	2 oz. blanched almonds,
Grated rind of 1 lemon.	to decorate with.
1 teasp. baking powder.	Milk, about ¼ pt.

Follow the rules for cake-making, Class II Method, page 314. Cover the top of the cake with the whole almonds, and bake for about 3 hours in a moderate oven.

This recipe gives an excellent fruit cake, but where a richer recipe is desired 1 or 2 more eggs may be used.

EASTER CAKES (18 to 20 cakes)

10 oz. flour.	2 oz. currants.
8 oz. butter.	A pinch of saffron
4 oz. sugar (fine).	steeped in a little
1½ yolks of eggs.	brandy.

Beat the sugar and butter to a cream. Add the yolks and sift the flour and brandy (strained). Let the paste stand a while (all night if possible). Roll out ⅛ inch thick. Cut in good-sized biscuits with fluted cutter. Bake in moderate oven very carefully for 10 to 15 minutes.

* FANCY CAKES, SMALL (12 to 16 cakes)

Plain	Richer
8 oz. flour.	4 oz. flour.
3–4 oz. fat.	4 oz. fat.
4 oz. sugar.	4 oz. sugar.
3 large eggs.	2 large eggs.
4 tablesp. milk.	Flavouring.
1 teasp. baking powder.	

2 oz. of any dried fruits, preserved ginger, pineapple, cherries, apricot, and, if liked, a little liqueur, may be added to either of the above recipes.

Follow the rules for cake-making, Class II Method, page 314. Dust with sugar before baking 15 to 20 minutes in small fancy tins.

FLORIDA ORANGE CAKE

(2 7-inch sandwich tins)

2 eggs, their weight in each of flour, fat, and sugar.   The grated rind and ½ the juice of 1 orange.   1 small teasp. baking powder.

Follow the rules for cake-making, Class II Method, page 314. Prepare a shallow tin, and bake 20 to 30 minutes in a moderate oven.   Ice when cold.

FRUIT AND CREAM CAKE

(2 7½-inch sandwich tins)

4 oz. flour.	4 oz. sugar.
4 oz. fat.	2 eggs.

If for bananas, use ½ banana flour, ½ teasp. baking powder.

Follow the rules for cake-making, Class II Method, page 314. Bake in a shallow tin.   When cold, cut into rounds 1 inch thick. Cover the bottom with thin slices of banana or other not too juicy fruit.   Sprinkle with sugar, and spread with stiffly whipped cream.   Replace the next round of cake and repeat till the cake is filled.   Coat with glacé icing.   Decorate to taste.

GENOA CAKE (9-inch tin)

1 lb. flour.	Grated rind of 1 lemon.
¾ lb. fat.	¼ lb. candied peel.
¾ lb. castor sugar.	½ lb. sultanas.
7 or 8 eggs.	½ lb. currants.
¼ lb. cherries.	1 teasp. baking powder.

To cover the top, 2 oz. almonds, blanched and sliced thinly.

Follow the rules for cake-making, Class II Method, page 314. Prepare a large shallow tin.   Cover the top of the cake thickly with almonds.   Bake in a moderate oven 1½ hours.   When cold, cut into nice-sized slabs.

GERMAN BISCUITS (8 to 10 biscuits)

3½ oz. flour. ¼ egg.	¼ teasp. ground cinnamon.
2 oz. margarine.	Milk, if necessary.
2 oz. sugar.	Glacé icing.
¼ teasp. baking powder.	Jam, cherries.

Mix the dry ingredients together.   Rub in the butter and mix to a firm paste with the egg.   Roll out thinly, cut into rounds, and bake till firm—about 15 minutes. When cool, sandwich two together with jam, glacé ice the top and place a piece of cherry in the centre.

* GERMAN POUND CAKE (8-inch tin)

10 oz. flour.	From ½ to 1 lb. mixed
8 oz. fat. 4 eggs.	fruits and peel.
8 oz. sugar.	1 teasp. baking
Grated rind 1 lemon.	powder.

Follow the rules for cake-making, Class II Method, page 314. Bake in a moderate oven for about 2 hours

N.B. 4 oz. ground rice may be added to ingredients if wished.

HARLEQUIN or RUSSIAN CAKE
(3, 6 by 4-inch, tins)

4 eggs; their weight in flour, fat, and sugar. ½ teasp. baking powder.

Follow the rules for cake-making, Class II Method, page 314. Divide the mixture equally into four portions. Leave one plain. Colour and flavour the other three to taste (e.g. (1) pink colour with vanilla flavouring; (2) chocolate or coffee; (3) green with lemon). Bake in equal-sized narrow, flat harlequin tins, greased and lined, for 15 to 20 minutes. Leave, if possible, till next day. From each cake cut (lengthwise) four strips 1 inch square. Soften red currant or other jelly with a palette knife. Stick the sixteen strips together with this in rows of four, using four colours in each row. The first colour of the second layer must be the second colour of the bottom layer, and the same sequence of colours must be used.

The third and fourth layers should be made in the same way, which will give diagonal squares of the same colour. Wrap the cake firmly in kitchen paper to stick the squares together, and leave till next day. Roll 1 lb. almond icing ⅛ inch thick, brush it with jelly, and wrap the cake in it. Trim the ends to show the coloured squares. Decorate with diagonal trellis work in butter or royal icing.

* JUMBLES (18 to 24 cakes)

Prepare mixture as for Shrewsbury Biscuits. Flavour with lemon, spice, or to taste. Divide into equal pieces the size of a walnut. Roll on a board with the hands into strips 8 inches long. Shape these into the letter S or fancy shapes. Bake in a moderate oven for 15 to 20 minutes. When cold, dust with castor sugar.

* MADEIRA CAKE (6-inch tin)

Plain	Richer
8 oz. flour.	8 oz. flour.
4 oz. fat.	6 oz. fat.
6 oz. sugar.	6 oz. sugar.
3 eggs.	4 eggs.
1 teasp. baking powder.	½ teasp. baking powder.
Grated rind of 1 lemon.	Grated rind of 1 lemon.

Follow the rules for cake-making, Class II Method, page 314. Dust with sugar. Bake for 1¼ hours in a moderate oven. When semi-cooked, place a strip of peel on the top.

* MARBLE CAKE (6-inch tin)

8 oz. flour.	3 eggs.
¼ lb. fat.	½ teasp. baking
6–8 oz. sugar.	powder.
½ gill milk.	

Follow the rules for cake-making, Class II Method, page 314. Divide into three or four portions, and colour as for Harlequin Cake. Fill the tin with alternate spoonfuls to give marbled effect. Bake in a moderate oven for 1½ hours.

* OATEN MACAROONS (12 to 16 cakes)

1 teacup flour.	2 oz. sugar.
2 oz. fat. 1 egg.	2½ teacups Quaker oats.
1 teasp. almond essence.	1 teasp. baking powder.

Follow the rules for cake-making, Class II Method, page 314. The mixture should be very dry. Form into small rocky cakes. Bake in a moderate oven for about 15 minutes. Leave on the greased tin to cool and dry.

* ONE EGG CAKE (5-inch tin)

½ lb. flour. 1 egg.	1 teasp. vanilla.
¼ lb. butter.	1 cup of milk.
¼ lb. castor sugar.	2 teasp. baking powder.

Follow the rules for cake-making, Class II Method, page 314, adding the milk and flour alternately. Bake in a prepared shallow tin about 30 minutes.

*ORANGE CAKE (Plain)
(5-inch tin)

6 oz. flour. 2 eggs. Rind of 1 or more oranges. ½ teasp. baking powder.	4 oz. sugar. 4 oz. fat (margarine **or** butter).

Follow rules for cake-making, Class II Method, page 314.
N.B. The juice can be used for icing.

* PAVINI CAKE (9-inch tin)

¼ lb. flour. ¼ lb. butter. ¼ lb. sugar. ½ lb. raisins. 2 oz. almonds (optional).	½ pt. milk (or less). ¼ lb. ground rice. ¼ lb. currants. ½ nutmeg grated. 1 teasp. bicarbonate of soda.

Cream the butter and sugar. Warm the milk. Mix the soda with some of the milk. Add this alternately with the flour to the butter and sugar. Mix well and quickly. Add the fruits, and as much milk as is needed to make the right consistency. Success in this cake depends on its being quickly made after the initial creaming is completed. Bake for 1½ to 2 hours in a moderate oven.

* QUEEN CAKES (16 to 20 cakes)

6 oz. flour. 4 oz. fat. 4 oz. castor sugar.	1 or 2 oz. currants. ½ teasp. baking powder. 1 or 2 oz. candied peel.
2 large or 3 small eggs.	

Follow the rules for cake-making, Class II Method, page 314.
Half fill some small greased fancy tins. Bake in moderate oven 15 to 20 minutes.

* RICE CAKE (6-inch tin)

4 oz. flour. 6 oz. fat. 6 oz. sugar. 3 eggs.	4 oz. ground rice. ½ teasp. baking powder.

Follow the rules for cake-making, Class II Method, page 314.

SEED CAKE (8-inch tin)

1 lb. flour. ¾ lb. fat.	½ lb. sugar. 5 eggs.
1 small tablesp. carraway seeds.	1 teasp. baking powder. 2 oz. citron peel.

Follow the rules for cake-making, Class II Method, page 314. Sprinkle with sugar. Bake in a moderate oven for 2 hours. When semi-cooked place a strip of peel on the top.

* SHREWSBURY BISCUITS (24 biscuits)

¼ lb. flour.	1 egg.
¼ lb. fat.	Grated rind
¼ lb. sugar.	of 1 lemon.
Allspice.	

Follow the rules for cake-making, Class II Method, page 314. Roll out, and cut into rounds. Bake in a moderate oven 10 to 15 minutes, till of a golden brown colour.

* SULTANA CAKE (6-inch tin)

½ lb. flour. 6 oz. fat.	Grated rind of 1 lemon.
6 oz. sugar.	4 oz. sultanas.
3 large eggs.	2 oz. candied peel.
1 teasp. baking powder.	

Follow the rules for cake-making, Class II Method, page 314.

* SWISS ROLL (I)
(10 by 12-inch tin)

The weight of 3 eggs in flour and sugar.	1 tablesp. milk.
	4 oz. jam.
3 oz. butter.	½ teasp. baking powder.

Follow the rules for cake-making, Class II Method, page 314. Spread evenly on a greased tin. Bake for 10 minutes in a hot oven, turn on to a sugared paper. Trim the edges, spread with jam, and roll up quickly.

SWISS ROLL (II)
(10 by 12-inch tin)

2 eggs.	¼ teasp. or pinch of
The weight of 2 eggs in sugar and 1 in flour.	baking powder.
	2 tablesp. of jam or curd.

Beat the eggs and sugar together until quite thick (about 10 to **15 minutes).** Sift in the flour and baking powder. **Mix** lightly and do not stir the mixture or it will be tough.

Have ready a greased Swiss roll tin, line it with paper and grease and flour the paper slightly. Turn the mixture into the tin and bake in a quick oven 5 to 8 minutes. Turn it on to a sugared paper. Remove the greased paper and spread with the jam or curd and roll it up at once.

SWISS ROLL (III)

(13 by 11-inch or 13 by 9-inch tin, thicker roll)

3 eggs. 1 gill flour.	1 gill castor sugar.
$\frac{1}{4}$ teasp. baking powder.	1 tablesp. boiling water.

Grease a Swiss roll tin and line it with greased paper. Divide yolks from whites of eggs. Whisk the yolks and sugar very thoroughly. Beat the whites very stiffly. Add the boiling water to the yolks and sugar, fold in the sifted flour and baking powder. Mix a little, folding in the whites also until evenly mixed but being careful not to destroy the lightness. Put into the prepared tin. Bake for 15 minutes in a moderate oven. Turn out and roll up as for other Swiss Rolls. The same recipe with water omitted makes 2 good sandwich cakes of 8-inch diameter.

SWISS ROLL, CHOCOLATE (12 by 10-inch tin)

The weight of 2 eggs in flour, fat, and sugar.	1 oz. chocolate or $\frac{1}{2}$ oz. cocoa.
A small $\frac{1}{2}$ teasp. baking powder.	1 or 2 tablesp. water (not milk).

Follow the rules for cake-making, Class II Method, page 314. If cocoa is used, dissolve it in the water, but if chocolate is used, mix the powder with the flour. Spread the mixture evenly on a well-greased tin. Bake for 10 minutes in a hot oven. Turn out on to a sugared paper, sprinkle at once with sugar, trim off the crisp edges, and roll up very quickly.

When quite cold, unroll, and spread with a good filling.

FILLING

3 oz. butter (fresh) or 3 tablesp. cream.	1 oz. ground almonds.
3 oz. icing sugar (sifted).	Vanilla or cinnamon to taste.

Cream these ingredients together and spread this on the cold roll. Roll it up again, sprinkle with icing sugar and use.

OR, the recipe for Swiss Roll (III) may be used, substituting 1 tablesp. chocolate powder for the flour.

WALNUT CAKE (6½-inch tin)

10 oz. flour.	½ teasp. vanilla essence.
4–6 oz. fat.	4 eggs. ¼ pt. milk.
8 oz. castor sugar.	1 large teasp. baking
2 oz. chopped walnuts.	powder.

Follow the rules for cake-making, Class II Method, page 314.
Bake in 2 prepared tins about 7 inches in diameter in a moderate oven for 30 to 40 minutes. When cold, divide each cake into two rounds. Spread each layer with walnut or almond filling, and coat the top and sides with American frosting (icing). Decorate with shelled halves of walnut.

WEDDING CAKE (12 to 13-inch tin)

2 lb. flour.	
2 lb. butter. 7 eggs.	SPICES
2 lb. castor sugar.	½ oz. allspice.
¼ lb. citron peel.	¼ oz. ground corian-
½ lb. orange peel.	der seed.
½ lb. lemon peel.	¼ oz. ginger.
3 lb. currants.	¼ oz. mace.
1 lb. raisins, chopped.	½ oz. ground cinna-
¼ lb. finely chopped	mon.
almonds.	1 grated nutmeg.
1 large teasp. baking	
powder.	
1 large glass brandy.	

Follow the rules for cake-making, Class II Method, page 314, with the following exceptions:

(1) Put sand or salt on a baking tin. On this stand the prepared cake tin. Prepare the tin by lining it with 4 layers of greased paper round the sides and bottom. Make a thick paste of flour and water, put this at the bottom of the tin and cover it with 2 layers of greased paper. These precautions are to prevent burning.

(2) Cream the butter, sugar, and spices.

(3) Beat for at least ½ hour before adding the fruit. When the cake is in the tin, smooth the top with a little milk.

Bake in a slow oven for at least 4 hours. Leave in the tin for some time (about ¾ hour) before turning out.

CAKES—Class III

SPONGE CAKES

ANGEL CAKE (6-inch tin)

6 whites of eggs.	1 teasp. vanilla essence.
4 oz. castor sugar.	3 oz. Vienna or house-
1 teasp. cream of tartar.	hold flour.

Beat the whites very stiffly. Sieve twice the flour, cream of tartar, and sugar. Lightly fold these into the eggs. Add the vanilla. Poured into a floured, ungreased mould. Bake from 40 to 60 minutes. Ice with fondant icing, if liked.

GENOESE PASTE

3 oz. Vienna or	3 oz. butter.
household flour.	4 oz. sugar.
3 large eggs.	

The size of tin required depends on the use of Genoese: for slab cake, to cut up and ice, a straight-sided tin 12 by 8 inches.

Beat the eggs, add the castor sugar, and whisk over boiling water till thick and creamy. Remove from the fire and whisk till cold. Sift the flour. Melt the butter. Fold these ingredients lightly to the egg mixture; add, if wished, the grated rind of half a lemon. Pour into tins prepared as for sponge cake (see rules for cake-making, Class III Method, page 315). Bake in a moderate oven for about 30 minutes, or according to the size of the cakes.

GENOESE PASTE, CHOCOLATE

Make as above, but mix 1 oz. grated chocolate and, if liked, 1 or 2 oz. ground almonds with the yolks and sugar after they have been whisked. Finish as for ordinary Genoese Paste.

GENOESE PASTE, COFFEE

Add 1 dessertsp. of coffee extract to the eggs and sugar after they have been whisked. Then proceed as for ordinary Genoese Paste.

*JAM SANDWICH (2 7½-inch tins)

2 eggs, their weight in fat, sugar and flour.   ⅛ teasp. baking powder.
Flavouring to taste.

Follow the rules for cake-making, Class III Method, page 315, and bake in 2 prepared flat tins in a quick oven for 10 minutes. Turn out on to a paper sprinkled with sugar. When cold spread one with jam and place the other over. The same mixture may be spread on one flat tin, baked and spread with hot jam, and rolled at once to make a Swiss roll.

SAVOY CAKE (2 lb. loaf tin)

| 4 small eggs. | ½ lb. sifted and dried |
| ½ lb. sugar. | Vienna or household flour. |

Follow the rules for cake-making, Class III Method, page 315. Bake in a moderate oven about 35 minutes.

*SPONGE CAKES, SMALL (8 or 9 tins)

2 oz. Vienna or	1 dessertsp. milk.
household flour.	3 oz. castor sugar.
2 eggs.	

Follow the rules for cake-making, Class III Method, page 315. Prepare some small sponge finger tins and half fill them with the mixture. Dust the tops with sifted sugar and fine flour, and bake 15 minutes in a moderate oven.

SPONGE SANDWICH CAKE

(2 7½-inch tins or 2 8-inch tins)

3 eggs.   3 oz. flour.   3 oz. sugar.

Whisk the eggs and sugar for about 10 minutes. Fold in the sifted flour quickly. Put into 2 round tins prepared as for sponge cakes, Class III Method, page 315. Bake 10 minutes in a quick oven. When cold, put a coffee or nut filling on one, cover with the other, and ice with any suitable icing. This recipe makes an excellent Swiss roll.

CAKES—Class IV

MISCELLANEOUS

ALMOND CAKES (I)

(24 cakes)

2 eggs, their weight in sugar, flour, and margarine.	MERINGUE
	Whites of the eggs.
	3 oz. castor sugar.
1½ tablesp. water.	1 oz. almonds.
¼ teasp. baking powder.	6 drops almond essence.

Cream fat and sugar together till soft. Add the yolks of the eggs not too closely drained from the whites. Mix smoothly and add the flour, water, and lastly the baking powder. Put into a flat greased tin and bake 10 to 15 minutes. The mixture should be pale in colour and just firm. Turn out to cool. Blanch and shred the almonds. Beat the whites of the eggs as stiffly as possible. Add the sugar to the whites of eggs, also almond essence. Put this on the cakes, which should be cut into fancy shapes in readiness. Sprinkle the almonds on top and place the cakes on a greased tin and bake slowly until the meringue is set. The cake mixture can be baked in small tins and is then less likely to dry in the second baking.

ALMOND CAKES (II)

(about 18 cakes)

½ lb. ground almonds.	¼ lb. castor sugar.
3 whites of eggs.	Rice paper.
Cherries and angelica for decoration.	

Whisk the whites very stiffly. Add the almonds and sugar. Force in fancy shapes on to rice paper.

Decorate and bake 10 minutes in a moderate oven.

ALMOND FINGERS (about 18 fingers)

½ lb. flour.	½ teasp. baking powder.
¼ lb. sugar.	2 yolks of eggs.
¼ lb. butter or margarine.	A little jam.

ALMOND MIXTURE { 6 oz. chopped almonds. 1 white of egg, whipped stiff. 2 tablesp. sugar.

Rub the fat in the flour, add the sugar and baking powder.

Mix to a stiff dough with the eggs. Roll into a paste ½ inch thick, spread with a little jam. Spread out the almond mixture Cut into fingers with a sharp knife. Place on a greased tin and bake in a good oven for about 20 minutes.

N.B. If liked, the mixture can be baked whole and cut into fingers afterwards.

BRANDY SNAPS (9 or 10 snaps)

2 oz. syrup.	2 oz. margarine.
1¾ oz. flour.	½ teasp. grated lemon
1¼ oz. castor sugar.	rind.
½ teasp. ground ginger.	½ teasp. brandy.

Melt the syrup, sugar, and margarine in a saucepan, then stir in the flour, ginger, lemon rind, and brandy. Mix the ingredients well together, then drop the mixture in small teaspoonfuls on a greased baking sheet about 3 inches apart. Bake in a cool oven from 7 to 10 minutes. When baked and slightly set, roll up at once round the greased handle of a wooden spoon. If overbaked, the snaps are too brittle to roll.

CHOCOLATE WAFERS (about 24 wafers)

4 oz. grated chocolate.	2 stiffly beaten whites.
¼ lb. castor sugar.	Vienna or household flour.

Add the sugar and chocolate to the eggs, adding enough flour to make a smooth paste. Roll to the thickness of a penny. Cut into wafers. Bake 12 to 15 minutes in a moderate oven. Remove, and set on a tin in an oven to dry.

COCONUT CONES (12 cones)

3 whites of eggs stiffly beaten.	6 oz. coconut.
	10 oz. sifted sugar.
Rice paper.	

Add the sugar and coconut to the whites of eggs. Pile on rice paper in the shape of cones, and bake in a cool oven till a very pale fawn colour.

GINGERBREAD (10 by 7-inch tin)

¾ lb. flour.	4 oz. margarine.
½ lb. treacle.	4 oz. sugar.
2 small eggs.	½ gill milk.
½ teasp. bicar-	1 teasp. ground
bonate soda.	ginger.

If liked, 2 oz. peel or 2 oz. preserved ginger may be added. 1 oz. almonds split and put on top when cake has been in oven 15 minutes.

Sieve flour, ginger, and soda. Add fruit if liked. Melt fat, treacle, and sugar over gentle heat. Beat eggs. Add milk. Add to flour with melted treacle, etc. Beat well, turn into lined and greased Yorkshire-pudding tin or cake tin. Bake in very moderate oven 1½ hours.

GINGERBREAD, FRUIT (9 by 6-inch tin)

6 oz. flour.	½ oz. ground ginger.
2 oz. butter.	½ teasp. spice.
1½ oz. sugar.	1 large egg.
6 oz. syrup.	1 oz. sultanas.
1 oz. chopped peel.	1 oz. chopped nuts.
1 oz. preserved ginger.	1 oz. cherries.

Follow rules for cake-making, Class I Method, page 313. Bake in slow oven.

*GINGERBREAD, INPARK
(10 by 7-inch cake, or cake tin 8-inch diameter)

¾ lb. flour.	½ teasp. bicarbonate
1 teasp. allspice.	of soda.
2 to 4 oz. fat.	½ oz. ginger.
1 egg (optional).	½ lb. treacle.
2 oz. coarse sugar.	½ gill warm milk.

Mix the flour, sugar, ginger, and allspice. Warm the butter, and add it, with the treacle, beaten egg, and soda (dissolved in the milk, which must be warmed to blood heat), to the dry ingredients. Mix thoroughly. Pour into a prepared shallow tin, and bake for about 1¼ hours. This is an excellent recipe even when egg is omitted.

* GINGERBREAD NUTS (18 to 24 nuts)

½ lb. flour.	3 oz. fat.
2 oz. sugar.	½ oz. ginger (or less to
1 teasp. baking powder.	taste).
2 tablesp. treacle.	Spice to taste.

Mix the flour, ginger, baking powder, and spice. Rub in the

fat and add the sugar. Warm the treacle, and add it to the dry ingredients to form a dough. Roll this into little balls the size of a walnut. Place these, slightly flattened, on a greased baking tin, and bake 10 to 20 minutes in a moderate oven. The dough may also be rolled and cut into biscuits.

MACAROONS (10 to 12)

¼ lb. ground almonds.	3 small whites of eggs.
1 oz. rice flour.	Vanilla.
¼ lb. castor sugar.	Few shredded almonds.

Beat the eggs very slightly. Add all the other ingredients and mix to a stiff paste. Line a tin with rice paper. Form the paste into small balls (walnut size), put them on the paper, leaving space to spread. Brush lightly with cold water, put a half-almond or a shred on each, and bake in a moderate oven 20 to 30 minutes.

MACAROONS, CHOCOLATE

Add 1½ oz. grated chocolate warmed in the oven and vanilla essence to taste to the ingredients given for Macaroons, and follow that recipe.

*OATCAKE (12 to 16 cakes)

7 oz. fine oatmeal.	1 tablesp. of drip-
½ teasp. salt.	ping or melted
1 oz. flour.	bacon fat.
Boiling water.	

Mix the oatmeal, flour, and salt. Add the melted fat and sufficient boiling water to bind the whole. Roll this in fine oatmeal. Roll as thinly as possible. Cut into triangles and bake in a moderate oven till crisp.

QUAKER OATS FINGERS (10 to 12 fingers)

4 oz. Quaker Oats.	3 oz. sugar.
2 oz. margarine.	1 teasp. treacle.

Melt the margarine and treacle in a saucepan. Add the sugar and Quaker Oats, and stir all together for a few moments, over gentle heat. Then turn the whole into a greased baking tin, and bake 15 to 20 minutes in a moderate oven until of a good brown colour. Leave in the tin until cool and then turn out and cut into neat fingers. This is an excellent recipe.

ROUT CAKES (about 24 cakes)

½ lb. flour.	2 or 3 eggs.
½ lb. ground almonds.	1 oz. butter.
	½ lb. sugar.

Mix and knead the dry ingredients with the well-beaten eggs to obtain a perfectly smooth dough. Leave this till next day. Roll it to ⅛ inch thick. Cut into fingers, diamonds, etc. Place these on rice paper, or on a greased, floured baking sheet. Leave in a cool place for ½ hour or more. Then bake in a moderate oven for about 10 minutes, or until golden. These cakes keep well.

* SHORTBREAD (I)

(12 to 16 biscuits)

6 oz. flour. 5 oz. butter.	2 oz. ground rice.
1 oz. chopped almonds.	1½ to 3 oz. castor sugar.

Sieve the flour, rice, and sugar. Rub the softened butter into these and knead till the whole is a pliable dough, adding no liquid. Form into 2 cakes 1 inch thick. Prick these, and lay a strip of candied peel on each. Let this stand for some time, then bake in a moderate (300° F.) oven for 40 minutes. The same mixture may be rolled to ¼ inch thick, and cut into fancy biscuits. Prick and bake these.

SHORTBREAD (II)

(12 to 16 biscuits)

[1] 6 oz. flour. ¼ lb. butter. 2 oz. castor sugar.

Mix the flour and sugar, rub in the butter, mix with the hand and knead till the mixture will bind, using no moisture. Form into round, square, or oval cakes. Prick these, and bake slowly on greased paper for ¾ hour.

This recipe may be varied by adding 1 oz. chopped almonds. Decorate the tops of the cakes with strips of almond or peel and mark the edges with a fork.

[1] 8 oz. flour are required in very hot weather.

SHORTCAKE, COCONUT (7-inch diameter)

4 oz. flour.	2 oz. butter.
2 oz. sugar.	2 oz. coconut.
Pinch of salt.	½ teasp. baking
1 yolk of egg.	powder.

Cream the butter, add the sifted flour, salt, and baking powder; then the yolk, sugar, and coconut by degrees. If absolutely necessary, add milk to bind, but the mixture must not be moist.

Flatten out to a cake ½ inch thick; mark it into quarters, decorate the edges, and bake (on a greased paper, placed on a baking tin) for 20 minutes in a moderate oven.

LUNCH BISCUITS (to eat with cheese)
(50 to 60 biscuits)

½ lb. flour.	Salt to taste.
½ to 2 oz. butter.	Cream to make.

Rub the fat in the flour, mix to a stiffish dough with the cream. Knead and beat with a rolling pin. Roll thinly, cut into rounds, prick well, place on a hot tin and bake in a hot oven.

VICTORIA SANDWICH CAKE
(2 7½-inch sandwich cake tins)

3 eggs.	3 oz. butter or margarine.
Their weight in flour and sugar.	1 tablesp. milk.

Follow the rules for cake-making, Class II Method, page 314. Bake in two sandwich tins (greased or greased and lined with greased paper) for 20–30 minutes. When cold spread with jam and sprinkle with sifted castor or icing sugar.

XVI. FILLINGS AND ICINGS FOR CAKES

FILLINGS

ANY plain sponge, Genoese, or suitable cake may be made very elaborate and delicious by cutting it into rounds and placing some good filling between the rounds, which are then fitted together again. The top one can then be iced and decorated.

ALMOND FILLING (3 sandwich cakes)

2 tablesp. ground almonds.	1 teasp. vanilla or liqueur.
2 tablesp. apricot jam.	1 tablesp. thick cream.

Mix thoroughly and use.

CHOCOLATE FILLING (I)
(4 sandwich cakes)

Dissolve 2 oz. chocolate in ½ pt. milk, then follow the recipe for Frangipane Custard.

CHOCOLATE FILLING (II)
(4 sandwich cakes)

Stiffly whip ¼ pt. of cream. Add 2 oz. grated chocolate, 2 oz. ground almonds, and 4 oz. sifted icing sugar. Mix and use. This does not keep.

COFFEE FILLING

Follow the recipe for Frangipane Custard, adding coffee essence to taste to the boiling milk. The whole amount must not exceed the ½ pt.

FRANGIPANE CUSTARD (3 or 4 sandwich cakes)

½ pt. milk (boiling).	1 oz. cornflour or flour.
1 oz. sugar.	2 or 3 yolks of eggs.
1 oz. butter.	Flavouring to taste.

Mix the cornflour to a smooth cream with a little cold milk or water. Pour the boiling milk on to this and boil for a few minutes, stirring well. Add the butter and sugar. Cool a little and add the eggs. Re-cook without boiling. Cool and use when cold. Chopped nuts, cut-up cherries, etc., may then be added if wished.

See also Custard, Confectioner's, page 221.

LEMON FILLING

Substitute lemon for orange, and follow the recipe for Orange Filling.

MACAROON FILLING (3 or 4 sandwich cakes)

4 oz. ground almonds.   ½ lb. castor sugar.   3 whites of eggs.

Mix these well together and pound them. Use as required. If stored in a jar, this will keep for some time.

ORANGE FILLING (I)

(2 sandwich cakes)

2 apples.	2 oranges.
2 lemons.	1 dessertsp. of
1 egg.	arrowroot.
2 oz. sugar.	1 oz. butter.

Grate the apples and the orange and lemon rind. Put all the ingredients, including the beaten egg and strained orange and lemon juice, into a pan and cook till thick. Use when cold.

ORANGE FILLING (II)

(1 sandwich cake)

½ oz. butter.	Grated rind and strained
2 yolks or 1 whole egg.	juice of 1 orange.
4 oz. castor sugar.	1 oz. cake crumbs.
Juice of ¼ lemon.	

Stir all the ingredients over the fire till mixture thickens. Use when cold.

PINEAPPLE FILLING (5 or 6 sandwich cakes)

2 pt. frangipane custard.	2 tablesp. whipped cream.
3 oz. preserved pineapple, cut small.	A few drops pineapple flavouring.
	1 tablesp. cake crumbs.

Preserved ginger or other fruit may be used in place of pineapple. Mix all together with the fruit.

RICH ALMOND FILLING (1 or 2 sandwich cakes)

2 oz. castor sugar.	2 tablesp. cream.
3 oz. almonds.	2 oz. butter. 1 egg.

Mix the pounded almonds, sugar, and butter. When well mixed, add the cream and egg. Flavour to taste and use.

WALNUT FILLING (1 sandwich cake)

1 tablesp. ground almond.	2 tablesp. chopped walnuts.
1 tablesp. royal icing.	Vanilla to taste.

Mix and use. Grated or desiccated coconut may replace almonds.

ICINGS

To ice successfully icing sugar must always be used. It requires pounding and passing through a hair sieve.

Exact proportions for mixing icings cannot be given, as some sugars absorb more liquid than others. In each case the right consistency must be obtained.

RULES FOR ICING A CAKE

(1) Trim the cake, if necessary, to an even shape.

(2) Remove all loose crumbs from the top and sides, first by brushing, and then by wiping with a damp cloth.

(3) Pound and sieve the icing sugar, and make the icing according to recipes.

(4) Place the cake on a wire tray, placed on a large dish or plate.

(5) Pour the icing over the cake, smoothing the top and sides with a palette (or broad-bladed knife), dipped in cold or hot water.

(6) Any icing that falls through the wire tray may be taken up and used for the sides.

(7) If decorated with fruits and nuts, put these in place before the icing sets; if with forced icing, let the surface coating set quite hard first.

ALMOND PASTE
(cover cake in 6-inch tin)

¼ lb. ground almonds.	¼ lb. very fine castor
¼ lb. icing sugar.	sugar, OR ½ lb. icing
Egg for mixing.	sugar only.

For keeping cakes use icing sugar only. Flavouring may be added if wished.

Whole egg may be used, or whites only, or yolks only, but if the latter a little brandy should be added with them. White of egg alone is the best. Beat the whites very slightly. Then mix the whole to a stiff paste. The desired consistency is that of short crust. Knead a little. Dust a board with sifted icing sugar, and roll to fit the cake. Before placing on the cake, brush the underside with white of egg to make it adhere to the cake. Unless whites only are used, stand the cake when almond iced in a cool oven with the door open for 20 to 30 minutes. This removes any taste of raw egg. In any case it requires to stand in a warm place for 24 hours or more.

AMERICAN FROSTING (cover 7½-inch cake)

1 lb. lump sugar. 1 gill water.

Boil to 240° F. Pour at once on to two stiffly beaten whites of egg. Whisk till thick enough to coat. Pour at once over the cake.

N.B. This can be also made by using one white of egg.

BUTTER or VIENNA ICING
(cover cake 8-inch diameter)

4 oz. butter.	Colouring and flavour-
6 or 8 oz. icing sugar.	ing to taste.

If used for filling one sandwich cake, 1½ oz. butter and 2 oz. sugar will be required.

Cream the butter. Add the sifted sugar. Beat well. Use as required.

CHOCOLATE BUTTER ICING

(cover cake 8-inch diameter)

Add 2 oz. grated chocolate, dissolved in 2 teasp. warm water and allowed to cool, to the ingredients given for Butter or Vienna Icing.

CHOCOLATE ICING

(cover 1 7-inch sandwich cake)

| 6 oz. icing sugar. | Barely ⅓ gill warm water |
| 2 oz. chocolate. | or thin sugar syrup. |

Dissolve chocolate in the liquid. Add butter. Cool well. Add sugar, which must be perfectly smooth. Mix till the mixture will coat the back of a spoon, adding more sugar if required. Warm slightly and use. If overheated, the icing discolours and cracks when cold.

COFFEE or MOCHA BUTTER ICING

Add 2 tablesp. of coffee essence to the ingredients given for Butter or Vienna Icing.

COFFEE MOCHA GLACÉ

(cover large thick sandwich)

To ½ lb. icing sugar add sufficient strained coffee to make a cream thick enough to coat the back of a spoon. Warm slightly, and pour quickly over the cake. If overheated, it will crack and discolour.

FONDANT ICING

(cover large thick sandwich)

1 lb. icing sugar.　1 gill water.

Dissolve the sugar in the water over gentle heat, then boil to 245° F. Then skim. Turn this into a basin, previously rinsed out with cold water, and stir until creamy. Add flavouring (e.g. 1 dessertsp. coffee essence), mix well, and dip the surface of the cake into the icing. If used too warm the icing becomes dull when cold. The sides may be spread with icing and sprinkled with chopped nuts, etc. The icing may also be spread on the cake.

ICING FOR GLAZING PASTRY

1 white of egg, slightly beaten.   1 oz. castor sugar.

Mix and spread this over the pastry. Dust with sugar and dry in a cool oven.

JELLY ICING

(1 slab Genoese 12 by 8 inches)

¼ pt. cream. ⎱
¼ pt. water. ⎰ OR ½ pt. milk.

¼ oz. gelatine.   1 oz. sugar.   Colouring and flavouring.

Dissolve the gelatine in the water. Add the sugar, cream, colouring, and flavouring. When just beginning to set, pour it over the cake.

LEMON WATER ICING

See Water Icings.

NOUGAT ICING

(1 slab cake 6 by 4 inches)

¼ lb. sugar.   2 tablesp. lemon juice.

Make a caramel of these (see page 219). Add 3 oz. blanched, chopped, and browned almonds. Pour at once on to a slab of cake. When set, turn the cake so that the icing rests on the board. Then cut the cake into fancy shapes.

ORANGE ICING

See Water Icing. Use orange juice.

ROYAL ICING

(cover cake in 6-inch tin)

About 1 lb. icing sugar.   2 or 3 whites of eggs.
1 dessertsp. lemon juice (optional).

Put the sugar in a bowl, add the lemon juice, and white of egg unbeaten. Gradually work in the sugar, beating well for 20 minutes or more with a wooden spoon. The mixture, when ready, should be sufficiently soft to enable it to be spread smoothly over a cake with a broad-bladed knife dipped occasionally into cold water, but too thick to flow at all. Before spreading,

M

a few drops of blue colouring can be added if wished. Leave the icing for an hour or two, when it can be decorated with crystallized fruits, etc.; but if the decoration required is to be made with forced icing, leave the first coating for 12 to 24 hours in a warm place to harden.

Icing made in the same way will be required for the decoration. This is forced through an icing syringe fitted with a fancy pipe.

WATER ICINGS

These are the simplest forms of icings. The icing sugar must be pounded and put through a hair sieve. It is then mixed with water, lemon juice, orange juice, or sieved fruit juice, e.g. raspberry, etc., to obtain whatever flavour is desired. For orange icing a little finely grated rind of orange may be added as well as the juice. The consistency of the mixture must be that of a coating sauce. To test it, coat the back of a spoon. The shape of the spoon must be visible, the colour of it entirely hidden, and the icing perfectly smooth. This icing will set in a few hours, but is never hard like Royal Icing. It is not suitable for decorating, as it cannot be forced through a syringe satisfactorily.

WATER or GLACÉ ICING
(large thick sandwich)

| ½ lb. icing sugar. | Little yellow colouring, |
| Strained juice 1 lemon. | if liked. |

Tepid water if required.

Follow directions given in previous recipe. Mix rather more stiffly, then place bowl in hot water. Stir gently till spoon is smoothly coated. Use at once.

OR, mix as above in a clean pan, stir gently over very gentle heat till spoon is smoothly coated.

N.B. The bottom of the saucepan must not be allowed to get at all hot or the icing will become dull, therefore stand pan in a tin of hot water.

WATER ICING BOILED or TRANSPARENT ICING
(cover cake 8 to 9-inch diameter)

1 lb. loaf sugar.   ½ gill warm water.

Dissolve the sugar over gentle heat, then boil it to 230° F. Pour into a basin, and stir till nearly cold. Use it for coating cakes before it gets quite cold.

XVII. BEVERAGES

CHOCOLATE

½ pt. milk. 1 egg.	1 teasp. castor
1 oz. chocolate.	sugar.

Pour the milk and chocolate into a rinsed pan and stir over the fire until the chocolate dissolves. Beat up the egg and pour over it the boiling chocolate. Put it in a jug and place the jug in boiling water and stir till thick and frothy. Add sugar.

N.B. The egg may be omitted, if liked.

CIDER CUP (I)

1 qt. cider.	1 pinch borage.
3 slices of lemon.	1 orange sliced.
1 small glass sherry.	1 small glass brandy.
A little maraschino.	2 bottles soda water.

Mix all these together. Stand on ice and add some broken ice.

CIDER CUP (II)

1 pt. cider.	Pinch of borage.
1 pt. soda water.	Few black grapes.
½ orange.	1 tablesp. sherry.
½ lemon.	½ tablesp. brandy.
Slice of cucumber (if liked).	

Cut a thin slice from the orange and lemon and squeeze the juice from the rest of the fruit. Add slices and juice to cider, with the rest of ingredients except soda water. Cool well. Add soda water and broken ice just before serving.

CLARET CUP (3 pt.)

1 bottle claret.	2 bottles iced soda water.
Some sliced cucumber.	1 sprig borage.
Sugar to taste.	The rind and juice of 1
1–2 glasses sherry.	lemon.
1 liqueur glass brandy.	

Mix these in the above order. Strain before serving.

COCOA

1 teasp. cocoa.   1 teacup milk or milk and water.

Blend the cocoa in a cup with a little of the cold milk. Boil the remainder, and pour it on to the blended cocoa. Rinse the pan, and pour the cocoa back. Boil for a minute or two and serve with sugar, if liked.

OR, the cocoa may be made less rich and more easily digested if about ⅓ water and ⅔ milk is used. Boil the cocoa in the water only, then add the milk and re-heat, but do not re-boil.

COFFEE

1 oz. mocha coffee.   ½ pt. freshly boiled water.

Have the coffee jug hot and the water freshly boiled. Put the coffee into the jug, pour in the water and infuse for 10 minutes by the side of the fire. Strain, re-heat if necessary, and serve with hot milk separately.

When the coffee has not been freshly roasted, place it in a lined saucepan and heat gently over the fire for a few minutes. Pour on the boiling water and proceed as above.

COFFEE, ICED

1 qt. strong coffee.	Sugar syrup to taste.
½ pt. milk.	½ pt. cream.

Mix the coffee, milk, cream, and syrup. Freeze until the whole resembles very thick cream.

Serve this in small glasses, handing castor sugar and whipped cream with it. If liked, whipped cream may be served on the top of each glass of iced coffee.

FISH HOUSE PUNCH, 1792
(12 pt.)

8 pt. water.	1 glass curaçao.
1 qt. Jamaica rum.	Sugar to taste.
1 tumbler French brandy.	1 pt. lemon juice.
Juice of 2 oranges.	½ tumbler peach brandy.
2 sliced lemons.	1 shredded pineapple.

Mix all together some time before using. About 1 hour

before serving add a large piece of ice and one bottle of iced champagne.

HOCK CUP (3 pt.)

1 bottle hock.	1½ bottles soda.
A large lump of ice.	A sprig of borage.
Some slices of cucumber and lemon.	1 glass brandy.
	1 liqueur glass curaçao.
1 glass Benedictine.	1 glass yellow Chartreuse.

Let the mixture stand for a few minutes. Remove the cucumber and lemon and add fresh strawberries.

LEMONADE (I)

(1 pt.)

2 lemons.   1 oz. sugar.   1 pt. boiling water.

Put the thinly cut rind and sugar into a jug. Pour the boiling water on to this. Cover and stand till cold, then add the juice of the lemons, strain and serve.

LEMONADE (II)

(for parties, 16 pt.)

Peel 12 lemons very thinly, and pour 3 qt. of boiling water on to the peel. Add the juice and sugar to taste. Mix well, and strain this to 5 qt. of cold water. Put on ice, then serve.

N.B. A less expensive lemonade can be made by omitting 4 lemons and adding ½ oz. of citric acid.

LEMON SYRUP

3 lb. loaf sugar.	Few pieces of whole
4 pt. water.	ginger.
2½ oz. citric acid.	Essence of lemon.

Boil the sugar, water, and ginger together for 10 minutes. Pour it over the citric acid and add 4 drops of lemon essence. Bottle and cork. To make a lemon drink, mix the syrup with water to taste.

MULLED WINE

The rind, thinly cut, of ½ orange and ½ lemon.

| 6 cloves. | Pinch of nutmeg. |
| 6 oz. loaf sugar. | ½ pt. water. |

Mix and heat these; strain, and add a bottle of wine. Heat as hot as possible without boiling. Serve at once.

ORANGE GIN

The rind, thinly cut, of 8 Seville oranges and 8 lemons. To these add 1 gal. unsweetened gin, also 3 lb. loaf sugar. Stir every day for a week, then strain and bottle.

RASPBERRY VINEGAR

| 2½ lb. raspberries. | 1 lb. sugar to each |
| 1 pt. best vinegar. | pt. of liquid. |

Bruise the fruit well and add the vinegar. Allow it to stand 3 days, stirring it well at intervals. Strain it and add the sugar. Boil 20 minutes. Put it into hot bottles.

Black currant vinegar is made in the same way.

SLOE GIN

| 1 gal. unsweetened gin. | 3 qt. sloes (well pricked). |
| 2½ lb. loaf sugar. | ½ oz. bitter almonds. |

Put these ingredients in a large jar, and shake it frequently.

TEA

Have water freshly boiled. Heat the teapot thoroughly and dry it. Put in the tea, allowing 1 teasp. for each person. As soon as the water boils pour it over the tea leaves, and leave the tea to infuse for 3 minutes, but not longer, or the tea will be bitter.

N.B. Less tea should be used when it is being prepared for a large number.

XVIII. INVALID COOKERY

THE food which is to be sent to the sick-room is amongst the most important items of household management. It needs special care, thought, and in many cases fresh methods of preparation. It is an interesting and necessary subject for all students of domestic subjects, and one of which most certainly they will need thorough knowledge. Certain concise rules in connection with the preparation of sick-room cookery are helpful and easy to carry in mind.

RULES

(1) The freshest and best materials should be used for sick people.

(2) The food should be prepared as far as possible on the day it is to be served, and only small quantities made at one time. Flavour and season all invalid food lightly.

(4) Special pans and utensils should be set aside for this purpose, and the actual china and silver in use should be beautifully clean and shining. Tiny cups, dishes, and glasses and moulds lend themselves to make an attractive tray for the invalid.

(4) Beef tea should not be boiled, or strained through a fine strainer. The cup in which it is served should be heated before putting in the beef tea.

(5) All food should be removed from the sick-room directly the invalid has finished the meal.

APPLE SOUFFLÉ (1 or 2 people)

2 large apples.	1 lemon (small).
1 tablesp. of sugar.	1 egg (new-laid).

Bake the apples and sieve them. Add the sugar, a little of the lemon rind grated, and the juice with the beaten yolk. Whisk the white stiffly. Fold it in lightly and pour into a dainty greased dish. Bake in a moderate oven for about 10 minutes.

ARROWROOT GRUEL (1 large cup)

½ tablesp. arrowroot.   1 large teasp. sugar.   ½ pt. milk.

Mix the arrowroot with a little of the milk. Boil the remainder. Pour some of this on to the arrowroot mixture, stir, and pour all into the pan, add the sugar and boil for 5 minutes.

ARROWROOT PUDDING (1 or 2 people)

1 tablesp. arrowroot.	½ tablesp. sugar.
½ pt. milk.	1 tablesp. brandy.
1 well-beaten egg.	

Make as for Arrowroot Gruel, add the egg, and pour into a very small buttered pie-dish. Brown the surface by placing it in a quick oven for a few minutes.

BARLEY WATER

2 oz. pearl barley.   1 oz. sugar.   1 qt. water.   1 lemon.

Wash and blanch the barley. Add the grated rind and the juice of the lemon and the sugar. Boil the water and pour it over this. Cover and let it stand till cold. Strain and use. The same barley may be used a second time.

BARLEY WATER, THICK

2 oz. pearl barley.	Rind and juice of
1 qt. water.	½ lemon.
Sugar to taste.	

Wash and blanch the barley by putting it into cold water and boiling it for 1 minute. Strain, rinse it, and put it with the thinly cut lemon rind and 1 qt. of fresh cold water into a double saucepan. Boil gently for 1 to 2 hours. Add the sugar and lemon juice. Strain, and use when cold.

BEEF SANDWICHES, RAW (3 or 4 sandwiches)

3 oz. lean beefsteak.	Thin slices of bread
A little salt.	and butter.

Scrape the meat finely, and pass it with the salt through a fine sieve. Form into sandwiches with the slices of bread and butter.

BEEF TEA

½ lb. good lean beef.   ½ pt. water.

Cut the beef into slices.   Scrape off as much meat as possible
from these, and then mince what remains very finely.   Put the
meat in the water as it is scraped off and minced, stirring
occasionally.   Let it stand for ½ hour.   Put the meat and water
in an earthenware jar, cover this closely by sealing the join
of the cover and jar with a paste made of flour and water.
Stand the jar in a saucepan of hot water which reaches rather
more than half-way up the side of the jar.   Simmer for ¾ to
1 hour, but do not boil.   Strain, remove any grease, and add
salt as required.   OR, a quicker method, mince the beef as finely
as possible.   Stir it well up in the cold water, and cook as above.

BEEF TEA, RAW

½ lb. beefsteak.   Pinch of salt.
1 gill soft water or water that has been boiled.

Remove the fat and skin from the meat.   Scrape it finely and
soak it in the water for 3 hours.   Stir occasionally.   Strain,
pressing the meat well.   This should be made in small quantities,
as it does not keep well.

BEEF TEA CUSTARD (1 person)

¼ pt. beef tea.   1 egg.   Seasoning.

Beat the ingredients together, and strain into a buttered cup.
Cover this with buttered paper and steam gently for about 20
minutes until firm, without letting the mixture bubble.   Serve
hot or cold.

BLACK CURRANT TEA (1 qt.)

2 tablesp. black | ¼ teasp. cornflour
currant jam. | (optional).
1 qt. water.

Boil the jam and water for ½ hour.   Stir in the cornflour
(if used), mixed smoothly with a little water, and boil for 3
minutes.   Strain and use.

OR, a simpler recipe, pour ½ pt. boiling water on 1 tablesp.
of jam.

*M

BREAD AND MILK (1 person)

1 slice of bread without crust cut into squares.   ½ pt. milk.

Put the bread into a china bowl, pour on the boiling milk, cover for 1 minute.   Serve with sugar or pepper and salt.

CAUDLE (I)

(3 or 4 people)

| 1 pt. gruel.   1 egg. | Lemon rind and sugar |
| 1 glass sherry. | to taste. |

Beat the egg to a froth, and add it to the other ingredients.

CAUDLE (II)

(2 people)

| ½ pt. gruel. | 1 glass port wine. |
| 1 white of egg. | Lemon to taste. |

Make rather thick gruel.   When boiling, add the wine and flavouring.   Cool, and add stiffly beaten white.

CHICKEN BROTH (I)

(about 1 qt.)

1 chicken.   1 qt. cold water.   A crust of bread.

Skin and cut the chicken into small pieces.   Place these in a pan with the water and crust.   Simmer very gently for 3 to 4 hours, or longer, if possible, skimming frequently.   Then strain through a sieve.   Remove all fat, and season to taste.

CHICKEN BROTH (II)

Use bones from chicken.   Just cover with water and simmer gently for 3 hours.   Strain, remove all fat, and season.   Serve hot or cold.

CHICKEN (or VEAL) CREAM

Made in the same way as Fish Cream, but the meat must be passed through the mincing machine before it is pounded.

CHICKEN SOUP

Use Chicken Broth (II). Add 1 beaten yolk and 1 tablesp. cream to each ½ pt., and heat carefully.

CHICKEN TEA

(about 1½ pt.)

½ a chicken.	1 pt. milk.
½ pt. water.	Pepper and salt.

Shred the chicken and soak it in the water for a few minutes. Add the salt and milk, and cover closely. Stand in a pan of water and simmer gently for 3 hours. Strain, add the pepper, remove all grease, and serve very hot with a little toast.

CORNFLOUR SOUFFLÉ PUDDING (1 or 2 people)

½ oz. of cornflour.	Small piece of
½ pt. of milk.	lemon rind.
1 egg.	½ oz. of sugar.

Boil the milk with the lemon rind. Mix the cornflour to a cream with a little of the cold milk. Strain milk on to cornflour and stir. Return it to the saucepan and cook 5 minutes, stirring all the time. Allow it to cool and add the sugar and yolk of egg. Whip the white of the egg stiffly. Fold this in lightly and turn into a pie-dish and bake till a very pale brown.

COUGH MIXTURE

1 gill of whisky.	2 oz. of glycerine.
¼ lb. of honey.	Juice of 2 lemons.

Mix all thoroughly together and take when needed.

CUSTARD (1 or 2 people)

1½ gills of milk.	¼ oz. of gelatine.
1 egg.	1 teasp. brandy.
¾ oz. of sugar.	Vanilla essence.

Heat the milk, add to this the sugar, egg (beaten), vanilla essence, and brandy. Dissolve the gelatine in two tablesp. of hot water. Add the gelatine to the milk and allow it to thicken slightly over the fire, but not nearly boil. Turn into a wet mould and allow it to set. When quite cold turn out and serve.

EGG DRINK (1 person)

1 egg.	1 tablesp. sherry.
1 teasp. castor sugar.	1 gill heated milk.

Beat the egg in a small basin till it is well mixed, add the sugar and sherry and pour on the heated milk, stirring all the time. Pour into a glass and serve.

EGG AND SODA WATER (1 person)

1 yolk (new-laid).	¼ pt. soda water.
2 tablesp. milk.	1 teasp. castor sugar.

Beat the yolk and sugar till thick and creamy. Add the milk, mix well. Put this into a glass and add the soda. If white of egg is used, it must be beaten to a stiff froth before adding it to the other ingredients.

EGG JELLY

See page 245.

EGG NOG (1 person)

½ pt. new milk.	1 new-laid egg.
1 teasp. sugar.	1 dessertsp. brandy.

Scald, but do not boil the milk. Leave it till cold. Beat the egg and sugar. Add the brandy and strain these into a tumbler. Fill the glass with the milk and serve.

FISH CREAM

4 oz. white fish (sole, haddock or whiting).	1 yolk of egg.
	½ oz. breadcrumbs.
½ oz. butter.	½ gill cream.
1 small tablesp. milk.	Squeeze of lemon juice.
1 beaten white of egg.	Salt and pepper.

Melt the butter in a small saucepan, add the crumbs, yolk, and milk, and cook till thick, and turn the sauce into a mortar. Wipe and shred the fish finely, add it to the sauce and pound well together. Then rub the mixture through a fine wire sieve. Season, then add the cream and the stiffly beaten white of egg. Turn the mixture into a greased basin or mould. Cover with greased paper and steam very gently 30 to 40 minutes. When firm, turn the cream out on to a hot dish. If liked, it may be coated with a white sauce.

FISH OMELET (1 or 2 people)

2 oz. cooked fish.	½ oz. of butter.
1 tablesp. of white sauce.	1 teasp. of anchovy essence.
½ teasp. of chopped parsley.	2 new-laid eggs. Pepper, salt.

Divide the fish into flakes and remove all bones and skin. Beat up the yolks of the eggs, add salt, pepper, anchovy essence, and a little fish. Beat the whites of the eggs stiffly and mix in lightly with the yolk. Cook in the butter until firm enough to fold. Mix and heat the fish sauce, parsley, salt and pepper. Put this mixture in the centre of the omelet and then fold and serve at once.

FISH, STEAMED

Sprinkle fillets of sole, etc. (whiting is a very light fish), with lemon juice and a little salt. Fold them neatly. Place them between 2 buttered plates. Put these over a saucepan of boiling water. Cook for 20 to 30 minutes, according to the thickness of the fish. It should look milky when done.

Serve on a dainty dish with the liquor poured round, garnish with lemon and parsley and rolls of thin bread and butter.

FLOUR, BAKED

This is often used to replace cornflour or arrowroot, as it is more nourishing, and equally digestible.

Sprinkle the flour on a baking tin. Cook it in a moderate oven until a pale brown colour. Store in airtight tins.

FRENCH EGG (1 person)

Whisk 1 yolk of egg with a teaspoon of sugar (castor) for 5 to 10 minutes till quite light. Add sherry or liqueur to taste. Whip the white very stiffly. Just mix the two and serve at once in a custard glass.

FRUIT TART (1 or 2 people)

1 small sponge cake.	1 large apple.
1 egg. 1 gill milk.	2 tablesp. water.
1 tablesp. castor sugar.	1 dessertsp. sugar.

Boil the 2 tablesp. of water with the dessertspoon of sugar for 5 minutes, then put in the peeled and sliced apple. Cook till tender; then beat the apple smooth and put in the bottom of a pie-dish. Cut the sponge cake into thin slices and place them on top of the apple. Beat up the egg, add the teaspoon of castor sugar and strain it on to the sponge cake. Soak the pudding for a few minutes, then bake in a moderate oven until the custard is set.

N.B. The appearance is improved if the milk is mixed with the yolk only, and the white is whipped stiffly, mixed lightly with 1 teasp. of castor sugar and piled on the pudding when it is set. Return to a very cool oven and crisp off for about ½ hour. The meringue should not be darker than a pale biscuit colour.

GRUEL (1 person)

1 oz. medium oatmeal.   3 gills whole milk or water.

Mix the oatmeal and water, cover it over and allow it to stand for 1 hour, then stir it up and strain it into a saucepan. Stir it over the fire until boiling. Allow the gruel to simmer for 15 minutes. Before serving, it may be salted or sweetened according to taste.

INVALID'S CHOP (1 person)

1 mutton chop.	2 tablesp. stock or
½ oz. breadcrumbs.	water.
Seasoning.	

Shred the meat, and put it with the other ingredients into a pan. Simmer for 10 minutes, and serve on toast.

INVALID'S ICE (1 person)

| White of 1 new-laid egg. | 1 teasp. of lemon juice. |
| 1 teasp. of castor sugar. | 1 teasp. of sherry or brandy. |

Beat up the white stiffly, add the lemon juice, sugar, and wine, stir lightly. Pile in the glass and serve at once.

IRISH MOSS JELLY (3 or 4 people)

| 1 pt. milk. 1 oz. sugar. | Thinly cut lemon |
| 1 oz. moss. | rind. |

Soak the moss for some hours in cold water. Then put it

into a pan with the milk, sugar, and lemon. Simmer very gently for ½ hour. Strain, pour into a wet mould, and turn out when cold.

LEMON WHIFFLE (2 or 3 people)

1 pt. boiling water.	6 or 8 oz. loaf sugar.
2 whites of eggs.	2 tablesp. arrowroot.
Rinds and juice of 3 large lemons.	

Soak the rinds, thinly cut, overnight in the water. Strain and boil the liquid with the sugar and lemon juice. Mix the arrowroot to a smooth cream with water and pour the boiling syrup to this. Return to the pan, re-boil. When thick, add the stiffly beaten whites. Whisk after adding stiff whites till mixture piles up. When cold, serve in custard glasses.

PORT WINE JELLY (5 or 6 people)

2 gills port.	1 in. cinnamon stick.
2 gills water.	Rind and juice of 1 lemon.
1 tablesp. red currant jelly.	¾ oz. gelatine (or 1 oz. in VERY hot weather).
2 oz. loaf sugar.	

Wash and peel the lemon thinly and strain the juice from it; then put all the ingredients into a rinsed, lined pan and stir over the fire till dissolved. Draw the pan to one side and allow it to infuse for 15 minutes. Strain through muslin when cold, pour into wine glasses or little moulds. When set, turn out and serve with whipped cream. The wine can be halved and the liquid made by the addition of extra water.

PORT WINE LOZENGES

1 gill port.	4 lumps sugar.
¼ oz. isinglass.	1 teasp. red currant jelly.
1 in. cinnamon stick.	Strip lemon rind.

Put all the ingredients into a pan and stir over the fire until dissolved; put the lid on the pan and infuse for 10 minutes. Strain through muslin and pour the mixture into a flat dish. When cold and set, cut into neat-sized pieces.

RESTORATIVE SOUP (1½ pt.)

1 lb. knuckle of veal.	1 lb. shin of beef.
1 lb. neck or knuckle of mutton.	2 qt. cold water.
	1 teasp. salt.

Put the water and salt into a strong pan. Wipe the meat, free it from fat and cut it into small pieces; put these at once into the water. Remove marrow, skin, and fat from the bones, wash them well and add them to the other ingredients. Bring slowly to the boil, skim if necessary and simmer 3 or 4 hours. Strain the soup through a hair sieve. When cold remove the fat and re-heat the soup.

If desired, this soup may be thickened with (a) tapioca, sago, rice; (b) arrowroot, cornflour, etc., allowing 1 teasp. of grain to ½ pt. of stock.

N.B. The meat and bones should be simmered further for household stock or soup.

SCALLOPED OYSTERS (1 person)

1 tablesp. bread-crumbs.	½ oz. butter.
4 oysters.	½ teasp. lemon juice.
	Salt and pepper.

Mix the crumbs and seasoning. Heat the oysters gently in their own liquor, do not boil them. Beard and remove the gristle. Cut in four. Butter a scallop shell. Arrange layers of crumbs, oysters, and butter alternately. Pour over the liquor and the lemon juice or a little sherry. Put tiny bits of butter on top and bake from 10 minutes.

TEA MADE WITH MILK (1 person)

1 teasp. tea.   ½ pt. milk.

Make as usual. Stand 1 minute only, pour out and serve.

TOAST WATER (1 qt.)

Toast the crust of a loaf of bread on each side. Pour over it 1 qt. of cold water. When the colour of sherry, strain and serve.

TREACLE POSSET (1 person)

½ pt. milk.   2 tablesp. treacle.

Boil the milk, add the treacle, re-boil, strain and use.

WHEY, FROM RENNET (1 person)

½ pt. milk.   1 teasp. rennet.

Make the milk lukewarm. Add the rennet. Leave for 1 hour. Then break the curd with a fork and strain it through fine muslin.

WHITE WINE WHEY (1 person)

½ pt. milk.   1 teasp. sugar.   1 wineglass sherry.

Bring milk to boiling point. Add sherry, stir, add sugar, and strain. Drink when very hot.

XIX. JAMS, FRUIT JELLIES, AND FRUIT CHEESES

FOOD PRESERVATION

DECAY in foods is caused largely by microscopic forms of life known as moulds, yeast, and bacteria. These are present in the atmosphere, and bring about destructive changes in food. The preservation of food therefore depends on the destruction or rendering inactive of any organisms which are present in the food and the protection of the food from further contamination. The methods in common use are the following:

(1) Application of heat and exclusion of air thereafter, as in jam- and jelly-making, bottling, and canning.

(2) Use of special antiseptic mediums, such as vinegar, salt, and sugar.

(3) Drying. For example, the treatment of herbs and fruits.

(4) Chilling such foods as meat, fish, game, fruit, and vegetables.

JAMS

GENERAL RULES

(1) The fruit should be gathered in dry weather, and should be fresh and whole.

(2) It should be under- rather than over-ripe, the latter being liable to ferment.

(3) Hard fruits should be wiped and prepared according to their kind, e.g. gooseberries topped and tailed; plums stalked, and stoned if wished.

(4) Equal quantities of fruit and sugar should always, if possible, be allowed. Jams made with a smaller proportion of sugar do not keep so well, with a few exceptions.

(5) The best quality of preserving sugar should be used.

(6) Jams must be stirred constantly with a wooden, not metal, spoon from the moment that the sugar and fruit begin boiling together.

TABLE FOR JAM-MAKING

If hard fruits can be cooked in the oven in a covered jar sufficient juice will flow, and no water will be needed. This is really by far the better method. But in making large quantities of fruit into jam this is not always convenient, and then the fruit can be cooked in the preserving pan with a little water until tender. This table shows the amounts of sugar and water.

KIND OF FRUIT.	AMOUNT OF SUGAR.	AMOUNT OF WATER.
To each lb. of APPLE (weighed after peeling and coring)	$\frac{3}{4}$–1 lb.	1 gill.
,, ,, APRICOT (weighed after stoning)	1 lb.	1 gill.
,, ,, BLACKBERRY	1 lb.	1 gill apple juice.
,, ,, CHERRY	$\frac{3}{4}$–1 lb.	1 gill red currant juice.
,, ,, RED CURRANT	1 lb.	Nil.
,, ,, BLACK CURRANT	1–1$\frac{1}{2}$ lb.	1$\frac{1}{2}$ gills.
,, ,, DAMSON	1 lb.	1 gill.
,, ,, GREENGAGE (weighed after stoning)	1 lb.	1$\frac{1}{2}$ gills.
,, ,, GOOSEBERRY	$\frac{3}{4}$–1 lb.	1–2 gills.
,, ,, PLUM	1 lb.	$\frac{1}{2}$–1 gill.
,, ,, RASPBERRY	1 lb.	Nil.
,, ,, RHUBARB	1 lb.	A very little.
,, ,, STRAWBERRY	1 lb.	1 gill red currant or gooseberry juice, or $\frac{1}{4}$ gill lemon juice.

(7) Jars must be prepared for jam by washing and drying them. They must then be heated thoroughly. Damp pots are often one of the causes of jams not keeping.

(8) Except for whole-fruit jams the fruit must always be brought to the boil before the addition of the sugar. Hard fruits must be cooked till soft, preferably in a covered jar in the oven, before the sugar can be added. When soft, put them in the preserving pan.

(9) As soon as the fruit boils in the preserving pan, add the sugar, commence stirring and boil rapidly, skimming as long as any scum rises, for from 15 to 35 minutes. No jam should need more boiling than this; and 20 minutes is a good average time. Just before the jam is ready add a small piece of fresh butter, $\frac{1}{4}$ oz. to 8 lb. This dissolves the scum.

(10) Test the jam by placing a little on a saucer. In about a minute it should have commenced to stiffen and will no longer flow freely. It is then ready.

(11) Either (1) Put it at once into the pots, filling them carefully or (2) If the jam is allowed to cool for a few minutes before potting, the fruit does not tend to rise to the top of the jar.

(12) Jars should be filled to within $\frac{1}{4}$ inch of the tops, and any jam spilt on the edges must be wiped off immediately with a hot, damp cloth.

This prevents the cover from becoming moist from the sticky particles of jam, thereby causing mildew.

(13) Place a round of waxed paper, dipped in brandy if liked, on the jam. It should cover exactly in order to exclude air.

(14) Damp and dry carefully a square of vegetable parchment, and tie the jars down at once with this.

Authorities differ about the last two points. Many prefer to leave the jam till cold before tying it down, but I find that the former method gives a more lasting result.

Whole-fruit Jam

SUITABLE FOR STRAWBERRY, RASPBERRY, BLACK CURRANT, CHERRIES, RHUBARB (cut into half-inch lengths), and MARROW. (See also Recipe for Marrow Jam)

RULES

(1) Choose the best fruit.
(2) Weigh it.
(3) Place it in bowls, sprinkling it in layers with half its weight in finest preserving sugar.

(4) Leave in a cool place for 24 hours to let the juice flow freely.

(5) Add the rest of the sugar, and unless the weather is so hot that fermentation would follow, leave for 24 hours more.

(6) Put the whole on to boil, stirring very gently to avoid crushing the fruit.

(7) Boil rapidly for 30 to 35 minutes. When done, the fruit will no longer float on the syrup, and the scum will cease to rise.

(8) Put into jars at once; if over-boiled, the jam becomes treacly and sticky.

The juice will not set, but should be thick, and the fruit quite whole.

If gooseberry jam is made in this way, a small quantity of any juice from fresh fruit must be put with it when it is first covered with sugar to start the dissolving process.

No water must ever be added to whole-fruit jam.

N.B. For this type of jam a patent pectin preparation is satisfactory. The jam is rather sweet and does not always keep as well as if made by the usual methods, but the flavour is fresh and colour good. The directions on the packet or bottle must be followed carefully.

Mixed-fruit Jams

The following mixed-fruit jams are most satisfactory:

> Blackberry and Apple.
> Loganberry and Rhubarb.
> Raspberry and Rhubarb.
> Strawberry and Gooseberry.

Different proportions of these fruits can be used; equal quantities give a good result, and equal weights of fruit and sugar should be used.

In each case the hard fruit should be well broken down in the preserving-pan first, cooking with a little water if necessary, then adding the soft fruit and proceeding with the directions for jam making on page 364 from Rule (9) onwards.

BLACK CURRANT JAM

4 lb. fruit.   6 lb. sugar.   2 pt. water.

Prepare fruit. Boil it with the water for 20 minutes. Add sugar and boil quickly for 10 minutes.

STRAWBERRY JAM

| 4 lb. fruit. | 4 lb. sugar. |

Acid fruit juice (1 pt. red currant or gooseberry juice OR 1 gill lemon juice).

Heat the fruit carefully with the fruit juice until softened but not pulped. Add the sugar and proceed with directions on page 364 from Rule (9) onwards.

VEGETABLE MARROW JAM

6 lb. ripe marrow cut into dice.	8 lb. sugar.
2 lb. apples reduced to pulp by gentle cooking.	¼ root ginger (crushed and tied in muslin). OR
juice of 3 or 4 lemons and grated rind of 1.	½ lb. preserved ginger, cut in dice, can be used instead of root ginger.

Cover marrow with half the sugar and flavourings and stand for 24 hours. Add to the apple pulp with the rest of the sugar and proceed with directions on page 364 from Rule (9) onwards.

DRIED APRICOT JAM

| 1 lb. dried apricots. | Rind and juice of |
| 4 lb. sugar. | 3 lemons. |

3 pt. water.

Wash the fruit well; soak in cold water for 2 days. Boil for 1 hour, add the sugar and lemon juice and rind (grated), and boil for ½ hour. Test as usual.

The lemon may be omitted if liked.

*GREEN TOMATO JAM

Green tomatoes, 6 lb. Peel these and cut them up. Boil them for 1 hour with a thinly cut rind and juice of 2 lemons. Then add 3 lb. sugar for this amount, and boil for another hour. This is a good, cheap jam.

FRUIT JELLIES

RULES

For these, only the JUICE of the fruit is needed. To obtain this:

(1) Cook the fruit in a covered jar in the oven, or in a lined stewpan, until the juice flows freely. The amount of water required depends on the kind of fruit; from ½ to 1 gill per lb. for juicy fruits, and sufficient water just to cover for hard fruits (crab-apples, etc.).

(2) Strain the juice by draining it through a coarse cloth or

hair sieve. A weighted plate may be placed on the top of it, but it must not be pressed or squeezed or the jelly will be cloudy.

(3) Measure the juice, bring to boiling point, add 1 lb. preserving sugar to each pt., dissolve the sugar, then boil rapidly until the jelly sets, usually 10 to 15 minutes.

(4) Test as for jams.

(5) Pour into hot dry jars and tie down as for jams.

Castor sugar may be used instead of preserving sugar, in which case it should be warmed in the oven before adding it to the fruit juice as it dissolves more readily.

N.B. The above method is satisfactory for fruits rich in pectin, i.e. apples, crab-apples, gooseberries, loganberries, etc.

For fruits lacking in pectin, e.g. rhubarb, blackberries, etc., the juice may need boiling (to obtain greater concentration) after straining.

To test fruits for pectin:

(*a*) Cool the fruit juice.

(*b*) Add 1 teasp. juice and 3 teasp. methylated spirit.

(*c*) Note the formation of clot. If solid and firm, the juice is ready for addition of sugar. If soft and broken, boil till the test is good.

There are various pectin preparations on the market that are useful for fruits lacking in pectin. **Blackberry Jelly** is much more satisfactory if a few apples or crab-apples are used with it.

REASONS FOR UNSATISFACTORY RESULTS IN JAM- AND JELLY-MAKING. If overboiled, jelly will be treacly and brown; if underboiled, it will not set (in this case re-boil it).

CRYSTALLIZATION is due to (*a*) overboiling; (*b*) undissolved sugar; (*c*) too much sugar; (*d*) keeping too long; (*e*) storing in too warm a place.

APPLE AND CRAB-APPLE JELLY

Choose hard, red, juicy apples. Wipe and halve these. Put them into a covered jar with ½ pt. water and the juice of half-lemon to each lb. of apples. Cook gently in a covered jar until quite pulpy. Strain them through a jelly bag or cloth. Measure the juice and to each pt. allow 1 lb. castor sugar. Then follow the rules for making jellies, page 366.

See also Red Currant Jelly (I).

MEDLAR JELLY

The medlars for this must still be hard. Wipe and cut them in halves. To each lb. allow 1 pt. of water. Cook them gently in a covered jar until pulpy. Strain them through a jelly bag or cloth, but do not rub or press them. Measure the juice and to each pt. allow 1 lb. castor sugar.

Then follow the rules for making jellies, page 366.

QUINCE JELLY

Wash and divide into quarters. Then follow the rules for Medlar Jelly.

RED CURRANT JELLY (I)

The currants should not be washed. Place them in a coarse cloth, a handful or two at a time, and squeeze with the hands till all the juice is extracted. Measure this into a preserving pan, add 1 lb. loaf sugar to each pt. of juice. Bring to the boil, skim well and boil for *exactly* 3 minutes, no longer. Dish up in pots.

RED CURRANT JELLY (II)
(Unboiled)

Squeeze the fruit as above. Allow 1 lb. loaf sugar to 1 pt. of juice. Pound and sift the sugar very finely and make very hot in the oven. Strain the juice and make it also as hot as possible without boiling. When all but boiling (be very careful not to let it actually boil) draw off from the fire and stir the hot sugar in gradually. Continue stirring until the last moment. When the sugar has entirely melted, the juice is ready to put into pots. It will jelly as well as if boiled and retain the flavour of the fresh fruit.

FRUIT CHEESES

These are an old-fashioned form of sweet or dessert. They are very wholesome and are so useful because of their keeping properties, providing fruit in winter.

Apple Cheeses

Follow the recipe for Apple Marmalade (p. 369), but store the cheese in slightly oiled moulds. When required, turn these out. Serve with cold meat.

Damson Cheese

Cook the damsons in a covered jar, adding no water. When quite soft, sieve them. Follow the recipe for Apple Cheeses. Some of the kernels of the damsons, blanched, may be added to the cheese.

Damson and Apple may be mixed if liked.

Quince and Apple Cheese

This may be made by mixing 1 part quince with 3 parts apple, or a larger proportion of quince can be added to taste.

MARMALADES

Apple Marmalade

6 lb. apples.   2 lemons (OR just under ¼ pt. water).

Wipe and halve the apples, and cook them with the lemon juice or water in a covered jar until tender. Sieve them, and cook the pulp obtained, stirring all the time, until it is thick enough to take up in heaped spoonfuls. Then weigh it, and take the same weight in castor sugar. Bring the pulp to the boil, add the sugar, and boil rapidly, stirring, for 15 to 20 minutes. If overboiled, it will be sticky and dark in colour, instead of firm and bright.

Jelly Marmalade

4 lb. Seville oranges. | 5 lb. crystallized sugar.
4 lemons.

Pare the rind very thinly from 6 of the largest oranges and cut into thin shreds (clean scissors are most useful for this), and boil slowly for ½ hour in 1 pt. of water. Take away rind, white, and pips from the other oranges and lemons, and break up the pulp with the hands into 3 pt. of water. Boil gently for ½ hour, then strain through a bag. Put the shreds, the water they were boiled in, and the strained juice into a pan with the sugar and boil for 30 minutes. Remove all scum. Test on a plate to see if it sets before removing it from the fire. Pour into pots and cover while hot. Best made in March or April.

Orange Marmalades

There are two different ways of making Orange Marmalade: one resulting in a solid jam, which is known as Scotch Marmalade; the other in a bright, clear jelly with finely shredded pieces of rind in it. The Clear Marmalade is by far the cheaper and also involves much less labour, but as the Scotch is a standard recipe, both are given. Seville oranges should be used, and 1 lemon may be allowed to 6 oranges, if wished. Preserving sugar should be used.

Orange Marmalade, Clear (I)

Wash the oranges and shred them very finely. To each orange add 1 pt. cold water and stand 24 hours. Peel the lemon thinly and shred, and add with the juice to the rest. Boil gently till peel is quite tender. Measure and to each pt. of pulp add 1 lb. preserving sugar and boil quickly till marmalade sets.

Orange Marmalade, Clear (II)

Wipe the oranges, divide them in two, remove all pips, and slice the oranges, rind and fruit, very thinly. This may be done by hand with a sharp knife, or with a machine. Weigh the sliced fruit, and to each lb. allow 2 or 3 pt. cold water (2 pt. make rather a better-flavoured jelly, but 3 pt. is excellent also and more economical). Leave this to soak for 48 to 60 hours.

Then cook very gently till the rinds are quite tender, but not pulped, and until the juice is reduced to about half the original amount.

Weigh this, and allow 1 lb. or, if a sweeter marmalade is desired, 1¼ lb. preserving sugar to each lb. of the fruit and juice. If to start with 12 lb. oranges were sliced and 24 pt. of water added, then, if the juice is properly reduced, the whole will now weigh 24 lb., and requires either 24 or 30 lb. sugar to taste. Bring the fruit and water to the boil, add the sugar, and boil rapidly for about 20 minutes.

IF A BITTER MARMALADE is desired, soak the orange pips in water for 24 hours, and add some of the jelly that will be found on these to the fruit and juice when the sugar is added.

Orange Marmalade, Scotch

Remove the rinds from the Seville oranges, being careful to take as little as possible of the white part. Put the rinds in plenty of cold water and cook them gently until so tender that a straw can pierce them easily. Pour away the water, and cut the rinds into very thin shreds. Remove all possible pith from the rest of the fruit and slice it thinly, removing all pips. Weigh this fruit and the sliced rinds, and to each lb. allow 1 lb. of preserving sugar. Bring the fruit and rinds to the boil, adding the sugar by degrees, and boil for about 25 minutes.

Orange Marmalade, A Simple Recipe

Use *two* lemons to every 6 oranges. Wash and slice fruit very thinly. Add 1 pt. of water for each orange. Steep for 24 hours with the pips tied in muslin. Boil till quite tender (1 or 2 hours). Remove the pips, add the lemon juice and 1 lb. of sugar to each pt. of cooked pulp. Boil till setting (30 to 40 minutes). Pot and finish as usual.

Quince Marmalade

Wash the fruit. Put it into a covered jar with water to cover it and cook till tender. Strain, peel, and core the fruit, and put it back into the same water in which it was cooked. Reduce it, cut the fruit into cubes. Weigh the fruit and juice, and to each lb. allow 1 lb. of sugar. Bring the fruit and juice to the boil. add the sugar and boil rapidly for about 20 to 35 minutes. Test. It should be of the consistency of whole-fruit jam.

XX. BOTTLING OF FRUITS AND VEGETABLES

THE best method is by sterilization. For this, a special deep sterilizing pan is the most convenient utensil. It is fitted with a false bottom attached to a handle, so that the bottles can be lifted in and out of the water without handling them.

In the absence of a proper pan, a deep fish kettle may be used. This must be fitted with a false bottom (strips of wood nailed together answer very well), and a hole must be cut in the lid to admit a thermometer.

The pan must be sufficiently deep for the bottles to be immersed totally in water after the false bottom is in.

Very good bottles are the ' Kilner ' patent glass bottles. These are fitted with a glass cap, a metal screw, and a rubber ring. A thermometer is essential, as it is impossible to guess the correct temperatures for fruit, though vegetables may be bottled successfully without one.

If bottles with metal tops and metal springs are used (e.g. Fowler-Lee's bottles), follow the directions issued by the maker.

RULES FOR BOTTLING FRUIT AND VEGETABLES IN KILNER BOTTLES

(1) See that the bottles are scrupulously clean.

(2) Examine the rubber rings and glass lids for possible flaws, as a single flaw will prevent success; if the rubber rings are stiff, soften them by putting them in warm water for a few minutes.

(3) Place a false bottom in the sterilizing pan, as, if the bottles are brought suddenly into contact with heat, they will crack.

(4) Examine the necks of bottles for possible flaws or cracks.

(5) After sterilization, lift the bottles on to wood to prevent cracking due to sudden cold on hot bottles.

(6) Store bottles when empty by putting them away in a clean condition with the rubber ring inside the bottle, and the glass cap and metal screw on the top.

(7) Keep a supply of spare rubber rings, glass caps, and metal screws in case of accident. See that the metal screws are not bent.

GENERAL RULES FOR BOTTLING FRUIT

(1) Pick the fruit when dry; prepare it (top and tail gooseberries, stalk currants, etc.).

(2) Wash the fruit. Hard fruits may be washed in fresh water and drained; soft fruits, currants, etc., must be put in the bottles; then add water to fill the bottles, shake gently, and, keeping back the fruit, pour off the water. Do this once or twice until clean, but do not break the fruit.

(3) Pack the bottles as full of the fruit as is possible. Soft fruits require shaking down by hitting the bottle gently on a pad or cushion.

(4) Put the rubber ring in place on the neck of the bottle.

(5) Fill the bottles to overflowing with either clean cold water or cold sugar syrup, made as follows: Dissolve ¼ lb. sugar in 1 pt. water; boil for a few moments and skim; use when cold.

(6) When the bottles are ABSOLUTELY full, and brimming over, put a lid quickly on. Keep it in place with the hand, and slip a metal ring on, never relaxing the pressure.

(7) Screw the metal ring firmly.

(8) Prepare as many other bottles as the sterilizing pan will hold, each in the same way.

(9) Place the bottles in the pan on the false bottom.

(10) Pour sufficient fresh cold water over the bottles to cover them to a depth of two or three inches.

(11) Under the water, unscrew the metal screws, until they are loose and rattle on the bottles without letting them slip right off. This is important, as during the heating the glass expands, and if this were omitted the bottles would crack. It must be done under water to prevent air from entering the bottles.

(12) Put a lid on the sterilizing pan and put the thermometer in place.

(13) Put the sterilizing pan on the stove and slowly heat the liquid, so that at the end of the first hour the thermometer registers exactly 130° F.

(14) Continue heating gently, so that at the end of another ½ hour the thermometer registers 150° F.

(15) Keep the temperature at 150° F. for 5 minutes.

(16) Lift the bottles out of the hot water. To do this, raise the handle fitted to the false bottom, and, at once, tighten the metal screws.

If there is no proper sterilizing pan fitted with a false bottom and handle, dip out sufficient water until the bottles can be grasped below the screw with a cloth. Lift each one out singly and tighten the screw IMMEDIATELY to prevent the admittance of any air. Tighten again after a short interval.

(17) Leave the bottles until next day. Then loosen the screws carefully and remove them. Hold the glass lids, and if they are firmly fixed in place by the pressure of outside air, caused by the ' vacuum ' in the bottles, the bottles will be so firmly sealed that they can be lifted by the lids.

The fruit inside will then keep in perfect condition for years.

(18) Replace the screws loosely (so that they may not be lost) and store the bottles in a cool, dry place. The fruit is quite cooked and ready for use when wanted.

The above rules are applicable to: Apricots, Bilberries, Blackberries, Cherries, Cranberries, Damsons, Gooseberries, Greengages, Loganberries, Mulberries, Peaches, Plums, Raspberries, Red and White Currants, Rhubarb.

The following fruits require a rather higher temperature for sterilization:

APPLES AND PEARS

Bring these to 150° F. in the first hour, then to 180° in the next ½ hour, and keep at 180° for 10 to 15 minutes. These fruits being harder, require longer in order to cook them properly.

BLACK CURRANTS

Bring the temperature to 130° F. in the first hour, then to 160° in the second ½ hour, and keep at 160° for 5 minutes.

STRAWBERRIES

Choose hard, sweet ones, at the end of the season. Stalk and sprinkle them with sugar. Pack them tightly in bottles, adding no water. Put the rubber rings, glass caps and metal screws on the bottles. Place these in the sterilizer on a false bottom with cold water up to the shoulder of the bottles only. Cover the sterilizer, and gently heat till the thermometer registers 150° F. Keep it at that temperature for 5 minutes. Lift out the bottles, unscrew and open them, and holding one with a dry cloth pour its contents into a second, until this is full to overflowing. Cover it at once with a warmed lid, and screw firmly down. Repeat, until as many bottles are filled to overflowing as possible.   Then put them back into the sterilizer, adding more water at the same temperature, till all the bottles are immersed in water.   Loosen the screws under water, and bring the temperature quickly up to 150° F.   Keep at that for 5 minutes.   Lift out the bottles and screw them tightly.   Next day, test as for ordinary bottling by sterilization, and store according to the rules given.

The only kind of strawberry that will keep its colour is the variety known as 'Leopold de Tardite '.

This method is excellent for **Raspberries** also.

A Simple Method of Bottling Fruit in the Oven without a Thermometer

(1) Fill some bottles or jars to within an inch of the top with any sound, dry fruit.   Pack this as tightly as possible into the bottle.

(2) Cover the tops of the bottles with patty pans to prevent fruit discolouring and place on wood or cardboard in a cool oven, 260° to 300° F.

A homely test is to place a saucer of cold water in the oven. In 5 minutes it should be steaming and hot to the touch, but bearable.

ADD NO LIQUID WHATEVER TO THE BOTTLES.

Leave in oven till fruit which was too firmly packed to be movable becomes loosened and the juice just begins to flow. This takes about 1 hour.   Gooseberries change colour slightly, becoming yellower.

(3) Have ready rapidly boiling water or sugar syrup; 4 to 8 oz. per pt., according to acidity of the fruit.

(4) Lift out one bottle on to wood and fill it immediately with boiling water just to cover the fruit.

(5) Cover the bottle AT ONCE with either: (a) Melted clarified mutton fat, or (b) Parchment paper, wetted or dried.   This must be tied on firmly, and then brushed with gum, melted resin, paraffin wax, lard, etc.

(6) Do each bottle separately and tie it down before lifting the next out of the oven.

(7) When cold, store in a cool, dry place.

N.B.   If Kilner jars are available they may be used.   In this case slip the warmed rubber ring on as soon as the bottle is removed from the oven. Fill the bottle to overflowing with boiling water, slip on the warmed lid and screw down firmly. Test next day as usual.

To Bottle Fruit without a Thermometer or Oven

(1) Take a pan sufficiently deep to contain the bottles.

(2) Place a false bottom in the pan.

(3) Pack the bottles tightly with fruit and fill to overflowing with clean cold water or cold syrup (strength 4 to 8 oz. per pt.) as above for ' Kilner ' or other patent bottles, and to within ½ inch of the top for ordinary bottles or jars.

(4) Put the bottles in the pan.

(5) For patent bottles adjust caps and slips or bands carefully; cover completely with cold water. For ordinary bottles or jars surround with cold water up the shoulders of the bottles.

(6) Put on the lid of the pan. This should fit well to prevent escape of steam. Bring gently to simmering point; the process takes about 1 hour. Keep at this temperature for about 15 minutes.

(7) Lift each bottle out singly and cover either with mutton fat or parchment (see next page); or for ' Kilner ' bottles put on the warmed rings, caps and screws, and screw down firmly.

To Cover Ordinary Bottles

(1) To Cover with Bladder. Soak the bladder overnight. Trim and wash it in several waters until sweet and clean. Cut it rather larger than required, keep it in water till wanted. Tie it loosely over the pots, then pull down and tighten the string as each bottle is sterilized.

(2) To Cover with Cloth and Wax. Required, strong unbleached calico. Wash to remove dressing and cut in squares large enough to cover the tops of the bottles well. Wax sealing mixture:

4 oz. resin.   ½ oz. vaseline.   ½ oz. beeswax.

Pound the resin and place in an old tin or stoneware jar. Add vaseline and beeswax. Place the tin or jar in a pan of hot water and heat until all ingredients are thoroughly melted. Stir with an old stick. This tin of sealing mixture may be kept from season to season and remelted as required.

To Use. Cut a circle of greaseproof paper a size larger than the mouth of the bottle to prevent wax dropping on fruit.   Mark size of bottle on the calico square and paint a circle of melted wax a little larger than the mouth of the bottle.   Stick the paper to the centre; the wax must come beyond the paper all round.   When the jar is removed from the oven, tie this cover still hot firmly over the top.   When beginning to harden, brush more wax over the top to make a thoroughly good seal.

N.B. For this method the syrup or water should just cover the fruit.   If it touches the paper the latter will come off and wax drop into the fruit.

(3) To Cover with Paper and Paste.   Three or four thicknesses of clean paper pasted together and tied over the mouth of the jar.   For this method also the syrup or water must not be allowed to come up to the cover.

(4) To Cover with Parchment.   Parchment paper, wetted or dried.   This must be tied on firmly, and then brushed with gum, melted resin, paraffin wax, lard, etc.

(5) To Cover with Clarified Mutton Fat.   This requires a paper cover as well.

PRESERVATION OF VEGETABLES

Vegetables are more difficult to preserve than fruit, because:

(1) Vegetables contain less acid.

(2) They are more solid in composition.

(3) Most kinds come more in contact with soil.   Some of the soil bacteria are of the sporing type which are very resistant to heat.   The process of preservation of vegetables must, therefore, be carried out by different methods from those used for fruits.   Sterilization of canned and bottled non-acid vegetables must be carried out in a pressure cooker.

Rules

(1) Choose young, but well-grown vegetables.

(2) Preserve as soon as possible after gathering.   This is most important because of the action of enzymes and bacteria.

(3) Wash very thoroughly.   Pea pods should be washed before shelling.

(4) Prepare according to their kind.

(5) Dip in boiling water (tied in muslin or in a vegetable basket) for 2 to 5 minutes according to kind and age of vegetable.

This blanching is done (a) to shrink the vegetables and make

N

them more pliable and easy to pack into the bottles; (b) to remove any strong flavour; (c) to cleanse.

(6) Dip into a bowl of cold water to make them easier to handle in packing.

(7) Pack loosely in THOROUGHLY CLEAN bottles. Tight packing prevents heat penetrating to the centre and does not allow for swelling. Do not fill too full, leave about ¼ inch to spare.

(8) Fill to overflowing with a covering liquid of the Acid Brine given below. The liquid must be cold.

(9) Adjust lids, RUBBER BANDS and clips or screw bands.

(10) Place in fish kettle or sterilizer and if possible cover completely with cold water: otherwise be very sure the lid is very tight fitting. Bring water in sterilizer to boiling point AS QUICKLY AS POSSIBLE and boil for 1½ hours. The time and temperature are important.

(11) Remove bottles one at a time, tighten bands and leave until next day, then test.

N.B. If on removing bottles the covering liquid no longer covers the vegetables, remove lids one at a time, pour in more boiling brine, fasten down and re-sterilize for another 20 minutes.

ACID BRINE COVERING LIQUID

The Lemon Juice Method has the disadvantage of slightly spoiling the colour of green vegetables, but it improves that of white ones.

1 gal. water.   2½ oz. salt.   5 fluid oz. lemon juice.

Bring water to boil, add salt and lemon juice, and cool before use. Measure the lemon juice very carefully with a fluid ounce measure obtainable at Woolworths or Boots.

The above method is very satisfactory for all vegetables except the following:

ASPARAGUS

Wash each stick and remove side-spurs. Cut the stalks to the length of the bottle—it must only reach to the shoulder. Pack it very tightly. Fill the bottle with cold water, empty this, and do this twice or thrice to wash away particles.

Then fill the bottle to overflowing with acid brine covering, and finish as usual.

MUSHROOMS

Choose fully expanded ones. Remove nearly all the stalk and the peel. Lay them on dishes and sprinkle them with salt and pepper. Leave them for a little while, then put them in a covered jar and cook them in the oven. Next day pack them in bottles, adding no water, but filling the bottles with the mushroom juices.

Finish according to the rules for bottling vegetables, page 377.

SALTED FRENCH BEANS

Put a layer of kitchen salt into an earthenware jar, add a layer of prepared young beans. Repeat in layers till the jar is full, finishing with salt. Stand for a few days, then turn occasionally until brine forms. Tie down.

To Use. Wash and soak in cold water till the bulk of the salt is removed. Cook as usual, omitting salt.

N.B. The jar need not be filled all at once.

TOMATOES

Choose sound, slightly under-ripe ones. Remove the stems and prick two or three times into the fruit (but not through the outer skin) from where the stems are removed. Place them in bottles, packing them tightly, but care must be taken not to break the skins.

Add ½ teasp. of salt to each bottle; fill them to overflowing with clean cold water, put on the ring cap and screw as for fruits. Submerge the bottles in cold water in the sterilizer, loosen the screws, place the sterilizer on the stove and heat it so that in 1 hour the thermometer registers 150° F. and in the second ½ hour 180°. Leave at 180° for 15 minutes, then lift out the bottles, tighten the screws, and test as usual next day.

HOME CANNING OF FRUIT AND VEGETABLES

Canning of fruit and vegetables can now be safely, easily, and quickly carried out at home if one uses modern lacquer-lined 'Sanitary Cans' and a hand can-closing machine.

Students requiring further information about canning, or more detailed knowledge of the processes of preserving fruit and vegetables by various methods, are advised to consult the firms who supply the apparatus.

XXI. PICKLES AND CHUTNEYS

PICKLES

To pickle food is to preserve it, so that it is often an economy to pickle any surplus vegetables or portions of meat that cannot be eaten at once.

THE PICKLING OF MEAT

Meat for pickling, by whichever method, must be sound and fresh. Remove all traces of blood, also any pipes and kernels. SUGAR is an improvement, and also a preservative, having great antiseptic properties.

SALTPETRE must be used with care, as if used in excess it renders the meat very hard.

BAY SALT should be used in preference to common salt, as it gives a better flavour.

There are two methods of pickling meat: The Dry and the Wet. The former gives the best flavour, but is more trouble. The latter is a cheaper method.

DRY PICKLING (I)
(4 to 6 lb.)

½ lb. bay salt (powdered).	1 teasp. allspice.
	1 teasp. black pepper.
½ lb. coarse sugar.	1 chopped onion.

Mix the ingredients, and rub them thoroughly into the meat, which must be turned daily, and rubbed over well. Leave the meat in this pickle for about 10 days.

(II)
(4 to 6 lb.)

½ lb. powdered bay salt.	½ teasp. ground mace.
¼ lb. treacle.	1 teasp. ground cloves.
½ teasp. black pepper.	¼ oz. saltpetre (ground).
½ a nutmeg.	

Mix thoroughly and warm these ingredients. Rub them into the meat as described above.

(III)
(4 to 6 lb.)

½ lb. bay salt.	½ lb. saltpetre.
1 lb. common salt.	6 oz. brown sugar.

4 oz. ground black pepper.

Mix together, warm, and rub into meat. Repeat daily for 3 weeks.

WET PICKLING (I)
(10 to 12 lb.)

6 to 8 oz. brown sugar.	3 lb. bay salt.
	¾ oz. saltpetre.

1 gal. soft water.

Boil all these ingredients, skimming, for about 20 minutes. Leave till cold. Then place the meat to be pickled in the prepared brine. It is better to place the brine in a tub or jar that has a lid to cover it. Leave the meat in the brine for a week or 10 days, according to the size of the joint. Tongue should remain in the brine for about 3 weeks. It should then be taken out and soaked in fresh cold water the night before cooking.

(II)
(8 to 10 lb.)

1 lb. bay or common salt.	1 oz. saltpetre.
	½ lb. brown sugar.

3 qt. water.

Sliced onions, etc., may be boiled in brine if liked. Boil 20 minutes. Skim and pour into earthen pot or wooden tub, and leave till cold. Completely immerse the meat in the cold brine 14 to 21 days.

PICKLED BEEF, PORK, Etc.

See Dry or Wet Pickling, above.

PICKLED TONGUE

3½ lb. salt.	1 oz. saltpetre.
1 oz. brown sugar.	1 gal. water.

Wash the tongue, and rub it with salt. Leave it till next day. Throw away the liquid.

Boil the above ingredients for 10 minutes, skimming well. When cold place the tongue in the pickle for about 2 weeks, according to size.

THE PICKLING OF VEGETABLES

Most vegetables are suitable for this purpose. They must be freshly gathered. Divide cauliflowers into sprigs; shred red cabbage finely, and cut marrows and cucumbers into slices.

The vegetables must be well wiped (not washed), and then covered by a brine made as follows: 1 lb. salt, 1 qt. water. Boil these together, and when cold pour them over the vegetables. Leave them in the brine for 3 days; then change it, and leave them for a fortnight in the second lot of brine. After this, wash the vegetables well, place them in bottles and cover them with vinegar and water. Leave them for 24 hours. Pour off the vinegar and water, and drain the vegetables thoroughly. Make a mixture of the following:

1 gal. vinegar.	4 oz. mustard seed.
4 oz. peppercorns.	2 tablesp. salt.
4 blades of mace.	Few small onions or
4 oz. bruised ginger.	3 cloves of garlic.

Boil all together for 5 minutes. Place the vegetables, either mixed or separately, into bottles, and when the mixture is cold, cover them with it.

A few chillies and peppercorns should be put on the tops of bottles of mixed pickles. Special corks must be bought for pickle bottles. A piece of bladder or parchment must be put under the cork, and the top must be closely sealed with bottling wax.

N.B. Copper or brass pans must NEVER be used for boiling vinegar in. Enamel or aluminium ones should be used, or, failing these, an earthenware jar or big casserole.

PICKLED CABBAGE

This is crisper if frost has touched the leaves.

Shred the cabbage finely, spread it on a flat dish, and cover it with salt. Cover and leave till next day. Drain away all moisture from it and put it into jars. Make a pickling mixture following the recipe given above, and, when cold, strain it over the cabbage, covering it entirely. Seal as described above.

This pickle does not keep very long, as the cabbage loses its crispness.

PICKLED ONIONS

Small ripe onions.	1 tablesp. allspice.
1 gal. vinegar.	1 tablesp. black
½ tablesp. salt.	peppercorns.

The onions must be dry. Remove the outer skins with a silver knife (steel spoils the colour). Put them quickly into jars or bottles. Cover with the cold vinegar and add the spices as on page 382. Tie down the jars with bladder. In 2 or 3 weeks they are ready for use.

Make this pickle in July or August.

PICKLED TOMATO

2 qt. green tomatoes.   ¼ teacup of salt.   2 large onions.

Slice the tomatoes and onions fairly thickly. Cover with the salt and leave them to stand all night. Drain well, and add 1 pt. of water and ½ pt. of vinegar. Boil for ¼ hour, drain well, and throw away the liquor. Make the following mixture: 1 pt. of vinegar, ½ lb. of castor sugar, 1 dessertsp. of cloves, cinnamon, and mustard seed (tied together in a bag), 1 saltsp. of cayenne, 1 dessertsp. of ground ginger. Add these to the tomatoes and boil for 15 minutes. Remove the bag of spices. Put into hot jars and cool before covering.

Seal as for all pickles.

PICKLED WALNUTS

These must be gathered early (in July) while still soft and before any shell can be felt when pierced with a needle.

Prick the walnuts right through the centre.

Cover them with a brine made of 1 gal. of water and 1½ lb. salt. Leave them for several days in the brine, changing it two or three times. Then drain them and lay them singly on flat dishes exposed to the air until they turn quite black. Place them in jars. Prepare a pickle, following the instructions for pickling on previous page. Strain it at once over the walnuts and tie down when cold. Keep for some months before use.

PICKLES, MIXED

1 gal. of vinegar.	2 oz. turmeric.
4 oz. of bruised ginger.	¼ oz. cayenne (or less).
4 oz. of mustard.	1 oz. salt.
1 oz. ground black pepper.	All kinds of vegetables.

Mix the mustard, turmeric, salt, and cayenne smoothly with a little of the vinegar. Add the rest of the ingredients, and place in a large jar. Keep in a warm place for 3 or 4 weeks, stirring daily. The jar must have a closely fitting lid. As the vegetables come into season, gather them when quite dry. Wipe (not wash) them and put them raw into the pickle. When all the vegetables have been added, store in jars in the usual way. All the time vegetables are being added the pickle must be stirred daily. Store it for a year before using it.

CHUTNEYS

APPLE CHUTNEY

4 lb. apples.	3 lb. brown sugar.
1 lb. raisins.	½ lb. salt.
1 lb. currants.	¼ lb. ground ginger.
3 oz. garlic.	1 oz. cayenne.

1 qt. vinegar.

Cut the apples into quarters and boil in 1 qt. of vinegar till tender. Boil the sugar in the other qt. Mix both together. When cold, add the raisins and currants chopped finely and the remaining ingredients well pounded.

GOOSEBERRY CHUTNEY

2 lb. green goose-berries.	2 teasp. ground ginger.
	1 lb. Demerara sugar.
¼ lb. shallots.	1 pt. vinegar.
¼ lb. sultanas.	¼ lb. currants.
1 teasp. cayenne.	1½ oz. salt.

Simmer together gently for 2 hours.

GREEN TOMATO CHUTNEY

4 lb. green tomatoes.	1 lb. sultanas.
2 oz. crushed mustard seed.	2 lb. apples.
	¼ lb. salt.
½ oz. chillies.	2 oz. garlic.
3 oz. root ginger.	2 lb. Demerara sugar.

1 qt. vinegar.

Weigh the ingredients when prepared for cooking. Peel and slice the tomatoes and apples. Shred the chillies, peel and mince the garlic, and clean the sultanas. Boil all together, tying the root ginger in muslin. When tender and of a good consistency remove the ginger and put the chutney into hot jars, and cover with air-tight covering.

INDIAN CHUTNEY

3 lb. quinces, apricots, or apples.	½ lb. dried chillies.
	1 lb. sugar.
1 lb. raisins.	¼ lb. ginger.
¼ lb. garlic.	1 lb. salt.

1 qt. vinegar.

Peel and cut the fruit. Boil it in 3 qt. of vinegar till soft. Mash in the sugar and other ingredients. Then add the rest of the vinegar. Cork. This will keep for years, and improve with age.

*N

XXII. BUTTERS, FORCEMEATS AND FARCES

BUTTERS

With many kinds of entrées, fish dishes, etc., butters are served in addition to, or instead of, sauces. They are composed of butter amalgamated with certain flavourings.

These BUTTERS are also most useful to add to certain sauces at the last moment, and for spreading on sandwiches or croûtes for savouries and for decoration.

When made, the BUTTERS are spread on a plate and left to get very cold. They can then be cut into neat shapes by using small fancy cutters dipped into hot water, or they can be worked up like butter with butter patters.

A few of the most useful recipes follow.

ANCHOVY BUTTER

5 anchovies.　2 oz. butter.　Lemon juice.

Wash the anchovies and remove all bones. Dry them. Pound them with the butter and add a squeeze of lemon. Rub through a very fine sieve. Spread on a plate and use when very cold.

BRANDY BUTTER

2 oz. butter.　1 oz. icing or fine castor sugar.

Beat these together and add brandy to taste. Serve cold with Christmas pudding.

DEVILLED BUTTER

| 2 oz. butter. Pepper, ground ginger. | A little cayenne. A good pinch of curry powder. |

Mash these together. Spread on a plate and use when cold for grilled game, cutlets, etc.

GOLDEN BUTTER

1 hard-boiled yolk of egg.	Salt, cayenne, and a squeeze
1½ oz. butter.	of lemon.

Pound and sieve, spread on a plate and use.

GREEN BUTTER

1 oz. spinach.	1 onion.	¼ oz. parsley, chervil,
2½ oz. butter.		chives.

Boil the spinach and other greens for a few moments. Drain and pound them. Fry the onion till golden in half the butter. Sieve these, mixed with the butter and herbs. Season, if needed add green colouring. Spread on a plate and use when cold.

* HAM BUTTER

2 oz. butter.	1 tablesp. cream.
1 egg yolk (boiled hard).	4 oz. minced cooked ham.
Seasoning and cayenne.	

Pound all together and sieve them. Spread on a plate. Use when cold.

HORSERADISH BUTTER

2 oz. butter. Cayenne.	¼ stick horseradish very
Lemon juice.	finely grated.

Mix together, sieve. When cold form into shapes and serve with fillets of beef.

LOBSTER BUTTER

1 oz. lobster coral. 2 oz. butter. Seasoning.

Pound and sieve these. Spread on a plate and use cold as needed.

MAÎTRE D'HÔTEL BUTTER

1 oz. butter.	1 teasp. very finely
1 teasp. lemon juice.	chopped parsley.
Salt, pepper, and cayenne.	

Mix all the ingredients, spread on a plate, and use when cold.

MONTPELIER BUTTER

2 or 3 sprigs of parsley, chervil.	1 or 2 spinach leaves.
2 oz. butter.	1 anchovy.
1 hard-boiled yolk of egg.	Salt, pepper, cayenne. Squeeze of lemon.

Cook the parsley, chervil, and spinach in boiling water for 2 or 3 minutes. Drain and press them. Pound them with the other ingredients. Sieve and use as directed when cold.

SHRIMP BUTTER

1 oz. shelled shrimps.	Cayenne and yellow and
1 anchovy. 2 oz. butter.	pink colouring.

Pound and colour. When the right shade is obtained, sieve and use cold.

TOMATO BUTTER

2 tomatoes. Their weight in butter.

Skin the tomatoes and put them in a pan with the butter. Cook quickly, season, sieve and use when cold.

FORCEMEATS AND FARCES

As a Substitute for Breadcrumbs, crusts of bread, soaked in cold water, strained well, and sieved, may be used in the following recipes for economy; or, a Bread Panada composed of ¼ lb. bread, free from all crust. Cut this up small and soak it in 1 pt. boiling milk, adding flavourings and seasoning to taste. Leave this for some time, then pour off some of the milk; add 1 oz. butter and cook gently. Cool and use as needed.

CHESTNUT FORCEMEAT (1 medium turkey)

1 lb. chestnuts.	2 oz. breadcrumbs.
1 teasp. chopped parsley.	¼ lb. ham or bacon (or sausage meat).
¼ teasp. grated lemon rind.	2 egg yolks or 1 whole egg.

Cut top off chestnuts, boil ten minutes, then peel, and remove inner skin. Cook gently in stock till tender. Drain and pound

them with the other ingredients. Season well. This is often
used for turkey.

* FISH FARCE or FORCEMEAT

1 oz. fat. 1 egg.	½ lb. fish (raw) freed
1 oz. flour.	from skin and bone.
½ gill fish stock.	Seasoning.

Make a panada of the fat, flour, and stock. Boil and add
the fish and egg. Pound well; it is often easier to pound half
at a time. Season with salt, pepper, cayenne, and lemon. Sieve
and use as directed.

FORCEMEAT BALLS (for Hare)

Mix the cooked and finely chopped liver of the hare with
4 oz. good forcemeat. Make into balls the size of a marble.
Flour or egg and crumb these and fry them.

GAME (or CHICKEN) FORCEMEAT

1 oz. fat.	½ lb. raw game
1 oz. flour.	or chicken.
½ gill game or	1 egg.
chicken stock.	Seasoning.

Make exactly as for Fish Farce.

* LIVER FARCE

¼ lb. liver.	Blade of mace.
Slice of carrot,	2 oz. bacon.
turnip, onion,	Bunch of herbs.
celery.	Nutmeg.
Seasoning.	

Cut up and fry the bacon. Add the sliced liver and finely
cut vegetables and the spices, seasoning, etc. Fry all for about
10 minutes. Remove the herbs and pound and sieve the rest
of the ingredients. The farce is then ready for use.

* SAGE AND ONION STUFFING (for Duck, Goose, etc.)
(2 ducks or 1 goose)

4 large onions.	¼ lb. breadcrumbs.
6 sage leaves.	1 teasp. salt.
½ teasp. pepper.	1 to 2 oz. butter.

Blanch the onions, and re-boil them in fresh water until tender, cooking the 6 sage leaves with them for the last few minutes. Drain and chop the onions and sage finely. Mix these with the rest of the ingredients. A chopped apple may be added if liked.

* VEAL FORCEMEAT

(2 chickens or rabbits or 1 turkey)

4 oz. breadcrumbs (or soaked bread).	Little grated lemon rind.
1 tablesp. chopped parsley.	½ to 2 oz. suet, or hard dripping (finely chopped), or butter or margarine rubbed in.
1 teasp. dried herbs (thyme, etc.).	¼ teasp. pepper.
½ teasp. salt.	Egg or milk for mixing.

Mix all the ingredients, adding the egg or milk last. The mixture when finished should be of a moist, crumbling consistency.

XXIII. MISCELLANEOUS RECIPES, AND HAY BOX COOKERY

BROWNED CRUMBS (PANURETTE)

PLACE any crusts on a tin in a cool oven. When well dried and of a good golden brown colour, crush them with a rolling pin. Sieve them through a wire sieve.

Use the crumbs for any au gratin dish, etc. Any pieces left over that will not crush and sieve can be re-dried and used up in the same way. Keep a supply of these crumbs (for daily use) in a tin.

CARAMEL (for Gravies)

¼ lb. brown sugar.   ½ pt. of water.

Put the sugar in an *iron* saucepan and heat until it burns and is very dark. Cool this. Then add ½ pt. of water and boil until the sugar is dissolved and thick. Bottle and use for colouring stews or gravies.

CLARIFIED BUTTER

Melt some butter in a pan over gentle heat. Remove any scum. Pour off the clear liquid, and throw away the sediment.

DEVILLED ALMONDS

Proceed as for salted almonds, but sprinkle with cayenne and salt and serve hot.

DEVILLING, PASTE FOR

1 teasp. mustard (made).   ¼ teasp. salt.
1 saltsp. pepper.   ½ saltsp. cayenne.

Mix these with sufficient oil (or oiled butter) and a few drops of vinegar till a soft paste is obtained. To apply this, make some lengthwise cuts in the legs, etc., fill these with the paste, and grill or broil or fry in a very small quantity of butter.

This is excellent for devilling legs of poultry, game, etc.

DEVONSHIRE CREAM

Place the new milk in a deep pan, and leave it standing for 12 to 24 hours, according to the weather—12 is the more usual time, and therefore milk from the evening milking should be used.

Then place the pan over another vessel containing boiling water, and bring the temperature slowly up to between 170° to 180° F. 175° is the usual, but in hot weather 180° is necessary.

Leave the pan undisturbed in a cold place for 24 hours. Then skim the cream.

N.B. If no vessel is handy over which to stand the pan of milk, it may be put on a cool part of the stove, and the temperature may thus be gradually brought up without risk of burning the milk.

FRIED PARSLEY

Choose fresh green pieces. Wash if necessary and dry without crushing. Pick off the larger stalks. After the deep fat has been used for other frying, draw it to a cool place, off the fire, and, keeping the basket in it, let it cool for 3 or 4 minutes. Then throw in the parsley, taking care not to be splashed with the hot fat, as the parsley contains so much water that the fat is inclined to spurt out. Leave the parsley in the fat for about a minute, when it should be quite crisp and of a vivid green. Drain well, and use as required.

MINCEMEAT (I)

(6 to 8 lb.)

1½ lb. stoned raisins.	2 lb. moist sugar.
1½ lb. currants.	½ lb. mixed peel.
1½ lb. suet.	2 lb. large apples.
3 large lemons (rind and juice).	3 tablesp. orange marmalade.

1½ teacups brandy.

Mince the raisins, half the currants, the peel, apples, and marmalade. Add the finely chopped suet, the grated lemon rind, sugar, rest of currants, and mix with the lemon juice and brandy. Mix every day for a week, then tie down as for jam. This is an excellent old-fashioned recipe.

MINCEMEAT (II)

(6 to 8 lb.)

1 lb. raisins (stoned and minced).	½ lb. grapes. 1 gill rum.
1 lb. apples (minced).	Rind (grated) and juice of
1 lb. currants (½ lb. minced).	1 lemon.
1 lb. sultanas (½ lb. minced).	1 grated nutmeg.
1½ lb. mixed peel (minced).	1 teasp. ground ginger.
	½ tumbler brandy.
	1 lb. beef suet, finely chopped.

Mix thoroughly, stirring daily for a week. Then tie down as for jam.

POTTED MEAT (about ¼ lb.)

6 oz. cooked meat.	Powdered allspice, cinnamon, nutmeg, and clove.
4 oz. clarified butter.	
Pinches salt and pepper.	

Put the butter in a saucepan over the fire, cook until a scum rises; draw from the fire, skim well and strain through muslin to keep back any sediment. Remove all fat, skin, and gristle from the meat and pass it twice through the mincing machine. Then pound the meat, seasonings, and two-thirds of the butter in a mortar. Place the meat in jars; make it smooth on top. Run the rest of the clarified butter on top to exclude the air. It will keep for some time.

N.B. If liked, the meat can be rubbed through a wire sieve after it is pounded.

PULLED BREAD

Tear from the loaf rough pieces the size of a small egg. Dip in milk and place on a tin in a moderately hot oven till golden brown. Serve on a napkin instead of bread or dinner rolls. May be kept for some time in an air-tight tin.

SALTED ALMONDS

½ lb. Jordan almonds.	A pinch of cayenne and a pinch of celery salt.
3 oz. clarified butter.	
Fine salt.	

Blanch and dry the almonds. (1) Fry them gently in the butter till of an even golden tint, drain them and sprinkle them well with salt. (2) Brown them in the oven, brush them with gum arabic and dredge with salt.

HAY BOX COOKERY

The idea of this method of cookery comes from the careful housewives of Norway, who do a great deal of their cookery in this way. It is to be recommended strongly to business people who are from home all day; they come back to a nourishing meal well cooked, only requiring to be heated up. It is an excellent method of rapidly preparing a warm breakfast. A well-cooked dish of porridge can be heated up in a few minutes in the morning, provided the porridge is prepared the previous evening and allowed to cook overnight in the hay box.

Box. A strong wooden box is required, an old wooden trunk or a ' Tate ' sugar box bought from the grocer (cost about 1s.), the lid fastened on with hinges, and a hasp and staple in front. Line with newspaper or brown paper (line lid as well); re-line with flannel—old blanket or scouring flannel—pack tightly with hay, and make a mattress of hay encased in flannel for the top, to exclude the air.

ADVANTAGES. Economy of fuel.
Economy of labour.
Food not spoilt or wasted if not attended to.
No smell of cooking.

SUITABLE FOODS. All dishes that can be prepared by boiling, steaming, or stewing.

METHOD OF COOKING. Prepare food in the usual way. Fire-proof dishes are excellent for this method of cookery, but any pan with a short handle is suitable.

Bring to the boil and cook well for a few minutes.

Take pan off the fire, being careful that no live sparks adhere to it, wrap in a piece of flannel, and put right down into the hay, pack it well round and over, put on mattress and lid, and leave till required.

Take pan out and heat upon range or gas. The food is then ready for dishing.

POINTS TO WATCH. The pan should be almost full, the better to retain the heat.

Start the cooking thoroughly on the fire.

Transfer the pan to the box as quickly as possible to prevent cooling.

Keep the lid tightly closed to retain the steam.

Bring the food to the boil after removal from the hay box.

TIME TABLE FOR COOKING IN THE HAY BOX. This method of cookery takes twice as long as the ordinary way, but dishes do not spoil if left longer. Porridge, rice, haricot beans, etc., may be left overnight.

PORRIDGE. Boil on fire 5 to 7 minutes. Cook in hay box 3 to 4 hours or all night.

IRISH STEW. Stew on fire ½ hour. Cook in hay box 4 to 5 hours.

MILKY RICE, OR SIMILAR GRAIN. Boil milk and rice 10 minutes. Cook in hay box 4 to 5 hours.

POTATOES. Place in cold water, bring to boil and cook for 2 or 3 minutes. Cook in hay box 2 to 3 hours.

XXIV. FOOD VALUES

FUNCTIONS OF FOOD

FOOD is composed of the same constituents as the body and is required for three essential purposes:

(1) The building of muscles, bones, and blood, and for the replacement of worn-out parts.

(2) The production of energy to maintain the body temperature and to provide for the internal and external activity of the body.

(3) For protection to aid in the proper utilization of the food and the normal functioning of the body as a whole.

CLASSIFICATION

The food constituents may be classified as follows:

Builders	*Energy Foods*	*Protectors*
Proteins	Carbohydrates	Mineral salts
Mineral salts	Fats	Vitamins
Water	Proteins	Water

SOURCES OF FOOD

(1) PROTEINS. First-class or animal proteins are most easily utilized by the body, so that milk, cheese, eggs, meat and fish are valuable sources.

Second-class proteins from cereals, vegetables, and nuts are useful especially when used in conjunction with first-class proteins. Although primarily muscle-building foods, proteins supply some energy.

(2) CARBOHYDRATES in the form of *starch* are found in cereal foods, vegetables and nuts, whereas *sugars* are supplied by fruits, cane and beet sugar, honey, and milk. Cellulose found in whole-grain cereals and some fruits and vegetables, is not digested but probably helps in the elimination of all undigested materials from the body.

(3) FATS are concentrated energy foods and are supplied in milk, butter, dripping, lard, cheese, eggs, meat and oily fish, and vegetable fats are used in margarine and salad oils.

(4) MINERAL SALTS are builders and protectors. If calcium, iron and iodine are adequate in the diet then the other essential mineral elements will also be present.

Calcium, found in cheese, milk and eggs, gives hardness to bones and teeth, with the help of vitamin D.

Phosphorus is found in milk, eggs, cheese, meat, and fish.

Iron, present in egg yolk, liver, green vegetables, wholemeal bread and oatmeal, is essential for the blood. *Iodine* is adequate if sea-fish is served once a week.

(5) VITAMINS are substances of widely varying composition, but they play an essential part in the human body.

A and D are fat soluble, being found in milk, butter, dripping, fish oils and vitaminized margarine. Vitamin A is also formed in the body from carrots, tomatoes, and green vegetables, while Vitamin D is formed in the body under the influence of sunlight. B and C are water soluble.

Vitamin B is obtained from yeast extracts, whole-grain cereals, milk, eggs, meat, fruit and vegetables.

Vitamin C is found in fresh green vegetables and fruits, especially citrus fruits and tomatoes. This vitamin is easily destroyed and deteriorates during storage.

(6) WATER forms seven-tenths of the weight of the body, and is essential for all reactions of the living cells.

FOOD REQUIRED

The quantity and kind of food required will vary with the rate of growth and the activity of the individual. The following foods should be present in a well-balanced diet:

MILK, 1 pint a day for adults and more for children.

CEREALS. Wholemeal bread and oatmeal are most useful.

MEAT or FISH once daily.

EGG, CHEESE or PULSES once daily.

FRUIT. Twice daily, including one citrus fruit or tomato.

VEGETABLES. Two daily besides potatoes and including one salad or green vegetable.

FAT. Butter or vitaminized margarine.

SUGAR. Preferably brown sugar and honey.

WATER. About three pints of fluid should be taken daily by an adult, some of which should be in the form of water.

XXV. MEALS AND MENUS

IT is perhaps a matter more for congratulation than regret that since the war our menus have been more simple and less expensive. This does not necessarily mean that our taste and standard are lower, but that there is less labour available and less time to spare for the work.

The following menus give suggestions for households where a reasonable amount of help is available.

BREAKFAST MENUS FOR ONE WEEK

The English breakfast has been in the past, and still is with many people, a substantial meal. There is another opinion now in vogue where a light breakfast is thought to be more suitable to the digestive organs and to encourage a healthy appetite by luncheon time. A wise housekeeper will cater for both tastes, unless very sure of the people she is preparing for. It would be well to make a rule that fruit in some form should appear on the breakfast table as well as at other meals.

SUMMER

The first menu is given in full: in the later ones only the particular dishes for the day are enumerated.

SUNDAY.—Tea or Coffee. Cold Ham. Watercress. Strawberries. Bread. Rolls. Toast. Butter, Marmalade, Jam, or Honey.

MONDAY (abbreviated menu).—Poached Eggs. Grilled Brawn. Tomatoes, Lettuce. Melon or Fruit.

TUESDAY (abbreviated menu).—Pressed Beef. Scones. Grilled Sausages. Watercress. Mulberries.

WEDNESDAY (abbreviated menu).—Kedgeree. Scrambled Eggs. Cress. Fruit.

THURSDAY (abbreviated menu).—Soused Herrings. Stewed Kidney on Toast. Lettuce. Strawberries.

FRIDAY (abbreviated menu).—Tomato Eggs. Veal Mould. Watercress. Fruit.

SATURDAY (abbreviated menu).—Finnan Haddock. Beef Roll. Cress. Tomatoes. Fruit.

SUNDAY (menu in full).—Tea or Coffee. Bacon and Fried Eggs. Hot Rolls. Bread, Butter, Marmalade, Jam, or Honey. Bananas.

MONDAY (abbreviated menu).—Porridge. Sausage. Apples.

TUESDAY (abbreviated menu).—Cereal and Cream. Kippered Herrings. Cold Pickled Pork. Fruit.

WEDNESDAY (abbreviated menu). — Fish Omelet. Grilled Ham. Bananas.

THURSDAY (abbreviated menu).—Porridge. Scrambled Eggs. Rissoles. Apples, fresh or baked.

FRIDAY (abbreviated menu).—Cereal and Milk. Kippered Herrings or Bloaters. Kidneys and Bacon. Fresh Fruit.

SATURDAY (abbreviated menu). — Porridge. Ham Toast. Brawn or Tongue. Apples and Pears.

FAMILY LUNCHEON

Luncheon is a meal which varies considerably in different households. It may consist of a joint, vegetables, and pudding, or an entrée made up from the remains of a previous meal with some sweets and cheese, or it may consist of four, five, and six courses, or again may be made up of vegetarian dishes.

The rule generally observed now is that if the evening meal is to be a substantial one, then the Luncheon will be light, and vice versa. Luncheon then may consist of Hors d'Œuvres, Soup, Fish, Roast Fowl or Joint, Sauces, Vegetables, Sweets, Savouries, and Coffee. It may also consist of Soup, Entrée, Vegetables, and Sweets, or it may be still more reduced as to the number of dishes placed on the table.

SUNDAY.—Cold Roast Fowl. Ham. Salad. Trifle. Strawberries and Cream.

MONDAY.—Mutton Cutlets. Peas. Potatoes. Tomato Sauce. Cold Tongue. Salad. Fruit Fool. Milk Pudding. Cheese Straws.

TUESDAY.—Fish Cakes and Sauce. Cold Fowl. Potatoes. Salad, Dressing. Red Currant and Raspberry Tart. Junket and Cream.

WEDNESDAY.—Salmon Mayonnaise. Salad. Potatoes. Curry of Cold Meat. Cream. Fruit Salad. Caramel Custard. Anchovy Creams.

THURSDAY.—Steamed Hake. Egg Sauce. Cold Lamb. Mint Sauce. Potatoes. Cauliflower. Summer Pudding and Custard. Fruit in Jelly.

FRIDAY.—Fish Pie. Galantine of Veal. Salad. Potatoes. Manchester Pudding. Chocolate Mould. Cheese Cream.

SATURDAY.—Fried Plaice. Anchovy Sauce. Fricassee of Eggs. Spinach. Chip Potatoes. Lemon Tart. Fruit Sponge Pudding.

WINTER

SUNDAY.—Boiled Fowl. Egg Sauce. Cold Mutton. Winter Salad. Potatoes. Fruit Fleur. Lemon Mould.

MONDAY.—Curried Fowl. Cold Beef. Potatoes. Winter Salad. Boiled Apple Pudding. Macaroni Cheese.

TUESDAY.—Fried Plaice. White Sauce. Irish Stew. Mashed Potatoes. Coconut Fleur. Stewed Prunes. Sago Pudding.

WEDNESDAY.—Fish Scallops. Steak and Kidney Pie. Potatoes. Sprouts. Steamed Canary Pudding. Lemon Sauce. Banana Custard.

THURSDAY.—Cheese Patties. Boiled Salt Beef. Potatoes. Carrots. Turnips. Fruit Salad. Custard Pudding.

FRIDAY.—Baked Turbot. Exeter Stew. Sauce Piquante. Boiled Celery. Mashed Potatoes. Treacle Layer Pudding. Stewed Figs. Tapioca Cream.

SATURDAY.—Roast Leg of Mutton. Sprouts. Potatoes. Cheese d'Artois. Apple Tart and Cream. Orange Trifle.

DINNERS

For many years there has been an increasing tendency towards simplicity in all the various meals of the day. Shortage of labour has had something to do with this and so also has later medical opinion as to the amount of food necessary to keep the body in health. A complete dinner consists of nine courses, but it can be abridged without a great amount of loss. The Hors d'Œuvres, Savoury, Fish, or Soup can easily be dispensed with.

EXAMPLE OF FULL MENU

Hors d'Œuvre
Huîtres au Naturel

Potage
Consommé à la Royale

Poisson
Sole à la Colbert

Entrée
Fillets à la Viennoise

Relevé
Selle d'Agneau à la Bretonne, Sorbets l'Ananas

Rôti
Lièvre rôti, Salade d'Orange

ENTREMETS:

Légume
Asperges Hollandaise

Entremets
Charlotte Russe, Pouding au Caramel

Bonne Bouches
Petites Crèmes de Fromage
Café

EXAMPLE OF ABRIDGED MENU

Asparagus Soup
Turbot, Dutch Sauce
Chicken in Casserole
Baked Cauliflower
Lemon Soufflé

OR

Apple Tart
Cheese Straws

EXAMPLE OF VEGETARIAN MENU

Artichoke Soup
Mushroom Omelet
Eggs on Spinach
Tomato Salad
Jellied Trifle
Apple Amber
Welsh Rarebit

XXVI. FOODS IN SEASON

All the Year

FRUIT.—Apples, bananas, dates, figs, lemons, nuts, oranges, prunes.

VEGETABLES.—Cabbage or greens, carrots (young or old), onions, parsley, potatoes.

FISH.—Dried haddock, hake, dried herrings, plaice, sole.

POULTRY.—Chickens or fowls, spring chickens in late spring and early summer.

MEAT.—Beef, mutton, veal.

FOODS OBTAINABLE IN DIFFERENT MONTHS

January

FRUIT.—Grapes, medlars, melons (Spanish water), pears, pines (St. Michael's), rhubarb.

VEGETABLES.—Artichokes (Jerusalem), beetroot, broccoli, brussels sprouts, carrots, celery, greens, horseradish, leeks, onions, ditto Spanish, parsnips, potatoes, salsify, savoys, Scotch kale.

FISH.—Cod, crabs, eels, flounders, haddocks, halibut, herrings, lobsters (scarce), mackerel, oysters, pike, plaice, prawns, soles, sprats, turbot, whiting.

GAME AND POULTRY.—Blackcock, chickens, ducks (wild), geese, ditto wild, hares, partridges, pheasants, pigeons, plovers, rabbits, snipe, turkeys, woodcock.

MEAT.—Lamb, pork, venison.

February

FRUIT.—Grapes, lemons, melons (Spanish water), nuts, oranges, ditto Seville, pears, pines (St. Michael's), ditto English, prunes, rhubarb.

VEGETABLES.—Artichokes (Jerusalem), beetroot, broccoli, brussels sprouts, carrots, celery, horseradish, kale, leeks, lettuce, onions, ditto Spanish, parsnips, potatoes, salsify, savoys, seakale.

FISH.—Cod, crabs, eels, haddocks, herrings, lobsters, mackerel, oysters, pike, salmon, smelt, sprats, trout, turbot, whitebait.

GAME AND POULTRY.—Blackcock, chickens, ducklings (very dear), ducks (wild), geese, ditto wild, hares, larks, partridges, pigeons, plovers, prairie hens, rabbits, snipe, teal, turkey, widgeon, woodcock. Game till middle of month.

MEAT.—Lamb, pork.

March

FRUIT.—Grapes, melons (Spanish water), oranges, ditto Seville, pines (St. Michael's), ditto English, prunes, rhubarb.

VEGETABLES.—Artichokes (Jerusalem and globe), beetroot, broccoli, cabbage (red), carrots, chervil, horseradish, leeks, lettuce, onions, ditto Spanish, parsnips, potatoes, ditto new, radishes, salsify, seakale, small salad, spinach.

FISH.—Cod, conger-eels, crabs, lobsters, mackerel, oysters, pike (till 15th), salmon, shrimps, smelts, sprats, trout, turbot, whitebait.

GAME AND POULTRY.—Blackcock, chickens, ducklings, ducks (wild), geese (wild), guinea-fowl, pigeons, prairie hens, quails, teal.

MEAT.—Lamb, pork, veal (best from March to July).

April

FRUIT.—Grapes, green gooseberries, lemons, oranges, pines (St. Michael's), ditto English, rhubarb.

VEGETABLES. — Artichokes (globe), asparagus, beetroot, broccoli, cabbage (spring), chervil, cucumbers, horseradish, lettuce, onions, parsnips, peas, potatoes, ditto new, radishes, seakale, spinach, small salad, tomatoes, turnip-tops.

FISH.—Cod, conger-eels, crabs, dory, flounders, herrings, ling, lobsters, mackerel, mullet, oysters, prawns, salmon, scallops, shrimps, skate, smelts, trout, turbot, whitebait.

GAME AND POULTRY.—Chickens, ducklings, guinea-fowl, leverets, pigeons, teal.

MEAT.—Lamb (best from April to June), pork.

May

FRUIT.—Cherries and currants, green gooseberries, grapes, nuts, pines (English), rhubarb, strawberries.

VEGETABLES.—Artichokes (globe), asparagus, beetroot, cabbages, carrots, cauliflowers, chervil, cucumbers, horseradish, lettuce, onions, peas, potatoes, ditto new, radishes, seakale, spinach, tomatoes, turnips.

FISH.—Bass, brill, conger-eels, crabs, crayfish, dory, eels, haddock, halibut, ling, lobsters, mackerel, mullet, plaice, prawns, salmon, scallops, shrimps, skate, smelts, sole, trout, turbot (at its best), whitebait, whiting.

GAME AND POULTRY.—Chickens and ducklings, guinea-fowls, leverets, pigeons.

MEAT.—Lamb.

June

FRUIT.—Apricots, bananas, currants, cherries, gooseberries, grapes, melons, pines, raspberries, strawberries.

VEGETABLES.—Asparagus, beans (French and kidney), cabbages, carrots, cauliflowers, chervil, cucumbers, endive, green peas, horseradish, lettuce, onions, potatoes, radishes, spinach, tomatoes, turnips.

For Drying.—Mint, tarragon, thyme.

FISH.—Bass, brill, conger-eels, crabs, crawfish, eels, haddock, halibut, lobsters, mackerel, mullet, plaice, prawns, salmon, shrimps, soles, trout, turbot, whitebait, whiting.

GAME AND POULTRY.—Chickens and ducklings, goslings, leverets, pigeons, snipe, venison.

MEAT.—Lamb.

July

FRUIT.—Apricots, cherries, currants, gooseberries, grapes, green figs, greengages, loganberries, melons, mulberries, peaches, pineapples (English), plums, raspberries, strawberries.

VEGETABLES.—Artichokes (globe), asparagus, beans, beetroot, cabbages, carrots, cauliflowers, chervil, cucumbers, green peas, horseradish, leeks, lettuce, marrows, onions, potatoes, salsify, spinach, tomatoes, turnips.

For Drying.—Marjoram, mint, thyme.

For Pickling.—Red cabbage, cauliflowers, cucumbers, nasturtiums, onions.

FISH.—Brill, conger-eels, crabs, dory, eels, gurnards, haddock, halibut, herrings, ling, lobsters, mullet, pike, plaice, prawns, salmon, sea-bream, shrimps, soles, trout, whitebait, whiting.

GAME AND POULTRY.—Bordeaux pigeons, ducks, goslings, leverets, venison.

MEAT.—Lamb.

August

FRUIT.—Apricots, currants, cherries, grapes, green figs, greengages, filberts, melons (hot-house and rock), mulberries, nectarines, peaches, pears, pines (English), plums, raspberries.

VEGETABLES.—Artichokes (globe), beans, beetroot, carrots, cauliflowers, chervil, cucumbers, leeks, lettuce, marrows, mushrooms, onions, potatoes, salsify, shallots, spinach, tomatoes, turnips.

For Drying.—Basil, sage.

For Pickling.—Capsicum, chillies, walnuts.

FISH.—Bass, brill, conger-eels, haddock, herrings, lobsters, mullet, pike, plaice, prawns, salmon, sea-bream, shrimps, soles, trout, turbot, whitebait, whiting.

GAME AND POULTRY.—Blackcock (from the 20th), chickens, ducks (wild), fowls, goslings, grouse (from 12th), leverets, pigeons (wild), plovers, ptarmigan (from 12th), quails, snipe, teal, widgeon, woodcock.

MEAT.—Lamb, venison.

September

FRUIT.—Apricots, blackberries, damsons, grapes, green figs, greengages, melons (hot-house and rock), nectarines, peaches, pears, pines (English), plums, quinces, walnuts.

VEGETABLES.—Beans, brussels sprouts, cabbages, capsicums, cauliflower, celery, chervil, chillies, cucumbers, horseradish, leeks, lettuce, marrows, mushrooms, onions, parsnips, potatoes, shallots, spinach, tomatoes.

FISH.—Bass, brill, cod, conger-eels, haddock, halibut, herrings, lobsters, mackerel, mullet, oysters, pike, plaice, sea-bream, shrimps, soles, sturgeon, whiting.

GAME AND POULTRY.—Blackcock, chickens, ducks (wild), fowls, geese, ditto wild, grouse, leverets, partridges, pigeons (wild), plovers, ptarmigan, pullets, rabbits, snipe, teal, turkeys, venison, widgeon, woodcock.

MEAT.—Pork (in season till April), venison.

October

FRUIT.—Apricots, blackberries, cranberries, damsons, figs, filberts, grapes, melons (Spanish water), nectarines, pomegranates, peaches, pears, pines (St. Michael's and English), quinces, walnuts.

VEGETABLES. — Artichokes (Jerusalem), beans, beetroot, broccoli, brussels sprouts, cabbages, capsicums, carrots, celery, chervil, chillies, horseradish, leeks, lettuce, marrows, mushrooms, onions, ditto Spanish and pickling parsnips, potatoes, savoys, shallots, spinach, tomatoes, turnips.

FISH.—Brill, cod, conger-eels, crabs, haddocks, halibut, herrings, ling, lobsters, mackerel, mullet, oysters, pike, plaice, scallops, sea-bream, shrimps, soles, whiting.

GAME AND POULTRY.—Blackcock, chickens, ducks (wild), geese, ditto wild, grouse, hares, partridges, pheasants, pigeons, plovers, ptarmigan, rabbits, snipe, teal, turkey, venison, widgeon, woodcock. Poultry is cheapest at this time when game first comes in.

MEAT.—Pork, venison.

November

FRUIT.—Chestnuts, cranberries, figs, grapes, medlars, melons (Spanish water), nuts, pears, pines (St. Michael's), quinces.

VEGETABLES.—Artichokes (Jerusalem), beetroot, broccoli, brussels sprouts, cabbages, carrots, celery, chervil, garlic, greens, horseradish, leeks, onions, ditto Spanish and pickling parsnips, potatoes, savoys, Scotch kale, shallots, spinach, tomatoes, turnips.

FISH.—Cod, crab, eel, haddock, halibut, herrings, ling, lobsters, mackerel, oysters, pike, plaice, salmon (Dutch), scallops, smelts, soles, sprats, whiting.

GAME AND POULTRY.—Blackcock, chickens, ducks (wild), geese, ditto wild, grouse, hares, partridges, pheasants, pigeons, plovers, ptarmigan, rabbits, snipe, teal, turkeys, woodcock.

MEAT.—Pork, venison.

December

FRUIT.—Chestnuts, cranberries, grapes, medlars, melons (Spanish water), nuts, pears, pines (St. Michael's), pomegranates, walnuts.

VEGETABLES.—Artichokes (Jerusalem), beetroot, broccoli, brussels sprouts, carrots, celery, garlic, horseradish, leeks, lettuce, onions (Spanish), parsnips, potatoes, salsify, Scotch kale, shallots, spinach, tomatoes, turnips.

FISH.—Cod, crabs, eel, haddock, halibut, herrings, ling, lobsters, mackerel, oysters, pike, plaice, soles, sprats, whiting.

GAME AND POULTRY.—Blackcock, chickens, duck (wild), geese, ditto wild, grouse (to the 10th), hares, partridges, pheasants, pigeons, plovers, ptarmigan, rabbits, snipe, teal, turkeys, woodcock, venison (doe).

MEAT.—Pork.

XXVII. COOKERY TERMS

ABSINTHE: a liqueur.

ANGELICA: Crystallized stem of umbelliferous plant.

À L'INDIENNE: Curried dishes.

AU GRATIN: This term is applied to dishes covered with sauce and breadcrumbs or grated cheese, and browned in the oven or under a grill or salamander. These dishes are served in the dish in which they have been baked.

AU MAIGRE: Lenten dishes without meat.

AU NATUREL: Food cooked plainly.

BABA (from the Polish word BABKA): A very light yeast cake, usually used as a sweet.

BAIN-MARIE: A 'water bath' where a set of small saucepans containing sauces, etc., can be placed, so that by boiling the water in the 'bain-marie' the sauces, etc., are kept almost at boiling point without fear of burning, or of reducing through evaporation.

BAY LEAF: Leaf of a laurel, strong in flavour.

BISQUE: Name given to soups usually made from shell fish.

BLANCH, i.e. *To Blanch*: To put anything in cold water; to place this on the fire until it boils. This water is then thrown away, and whatever has been blanched is placed into fresh cold water.

BOMBAY DUCK: Indian fish dried, served with curry.

BORAGE: Aromatic plant.

BOUILLON: A plain clear soup, or beef broth.

BOUQUET-GARNI, BUNCH OF HERBS, i.e. parsley, thyme, marjoram, bay leaf: These should be tied in muslin as they can then be removed. Their flavour only is required in sauces, stews, etc.

CANNELONS: Small rolls of pastry filled with meat and fried.

CARAMEL: Burnt sugar. This is made by boiling sugar to either (1) light or (2) dark brown, when it can be used (1) for coating moulds, or (2) as a brown liquid colouring.

O

CARDAMOMS: A spice plant, used for flavouring.

CASSEROLE: A stew jar, a shape of rice, a potato, or pastry filled with meat.

CAVIARE: Sturgeon's roe salted.

CHARTREUSE: A mould of fruit or vegetables, or game set in jelly or aspic.

CHERVIL: An aromatic herb.

CHIVES: A small kind of onions.

COMPOTE: Fruit stewed in syrup.

CONDIMENTS: Highly flavoured seasoning, spices, etc.

CREAM, i.e. *To Cream*: This term means to beat butter, etc., or butter and sugar to the consistency of whipped cream. To do this, beat with a wooden spoon.

CROQUETTES: Shapes of minced meat, coated with egg and crumbs and fried.

CROUSTADES: Shapes of bread, fried, and filled with minced meat or fish.

CROÛTONS: Small pieces of bread fried, used as a garnish.

CURAÇAO: A liqueur.

DARIOLES: Moulds for meat and puddings.

DAUBIÈRE: French oval stew pan.

DIABLE, Devilled: Dishes served with a very hot sauce or seasoning composed of peppers, mustard, etc.

DRAGÉES: Sugar plums.

ÉCLAIR: A French pastry, 'choux paste', shaped and filled with cream, etc.

ENTREMETS: Dishes of vegetables, dressed, or savouries and sweets.

FAIRE REVENIR: This means to partly 'fry', i.e. to brown slightly, meat or vegetables without really cooking them.

FAT: This term is applied in cookery to butter, lard, margarine, or dripping and clarified fat.

FÉCULE: A very fine flour of rice or potato, used for binding soups and sauces.

FENNEL: An aromatic plant used as a garnish or for flavouring.

'FINES HERBES': Chervil, parsley, tarragon, thyme, etc.

FLAN: A French tart, open or closed.

FOIE-GRAS: The liver from a specially fattened goose.

FORCEMEAT: This is also called a FARCE, and means a preparation of meat, etc., to be used as a stuffing.

FRICANDEAU: Braised fillet of veal, larded.

FRICASSEE: This term is applied to a stew made of white sauce and white meat.

FRITTER (Beignet): Anything dipped in batter and then fried.

FRUMENTY: Boiled wheat or barley served with milk and sugar or honey.

GALETTE: Light rolls or cake.

GHERKINS: Small cucumbers (pickled).

GLAZE: A meat jelly used for glazing cold or hot meat.

GNOCCI: A light dough, made of semolina, flour, etc., and served with grated cheese.

GRENADINS: Small fillets of meat larded and braised.

HOMINY: Maize preparation.

HORS D'ŒUVRE: Relish served before soup.

IRISH MOSS: Seaweed used for jellies (particularly nourishing).

ISINGLASS: Gelatine made from the swimming-bladder of sturgeon.

KETCHUP: A sauce made from mushrooms, etc.

KIRSCH: A spirit made from cherries.

KOUMISS: A beverage made from fermented milk.

KROMESKIES: Rolls of minced meat wrapped in bacon and fried after dipping in batter.

LARDING: Inserting strips of fat bacon in game or meat.

LIAISON: A 'binding', made either of starchy material (flour, etc.), or of egg and cream, and used to 'bind' soups and sauces, and so to prevent the separation of the vegetable particles from the liquid. Blood may also be used (see jugged hare). The blood should be mixed with a very little vinegar, and after its addition no boiling should take place.

MACEDOINE: A variety of vegetables or fruits mixed together.

MADELEINE: A small cake.

MAÎTRE D'HÔTEL BUTTER: Butter mixed with parsley, lemon juice and seasoning, used for garnish.

MARASCHINO: White liqueur.

MARINADE: A mixture of oil, vinegars, parsley, etc., i.e. a savoury pickle in which meats and fish are left to stand for a short time before being cooked.

MAZARIN: A small fancy shape of fish, game, or poultry.

MIREPOIX: A mixture of vegetables and herbs, forming the foundation of some soups and sauces, used in braising.

MOUSSE: Originally a very light ice cream mixture.

NEGUS: Mulled wine.

NOYEAU: A liqueur flavoured with peach kernels.

PANADA: A thick mixture, resembling a thick sauce, composed of fat and flour, blended, to which a little liquid is added, and the whole boiled.

PANURETTE: Browned crumbs.

PAPRIKA: Red pepper (Hungarian).

PARMESAN: Skim milk cheese.

PIÈCE DE RÉSISTANCE: The chief joint.

PILAU: Turkish dish, meat and fish and rice well seasoned.

PISTACHIO: Kernels of the terebinth nut, used for decoration.

POACH: To cook in boiling water for a few minutes.

PURÉE: A smooth mixture of vegetables, meat, etc., sieved or pounded and sieved.

RAGOUT: A rich highly seasoned stew.

RAMEQUINS: Small cases for serving cheese savouries, etc.

RASPINGS: A name given to grated crusts of bread, or to browned breadcrumbs.

RAVIGOTE: A sauce containing herbs.

RÉCHAUFFÉ: Means re-warmed, i.e. cold meats re-heated in various ways.

REDUCE: This means to boil rapidly, thus reducing in quantity by evaporation.

ROUX: This is a mixture of flour and fat blended together, i.e. melt the fat, and add an equal quantity of flour. Cook a little. This is a 'white' roux before it colours at all, and is then the foundation for white panadas and sauces; a 'fawn' roux when golden brown; or a 'brown' roux when the flour has been allowed to fry in the fat until a rich chestnut colour results. This last is the foundation for brown panadas and sauces.

SALAMANDER: An iron implement which can be made red-hot, and so browns the surface of things.

SALMI: A rich hash of game, duck, etc.

SALPICON: A well-flavoured mixture of minced meat, ham, tongue, etc., mixed with a well-flavoured panada, and used for rissoles, etc.

SAUTÉ-PAN: A shallow copper pan used for dry frying.

SAUTER: This means to toss over the fire with a little fat.

SIPPETS: Small slices of bread, daintily cut, fried or toasted and served with entrées, savouries, etc.

SOCLE: A name given to a foundation made of rice, or other edible material, used for the dishing of elaborate dishes. The socle itself is not usually eaten, but it may be highly decorative.

SOY: A Japanese sauce, dark brown.

SYLLABUB: A milk punch flavoured with liqueurs and spices.

TAMMY: A silk or woollen canvas cloth which is used for straining soups and sauces.

TARRAGON: A plant used for flavouring and vinegar.

TIMBALE: Mould lined with pastry, potato, or macaroni, and filled with savoury mince.

TOURNEDOS: Fillets of beef served as an entrée.

TRUFFLES: A kind of mushroom found growing under the ground. There are three varieties, black, grey, and red.

VOL-AU-VENT: A case of pastry filled with meat, game, fish, or vegetables, or fruit.

APPENDIX

ESPAGNOLE SAUCE

2 oz. butter or margarine.	6 mushrooms.
2 oz. flour.	1 pt. brown stock.
2 oz. raw ham or lean bacon.	Pepper and salt.
1 onion.	1 gill tomato pulp.
1 small carrot.	¼ gill sherry (optional).

Cut the ham or bacon into small pieces and fry it in a pan with the margarine or butter. Add the vegetables sliced and fry well; add the flour and fry to a rich brown colour. Add the stock and seasonings, and simmer for two hours. Add the tomato pulp and the sherry when half-cooked. Tammy and re-heat.

EGGLESS CAKE (optional; keeps fresh well)

½ lb. margarine.	1 tablesp. honey.	½ pt. water.
½ lb. sugar (brown or white).	1 tablesp. black treacle.	½ pt. mixed fruit.
	OR 2 tablesp. treacle.	Spices, ginger to taste.

Boil all these ingredients gently in a saucepan for 5 minutes. Cool.

1 lb. flour.	½ teasp. bicarbonate of soda.
Pinch salt.	½ gill milk.

Cake tin 8–9 inches in diameter.

METHOD. Boil ingredients as above and cool to about blood heat. Sift the flour and salt into a bowl. Dissolve the bicarbonate of soda in the milk.

Make a well in the centre of the flour mixture, add by degrees the cooled ingredients together with the bicarbonate of soda mixture—working in gradually and quite smoothly. Pour at once into a tin lined with greased paper.

Bake about 1½–2 hours in moderate oven. Cool a little before turning out of tin.

MILK MOULD

1 pt. milk.   Sugar and flavouring to taste.
¾ oz. gelatine (1 oz. in hot weather). Tear the gelatine into small pieces (if French leaf gelatine is used).

Dissolve the gelatine in a little water and add this to the milk. Flavour and sweeten to taste. Strain into a wetted mould and turn out when cold.

A pinch of bicarbonate of soda added prevents curdling.

ADDITIONAL RECIPES SUITABLE FOR PRESENT USE

FRUIT FOOL

½ pt. fruit purée. ½ pt. custard or 1 gill custard, and
1 gill whipped tinned milk.

(1) Prepare the above ingredients, mix well together.
(2) Serve in one large glass dish or in small custard glasses.

POTATO SCONES

½ lb. flour.	1½ oz. fat (margarine).
½ lb. sieved cooked potatoes.	Salt and pepper to taste.
1 teasp. baking powder.	Mix with a little milk if necessary.

(1) Rub the fat into the flour.
(2) Mix the remainder of the ingredients well together, add milk, if necessary, to make an elastic dough.
(3) Roll out 1 inch thick, cut into rounds.
(4) Cook in a moderate oven 15–20 minutes.

OATMEAL BISCUITS

5 oz. plain flour.	4 oz. rolled oats.
½ teasp. salt.	½ teasp. bicarbonate of soda.
1½ oz. sugar.	½ teasp. ground ginger (if liked).
2 oz. margarine.	
1 tablesp. vinegar.	

(1) Rub fat into flour.
(2) Add oats, salt, bicarbonate of soda, and ginger.
(3) Mix with vinegar and a little milk.
(4) Knead, then roll out ½ inch thick.
(5) Bake in a moderate oven for 15–20 minutes.

RICE CREAM

¼ lb. rice.	1 tin evaporated
1–1½ oz. sugar.	milk.
Vanilla.	1 pt. water.

(1) Cook rice in water with sugar until all liquid is absorbed.
(2) Allow to cool.
(3) Whip up milk as stiffly as possible. Flavour.
(4) Fold in rice.
(5) Serve in glass dish.
(6) A spoonful of jam on top improves appearance.

BREAKFAST FRITTERS

2 oz. self-raising flour.	Seasoning.
½ gill milk.	Chopped parsley.
½ dried egg (added dry).	Fat for frying.

(1) Mix all dry ingredients together. Add milk until a dropping consistency is formed.
(2) Fry in small rounds in shallow fat.
N.B. These fritters can be fried after the bacon.

YEAST SHORTCRUST

| 1 lb. flour. | 1 teaspoonful salt. |
| 4 oz. fat. | ⅛ oz. yeast. |

Tepid water to mix.

(1) Cream the yeast.
(2) Mix the flour and salt together, then add the fat and rub in finely.
(3) Add the creamed yeast and enough tepid water to make an elastic dough.
(4) Allow to stand for ½ hour in a warm place.
Use as for shortcrust pastry.
Bake in a hot oven.

YEAST PUDDING
(Useful for large-scale cooking)

1¾ lb. flour.	3 oz. margarine.
¾ lb. dried bread-crumbs.	½ oz. spice.
	½ oz. salt.
¾ lb. currants.	1 oz. yeast.
2 oz. sugar.	1 pt. milk.

(1) Warm the flour.
(2) Cream yeast and sugar.

(3) Melt margarine, add milk, and bring to blood heat.

(4) Mix the dry ingredients together.

(5) Add the creamed yeast and milk until an elastic dough is formed.

(6) Half fill warmed greased pudding basins.

(7) Place to rise in warm place until it rises to top of basins.

(8) Steam for $1\frac{3}{4}$ hours.

POTATO PASTRY (I)

6 oz. flour.	4 oz. mashed potato.
$\frac{1}{2}$ teasp. baking powder.	2 to 3 tablesp. cold water.
2 oz. lard and margarine mixed.	$\frac{1}{4}$ teasp. salt.

Sieve the flour with the salt and baking powder. Rub in the fat with the tips of the fingers. Sprinkle on the water and cut in with a knife. Knead into a dough and roll out.

POTATO PASTRY (II)

6 oz. flour.	3 oz. mashed potato.
$2\frac{1}{2}$ oz. fat.	Water to mix.

Cream the fat and potato. Fold in the flour and add enough water to make a pastry dough.

CHOCOLATE CAKE

3 oz. flour.	2 tablesp. chocolate powder.
2 oz. fat (butter or margarine).	$\frac{1}{4}$ teasp. bicarbonate of soda.
2 oz. sugar.	$\frac{3}{4}$ teasp. cream of tartar.
2 dried eggs (reconstituted).	

(1) Cream fat and sugar together.

(2) Beat in reconstituted eggs, a little at a time.

(3) Fold in the dry ingredients after sieving.

(4) When a dropping consistency half-fill greased sandwich tin (approximately $6\frac{1}{2}$ in. diameter).

(5) Bake in a very moderate oven for 30–40 minutes.

SANDWICH CAKE

4 oz. flour.	$\frac{1}{2}$ level teasp. bicarbonate of soda.
2 oz. fat (butter or margarine).	1 level teasp. cream of tartar.
2 oz. sugar.	Little milk to make a dropping
2 dried eggs (reconstituted).	consistency.

(1) Cream fat and sugar together.

(2) Beat in reconstituted eggs, a little at a time.

(3) Fold in the dry ingredients after sieving.

(4) When a dropping consistency half-fill greased sandwich tin approximately $6\frac{1}{2}$ in. diameter).

(5) Bake in a very moderate oven for 30–40 minutes.

*O

SPONGE CAKE

½ gill flour.	¼ teasp. bicarbonate of soda.
½ gill sugar.	2 level tablesp. dried egg.
⅜ teasp. cream of tartar.	3 tablesp. water.

(1) Pound granulated sugar or use castor sugar.
(2) Sift flour and raising agents three times.
(3) Mix water, egg, sugar and beat for five minutes.
(4) Fold in flour through a sieve in 2 lots.
(5) Bake for 15 minutes in a moderate oven.

This mixture can only be baked in flat tins and used for charlotte russe, gateaux, etc.

MOCK CREAM

1 oz. fat.	1 rounded teasp. cornflour.
1 oz. sugar.	Vanilla essence.
½ gill milk.	

(1) Blend cornflour with a little of the cold milk.
(2) Boil remainder of milk and pour onto the blended mixture. Return to the saucepan and reboil for 3 minutes.
(3) Stir as the mixture cools to prevent lumps forming.
(4) Cream fat and sugar very thoroughly till smooth and white.
(5) Beat in cornflour a small amount at a time.
(6) Add vanilla essence.

This can be used for piping, etc.

MILANAISE SOUFFLE

½ pint evaporated milk.	½ gill lemon squash. ⎫ mix together
1 egg.	½ gill water. ⎬
2 oz. sugar.	½ oz. gelatine. ⎭
2 tablesp. lemon curd.	

(1) Whisk yolk of egg, sugar, lemon curd and ½ gill liquid till thick, over hot water.
(2) Dissolve gelatine in the other half of the liquid.
(3) Beat up milk till half whipped.
(4) Beat up egg white.
(5) Fold in gelatine, then milk and lastly egg white to the first mixture.
(6) Pour into a prepared soufflé case so mixture is 2 in. above rim of case.
(7) Finish with stars of cream, chopped nuts, etc.

To Whip Evaporated Milk

(1) Remove label, but do not pierce tin.

(2) Cover with cold water and bring slowly to the boil.
(3) Simmer for 3 minutes.
(4) Plunge into cold water.
(5) Leave overnight in the refrigerator or in a cool place.
(6) Remove from tin and whip up.

(The milk will thicken much more quickly and better than if done without this heating-up process).

PETIT BEURRE BISCUITS

4 oz. flour.	1½ oz. sugar.
2 oz. margarine.	¼ teasp. baking powder.
Pinch of salt.	

(1) Melt the fat till golden brown.
(2) Sieve flour, salt, sugar and baking powder.
(3) Add fat and a little cold water if necessary to mix to a stiff dough.
(4) Roll out thinly, stamp into an oval or round, shape with a cutter.
(5) Bake in a cool oven till golden brown.

PARKIN BISCUITS

2 oz. flour.	Pinch of ginger.
2 oz. oatmeal.	½ level teasp. bicarbonate of soda.
½ egg (dry).	1½ oz. sugar.
1 oz. fat.	Milk to mix.
2 oz. syrup.	

(1) Rub in fat.
(2) Sieve all dry ingredients and add.
(3) Warm syrup and add with enough milk to form a dough.
(4) Shape into equal sized rounds, flatten.
(5) Bake in a moderate oven until golden brown.

APPLE CRUMBLE

4 oz. flour.	1 lb. apples + ½ oz. sugar.
1½–2 oz. margarine.	Rind and juice of 1 lemon.
1½–2 oz. sugar.	

METHOD:

(1) Peel and core apples, slice very thinly into shallow fire-proof dish. Add ½ oz. sugar in layers.
(2) Add grated rind and juice of lemon.
(3) Rub margarine into flour, add sugar and mix.
(4) Place the crumble mixture evenly over the sliced apples.
(5) Bake in a moderate oven 45-50 minutes.

DOUGH BUNS (12–14 buns)

¾ lb. flour (warmed).	1½ oz. sugar.
Pinch of salt.	1 egg (omit if economy essential).
2 oz. currants.	½ oz. yeast.
1 oz. chopped peel.	1½–2 oz. fat (butter or margarine).

Spice, if liked.

Warm the flour, cream the yeast, warm milk to blood heat. Make a well in the flour, add a little of the milk to the yeast, and pour into the well in the centre of the flour, making a 'sponge.' Cover this and set to rise in warmth for about 20 minutes. Work in the rest of the flour, using additional milk as required. Set to rise for about an hour, covered. Beat in the butter, sugar, fruits, and egg and beat till the dough leaves the hands clean. Turn on to a board and knead lightly. Form into buns. Set these to 'prove.' Bake in a quick oven about 15–20 minutes. Glaze if wished.

MOCK CREAM

2 oz. sieved icing sugar.	1 teasp. boiling water.
2 oz. margarine or butter.	1 teasp. milk.

A few drops of vanilla.

Cream margarine (or butter), add sugar; beat well; add liquid; add flavouring. Use as required for piping.

MACARONI CHEESE CUTLETS

2 oz. macaroni.	Pinch of cayenne pepper.
3 oz. grated cheese.	1 gill panada (1 oz. margarine,
Yolk of egg.	1 oz. flour, 1 gill milk).
Seasoning.	

Cook macaroni, dry well, and chop up. Make panada. Mix together all ingredients; cool on greased plate. Shape into cutlets (4). Coat with egg and breadcrumbs. Fry in deep fat.

SAVOURY RICE

8 oz. rice.	1 oz. dripping.
6 oz. grated cheese.	2 teasps. chutney.
8 tablesps. tomato pulp.	2 teasps. curry powder.
4 oz. finely chopped onion.	Salt to taste.

Cook rice and drain well. Grate cheese. Fry onion in 1 oz. dripping. Add curry powder to onion and fry gently. Mix all ingredients together. Put into entrée dish, sprinkle with raspings, and heat through. Serve piping hot.

N.B. If entrée dish is not fireproof, use suitable fireproof dish.

FOR ADDITIONAL RECIPES

INDEX

Almond cheesecake, 190
—— devilled, 391
—— filling, 340, 342
—— fingers, 334
—— paste, 343
—— rings, 320
—— salted, 393
—— tartlets, 188
Anchovy biscuits, 286
—— butter, 386
—— creams, 281, 287
—— eggs, 277
Angels on horseback, 282
Apple amber, 188
—— and crab-apple jelly, 366
—— and rice, 210
—— charlotte, 211
—— —— Swiss, 211
—— cheesecakes, 190
—— cheeses, 368
—— crumble, App. 419
—— dumplings, 189
—— fritters, 232
—— jam, 363
—— meringues, 260
—— mould, 208
—— puddings, small, 182
—— roll, 179
—— snow, 258
—— soufflé, 351
—— trifle, 224
—— turnover, 197
Arrowroot gruel, 352
—— pudding, 352
Artichokes and oysters, 282
—— au gratin, 154
—— bottoms, 130
—— chips, fried, 131
—— fritters, 143
—— globe, 131
—— Jerusalem, 131
Asparagus, 131
—— tips in basket, 142
Aspic jelly, 244
—— mayonnaise, 122

Aspic olives in, 288
—— peas in, 141
—— plovers' eggs in, 105
—— quenelles in, 105
Aspics, 104, 288
Austrian fritters, 177

Baba, 305
Bacon, 290
—— and beans, 64
—— —— eggs, 290
—— —— haricot beans, 290
—— —— kidney, 291
—— —— mushrooms, 291
—— —— potatoes, 291
—— —— tomatoes, 291
—— broiled, 290
—— fried, 290
Baking, blind, 168
—— powder, 307
—— —— breads, 308
—— —— rolls, 308
—— rules for bread, 297
—— —— meat, 52
—— —— pastry, 167, 168, 171
Banana chartreuse, 245
—— fritters, 233
—— turnover, 197
Banbury cakes, 199
Barding, 53
Barley water, 352
—— —— thick, 352
Bartle, 32
Basting, 53
Bath buns, 301–2
—— chaps, 291
Batter, 142, 229, 279
—— baked, 231
—— —— with fruit, 231
—— boiled, 232
—— —— with fruit, 232
—— cases, 230
—— cheap, 229, 230
—— coating, 230
—— for fish, 230

Batter for fish pancakes, 230
——— savouries, 280
—— plain, 229
—— rich, 229
—— yeast, 231
Bavaroise au chocolat, 250
Beans, baked, 154
—— broad, 131
—— cutlets, 155
—— French, 131
—— salted, 379
—— —— in batter cases, 142
—— haricot, 132, 144, 153
—— curried, 144
—— timbale, 155
Beef and rice stew, 63
—— boiled, 62
—— —— (salted), 64
—— braised fillet of, 62
—— choice of, 51
—— fillets à la Bearnaise, 101
—— —— maître d'hôtel, 101
—— galantine, 69
—— olives, 63
—— pressed, 63
—— roast, 52
—— roll, 64
—— sandwiches, raw, 352
—— tea, 353
—— —— custard, 353
—— —— raw, 353
Beefsteak and kidney mould, 82
—— and kidney pie, 198
—— fried, 64
—— grilled, 64
—— pudding, 177
Beetroot, 132
Beignets, 97
Beverages, 347
Biscuits, anchovy, 286
—— cheese, 286
—— chocolate macaroon, 337
—— German, 325
—— lunch, 339
—— macaroon, 337
—— oatmeal, 318, 415
—— parkin, App. 419
—— petit beurre, App. 419
—— Shrewsbury, 329
Bisque, 26
Blackcock, 91
Black currant jam, 366
—— —— tea, 353
Blancmange, 206, 207
Blanquette of veal or rabbit, 65

Bloaters, fried, 291
—— grilled, 291
Boiling of meat, rules for, 57
Bombay toast, 282
Boning, rules for, 90
Borders, 137, 162
Bottling, 372
—— apples, 374
—— asparagus, 378
—— black currants, 374
—— fruit, 372, 375
—— in the oven, 375
—— mushrooms, 379
—— pears, 374
—— raspberries, 375
—— strawberries, 374
—— tomatoes, 379
—— vegetables, 372, 377
—— without thermometer or oven, 376
Bouchées, 97, 280
Brain fritters, 65
Braised meat, 60
Braising of meat, rules for, 59
Brandy snaps, 335
Brawn, 65
Bread and milk, 354
—— cottage loaf, 298
—— currant, 299, 303
—— household, 297
—— milk, 299
—— panada, 388
—— pulled, 393
—— rules for baking, 297
—— rules for making, 296
—— tin loaf, 298
—— Vienna, 300
—— wheatmeal, 299
—— wholemeal, 299
Breadcrumbs, browned, 96
Breakfast dishes, 290
Bream, 32
Bretzels, 317
Bridge rolls, 301
Brill, 32
Brioche, 305
Broccoli, 132
Broiling of meat, rules for, 54
Broths, 5, 24
—— chicken, 354
—— mutton, 25
—— Scotch, 26
—— sheeps' head, 26
Brussels sprouts, 132
—— —— à la veloutée, 146

Bubble and squeak, 83
Buns, Bath, 301–2
—— Chelsea, 302
—— dough, App. 420
—— hot cross, 302
—— raspberry, 319
Burmese Croûtons, 155
Butters, 386
—— anchovy, 386
—— brandy, 386
—— cassolettes, 280
—— clarified, 391
—— devilled, 386
—— golden, 387
—— green, 387
—— ham, 387
—— horseradish, 387
—— lobster, 387
—— maître d'hôtel, 387
—— melted, 128
—— Montpelier, 388
—— shrimp, 388
—— tomato, 388

Cabbage, 132
—— pickled, 382
—— rolls, stuffed, 88
Caisses petits, 97
Cakes, 312
—— almond, 334
—— —— fingers, 334
—— —— rings, 320
—— angel, 332
—— Banbury, 199
—— Boodle Club, 316
—— Bretzels, 317
—— cherry, 314, 320–1
—— chocolate, 321, App. 417
—— —— kisses, 322
—— —— marble, 322
—— —— sandwich, 322
—— —— small, 321
—— Christmas, 323
—— coconut, 314, 323, 335
—— coffee, 323
—— —— kisses, 323
—— cornflour, 323
—— —— small, 324
—— Cornish, 317
—— Cumberland bun loaf, 317
—— Devon, 318
—— dough, 305
—— Dundee, 324
—— Easter, 324
—— Eccles, 200

Cakes, eggless, App. 414
—— fancy, small, 324
—— fillings for, 340
—— Florida orange, 325
—— fluffy, 323
—— fruit and cream, 325
—— Genoa, 325
—— German pound, 320
—— gingerbreads, 336
—— harlequin, 326
—— icings for, 342
—— jam sandwich, 333
—— lardy, 306
—— Madeira, 327
—— made with yeast, 296
—— made without yeast, 312
—— marble, 327
—— oat, 337
—— one egg, 327
—— orange, 328
—— parkin, 318
—— Pavini, 328
—— plain, 316
—— —— standard recipe for, 313
—— pound, 323
—— Quaker oats fingers, 337
—— queen, 328
—— raisin without egg, 319
—— raspberry, 210
—— —— buns, 319
—— rice, 314, 328
—— rich, 320; standard recipe for,
—— rock, 319   [314
—— rout (for keeping), 338
—— rules for making:
        Class   I method, 313
        Class II method, 314
        Class III method, 315
—— sandwich, App. 417
—— Savoy, 333
—— seed lunch, 320
—— —— plain, 320
—— —— rich, 329   [338–9
—— shortbread and shortcakes,
—— simnel, 306
—— sponge, 332, App. 418
—— —— sandwich, 333
—— —— small, 333
—— —— standard recipe for, 315
—— sultana, 329
—— tipsy, 223
—— Victoria sandwich, 339
—— walnut, 331
—— wedding, 331
Calf's brains à la maître d'hôtel, 66

Calf's brains fritters, 65
—— feet, 66
—— foot jelly, 245
—— head, 66
Canadian fruit mould, 209
Canapés, 281
—— lobster, 284
Cannelons, 98
Caramel, 219
—— for gravies, 391
—— puddings, 219
—— rice, 220
—— sago, 220
—— tapioca, 220
Carp, 32
Carrots, boiled and braised, 133
Casserole of potato and meat, 83
Cassolettes, 98
—— butter, 280
Caudle, 354
Caul or Leaf, 53
Cauliflower, 133
—— au gratin, 143
—— soufflé baked, 145
Caviare, 279
—— tartines, 287
Celeriac, 134
Celery, 133
—— bouchées, 142
—— cream, 287
Charlotte, apple, 211
—— russe, 250
—— —— apricot, 251
—— —— chestnut, 251
—— —— economical, 251
—— —— orange, 251
Chartreuse of bananas, 245
—— grapes, 245
—— pheasant, 104
Chaudfroid of chicken, 106, 107
—— sauce, 105
Cheese, 153
—— aigrettes, 281
—— and rice, 162
—— apple, 367
—— biscuits, 286
—— bombs, 155
—— cakes, 190
—— —— almond, 190
—— —— apple, 190
—— —— curd, 190
—— —— lemon, 191
—— —— Welsh, 191
—— damson, 368
—— —— and apple, 367

Cheese, d'Artois, 155
—— macaroni, 159
—— —— cutlets, App. 420
—— muff, 282
—— pastry, 286
—— patties, 156
—— potato, 161
—— puddings, 156
—— —— Yorkshire, 163, 234
—— pyramids, 287
—— quince and apple, 369
—— soufflé, 236
—— straws, 286
Chelsea buns, 302
Chestnut charlotte russe, 251
—— patties, 145
—— with sauce, 157
Chicken à la Marengo, 93
—— broth, 354
—— chaudfroid, 106, 107
—— cream (cold), 107
—— —— (hot), 100, 354
—— custard, 275
—— fricassée, 69
—— galantine, 94
—— livers, devilled, 283
—— mayonnaise, 107
—— patties (see egg patties), 274
—— roast, 91
—— soufflé, 236
—— tea, 355
Chining, rules for (see cutlets), 98
Chocolate, 347
—— Bavaroise au, 250
—— filling, 340
—— kisses, 322
—— mould, 202
—— pie, 191
—— roll, 330
—— soufflé, 268
—— tartlets, 192
—— wafers, 335
Chopped meat puddings, 178
Chops, invalid's, 358
—— mutton, 75
—— pork, 78
Choux paste, 175, 280
—— —— for savouries, 280
Christmas puddings, 186
Chutneys, 384
—— apple, 384
—— gooseberry, 384
—— green tomato, 385
—— Indian, 385
Cider cups, 347

Claret cup, 347
Clarified fat, 56
Cocoa, 348
Coconut cones, 335
—— mould, 202
—— pudding, 192
—— shortcake, 339
Cod, 32
—— cutlets, 41
—— —— à la crevette, 41
—— dressed, 41
—— roe, 32
—— —— toast, 282
—— salt, 32
—— sounds, 33
—— steaks à la maître d'hôtel, 41
Coffee, 348
—— filling, 340
—— iced, 348
—— kisses, 323
Cold meat gâteau, 86
Collops, minced, 74
Compote of pigeons, 93
Consommés, 5, 20
—— à la Brunoise, 21
—— —— Condé, 22
—— —— Jardinière, 22
—— —— Princesse, 22
—— —— Royale, 23
—— —— Tortue, 23
—— au macaroni, 22
—— au riz, 23
—— aux quenelles frites, 23
—— Carmen, 22
—— Fleuri, 22
—— Julienne, 22
—— Rothschild, 23
Coquilles, 98
Corn, sweet, 154
Cornets, 200
Cornflour fruit mould, 209
—— gnocci, 157
—— mould, 203
—— soufflé, 355
Cornish pasties, 66
Cottage pie, 83
Cough mixture, 355
Cow heel, 67
—— —— jelly, 245
Crab, curried, 41
—— dressed, 33
—— rich mock, 162
—— scrambled, 42
Creams, 98, 248
—— anchovy, 281, 287

Creams, apricots with gooseberry, 249
—— Bavaroise au chocolat, 250
—— brown bread, 250
—— celery, 287
—— chestnut, 252
—— chicken (cold), 107
—— —— (hot), 100
—— —— invalid's, 354
—— chocolate, 252
—— coffee, 252; jelly, 253
—— cold, 107
—— custard, 249
—— Devonshire, 392
—— everlasting, 253
—— fairy, 258
—— fish, 356
—— fruit, 248
—— ginger, 254
—— honeycomb, 254
—— hot, 98
—— lemon, 254
—— mock, App. 418, App. 420
—— mosaic, 254
—— moulded, 248
—— orange, 255
—— pineapple, 255
—— plain orange, 255
—— rice, App. 416
—— sago, 256
—— stone, 256
—— strawberry, 256
—— tapioca, 257
—— unmoulded, 258
—— —— apple snow, 258
—— —— lemon, 258
—— —— orange, 258
—— —— pineapple, 258
—— —— raspberry, 259
—— —— strawberry, 259
—— veal, 354
—— velvet, 257
Crème frite, 221
Crepinettes à la Française, 67
Croquettes, 84
—— description of, 98
Croustades, 98, 281
Croûtes, 281
—— à la Midas, 283
—— à la Royale, 287
—— de Coburg, 283
—— pastry, 286
—— savoury, 285
Croûtons, Burmese, 155
—— Haddock, 283
Crunbs, browned, 391

Crumpets, 305
Cucumber, 134
Curd cheesecakes, 190
—— lemon, 195
Curly greens, 134
Currant loaf, 299
Curried crab, 41
—— mutton cutlets, 67
Curry, 68
—— croquettes, 84
—— of cold meat, 84
Custards, baked, 217
—— boiled, 217
—— caramel, 219
—— cheap, 221
—— chocolate, 221
—— coffee, 221
—— confectioner's, 221
—— cup, 217
—— game or chicken, 275
—— invalid's, 355
—— macaroon, 222
—— moulded, invalid's, 355
—— steamed, 218
Cutlets, 98
—— à la Russe, 105
—— Durham, 85
—— lamb à la Princesse, 102
—— lentil, 158
—— loin, 98
—— mutton, 98
—— —— à la Milanaise, 103
—— —— à la Reforme, 103
—— —— à la Soubise, 103
—— nut, 160
—— pigeon, 77

Dabs, 33
Dace, 33
Dahl, 157
Darioles, 99
—— cold meat, 85
Dauphins au citron, 192
Devilling, paste for, 391
Devils on horseback, 284
Devonshire cream, 392
—— tartlets, 193
Dough buns, App. 420
—— cake, 303
—— nuts, 303
Dresden patties, 85
Duck, choice of, 89
—— mock, 74
—— roast, 91
—— wild, 93

Dumplings, apple, 189
—— cheap, 7
—— currant, 183
—— for boiled beef, 62
Durham cutlets, 85
Dutch hare, 68
—— stew, 68

Eccles cakes, 200
Éclairs, 176
Eels, 33
—— pie, 33
—— stewed, 33
Egg and soda water, 356
—— drink, 356
—— gâteau, 275
—— jelly, 245
—— nog, 256
Egging and crumbing, 56
Eggless cake, App. 414
Eggs, 270
—— à la crème, 274
—— à la Mandolin, 277
—— anchovy, 277
—— baked, 270
—— boiled, 270
—— buttered, 270, 271
—— chaudfroid, 273
—— croquettes, 274
—— curried, 271
—— cutlets, 274
—— devilled, 271
—— dishes, 270
—— duck, 271
—— farced, 275
—— French (invalid), 357
—— fricassée, 275
—— fried, 272
—— —— in butter, 272
—— fritters, 274
—— in aspic, 273
—— kromeskies, 274
—— of the rising sun, 275
—— patties, 274
—— plover's, 273
—— —— in aspic, 105
—— poached, 272
—— —— and tomato sauce, 272
—— —— in sauce, 273
—— —— with cheese, 273
—— scalloped, 276
—— Scotch, 276
—— —— vegetarian, 163
—— scrambled, 270, 271

Eggs, stuffed, 277
—— —— (cold), 277
—— —— (hot), 278
—— —— with prawns, 277
—— suprème, 276
—— turkey, 273
Endives, 134
Entrées, 97
—— cold, 104
—— hot, 97
Epigrammes, 99
—— d'agneau à la Dauphine, 101

Farces, 388
—— fish, 389
—— liver, 389
Fat clarified, 56
Fig pudding, 181, 184
Fillets, 99
—— of beef à la Béarnaise, 101
—— —— braised, 62
—— —— à la maître d'hôtel, 101
—— veal à la Talleyrand, 101
—— à la Viennoise, 102
Fillings, 340
—— almond, 340, 342
—— —— rich, 342
—— chocolate, 340
—— coffee, 340
—— chestnut, 388
—— for coconut fleur, 193
—— for fleurs and tarts, 193
—— for orange tart, 193
—— Frangipane custard, 341
—— lemon, 341
—— macaroon, 341
—— orange, 341
—— pineapple, 342
—— rich almond, 342
—— walnut, 342
Fish, baking, 30
—— batter, 230
—— boiling, 30
—— braising, 31
—— broiling, 30
—— cakes, 46, 47
—— choice of, 28
—— cream, 356
—— croquettes, 47
—— cutlets, 47
—— filleting, 29
—— frying, 30
—— grilling or broiling, 30
—— kedgeree, 47
—— kromeskies, 48

Fish, mock, 157
—— omelet, 357
—— pie, 48
—— —— Russian, 48
—— preparation of, 28
—— pudding, 48, 49
—— rechauffés, 46
—— rules for cooking, 30
—— salad, 147
—— soufflé (cold), 49
—— —— with asparagus, 49
—— steamed, 31
—— —— for invalids, 357
—— stewed, 31
—— stock, 2
Fish House punch, 348
Flapjacks, 232
Fleur filling for chocolate, 193
—— —— coconut, 193
—— —— orange, 193
—— paste, 167, 196
—— rings, 167
Flounders, 34
Flour baked for invalids, 357
Food preservation, 362
Food values, 396
Foods in season, 403
Fools, 225
—— cheap fruit, 225
—— chestnut, 225
—— fruit, App. 415
—— gooseberry, 225
Forcemeat, 388
—— balls, 389
—— chestnut, 388
—— fish, 389
—— game or chicken, 389
—— veal, 390
Fowl, boiled, 91
—— roast, 91
—— steamed, 91
Freezing machine, 261
French egg, 357
—— pancakes, 215
Friars omelet, 213
Fricassée of chicken or veal, 69
Fritters, 97
—— apple, 232
—— Austrian, 177
—— banana, 233
—— batter for, 231
—— breakfast, App. 416
—— calf's brain, 65
—— —— à la maître d'hôtel, 66
—— orange, 233

Fritters, vegetable, 143
Frosting, 343
—— American, 343
Fruit, 207
—— bottling, 372
—— cheeses, 368
—— compote, 207
—— dried, 207
—— fool, 226, 415
—— jellies, 366
—— meringues, 260
—— mould, 208
—— salad, 151
—— —— orange, 151
—— sponge, 215
—— stewed, 207
—— tarts, 168
—— —— invalid, 357
—— tivoli, 257
Frying, English, 55
—— French, 54

Galantine, boning for, 90
—— of beef, 69
—— chicken, 94
—— veal, 70
Game, choice of, 89
—— custards, 275
—— roast, 91
Gâteau de fruits, 253
—— of cold meat, 86
—— of eggs, 275
Gelatine, 241
Genoese paste, 332
Gin, orange, 349
—— sloe, 350
Gingerbread, 336
—— fruit, 336
—— Inpark, 336
—— nuts, 336
Glaze, 66
—— for pastry, 345
Gnocci, cornflour, 157
—— semolina, 162
Goose, choice of, 89
—— roast, 91
Gooseberry turnover, 197
Gravies, 61, 62
—— thickened, 61
Greens, cooking of, 129
Grenadine of veal, 70
Grilling, rules for, 53
Ground rice, mock fish, 157
—— —— mould, 203
Grouse, 91

Gruel, 358
Gurnet, 34

Haddock, 34
—— creamed, 282
—— croûtons of, 283
—— Finnan, 34
Haggis, 70
Hake, 34
Ham, baked, 70
—— boiled, 71
—— mousse, 107
—— toast, 295
Hamburg steak, 71
Hares, choice of, 89
—— jugged, 94
—— roast, 91
Haricot beans and bacon, 71
—— mutton, 71
Hash, 86
Hay box cookery, 394
Heart, sheep's, 78
Herrings, 34
—— soused, 34
Hock cup, 349
Hominy, 292
Honey twist, 303
Honeycomb mould (see cream honeycomb), 254
Hors d'œuvres, 279
Hot cross buns, 302
Hot pot, 72
Huîtres croûtes, 284

Iced apricot mousse, 265
—— brown bread pudding, 266
—— chocolate and vanilla pudding, 266
—— —— soufflé, 268
—— coffee, 348
—— —— mousse, 265
—— —— soufflé, 268
—— mousses, 265
—— puddings, 266–7
—— —— glacé tutti frutti, 266
—— sorbets, 267
—— soufflés, 268–9
Ices, 261
—— Algerian, 262
—— banana, 262
—— black currant, 262
—— chocolate, 263
—— compound, 265
—— cream, New York, 263
—— —— strawberry, 264

Ices, cream, vanilla, 265
—— crème de fruits à la Monaco, 263
—— invalid's, 358
—— la dame blanche, 267
—— lemon water, 263
—— melon, 263
—— orange water, 264
—— pêche Melba, 264
—— simple, 262
—— strawberry water, 264
—— syrup for, 262
Icings, 342
—— almond paste, 343
—— American frosting, 343
—— butter, 343
—— chocolate, 344
—— —— butter, 344
—— coffee butter, 344
—— —— Mocha glacé, 344
—— fondant, 344
—— for glazing pastry, 345
—— frosting, 343
—— jelly, 345
—— lemon water, 345
—— nougat, 345
—— orange, 345
—— royal, 345
—— transparent, 346
—— Vienna, 343
—— water, 346
—— —— boiled, 346
—— —— glacé, 346
Indian dahl, 157
Invalid's chop, 358
—— cookery, 351
—— ice, 358
Irish moss jelly, 358
—— stew, 59, 79

Jamaica pudding, 216
Jams, black currant, 365
—— dried apricot, 366
—— green tomato, 366
—— mixed fruit, 365
—— rules for, 362
—— sandwich, 333
—— strawberry, 366
—— table for making all kinds, 363
—— vegetable marrow, 366
—— whole fruit, 364
Jellies, 241
—— apple and crab, 367
—— aspic, 244
—— calf's foot, 245
—— claret, 242

Jellies, clear, 241
—— coffee cream, 253
—— cow heel, 245
—— egg, 245
—— fruit, 365
—— Irish moss, 358
—— lemon, 242
—— marmalade, 368
—— medlar, 367
—— milk, 205
—— —— chocolate, 206
—— —— coffee, 206
—— —— lemon, 205
—— orange, 242
—— port wine, 359
—— quince, 368
—— rainbow, 246
—— red currant, 368
—— rules for making, 241
—— to line a mould with, 243
—— to turn out, 244
—— veal, 81
—— whisked, 248
—— wine, 242
John Dory, 34
Jugged hare, 94
—— rabbit, 95
Jumbles, 326
Junket, 204
—— chocolate, 204
—— coffee, 204
—— Devonshire, 204
—— rum or brandy, 205

Kedgeree, 47
Kidneys, broiled, 72
—— grilled, 72
—— stewed, 72
Kippers, filleted, 292
—— fried, 292
Kneading, rules for, 298
Kohlrabi, 134
Kromeskies, 99

Larding, 53
Lardoon, 53
Lamb, choice of, 51
—— cutlets, à la Princesse, 102
Leaf, 53
Leeks, 134
—— au jus, 144
Lemon cheesecakes, 191
—— curd, 195
—— —— roll, 179
—— mould, 205, 206, 209

Lemon pie, 195
—— pudding, 195, 213
—— rice, 205
—— roll, 179
—— snow, 258
—— sponge, 246
—— syrup, 349
—— whiffle, 359
Lemonade, 349
Lentils, 134
—— cutlets, 158
—— patties, 158
—— roast, 158
—— stewed, 158
—— timbales, 159
Lettuce, 134
Liver à la Française, 73
—— and bacon, 72
—— fried, 73
—— stewed, 73
Lobster, 35
—— canapés, 284
—— croquettes, 42
—— cutlets, 42

Macaroni, 153
—— à la Milanese, 159
—— cheese, 159
—— —— cutlets, App. 420
—— pudding, 205
—— timbale, 86
—— with cheese and tomato, 159
Macaroons, 337
—— chocolate, 337
—— oaten, 327
Macedoine of fruit, 246
Mackerel, 35
—— à l'Anvers, 35
—— baked, stuffed, 35
—— fried, 35
—— grilled, 35
—— pickled, 42
Marmalades, 369
—— apple, 369
—— bitter, 369
—— clear, 368
—— jelly, 369
—— orange, 369–71
—— quince, 371
—— Scotch, 369
—— simple recipe, 369
Marmite, 152
Marrow bones, 292
—— toast, 295
—— vegetable, 141

Marrow, stuffed, 146
Mayonnaise aspics, 123
—— chicken, 107
—— mock, 148
—— sauce, 111, 123
Meals, 398
Meat, baking, 52
—— braised, 60
—— braising, 59
—— broiling, 54
—— choice of, 51
—— cooking, 52
—— frying, 54, 55
—— grilling, 53
—— hot or cold, 51
—— pickling, 380
—— porcupine, 73
—— potted, 393
—— puddings, 177
—— roasting, 52
—— steaming, 58
—— stewing, 58
Menus, 398
Meringues, 259
—— apple, 260
—— fruit, 260
Milk, evaporated, App. 419
Mince, 87
—— en coquilles, 87
—— pies, 200
Minced collops, 74
Mincemeat, 392–3
Miscellaneous Recipes, 391
Mock duck, 74
—— fish, 157
—— goose, 77
—— mayonnaise, 148
Moulds, 74, 205
—— apple, 208
—— beefsteak and kidney, 82
—— Canadian, 209
—— chocolate, 202
—— coconut, 202
—— cornflour, 203
—— —— fruit, 209
—— fruit, 207–10
—— ground rice, 203
—— lemon, 205, 206, 209
—— milk, 205, 206, App. 414
—— —— puddings, 201
—— picnic, 144
—— prune, 209
—— rabbit, 82
—— rhubarb, 210
—— salmon, 50
—— savoury, 88

Moulds, syrup, 210
—— tomato and egg, 144
—— veal, 82
Mousses, 99, 107, 238
—— coffee iced, 265
—— cold, 107
—— de jambon, 107
—— (hot), 99
—— iced, 265
—— —— apricot, 265
—— lemon, 238
—— orange, 238
—— raspberry, 238
—— —— and banana, 259
—— strawberry, 238, 256
Mousseline, cold, 108
—— de canards, 108
—— duck, 108
—— hot, 99
Muffin, 305
Mulled wine, 350
Mullet, au gratin, 36
—— baked, 36
—— en caisses, 36
—— fried, 36
—— grey, 35
—— red, 36
Mushrooms, 134
—— devilled, 143
—— farce, 143
—— vol-au-vent, 147
Mutton, 74
—— boiled, 75
—— braised leg, 75
—— choice of, 51
—— chops, 75
—— cutlets, 103
—— —— curried, 67
—— haricot, 71
—— pie, 76
—— roast, 52
—— stewed with rice, 75
—— three ways of cooking one leg, 74

Nettles, 135
Noisettes, 100
—— de mouton à la Jardinière, 103
—— de mouton à la Maintenon, 103
Norman pie, 292
Nut and fruit roll, 160
—— cutlets, 160
—— roast, 160

Oatcake, 337
Oaten macaroon, 327
Oatmeal, 153
—— biscuit, 318, 415
—— parkin, 318
—— porridge, 292–3
Olives, farced, 287
—— in aspic, 288
Omelets, 234
—— English, 234
—— French, 235
—— Friar's, 213
—— rum, 235
—— sweet, 235
—— vegetable, 145
Onions, 135
—— fried, 135
—— spring, 135
Orange fritters, 233
—— gin, 350
—— salads, 151
—— snow, 258
—— sponge, 247
—— tart, 195
Ortolans, 92
Ox cheeks, 76
—— palates, 76
—— tail, 76
—— tongue, 77
Oysters, 36, 279
—— baskets, 42
—— bonnes bouches, 284
—— fritters, 43
—— in batter, 279
—— patties, 43
—— rarebit, 289
—— scalloped, 360
—— stewed, 43

Pains, petits, 99
Panada, 109, 110, 388
Pancakes, batter for, 230
—— French, 215
—— savoury, 88, 280
—— snow, 233
—— to cook, 230
Parkin, 318
Parsley, fried, 392
Parsnips, 136
Partridge, 92
Paste, almond, 343
—— choux, 175
—— fleur, 167, 196
—— for devilling, 391

Pastry, 164
—— cheese, 286
—— choux paste, 175
—— —— for savouries, 176
—— —— to fill, 176
—— cornets, 200
—— croûtes, 286
—— flaky, 169
—— fleur paste, 167
—— for patties, 173
—— for pies, 170
—— for vol-au-vent, 173
—— Genoese, 332
—— glazing for, 345
—— hot water crust, 173
—— paté foncé, 167
—— potato, 417
—— puff, 171
—— rough puff, 170
—— short baking of, 167
—— —— crust, 166
—— —— plain, 167
—— —— sweet, 167
—— suet crust, 164
—— to line pie-dishes and tins, 166, 167
Patties, cheese, 156
—— chestnut, 145
—— chicken (see egg patties), 274
—— egg, 274
—— lentil, 158
—— meat (see egg patties), 274
—— pans to line with pastry, 168
—— pastry, 173
—— vegetable, 145
Peas, 130, 153
—— dried, 136
—— green, 136
—— in aspic, 141
—— pudding, 161
Pêche Melba, 264
Perch, 36
Petits caisses, 97
Petits pains, 99
Pheasant, 92, 104
Pickled beef, 381
—— cabbage, 382
—— onions, 383
—— pork, 381
—— tomato, 383
—— tongue, 381
—— walnuts, 383
Pickles, 380
—— mixed, 384
Pickling, dry, 380

Pickling meat, 380
—— vegetables, 382
—— wet, 381
Pies, 170, 173
—— beefsteak and kidney, 198
—— chocolate, 191
—— cottage, 83
—— fish, 48
—— game, 173
—— giblet, 198
—— lemon, 195
—— meat, 170, 173
—— mince, 200
—— mutton, 76
—— Norman, 292
—— ordinary, 170
—— pork, 174
—— rabbit, 198
—— raised, 170, 173
—— Roman, 87
—— Russian, 87
—— sea, 178
—— three-decker, 178
—— veal and ham, 199
—— vegetable, 145, 163
Pigeon, choice of, 89
—— compote, 93
—— cutlets, 77
—— roast, 92
Pig's cheek, 291
—— fry, 77
Pike, 36
Pikelets, 305
Pineapple snow, 258
—— sponge, 247
Plaice, 37
Plover, 92
—— eggs, 273
—— —— in aspic, 105
Pork, choice of, 51
—— chops, 78
—— roast, 52
Porridge, 292–3
Port wine lozenges, 359
—— jelly, 359
Potage à la bonne femme, 18
—— d'amande, 18
—— reine Margot, 18
Potatoes, baked, 136
—— boiled, 136
—— border, 137
—— cheese, 161
—— chips, 138
—— croquettes, 137
—— French, 138

Potatoes, fried, 137
—— mashed, 138
—— new, 138
—— olive, 139
—— puff, 139
—— roast, 137
—— salad, 150
—— sauté, 137
—— savoury, 88, 161
—— soufflé, 139
—— steamed, 137
—— surprises, 161
Poultry and game pudding, 178
—— boning, 90
—— —— for galantine, 90
—— choice of birds, 89
—— preparation of, 89
Pout, 37
Prawns, 37
Profiteroles, 176
Prune gâteau, 246
—— mould, 209
Ptarmigan, 92
Puddings, 164
—— apple amber, 188
—— —— dumplings, 189
—— —— roll, 179
—— —— small, 182
—— —— turnover, 197
—— arrowroot, 352
—— baked batter, 231
—— —— batter and fruit, 231
—— —— custard, 217
—— —— lemon, 213
—— Bakewell tart, 189
—— banana turnover, 197
—— beefsteak, 177
—— black cap, 232
—— Blakemore, 189
—— boiled batter, 232
—— —— batter and fruit, 232
—— bread, 212
—— —— and butter, 212
—— —— crumb, 212
—— cabinet, 218, 219
—— canary, 214
—— caramel, 219, 220
—— —— rice, 220
—— —— sago, 220
—— —— tapioca, 220
—— castle, 214
—— cheese, 156
—— cherry, 214
—— chocolate, 192, 214
—— —— small, 215

Puddings, chopped meat, 178
—— Christmas, 186
—— —— cheap, 186
—— coconut, 192, 220
—— coffee cabinet, 219
—— college, 183
—— conservative, 213
—— cornflour, 203
—— —— soufflé, 355
—— crème frite, 221
—— currant dumplings, 183
—— custards, 217
—— dampfnulden, 227
—— date, 183, 184
—— Devonshire tartlets, 193
—— equality, 183
—— fig, 181, 184
—— fish, 48, 49
—— flavoured suet, sweet, 180
—— fool (see fools), 225
—— French rice, 184
—— fruit, 207
—— —— sponge, 215
—— —— with suet crust, 182-8
—— general favourite, 222
—— ginger, 181
—— Gloucester, 184
—— golden, 184
—— gooseberry, 194
—— —— turnover, 197
—— Gretna, 184
—— ground rice, 203
—— hasty, 203, 204
—— iced, 266-7
—— Ingoldsby plum, 186
—— Isle of Wight, 194
—— jam, 175, 195, 215
—— —— layer, 179
—— Jamaica, 216
—— lemon, 185, 195, 213
—— —— curd roll, 179
—— —— open, 195
—— —— pie, 195
—— rice, 205
—— rich, 195
—— roll, 179
—— little apple, 182
—— macaroni, 205
—— made with cake mixture, 214
—— —— yeast, 226
—— Manchester, 196
—— marmalade, 185
—— —— and vermicelli, 222
—— —— cheap, 185
—— meat, 177

Puddings, milk, rules for, 201
—— mincemeat roly poly, 180
—— Nantes, 216
—— Newcastle, 196
—— peas, 161
—— pineapple sponge, 247
—— plum, 186
—— —— duff, 185
—— princess, 216
—— prune capped, 186
—— queen of, 222
—— rabbit, 178
—— railway sponge, 216
—— raisin, 184
—— Randall, 215
—— rice with apple, 210
—— roly poly, 166
—— Scotch plum, 186
—— scrap bread, 212
—— six cup, 187
—— Snowden, 187
—— sponge, 187
—— suet, 177
—— —— methods of making, 180
—— —— plain, 181
—— —— rich, 187
—— sultana, 181, 216
—— summer, 213
—— Swiss roll, 329–30
—— syrup sponge, 188
—— treacle roly poly, 180
—— Upwey cake, 197
—— Viennese, 224
—— yeast, App. 416
—— yeast klosze, 227
—— Yorkshire, 234
—— —— cheese, 163, 234
Pulses, cooking of, 130
Punch, 267
—— Fish House, 348
—— rum, 267
Purées, 3, 5
—— d'Artoise, 11
—— game, 8

Quail, 92
Quaker oats fingers, 337
Quenelles, 103
—— in aspic, 105

Rabbit à la Tartare, 95
—— baked, 96
—— blanquette, 65
—— boiled, 95

Rabbit, choice of, 89
—— jugged, 95
—— mould, 82
—— pudding, 178
—— ragout, 96
—— roast, 96
—— stewed, 96
Rainbow jelly, 246
Raspberry buns, 319
—— cakes, 210
—— mousse, 238
—— sponge, 247
—— vinegar, 350
Rechauffé, fish, 46
—— meat, 82
Rhubarb mould, 210
Rice, 153
—— à l'Impératrice, 255
—— and cheese, 162
—— borders, 162
—— cream, App. 416
—— croquettes, 223
—— ground, 203
—— —— vegetarian, 157
—— lemon, 205
—— puddings, 201
—— savoury, App. 420
—— socle, 162
—— to boil, 153
—— with apple, 210
Risotto, 162
Rissoles, 87, 100
Roach, 37
Roasting, rules for, 52
Roll, apple, 179
—— chocolate, 330
—— lemon, 179
—— —— curd, 179
—— Swiss, 329–30
Rolls, baking powder, 308
—— bridge, 301
Roly poly, 166
—— mincemeat, 180
—— treacle, 180
Roman pie, 87
Roots, cooking of, 129
Roux, 109
Rum punch, 267
Russian pie, 87

Salads, 147
—— banana, 148
—— Chinese, 149
—— dressings, 148

Salads, dressings, boiled, 149
—— —— cheap, 149
—— —— chiffonade, 149
—— —— English, 150
—— —— French, 150
—— —— mock mayonnaise, 148
—— —— plain, 150
—— —— without oil, 150
—— egg, 149
—— fruit, 151
—— fish, 147
—— meat, 147
—— orange, 151
—— potato, 150
—— rules for making, 147
—— Russian, 147
—— tomato, 150
—— vegetable, 147
Sally Lunn teacakes, 304
Salmi, 100
Salmon, 37
—— mould, 50
Salsify, 139
—— à la béchamel, 142
Sardine à la noisette, 284
—— and oysters, 285
—— aux Piedmontaise, 285
—— curried, 293
—— toast, 295
Sauces, 109
—— Agro dolce, 122
—— anchovy, 112
—— apple, 126
—— apricot, 125
—— aspic mayonnaise, 122
—— béchamel, 110
—— Béarnaise, 120
—— Bigarade, 122
—— Bordeaux, 112
—— brandy, 112, 126
—— bread, 127
—— brown, 109, 113
—— caper, 113
—— caramel, 126
—— cardinal, 113
—— celery, 113
—— champagne, 113
—— chaudfroid, 105, 111, 122, 123
—— chocolate, 114
—— coating, 109
—— coffee, 114
—— cold, 111
—— Cumberland, 123
—— curry, 114

Sauces, demi-glacé, 114, 414
—— diable, 115
—— egg, 115
—— Espagnole, 115 App. 414
—— German, 121
—— gooseberry, 127
—— hollandaise, 111, 120
—— horseradish, 115, 116
—— Italian, 116
—— jam, 112, 125
—— King of Oude, 123
—— lemon, 116
—— —— superior, 121
—— lobster, 116
—— Madeira, 116
—— maître d'hôtel, 117
—— marmalade, 125
—— mayonnaise, 111, 123
—— —— aspic, 123
—— melted butter, 110, 117, 128
—— mint, 128
—— mousseline, 111, 121
—— mustard, 117
—— Normandy, 121
—— oiled butter, 128
—— onion, 117
—— orange, 124
—— oyster, 117
—— parsley, 118
—— piquante, 124
—— plain, 110, 111
—— plain custard, 111
—— poivrade, 118
—— reforme, 118
—— Robert, 118
—— rules for making, 109
—— rum, 126
—— Sabayon, 121
—— salmi, 118
—— Senior Wrangler, 128
—— shrimp, 119
—— Soubise, 119
—— suprème, 119
—— sweet, 119
—— —— arrowroot, 124
—— —— chaudfroid, 123
—— syrup, 112, 126
—— tartare, 124
—— thickened with egg, 111, 120
—— tomato, 119
—— treacle, 125
—— veloutée, 110, 120
—— whipped custard, 111, 122
—— —— egg, 121

Sauces, whipped, white, 109
Sausage rolls, 199
Sausages, 293–4
Sauté, 4, 59
Savarin, 305
Savouries, 279
—— anchovy and cream, 281
—— —— biscuits, 286
—— —— creams, 287
—— angels on horseback, 282
—— artichokes and oysters, 282
—— aspic (made with), 288
—— batter, 279
—— boats, 288
—— Bombay toast, 282
—— bonne bouchées, 284
—— bouchées, 280
—— butter cassolettes, 280
—— canapés, 281
—— cassolettes, 280
—— celery creams, 287
—— cheese aigrettes, 281
—— —— biscuits, 286
—— —— muff, 282
—— —— pastry, 286
—— —— pyramids, 287
—— —— soufflé, 236
—— —— straws, 286
—— choux paste, 280
—— cod's roe toast, 282
—— creamed haddock, 282
—— croustades, 281
—— croûtes, 281
—— —— à la Midas, 283
—— —— à la Royale, 287
—— —— de Coburg, 283
—— croûtons of haddock, 283
—— devilled chicken's livers, 283
—— devils on horseback, 283
—— farced olives, 287
—— French omelet, 235
—— lobster canapés, 284
—— mould, 88
—— olives in aspic, 288
—— oysters, 285
—— —— croûtes, 284
—— —— in batter, 279
—— —— rarebit, 289
—— pancakes, 88, 280
—— pastry croûtes, 286
—— potatoes, 88, 161
—— rice, App. 420
—— sardines à la noisette, 284
—— —— Piedmontaise, 285
—— Scotch woodcock, 289

Savouries, tartines de caviare, 287
—— tartlets, 288
—— Welsh rarebit, 289
Scalloped oysters, 360
Scallops, 37
Scones, 307
—— Balmoral, 308
—— butter with currants, 309
—— cream, 309
—— drop, 309
—— girdle, 310
—— potato, 310, App. 415
—— Raisley, 311
—— rules for baking, 308
—— —— making, 308
—— soda, 310
—— sultana, 311
—— tea, 311
—— treacle, 311
—— wholemeal, 312
Seakale cornets, 142
—— fried, 139
Sea pie, 178
Semolina, 162
Setting the sponge, 298
Shad, 38
Sheep's head, 78
—— heart, 78
—— trotters, 79
Shortbread, 338
Shortcake, coconut, 339
Shortcrust, 166
—— baking of, 167
—— yeast, App. 416
Simnel cake, 306
Skate, 38
Sloe gin, 350
Smelts, 38
Snipe, 92
Socle, 162
Sole, 38
—— à l'Olga, 43
—— à l'Orly, 43
—— à la suprême, 44
—— à la whitebait, 38
—— au gratin, 44
—— au vin blanc, 44
—— en mayonnaise, 45
—— fillets fried, 38
—— —— à la Michel, 45
—— —— with cheese, 45
—— —— with tomato, 45
—— fried, 38
Sorbets, 267
—— lemon, 267

Sorbets, orange, 267
Sorrel, 140
Soufflés, 236
—— apple, 351
—— au Sabayon, 239
—— cases, how to prepare, 236
—— —— for cold, 238
—— cheese, 236
—— chestnut, 237
—— chicken, 236
—— chocolate, cold, 239
—— —— hot, 237
—— —— iced, 268
—— coffee, cold, 239
—— —— hot, 237
—— —— iced, 268
—— fish, cold, 49
—— ginger, 237
—— iced, 268–9
—— —— chocolate, 268
—— —— coffee, 268
—— lemon, iced, 269
—— —— Milanese, 239
—— meat, 236–7
—— Milanaise, App. 418
—— orange, cold, 239
—— pineapple, 237
—— raspberry, cold, 239
—— strawberry, 239
—— sweet, cold, 238
—— —— hot, 237
—— vanilla, cold, 240
—— hot, 237
—— vegetable, 145
Soups, 1, 3
—— à la Palermo, 11
—— artichoke, 5
—— asparagus, 6
—— barley cream, 13
—— beef, 13
—— brown vegetables, 6
—— cabbage, 13
—— calf's head, clear, 24
—— —— thick, 14
—— cauliflower, 6
—— celery, 7
—— cheap pea, 7
—— chestnut, 14
—— —— purée, 7
—— chicken, 355
—— clear, 5, 20
—— —— mock turtle, 24
—— cock-a-leekie, 14
—— consommé (see Consommé),
      20

Soups, cressy, 8
—— croûte au pot, 24
—— fish, 26
—— —— white, 27
—— game, 15
—— —— purée, 8
—— giblet, 15
—— gravy, 15
—— green pea, 8
—— hare, 16
—— haricot, 8
—— —— and tomato, 9
—— hollandaise, 16
—— hotch-potch, 25
—— imitation hare, 9
—— kidney, 9
—— lentil, 10
—— lobster bisque, 26
—— maigre, 20
—— mock turtle, 14
—— —— hare, 17
—— mulligatawny, 10
—— mutton broth, 25
—— Normandy, 17
—— onion, 10
—— oxtail, 17
—— oyster, 27
—— potage à la bonne femme,
      18
—— —— d'amandes, 18
—— —— reine Margot, 18
—— pot au feu, 25
—— potato, 11
—— purées, 3, 5
—— —— d'Artoise, 11
—— rabbit, 19
—— restorative invalid, 360
—— sago, 19
—— Scotch broth, 26
—— sheep's head broth, 26
—— spinach, 11
—— tapioca cream, 19
—— tomato, 12
—— turtle, clear, 24
—— —— thick, 19
—— vegetable marrow, 12
—— vegetarian, 4
—— white fish, 27
—— —— foam, 20
—— —— vegetable, 20
Spatchcock, 294
Spinach, 140
—— à la crème, 142
Sponge cakes, 332, App. 418
—— fruit, 215

Sponge cakes, lemon, 246
—— orange, 247
—— pineapple, 247
—— raspberry, 247
—— semolina, 247
Sprats, 39
—— and rice pie, 46
Steak, grilled, 64
—— Hamburg, 71
Steaming, rules for, 58
Stew, beef and rice, 63
—— brown, 59, 79
—— Irish, 59, 79
—— white, 59, 79
Stewing, 58
Stockpot, care of, 2
Stocks, 1
—— fish, 2
—— first, 1
—— household, 2
—— plain household, 2
—— second, 1
—— vegetable, brown, 2
—— —— white, 3
Strawberry mousse, 238, 256
Stuffing, sage and onion, 389
Sturgeon, 39
Succotash, 162
Suet crust, 164
—— puddings, meat, 177
—— —— sweet, 179
Sugar, to colour, 260
Swedish tea ring, 303
Sweetbread, braised, 80
—— fried, 80
Sweet corn, 154
Swiss roll, 329–30
—— —— chocolate, 330
Syrup mould, 210

Tart, Bakewell, 189
—— fillings, 193
—— fruit, 168, 357
—— lemon or orange open, 195
—— open, 169
—— orange, 195
—— pineapple Swiss, 197
—— Waterloo, 200
Tartlets, almond, 188
—— chocolate, 192
—— Dauphins au citron, 192
—— Devonshire, 193
—— fruit and meringue, 194
—— orange, 193

Tartlets, raisin and lemon, 196
—— small, 169
—— Swiss, 196
Tea, 350
—— made with milk, 360
Teacakes, 301, 302
—— flat, 305
—— hot, 311
—— Sally Lunn, 304
Teal, 92
Temperatures, viii
Tench, 39
Terms used in cookery, 409
Timbale, 100
—— bean, 155
—— lentil, 159
—— macaroni, 86
—— vegetable, 146
Tipsy cake, 223
Tivoli of fruit, 257
Toad in the hole, 233
—— —— vegetarian, 163
Toast, 294–5
—— water, 360
Tomatoes, 140
—— omelet, 145
—— stuffed, 146
Tongue, ox, 77
—— pickled, 381
Treacle posset, 360
Trifle, 223
—— apple, 224
—— chocolate, 224
—— fresh fruit, 224
—— jellied, 224
—— stewed fruit, 224
Tripe, 80
—— and onions, 81
—— braised, 80
Trout, 39
—— fried, 39
—— grilled, 39
Trussing, rules for, 90
Turbot, 40
—— à la florentine, 46
Turkey, 92
Turnips, 140
—— tops, 141
Turnover, apple, 197
—— banana, 197
—— fruit, 197
—— gooseberry, 197

Veal, blanquette, 65
—— breast of, stewed, 81

Veal, choice of, 51
—— fillets à la Talleyrand, 101
—— fricassée, 69
—— galantine, 70
—— grenadines, 70
—— jelly, 81
—— knuckle, stewed, 81
—— mould, 82
—— roast, 52
—— —— shoulder, 82
Vegetable marrow, 141
—— —— stuffed, 146
Vegetables, 129
—— à la béchamel, 142
—— à la crème, 142
—— à la diable, 143
—— à la veloutée, 146
—— à l'Indienne, 144
—— aspic, 141
—— au gratin, 143
—— au jus, 144
—— baskets, 142
—— batters, 142
—— bottling of, 372, 377
—— bouchées, 142
—— cornets, 142
—— dressed, 141
—— dried (see Pulses)
—— farces, 143
—— fritters, 143
—— home canning of, 379
—— omelets, 145
—— patties, 145
—— pickling of, 382
—— pies, 145, 163
—— rules for cooking, 129
—— salads, 147
—— salted, 130

Vegetables, soufflés, 145
—— stock, 2
—— stuffed, 145
—— timbale, 146
—— vol-au-vent, 147
Vegetarian cookery, 152
—— Scotch eggs, 163
—— soups, 4
—— toad in the hole, 163
Venison, 92
Victoria sandwich cake, 339
Vienna bread dough, 300
Viennoise pudding, 225
Vol-au-vent, 100, 173
—— de fruits, 257
—— mushroom, 147
—— vegetable, 147

Walnuts au gratin, 163
Waterloo tarts, 200
Welsh cheesecakes, 191
—— rarebit, 289
Whey, 361
—— white wine, 361
Whisked jellies, 248
Whitebait, 40
Whiting, 40
Wine, mulled, 349
Woodcock, 93
—— Scotch, 289

Yeast, 296–7
—— batter, 231
—— klosze, 227
—— pudding, App. 416
—— shortcrust, App. 416
Yorkshire cheese pudding, 163, 234
—— pudding, 234